The
"Rape" of
JAPAN

T0282786

The "Rape" of JAPAN

THE MYTH OF MASS SEXUAL VIOLENCE DURING THE ALLIED OCCUPATION

BRIAN P. WALSH

Naval Institute Press
Annapolis, MD

Naval Institute Press
291 Wood Road
Annapolis, MD 21402

Library of Congress Cataloging-in-Publication Data
Names: Walsh, Brian P., author.
Title: The "rape" of Japan : the myth of mass sexual violence during the Allied occupation / Brian P. Walsh.
Description: Annapolis, MD : Naval Institute Press, [2024] | Includes bibliographical references and index.
Identifiers: LCCN 2023054956 (print) | LCCN 2023054957 (ebook) | ISBN 9781682479308 (hardcover) | ISBN 9781682479315 (ebook)
Subjects: LCSH: United States. Army. General Headquarters | Soldiers—Sexual behavior—United States. | Sex crimes—Japan—History—20th century. | Rape—Japan—Public opinion. | United States—Foreign relations—Japan. | Japan-—Foreign relations—United States. | Japan—History—Allied occupation, 1945-1952—Historiography. | BISAC: HISTORY / Wars & Conflicts / World War II / Pacific Theater | HISTORY / Military / United States
Classification: LCC DS889.16 .W35 2024 (print) | LCC DS889.16 (ebook) | DDC 940.54/26—dc23/eng/20240325
LC record available at https://lccn.loc.gov/2023054956
LC ebook record available at https://lccn.loc.gov/2023054957

♾ Print editions meet the requirements of ANSI/NISO z39.48-1992 (Permanence of Paper).
Printed in the United States of America.

32 31 30 29 28 27 26 25 24   9 8 7 6 5 4 3 2 1
First printing

To my parents, Irene Walsh and Jerry Walsh,
who raised me to love and to think

CONTENTS

ILLUSTRATIONS

TABLES & MAP

Tables

Map

ACKNOWLEDGMENTS

Though it is conventional to include those closest to you last, I must include one first. My first acknowledgment goes to my wife, Ayumi, who has been a part of this project from its inception. She looked some things up and ran others down. She brought things to my attention, secured appointments with librarians, ordered articles, helped secure permission to use images, and checked my translations. She suggested possibilities that I hadn't even considered. She has read every draft I wrote and challenged me on my every assumption. She pointed out things that I had just plain missed. She argued with me until I had either yielded the point or strengthened my argument against it. Whatever the shortcomings of this work, they are far fewer and less egregious thanks to her. She is my one and *onrii*.

Kenneth Pyle of the University of Washington and Sheldon Garon of Princeton University both continued to support me long after return on their investment was overdue. Ken Pyle made a gamble on me more than two decades ago, and though it hasn't yet paid off, it's getting closer to breaking even. Shel Garon continued advising me despite interminable delays in completing the manuscript. In addition, his work on prostitution in Japan provided a model of nuance and balance in scholarship that has served to smooth at least a few of the rougher of my edges.

Harold James of Princeton University and David Howell of Harvard University served on my dissertation committee and gave me valuable feedback as well as suggestions for expanding my work to prepare as a monograph. Sarah Kovner of Colombia University also served on my committee and, before that, was extremely generous with her time in discussing with me some of the issues raised in her excellent book, *Occupying Power: Sex Workers and Servicemen in Postwar Japan*. In addition, she generously provided me with some of the documents she used in preparing it. *Occupying Power* also made me aware of some of the work of Roger Brown of Saitama University. This spurred me to begin a very fruitful correspondence with Roger that has covered a number of topics, most pertinently sexual violence and prostitution during the Occupation. Evan and Oscie Thomas were extremely helpful, sharing the hard-won wisdom of their years of experience in the world of publishing. Brian Ashcraft was also very helpful to me in this way. Dr. Claudio Mosse of the Vanderbilt University Medical School provided me with historical information on the extent of venereal infection in the United States in the mid-twentieth century.

Historian and Occupation veteran Stanley Falk gave me great encouragement and graciously endured my endless questions about his experiences. He also provided me with an introduction to Edward Drea. Ed, in turn, gave me a wealth of historical materials, encouraged my efforts, and helped me to sharpen my prose on a number of projects, including the proposal for this book. Richard B. Frank has long encouraged me in my work, helping me to get my first-ever publication and giving suggestions about my work. Kenneth (K. J.) Moore was a source of great encouragement when it was sorely needed.

The staff at the *Journal of Military History*, including the late Bruce Vandervort, Timothy Dowling, Kachina Johnson, Roberta Wiener, and Anne Wells, were without exception a pleasure to work with. Their unflagging good cheer and conspicuous ability were of inestimable value to me in preparing the two articles that form the basis of the first two chapters. I gratefully acknowledge the *Journal*'s permission to use these articles.

Professor Iokibe Makoto, former president of the Japan's National Defense University, and the members of the Iokibe group all provided me with insights into the diplomatic background in which many of the events I describe in this book took place. Inoue Masaya and Shibayama Futoshi served as role models in the use of primary sources. Futoshi also introduced me to Christopher Szpilman, who first made me aware of Kanō Jigorō's concerns about venereal disease. The extremely talented Yasuoka Akio very generously shared his experiences of the war, Occupation, and postwar decades. He also kindly allowed me to use one of his works as the book's final illustration.

I would also like to thank the many friends who read and commented on earlier versions of this book. Daniel Albert, James Llewellyn, Josh Redstone, Rolf Russell, John Garras, Jim Hudgens, and Kurt Hoverson all contributed observations and suggestions that helped make the book better. Raymond Malone and Randy Pitzer indulged me in listening to half-baked arguments I have subsequently refined.

Numerous librarians and archivists helped me to find material. Among these, one in particular stands out: Eric Van Slander of the National Archives and Records Administration more completely combines the qualities of courtesy and competence than anyone else I have ever met working in a profession where both those qualities are prerequisites. His suggestions on where to look were invaluable and his ability to decipher sometimes cryptic or even erroneous citations is uncanny. He is a national treasure.

Padraic (Pat) Carlin of the Naval Institute Press proved remarkably adept at repeatedly coaxing better work from me without ever exciting my sensitivities. A rookie could not ask for a better coach. In addition, Pat led a team of extremely helpful and talented people who helped to make this a better book than the one I had initially envisioned. I am particularly grateful to Christi Stanforth, Brennan Knight, Jack Russell, and Robin Noonan.

My parents, Irene and Jerry Walsh, both read earlier drafts and gave me useful suggestions. In addition, they gave me financial and personal support without which I could not have completed my work. For financial and personal support, I am also indebted to my stepmother, Debbie Walsh. My in-laws, Makino Fumio and Makino Motoko, also provided generous financial support.

Finally, I would like to thank my *konketsuji*, Alex, who patiently (and sometimes not so patiently) endured my absorption in my work at the expense of time he deserved with his father.

Naturally, both the views expressed in this work and any errors in fact that might appear are mine alone.

INTRODUCTION

On May 18, 2014, right-wing activist Sakurai Makoto led a group of protestors through Tokyo's Akihabara district. The group he led, Zainichi Tokken wo Yurusanai Shimin no Kai (Citizens against the Special Privileges of Resident Foreigners), colloquially known as the Zaitokukai, had frequently been in the news. Usually targeting Koreans, the group achieved notoriety for its unabashed racist venom. At one rally in the Tsuruhashi district of Osaka, a neighborhood with a large number of ethnic Korean residents, a junior high school girl shouted that such people should be killed.[1] At another rally a man carried a sign reading, "Good Koreans, Bad Koreans, Kill Them All."

This time, however, the target of their ire was not Koreans but Americans, specifically the American servicemen who occupied Japan from 1945 to 1952. Claiming that Americans had coerced Japanese women into serving

FIGURE 1 • On May 18, 2014, Zaitokukai members marched to demand an apology from the United States. The banner reads, "Never forget the women whose virtue was robbed by the U.S. Military." (*Kyodo News*)

them sexually, they called for an apology from the American government and a recognition that similar charges leveled against the Imperial Japanese government were nothing but a "Korean lie." Marchers carried signs that read, "Shame on America! We will never forgive the anti-Japanese judgment passed down on the fabrications about the comfort woman system! In defeated Japan, the American Occupation army raped an enormous number of Japanese women and ordered the establishment of a system of prostitution to serve its personnel."[2]

The claim that similar charges leveled against Japan were nothing but a Korean lie is of particular note. Accusations that U.S. military personnel engaged in mass rape and sexual exploitation, and forced Japanese women into prostitution, are often made in a context of minimizing Japan's own maltreatment of women in conquered territories during World War II. Thus, American behavior during the Occupation is often the object of invidious comparison in discussions of the Nanjing Massacre and the so-called comfort woman system of military prostitution and sexual slavery, two issues of particular salience in Japanese politics and diplomacy.

The association of Nanjing with sexual violence is so intimate that many refer to the atrocity as "The Rape of Nanking." According to estimates delivered to the International Military Tribunal for the Far East (IMTFE, the so-called Tokyo Trials), Imperial Japan's armed forces raped more than 20,000 women.[3] Though this estimate is bitterly contested by many Japanese nationalists, it is indisputable that sexual violence during the Japanese army's Nanjing campaign was commonplace. It proved to be such an international embarrassment that it spurred the establishment of so-called comfort facilities, staffed by local women in Nanjing and elsewhere in central China.[4]

Such widespread and systematic abuse of women flies in the face of traditional masculine notions of martial honor and nobility toward the weak. Thus, the idea that this was a defining feature of the Imperial Japanese Army (IJA) is anathema to many Japanese nationalists. They attempt to dispose of charges of mass rape and forced prostitution using a variety of ruses. One method is outright denial mixed with a tu quoque (a sort of we-didn't-do-it-and-besides-so-did-everyone-else argument) aimed at foreign critics of Japan's handling of the issue. In this telling, forced military prostitution was widespread throughout the world in the mid-twentieth century, and Japan's system was no worse than any other, so foreign criticism of Japan is hypocritical. Advocates often single out the United States for particular censure because, the argument goes, contrary to popular American beliefs about the good behavior of U.S. servicemen during their Occupation of Japan, GIs in fact used tens of thousands of Japanese women as prostitutes, many and perhaps most of whom they knew to have been coerced into servitude. Worse, Americans perpetrated gut-wrenching atrocities against Japanese women in a storm of sexual violence that began as soon as they landed and continued throughout the Occupation. In this view, Americans, who have often put themselves in the role of moral scolds regarding the treatment of women throughout the world, should first look to their own monstrous history of abuse of the women of Japan.[5]

In *"Za Reipu obu Nankin" no Kenkyū* (Research on "The Rape of Nanking"), Higashinakano Shūdō and Fujioka Nobukatsu employed such an argument in an attempt to refute Iris Chang's *The Rape of Nanking*. In order to establish rough equivalence between the actions of the IJA in Nanjing and those of the U.S. Army in Japan, they claimed that "on just the single day of August 30, 1945, the day on which MacArthur landed at Atsugi Airbase, there were 315 cases of rape by American soldiers in Kanagawa prefecture alone."[6]

Miyake Hisayuki, formerly a journalist for the *Mainichi Shimbun*, used similar tactics in a panel discussion on Yashiki Takajin's popular Sunday afternoon television show, *Takajin no Soko Made Itte Iinkai*. During a staged debate, ostensibly to determine if there really was a Nanjing Massacre or if it was merely a fabrication of Chinese and American propagandists, Miyake sought to diminish the significance of the sexual violence in Nanjing by claiming that American troops committed 30,000 rapes during the Occupation.[7]

Accusations of widespread and systematic violation of Japanese women's human rights by American occupation forces have also been used to deflect criticism of the Japanese empire's comfort woman system. On May 5, 2015, a group of mostly Western academics issued a statement concerning comfort women and the then-upcoming seventieth anniversary of the end of World War II. In response, a group of right-wing Japanese academics convened a press conference to criticize the statement and its authors. One member of the panel, Takahashi Shirō, an education professor at Meisei University, claimed that the United States had no room to criticize Japan in light of the "massive" outbreak of rape by American soldiers during the Occupation.[8]

In 2008, General Tamogami Toshio, chief of staff of Japan's Air Self-Defense Forces, was removed from his position, demoted in rank, and forced into retirement after the discovery of an essay he wrote extolling the righteousness of Japan's cause in World War II. Soon thereafter, Tamogami became a fixture in right-wing circles. Appearing on an episode of Takeshi Kitano's *TV Takkuru* (TV Tackle), Tamogami minimized the significance of Japan's World War II comfort woman system by claiming that the very first order the United States gave the Japanese government at the outset of the Occupation was to set up a brothel for American troops in Yokohama.[9]

Hashimoto Tōru, an outspoken former mayor of Osaka, created controversy with his comments about the comfort women, making oblique and sometimes not-so-oblique references to the behavior of American troops. In May 2013, a U.S. official, responding to a request from Japan's foreign ministry, met with Hashimoto at Marine Corps Air Station Futenma in Okinawa. Afterward, Hashimoto addressed the assembled media, telling them that he had told the commander that the comfort woman system had been necessary for the maintenance of discipline in the IJA even if the system relied on coercion. He also noted that the Japanese government had set up brothels for Allied Occupation troops, and he urged the commander to have the Marines patronize the local red-light district in order to reduce crime. Hashimoto asserted, "There are places where people can legally release their sexual energy in Japan. Unless they make use of these facilities, it will be difficult to control the sexual energies of the wild Marines."[10]

In 2014, Momii Katsuo, shortly after being appointed as head of NHK's board of governors, also attempted to normalize sexual exploitation. Momii asserted that the comfort women system was "bad by today's morals, but this was a fact of those times. Korea's statements that Japan was the only nation that forced this are puzzling."[11]

Such views are now widely regarded as established truth by the Japanese right. At first blush, this may appear to be a simple case of psychological projection on the part of nationalist extremists. However, over the last three decades, claims like these have become increasingly common in mainstream Occupation historiography. Yuki Tanaka, a former professor at the Hiroshima Peace Institute of Hiroshima City University has done extensive work on both Japanese and Allied war crimes. Concerning the behavior of GIs in the opening days of the Occupation, he wrote,

> From the day they landed, U.S. soldiers engaged in the mass rape of Japanese women. . . . After that the incidence of rape spiraled upward throughout the period of the occupation, and the standard atrocities

began to occur: young girls raped in front of their parents, pregnant women raped in maternity wards, and so on. Over a period of 10 days (August 30–September 10) there were 1,336 reported cases of rape of Japanese women by U.S. soldiers in Kanagawa prefecture (where Yokosuka and Yokohama are situated) alone.[12]

Tanaka's claim comports with the writing of Fujime Yuki, now a professor at the Osaka University School of Human Sciences. In her *A History of Sexuality*, an award-winning survey of the evolution of public policy toward sexuality in Japan, Fujime touched on the subject of sexual violence by GIs: "In the first month after landing, American servicemen raped at least 3500 Japanese women." She then asserted, "The beginning of the Occupation was the beginning of the American military's sexual despoliation of Japanese women."[13]

In his Pulitzer and Bancroft Prize-winning *Embracing Defeat: Japan in the Wake of World War II*, historian John W. Dower cited a claim put forth by several authors that American soldiers had become so accustomed to the idea of sexual privilege with Japanese women that when the Supreme Commander of the Allied Powers, General of the Army Douglas MacArthur, placed brothels off-limits to them, they went on a rampage, and "the number of rapes and assaults on Japanese women," which had "amounted to around 40 *daily*" before the ban, "then rose to an average of 330 a day" (emphasis in original).[14] More recently, both Thomas U. Berger and Ian Buruma have written that were forty reported incidents of rape by American soldiers every day in 1945; Buruma added, "The figure was probably an underestimation, since many cases would not have been reported, out of shame."[15]

Many accounts of the Occupation present it as a time of near-lawlessness in which American soldiers did what they wanted, had their way with Japanese women, murdered civilians indiscriminately, and committed innumerable casual cruelties. They allegedly got away with this because their commanders were hostile and vindictive toward Japanese people and thus indifferent to their plight. Consequently, they made no effective efforts to discipline their troops. In this narrative, Japanese police were helpless before armed perpetrators, and American MPs were worse, turning blind eyes or even taking advantage of their authority to commit crimes themselves, sometimes against the very women whose cases they were supposed to be investigating.[16] Wherever Americans were stationed, the story goes, they destroyed communities, demoralizing the young women by raping them so that in their despair they turned to prostitution and invariably contracted the venereal diseases that were epidemic in the ranks of the occupiers.[17]

In terms of scale, the figure cited by Dower and many others would mean that there were more than 700,000 reported rapes of Japanese women during the Occupation. Thus, judging from the sheer numbers of incidents, the U.S. Occupation of Japan would have been one of the worst occurrences of mass sexual violence in world history, with *reported* cases being more than ten times the number of *estimated* rapes in Bosnia during the breakup of the former Yugoslavia and seven times the *estimated* number of incidents during the Bangladeshi War of Independence.[18]

Nor is the critique of sexual predation limited to rape. According to a good deal of recent writing, the U.S. Army was complicit in, encouraged, or even ordered the Japanese government to set up brothels exclusively for American troops.[19] Gender theorist and sociologist Hirai Kazuko has asserted that where war rape and military prostitution were concerned, "The mentality of the Occupation Army was astonishingly similar to that of the old Japanese Army."[20] Hirai has even explicitly endorsed Hashimoto's comments about Japan's actions during World War II being fairly standard for militaries of that time.[21]

Though few writers have gone as far as Hirai, accusations of American moral turpitude are common. The General Headquarters of the American military in Japan (GHQ, also sometimes referred to by the acronym SCAP [for Supreme Commander Allied Powers], an appellation that in common usage can refer to both the commander personally and to his command) has frequently been accused of depraved indifference to the fates of women who were allegedly forced to serve as prostitutes for U.S. military personnel. In a 2007 AP article carried in newspapers around the world, veteran Far East journalist Eric Talmadge asserted that Americans were participants in a forced prostitution network of their own:

Japan's abhorrent practice of enslaving women to provide sex for its troops in World War II had a little-known sequel: After its surrender—with tacit approval from the U.S. occupation authorities—Japan set up a similar "comfort women" system for American GIs.

An Associated Press review of historical documents—some never before translated into English—shows American authorities permitted the official brothel system to operate despite internal reports that the women were being coerced into prostitution.[22]

In 2005 the United States probably came as close as it ever will to tacitly admitting these charges. On a trip to the Far East, U.S. president George W. Bush was flummoxed by the intense passions aroused by Japanese prime minister Koizumi Junichirō's visit to Japan's controversial Yasukuni Shrine. Built to honor those who died fighting for the emperor, it also enshrines the souls of convicted war criminals who either died in custody or by execution of sentences. As such, visits by Japanese prime ministers are seen as provocative insults by some neighboring countries. Christopher Hill, the assistant secretary of state for East Asian affairs, recommended that Bush issue a statement condemning the visits to Yasukuni. Michael Green, a Japan expert on Bush's team, counseled strongly against such a step. Green said that Japan could deeply embarrass the United States with police reports of rape during the Occupation that had never been prosecuted. Bush chose to let the matter drop.[23]

Such allegations may be shocking to nonspecialists. Most Americans tend to regard the postwar American Occupation of Japan as the quintessential example of their nation's beneficence and magnanimity. There is, of course, nothing unusual about there being a vast gulf between the popular understanding and the expert consensus on a given subject. In this case, the extraordinary feature is that popular understanding comes closer to the truth. Bluntly stated, there is no credible evidence of the mass rape of Japanese women by American servicemen during the Occupation. Nor is there any reliable evidence of GHQ's collusion, involvement in, approval of, or connivance in any system of involuntary prostitution involving Japanese women. Moreover, the documentary record is unambiguous, and in many cases the emerging historical consensus on these issues inverts reality. With a few notable exceptions, those who have concerned themselves most intensely with the subjects of sexual violence and prostitution during the Allied Occupation of Japan are precisely those whose work is least substantiated by the historical record and most influenced by folklore.[24] This is a peculiar situation. It requires explanation.

The near-unanimity enjoyed by these interpretations is not the result of a sudden increase in rigorous and thorough research on the subjects. Rather, it is the result of the influence that myth, legend, political bias, historiographical fads, and the popular imagination can exercise on historians' judgment when they are allowed to operate unchecked. The currency of these legends has now reached a critical mass. Almost any disinterested observer surveying the literature could scarcely arrive at any other conclusion than those put forth by many apologists for Japan's war crimes.

It is a textbook example of incestuous amplification.

It has gone, for the most part, unchallenged for so long because the basic narratives, forged in the immediate postwar years, addressed and in some sense continue to address deep-seated emotional needs in both the Japanese popular consciousness and within the academic community. Depictions of mass rape and sexual slavery during the Occupation are best regarded not as factual accounts but, rather, as expression of internalized metaphors for Japan's defeat in World War II and its subsequent and continuing strategic subordination to the United States. Increasingly, these narratives appeal to Western critics of Japan's perceived fealty to American strategic objectives.

These are no small claims, and prudent readers will naturally be skeptical. To overcome that skepticism, I must satisfy three criteria. First, I must show that the historical consensus, which includes even an adviser to a decidedly conservative American president, is in fact wrong. Second, I must demonstrate that it would even be possible for so many people in the immediate post-Occupation period to be susceptible to believing outlandish stories about events of which they themselves had direct personal experience. Third, I must also show that legends created at this time indeed made the transition from the popular imagination to the historical consensus.

To achieve these goals, this book is divided into three parts. The first part consists of three chapters that use contemporary documents to analyze, respectively, crime, especially rape, committed by U.S. servicemen during the Occupation, GHQ's handling of the issue of prostitution, and GHQ's handling of the issue of venereal disease.

Chapter 1 discusses the behavior of American troops during the Occupation, with a focus on their treatment of women and especially on the troops' propensity for sexual violence. It deals with both the early Occupation, a time about which allegations of mass rape are most common, and with the Occupation as a whole. During the early Occupation the historical record is particularly rich. The Japanese government was deeply concerned about rape during this time and so instructed both its officials and its subjects to be vigilant in watching the Americans. This was also the time during which GI crime was at its highest. Relatively few military police entered with the first troops. The American vanguard routinely swept the Japanese police aside and deprived them of their weapons. Moreover, the Japanese government persuaded Occupation authorities to reverse their decision about using military scrip. As a result, the first troops to enter the country discovered that they could acquire nothing honestly. After American authorities came to believe that the Japanese population presented little physical danger to its troops, they dispatched more MPs, and this initial crime wave abated. Even during this time, violent crimes like rape and murder were rare.

Documentary evidence about American criminality is far scarcer after the first few weeks of the Occupation. There is nevertheless enough so that one can understand the approximate scale of crime during the Occupation as a whole and conclude that claims of mass rape are fundamentally false. The picture that emerges is one of occasional criminality sometimes including rape. However, contrary to myth, there is no time period during which mass rape can reasonably be alleged.

Finally, GI behavior during the Occupation is compared to the behavior of the troops of other occupying armies in World War II. The frequency of rape is compared to that of the Soviet Red Army in Europe, the Imperial Japanese Army in Asia, and the U.S. Army in Germany. The contrast with the behavior of Japanese troops in Asia is especially instructive, as numerous writers have, often misleadingly or incorrectly, compared the Imperial Japanese military and the U.S. military. Though the data analyzed for the behavior of these other armies is nowhere near as thorough as that for the U.S. military in Japan, it nevertheless provides a good basic understanding of how American troops in Japan compared to those of other occupying forces.

Chapter 2 discusses how GHQ dealt with the issue of prostitution in Japan. As with sexual violence, there are many legends about this subject. Many allege American initiative in the organized sexual exploitation of Japanese women. As was the case with sexual violence, the more sensational claims about GHQ's involvement in prostitution do not bear scrutiny. Nevertheless, the story of how the Americans handled the issue is an interesting one. GHQ found the problem vexing from the outset. The spread of venereal disease through American ranks soon made it imperative that some sort of action be taken. In addition, the revelation that many women in Japan's established licensed prostitution system were employed under duress brought the question of personal liberty to the forefront. Finally, the long-standing and deeply engrained cultural acceptance of prostitution in Japan constrained would-be reformers in GHQ. In this atmosphere GHQ made two major decisions regarding prostitution. First, it decided to abolish the institution of licensed prostitution as it had been traditionally practiced from the early Tokugawa period (early seventeenth century) and codified in Imperial Japan at the end of the nineteenth century. Second, it left the question of whether to completely outlaw prostitution to the Japanese.

GHQ began grappling with the issue of prostitution in the context of its public health implications, especially for U.S. personnel. American officials from GHQ's Public Health and Welfare Section (PHW) were largely ignorant about the subject and sought information from Japanese public health officials. They learned that in the licensed prostitution system, sex workers were confined to specified areas and subject to periodic health examinations but that regulation had become increasingly lax during the war years. PHW initially sought to reinvigorate the system with stronger enforcement and oversight. Later, when health officials discovered that many women and girls had been impressed into the system against their wills, they recommended eliminating the system altogether. Two weeks later, on January 21, 1946, SCAP duly ordered the abolition of licensed prostitution and declared all debts that bound women and girls in prostitution to be null and void. The intention was to eliminate all involuntary prostitution in Japan. Thenceforth GHQ continually ruled against the validity of any debt, no matter how incurred, that had the effect of trapping any woman in any form of sexual servitude. Nevertheless, brothel proprietors, often with the connivance or even assistance of Japanese officials, frequently stymied American intentions.

Shortly afterward, GHQ faced pressure to prohibit prostitution altogether. Pressure came from Japanese women's and Christian groups, and also from within the ranks of the occupiers themselves. The Japanese groups were unsuccessful primarily because they could not mobilize Japanese public opinion. American military men came much closer to success because they had ultimate authority, and their concerns were primarily practical and bore directly on their operations. Health officials and commanders came to a general consensus that an outright ban on prostitution and its related activities was the surest path to controlling venereal disease. They also shared with the Japanese public an aversion to the proliferation of streetwalkers that had begun near the end of the war and had been exacerbated by GHQ's abolition of licensed prostitution and its later order placing all brothels in Japan off-limits to American servicemen. In 1947 it briefly appeared that prostitution in all forms including voluntary prostitution would be abolished. PHW drew up a draft directive to outlaw prostitution and forwarded it to SCAP's Government Section (GS) and G-2 (Intelligence) for approval. G-2 was opposed to prohibition, believing it would be an exercise in futility that would invite scorn and hostility from the Japanese populace. GS, on the other hand, was generally in favor, but intended to support a ban only if it enjoyed popular backing. It became clear that such a ban did not. GHQ elected to leave the matter to the Japanese. Prostitution remained legal in most areas for the remainder of the Occupation. The Japanese government later technically outlawed the practice in 1956 (in a law that went into effect in 1957), but it remains both prevalent and open to the present day.

Chapter 3 deals with the problem of venereal disease during the Occupation. Venereal disease was a major problem for American Occupation authorities, who struggled mightily to control its prevalence among the troops. Many writers have consequently subscribed to fundamentally false narratives of both the source of the problem and American handling of it. In the presentations of many scholars, the venereal disease epidemic in Japan was the result of libidinous Americans infecting large numbers of Japanese women, mainly prostitutes, who then passed the diseases on to other Americans and Japanese as well.

While there was no shortage of infected personnel prior to the Americans' arrival in Japan, the levels of venereal disease were far higher in the Japanese civilian population, especially among prostitutes. Syphilis had been a problem in Japan since the beginning of the sixteenth century. Syphilis and other venereal diseases spread throughout the archipelago and became endemic. These were so prevalent that foreign visitors to Japan almost invariably commented on both the high level of infection and its association with prostitution. This was despite their generally high evaluation of Japanese hygiene and health in comparison to their home societies. In the early twentieth century, venereal disease was a major concern of some Japanese health officials, as well as of such diverse groups as women's rights activists and physical fitness advocates.

GHQ's handling of the problem of venereal disease met with only limited success for the first few years, but the measures American authorities introduced, most consequentially the use of antibiotics, finally began to have a positive effect. In the years immediately after the Occupation, using the methods introduced by PHW, authorities succeeded in the virtual elimination of venereal disease as a public health menace after centuries of futility. Many writers have suggested that the Americans were uniquely fixated on the elimination of venereal disease either because they could not control their troops' behavior or because they were obsessed with providing safe sexual entertainment for their troops. In reality, the handling of the venereal disease problem was consistent with the treatment of other infectious agents. Ultimately, it was not only successful but also a significant contribution to Japanese public health.

Having demonstrated that narratives stressing mass rape, systematic sexual exploitation, and the unchecked spread of disease are not supported by the historical record, the book then explores the process by which such false narratives came to enjoy currency in Occupation historiography. Chapters 4 and 5 discuss the psychological environment in which legends flourished.

Chapter 4 discusses the intimate association between rape and war in the human psyche and in history and literature. It shows that the fear of rape during wartime is ubiquitous and deeply ingrained. It is a major factor in people's emotions in situations of tense conflict regardless of whether the possibility of rape is remote or acute. There is a (sometimes altogether justified) fear that a nation's women will become the spoils of an invader. This fear can be a powerful motivator for troops who regard protection of these women as one of their cardinal duties. Propagandists have frequently employed these fears to motivate men to fight.

The chapter then examines how Japanese viewed the connection between rape and war before and during World War II. Even before the outbreak of full-scale war in China, many considered rape the natural corollary of conquest. Japanese servicemen tended to regard sexual license with the women of overseas territories as their due, thus they committed countless rapes. Accounts of sexual violence and the frequency with which their troops engaged in it became a major concern for the Imperial Japanese Army. This experience colored the way that Japanese anticipated the behavior of victorious Americans, and a miasma of dread descended on the crumbling empire in the war's final stages, becoming especially prevalent in areas considered likely targets of invasion. Japanese authorities played on this fear, disseminating rape propaganda to unite the populace against the invader. In the wake of Japan's sudden and unexpected surrender, this atmosphere of terror lingered. Rumors of mass sexual atrocity spread like wildfire as the Americans landed, and persisted for some time thereafter.

Chapter 5 deals with the reaction of Japanese conservatives and Japanese men across the political spectrum to the drastically changed position of women in Japanese society as a result of defeat and Occupation reform. The Occupation implemented what political scientist Susan J. Pharr has aptly called a "truly radical set of laws and policies" regarding women.[25] These enforced on Japan an American ideal of individual liberty that ran counter to traditional Japanese ideas of a patriarchal household as the fundamental unit of society. As part of this overhaul, the Americans sought to restructure sexual and marital relations on bases of equality and individual autonomy. Many Japanese men resented being deprived of their traditional privileges. In addition to presuming to dictate to Japanese men how they should deal with Japanese women, Americans further embittered many Japanese men with the example of how they dealt with Japanese children and especially Japanese women. Their cheerful and apparently happy-go-lucky attitude struck Japanese conservatives as the opposite of masculine. While Japanese had been taught that military men should be stern and serious, Americans, even when on duty, were casual, approachable, and sometimes downright playful. If not for the fact of their victory it would have been easy to dismiss them as frivolous.

FIGURE 2 • American serviceman with Japanese children (U.S. Army)

While the relations between GIs and Japanese children was galling to many, it was nothing compared to the downright humiliation many felt at the free and casual relations Americans often had with Japanese women. The widespread consorting of Japanese women with American men infuriated many Japanese men and quite a few women as well. Many saw Americans as little more than sexual interlopers who hypocritically used the rhetoric of autonomy and individual rights to seize control of Japanese women's sexuality from Japanese men and exploit it for their own pleasure.

The final part of the book shows how this psychological environment of fear and bitterness presented fertile ground for exploitation both commercially and politically.

Chapter 6 describes how left-wing forces in Japan capitalized on the resentment of relations between American servicemen and Japanese women to tie issues of sexual violence, perceived racial contamination, and prostitution to their campaign against the U.S.-Japan security treaty and the basing rights it gave to the American military. It also shows how the discourse about rape, prostitution, and mixed-race children appealed to prurient as well as to nationalist interests. The result was a subgenre of exploitation fiction. This sensational *panpan* (prostitute) literature was widely popular and many examples of it were falsely presented as reportage on actual incidents.

Chapter 7 discusses the work of those scholars most responsible for introducing the sensational stories that first appeared in *panpan* literature into mainstream historiography. It shows that some prominent writers in the field of Japanese studies either knew or should have known that what they were writing was false. However, in many cases these writers failed to exercise their critical faculties and let their political biases get the better of their judgment.

Legends of mass rape and sexual exploitation have long been staples of leftist activists in Japan. They were an essential ingredient of the historical narratives crafted in the service of protest movements against American military bases and the U.S.-Japan security treaty. Many of the scholars who have incorporated these narratives into their own accounts have denounced the U.S. military and the U.S.-Japan alliance as oppressive forces in the world. Moreover, some of the most prominent among them have explicitly argued that the purpose of scholarship should be not to analyze the evidence but, rather, to advance political agendas. The behavior of these scholars ranges from the incompetent to the unethical. The myths they have promoted are, at least in part, a deliberate fabrication intended to advance specific political outcomes.

The concluding chapter discusses the resilience of the myth and explores the reasons behind it. It demonstrates how Japan's subordination to the United States in diplomatic and strategic affairs has often been expressed in a metaphor of sexual conquest and domination. Writers and cartoonists across the political spectrum have invoked the metaphor in denouncing the United States. Many works of *panpan* literature, some created for a specific political purpose and others originating as sensational pornography, subsequently came to be seen as nonfiction by a large portion of Japanese society and later scholars. This literature has had an outsize effect on writing about the Occupation, and these works have been incorporated into the academic and popular mainstream understandings of American treatment of Japanese women.

As a whole, the work shows that portrayals of mass rape and sexual atrocities committed by GIs are best regarded as metaphoric expressions of the experience of defeat, occupation, and continued subordination rather than as factual accounts. That metaphor has a great appeal to those who resent Japan's continuing policy of subordinating itself to the United States on the international scene. Thus, the myth of mass rape will likely abide so long as that policy does.

CHAPTER I

GI BEHAVIOR DURING THE OCCUPATION OF JAPAN AND IN COMPARATIVE PERSPECTIVE

 ## THE EARLY OCCUPATION

In recent decades many writers have alleged that American forces committed numerous crimes, especially rape, during the Occupation of Japan. Most often they allege this about the operation's opening weeks and months, a period fraught with tension and uncertainty. Such claims cannot withstand scrutiny. Allegations of mass rape during any period of the Occupation are not supported by police records, and they are flatly contradicted by many contemporary accounts.

In its initial phase, the Occupation was solely an American operation, and its chief objective was to establish control. The Americans planned to move combat ground troops throughout the country as quickly as possible.[1] In the words of Maj. Gen. William C. Chase, commander of the First

Cavalry Division, "We planned an assault landing so we could be ready for anything."[2] Naturally, in these circumstances military police were not a priority. American officers were surprised to have more trouble with unruly GIs than with enemy irreconcilables in those opening days.

This mildly chaotic time has become the subject of legend, and many writers have claimed that American forces committed numerous heinous crimes, especially rape. These assertions are superficially plausible because of the initial disorder and because it would follow a pattern of rape and war seen elsewhere. There is often a period of lawlessness after a defeated regime has been ousted but the conquering power has yet to establish itself. During this time rape is sometimes widespread, and even when it is not common, it is more frequent then than in later periods. This happened with the Soviet Red Army in Germany, the Imperial Japanese Army in China, and (though on a vastly smaller scale) the U.S. Army in Germany.[3]

Some writers limit their allegations of mass rape to this time. As discussed at the introduction, Fujime Yuki and others state that there were 3,500 rapes during the first month of the Occupation. However, Fujime also gives the incongruously (and factually) low figure of 30 rape reports for all of 1946.[4] Similarly, Takemae Eiji asserted that there were 1,336 reported rapes of Japanese women by American servicemen in the first ten days of the Occupation but that after the initial crime wave, "military discipline took hold" and "the worst fears of both sides proved groundless."[5] Whatever the cause, many (but by no means all) writers acknowledge a conspicuous decrease in the reported number of rapes after the first weeks of the Occupation but assert that during this early period, sexual violence was rampant.

Claims such as these are easily investigated because both Japanese and American authorities closely observed the behavior of American servicemen, with a particular focus on rape. In fact, one set of Japanese reports listed only three categories of crime: rape, offenses against the police, and "other," in that order.[6] Another lists rape, offenses against the police, and offenses against ordinary citizens, again in that order.[7]

Similarly, American commanders took rape accusations very seriously. On September 2, 1945, just after the surrender ceremony on USS *Missouri*,

General of the Army Douglas MacArthur, Supreme Commander of the Allied Powers (SCAP), summoned Lt. Gen. Robert Eichelberger, commander of the U.S. Eighth Army and his top military lieutenant, "for a conference concerning some reported rape cases on the part of Marines."[8] According to Japanese police records, there were only six reported rape cases at the time.[9] On September 11, Brig. Gen. William T. Clement, USMC, brought Eichelberger a report on the rape cases in his area.[10] As of the previous day, there had been nine reported cases in the entire country.[11] Both the Japanese and the Americans took cases of misconduct, and especially of rape, very seriously, and they kept detailed records. Many of these records survive. Those records reveal that though there is a kernel of truth to accounts of lawlessness in the Occupation's opening days, the stories that have sprouted from that kernel are manifestly, often outrageously, false.

In the particular case of the Americans in Japan, the disorder attendant to the changeover in regimes was exacerbated by the fact that Japan capitulated about a year prior to expectation. Americans entering the country were thus relying on a hurried contingency plan they had drafted only weeks earlier.[12] MacArthur further aggravated the chaos with a poorly timed reversal of currency policy. At the behest of the Japanese government, SCAP repudiated military scrip after it had already been printed and distributed to American troops. GIs suddenly found themselves penniless, and many turned to crime. In the opening days of the Occupation, robberies, carjackings, and thefts were common. GIs seemed to especially prize the weapons of the Japanese police. Nevertheless, serious violent crimes like rape and murder were rare during even this time.[13]

The most easily obtained sources on GI crime come from Japanese media coverage. Due to fears of anti-American agitation, GHQ established a press code on September 18, 1945. This curtailed the ability of the vernacular media to criticize the Occupation or call negative attention to the behavior of its troops. However, prior to that time the Japanese media was free of American interference and did not hesitate to criticize the United States.[14] Moreover, the figures carried in the media about American crimes make clear that they had well-informed sources within the Japanese domestic security bureaucracy.

The *Asahi Shimbun*, one of Japan's largest papers, contains a number of accounts of petty crimes and of some more serious offenses. A survey of its coverage provides insight into the behavior of GIs. For example, a September 2 article described criminal actions that had occurred on the first two days of Occupation. According to this account, on August 30 American troops had committed two rapes and had attempted two others. On August 31, they stole a Japanese sword and several bicycles, robbed a beer truck, and committed several other thefts.[15]

A September 7 article carried the most detailed information about GI crime. There "was a fair amount of crime in the first two or three days," which caused some alarm. However, due to an increase in the size of the U.S. military police force, the number of incidents had drastically decreased.[16] Moreover, many of the complaints were registered by the police themselves.[17] The figures for crime are shown in table 1.

The paper carried more information on GI behavior on September 11, when it discussed the actions of troops entering Tokyo. According to this account, the Americans had entered the city on September 8, and up through the evening of the 9th, things had proceeded relatively smoothly. There were twenty-nine complaints against American officers and soldiers in Tokyo. These were mostly petty crimes such as theft, robbery, and dining without compensation. The article made a special point of the fact that no rapes had been reported. In fact, its title was "Absolutely No Violation of Women."[18] This was the last article in the *Asahi* with any concrete information about rape.

Aside from press reports, the next most easily obtainable resources are the testimonies of individuals with direct experience of the Occupation's advance. These are available in memoirs, latter recollections, and, more formally, in the official histories of the various Japanese prefectural police departments. These accounts reinforce the image of a relatively tranquil Occupation. The general feeling of Japanese authorities was one of profound relief. For example, there is the testimony of Hattori Ichirō, a police officer from Aichi Prefecture. Hattori's superiors dispatched him to aid local law enforcement in Kanagawa Prefecture, where the Americans made their first landings. He later recalled, "The city was surprisingly quiet. As

TABLE 1 • Reported crimes committed by American servicemen carried in the *Asahi Shimbun* on September 7, 1945

Date	Number of Incidents	Number of Incidents Involving Japanese Policemen
August 30	311	196
August 31	216	167
September 1	160	50
September 2	179	88
September 3	85	4
September 4	33	2
September 5	2	—

far as I am aware there was no especially big trouble."[19] In Kōchi, on the island of Shikoku, the arrival of the troops was "extremely peaceful."[20] In Shizuoka, near Mt. Fuji, "the advance of the Allied armies was extremely peaceful."[21] In Yamagata, on the Japan Sea coast of northeastern Honshū, "the strict discipline of the American troops completely allayed the fears of the populace."[22] The situation was the same throughout the country: an initial period of uncertainty and anxiety was soon followed by reassurance at the discipline and good behavior of the American troops.[23]

Civilians recorded or remembered the advance similarly. In his diary, the writer Yamada Fūtarō wrote down his conversations with people who had interacted with the American troops. One student remarked that the troops were maintaining strict discipline in Tokyo. A factory manager friend of Yamada's, "Old Man Saitō," was shocked at how pleasant the Americans were, remarking that from their attitudes one would be hard pressed to even know which side had won the war. Yamada himself wrote that though it was hard to admit, he could see why MacArthur was so proud of his troops.[24] By December 1, Yamada was so impressed that he wrote an entire entry about the behavior of the Americans. Recording his own impressions as well as those of people he talked with or overheard, he could barely contain himself, writing four pages of uninterrupted praise.[25] Similarly, the writer Nagai Kafū recorded an encounter at a restaurant where a number of young American officers were also dining. To Nagai, they seemed quite noble in their bearing and made efforts to communicate with Japanese in their own language. He could not help but feel that they were "far and away more genial than Japanese military men."[26] Many years later, ultranationalist Ishihara Shintarō, certainly no fan of the United States, recalled, "Everyone in my neighborhood watched Americans with great fear, but nothing really happened."[27]

Japanese police records corroborate such testimony. Authorities and civilians alike were consumed with dread that vengeful Americans, flush with victory, would go on a rampage. The specter of large-scale sexual violence haunted them all. Throughout the archipelago people from all walks of life sought ways to stem the expected onslaught. However, of most interest to the historian is that one of the actions taken by the Japanese government was to put its formidable domestic surveillance apparatus to work. The authorities instructed civilians to report any type of misconduct whatsoever and ordered police officers to investigate and report every allegation, even if they were nothing more than rumors.[28]

Evidence suggests that civilians followed these instructions to the letter. In one case, American investigators looking into a reported case of rape found that neither civilian nor military police knew anything about the allegation: "There is no record of this alleged offense at the police station and the police have no recollection of this occurence [sic]."[29]

In the early stages of the Occupation, the Home Ministry compiled reports from police departments, the Tokubetsu Kōtō Keisatsu (known as the Tokkō, or Special Higher Police) and local officials into extensive files on any misconduct of American troops. They distributed these files widely throughout the Japanese government, with copies forwarded to the home minister; the vice minister; the chief of the Tokkō; the headquarters of the Kempeitai, the notorious Japanese gendarmerie; the Lord Keeper of the Privy Seal; Deputy Prime Minister Prince Konoe Fumimaro; the Central Liaison Office (CLO); and ten more recipients.[30] Copies of some of these reports are currently available in the Japanese National Diet Library, the Japanese National Archives, the Japanese Foreign Ministry's Diplomatic Records Office, and two published volumes.[31] The reports are not always legible. In addition, some reports classify some crimes or other actions in questionable ways, and some reports are missing. Those caveats notwithstanding, when added to newspaper reports and personal recollections, they help to give a clear picture of GI behavior during the early Occupation.

The local population observed and reported almost everything the Americans did—often down to the most trivial detail. For example, in one case, three Americans approached Otohara Shichizō, a roof tile maker in Kawasaki. After offering him a cigarette, they pointed to a phrase in an English-Japanese dictionary that read, "I want a red kimono." After extensive difficulties in communication and an inability to procure red kimonos for the three men, a prefectural assemblyman with some knowledge of English happened by, and the men were satisfied with two red kimonos and one white one. After negotiating over price, the men paid for the garments. Mr. Otohara saw no reason to report the encounter, as the soldiers had paid. However, the local rumor mill went into action, and the police learned of the exchange. As per their instructions, the police investigated and filed a report.[32] In another case, a department chief (部長) of the Morioka police department thought it necessary to report on the activities of two Allied servicemen who had gotten their laundry done in town. The men tried to pay for their laundry with twenty yen, perhaps in worthless Occupation scrip, but the man who performed the service requested canned goods instead. They gave him four cans of food for washing four uniform shirts, two pairs of long underwear, two towels, two sheets, and four pairs of socks.[33] Another report detailed an encounter with a group of eleven soldiers who came to the residence of a Satō Fukuharu and bartered two packs of cigarettes, two cans of food, five pieces of chewing gum, and two bags of bread in exchange for an unknown number of tomatoes, spring onions, and cucumbers. Upon departing, the soldiers used an English-Japanese dictionary and pointed to a phrase that was something to the effect of "It was nice to meet you."[34]

Not all of the encounters between Allied personnel and Japanese civilians were so innocuous. American troops also committed crimes. Reports on these cases were every bit as detailed as those describing their harmless activities. The most numerous victims were Japanese police. Whether because of desire to disarm a potentially hostile force, humiliate a beaten

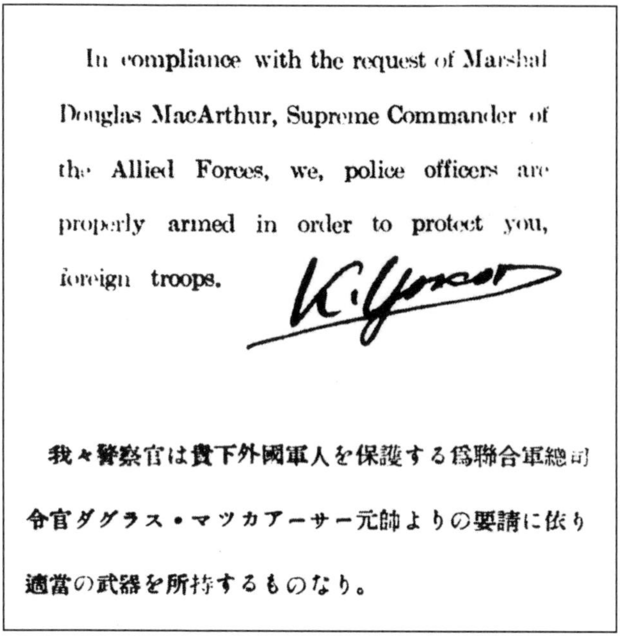

In compliance with the request of Marshal
Douglas MacArthur, Supreme Commander of
the Allied Forces, we, police officers are
properly armed in order to protect you,
foreign troops.

我々警察官は貴下外國軍人を保護する爲聯合軍總司
令官ダグラス・マツカアーサー元帥よりの要請に依り
適當の武器を所持するものなり。

FIGURE 3 • Example of flyer distributed to Japanese police
in an effort to stop the robbery of their service weapons by
American troops (Ehime Prefectural Police History)

foe, or simply to procure souvenirs, in the opening weeks of the Occupation GIs frequently robbed policemen of their swords and pistols.[35] This
happened so frequently that GHQ authorized the printing of a special flyer
to be distributed to policemen that noted that they were armed with the
understanding and approval of SCAP.

Americans also had a penchant for joyriding. Afterward, they often
simply abandoned vehicles when they would no longer function. This
pattern became so frequent that at one point the Japanese government
forwarded a request from a company that had suffered numerous thefts
petitioning GHQ to tell its soldiers to please just return the vehicles to the
place they had taken them from.[36] According to one official memo, in the
first twelve days of the Occupation, servicemen stole no fewer than 170
vehicles.[37] By the end of September, they had stolen 222 vehicles, including

five fire engines.[38] They also hijacked a tram and two trains and stole two buses.[39] At the time there was a grand total of 750 serviceable passenger cars in the entire Kantō area (which includes Tokyo and Yokohama). Of these only about 225 were gasoline-powered, and most were "nearly worn out."[40] Inevitably, a disproportionate number of victims were high-placed and influential Japanese. Two GIs stole a car from the Japanese Foreign Ministry.[41] In another case, Americans took a Welfare Ministry vehicle at gunpoint.[42] They also stole the car of Diet member Kōno Hachirō.[43] Another time, two Americans (the report said it was unclear if they were soldiers or journalists) carjacked a vehicle in broad daylight right in front of the police headquarters in Hibiya. One of the passengers had been future prime minister Ikeda Hayato.[44] In the highest-profile case, a GI approached future prime minister Kishi Nobusuke, who was watching over the official vehicle of then–prime minister Shidehara Kijurō. After feigning illness, he convinced Kishi to allow the prime minister's driver to take him to the hospital. En route, the soldier forced the driver from the car and drove away.[45] Though the memo detailing this incident to the Americans was stamped "Immediate Action" in red letters, the investigators never found the culprit.[46] After carjacking and theft of arms, the most frequent GI crimes were robbery, forced bartering, dining without compensation, and the like.

Ironically, very often the Japanese targets of these crimes were as much victims of their own government as they were of the occupying army. Before the surrender, American policymakers had assumed that in Japan, as in Germany, they would rule the country by direct military administration. Accordingly, they began assuming the functions of the Japanese government even before they landed. On August 22, a top-secret cable from Dōmei News Agency to the Japanese government indicated that a shipment of $100 million worth of military scrip was on its way from San Francisco to Manila.[47] Realizing that they were in danger of losing control over their economy, the next day the Japanese government sent an urgent telegram to MacArthur in the Philippines:

The Japanese Government wishes to be informed of the currency to be used in Japan by the Forces of Occupation.

> We hope that they will use the Bank of Japan notes for this pur-
> pose, and are ready to deliver the currency at Atsugi, Yokohama and
> Yokosuka.[48]

The United States apparently did not respond as the time of the troops' arrival drew ever closer. Finance Minister Tsushima Juichi proposed having the Bank of Japan print its own currency to distribute to the Americans. The cabinet agreed and ordered the money printed.[49] On August 28, the day the first American troops landed, the government again tried to persuade the United States to drop plans for military scrip. They cabled,

> Referring to our radio gram number 28 date 23 August, in which we
> expressed our hope that the Occupation forces would use the bank
> of Japan notes in Japan, we would like to submit the following to your
> special consideration, in view of a recent foreign broadcast. We are
> to deliver the Japanese currency as much as required by your head
> quarters for the expenditure of the Occupation forces, as informed
> to you in our radiogram under reference. If they are [sic] the military
> currency in the main island of Japan, it will disturb the monetary and
> financial situation in Japanese homeland in such a degree as to cause
> uncontrollable confusion of our system of currency and finance.[50]

Receiving no reply, the government dispatched Lt. Gen. Arisue Seizō to meet the advanced team landing at Atsugi airfield with 10 million yen in cash. Arisue spoke with the American officer in charge of the advanced team, Col. Charles Tench. Tench said that his men had no intention of leaving the base and that there was thus nothing to fear.[51]

However, on September 2, after the surrender ceremony on *Missouri*, and after there were many more Americans in the country than Tench's small group, Suzuki Tadakatsu, head of the newly established Central Liaison Office, learned that GHQ was planning to issue a number of bombshell directives the next day. Among other things, these would have established direct military government and decreed that GHQ's military scrip would be treated as the equivalent of Bank of Japan bills. After a flurry of activity, the Japanese government arranged a meeting between MacArthur and

Foreign Minister Shigemitsu Mamoru for the following morning. There Shigemitsu persuaded MacArthur to rescind the orders and let Japan maintain control of its currency.[52]

This diplomatic success instantly rendered penniless tens of thousands of armed young men on the streets of Japan. Many attempted to solve their conundrum by selling things to Japanese. Nagai Kafū related an incident as late as mid-October 1945 in which an acquaintance saw American soldiers selling chocolate in front of Atami station until they had collected enough money to patronize a nearby brothel.[53] Others attempted to buy things with American dollars or Filipino pesos. Some attempted to barter cigarettes, canned food, chocolates, and other goods.[54] Some chose more direct methods. Even among those relatively honest men who tried to deal squarely with civilians, a significant number lost their tempers once their initial offers were refused and made their opposites another offer, à la Vito Corleone.[55] Others simply paid in whatever money they had and forced Japanese to accept it.[56] In one case American frustration resulted in a terrifying experience for a group of Japanese women. A group of American soldiers burst into a brothel, and while they were robbing the place one of their number climbed the stairs, cornered one of the prostitutes, and, brandishing a pistol, raped her. When he was finished, he left her 100 yen in military scrip.[57] Others simply robbed passersby of portable wealth, including watches, cash, and fountain pens.[58] By the end of September, 439 watches had been reported stolen.[59] One particularly intrepid group apparently decided against molesting workaday Japanese and went straight to where the money was, the Yokohama branch of the Sumitomo Bank.[60] Later, in Tokyo, the Home Ministry, which ran the entire police force, found that its official seal was missing, and it was not able to conduct business until someone found an older seal.[61]

GIs could be brazen about their criminality. In one case a group of Americans patronized a brothel, and when the time came to pay the bill, they opened a black doctor's case and produced Japanese currency and a ladies' wristwatch and paid with a combination of the two.[62] GIs also patronized brothels, bars, and restaurants without paying and frequently stole any alcohol they could lay their hands on.[63] Americans sought alcohol so fervently that they sometimes came to grief in their pursuit of it. One GI robbed a miso ration shop of bottled shoyū and left the shop. Later, apparently realizing his mistake, he tossed it aside, returned to the store, and stole a flag.[64] Another demanded alcohol of the workers in a factory, only to be told that they had none. Apparently the GI in question had already acquired some familiarity with Japanese alcoholic beverages, because he immediately spotted a beer can. Triumphantly grabbing it, he poured the contents into his mouth—but the factory workers had been using it to store exhausted oil. In short order the soldier admitted the correctness of the Japanese claims, if not in so many words.[65] One incident ended tragically. On October 12, three GIs in Kure died after drinking methyl alcohol they had obtained from local black marketeers.[66]

After the currency problem was solved and Americans understood that their own troops were more a source of disorder than most Japanese civilians were, they began more rigorous policing. Crime dropped precipitously but did not disappear altogether.[67] As late as the following June, in an incident that surely must have set a record of some sort, an American soldier held up and robbed future prime minister Ashida Hitoshi on a train from Tokyo to Kyoto.[68]

While these reports certainly complicate the picture of an orderly and peaceful Occupation, they also make clear that serious violent crimes like rape and murder were rare. For example, a daily series of crime charts covering the period from August 30 to September 25 includes nine reported cases of rape and twenty attempts from various precincts in Kanagawa Prefecture.[69] In a chart covering Kanagawa, Chiba, Hokkaido, and Shizuoka Prefectures from August 30 to September 5, there were six reported cases of rape and four attempts. These totals do not include one case of abduction near Yokosuka.[70] Another chart covering the same area from August 30 to September 10 and updated to include a previously unreported case in Yokosuka (most likely the abduction) records a total of nine reported cases of rape and six attempts.[71]

Another file consists of a group of numbered reports including charts and details of various cases, plus one miscellaneous report attached to the end. The first report was filed on August 31, detailing events of the previous day and the final report, number 22, was filed on September 29 and covers events up to the 25th. Report number 5 or 6 (the number of the remaining report is illegible) is missing. The surviving reports detail twelve rape cases from August 30 to September 25 in Kanagawa, Tokyo, and Chiba. (The total here presented includes one case of rape of a prostitute not tallied in the records and one abduction later determined to be a rape.)[72]

Another collection of reports from various Home Ministry officials (principally from the governor of Kanagawa Prefecture) details GI crimes during the early Occupation, beginning on August 30. These reports are not regular or well organized; some are numbered, others are not. In the numbered sequence, the file includes reports 2 and 17, filed on September 17, and reports 18–33; the final, thirty-third report was filed on October 5. There are many unnumbered reports that deal principally with the beginning of September, and there are redundancies in these reports. It is impossible to say with certainty that these reports cover the period in question exhaustively, but especially when viewed in light of other sources, it is clear that these reports provide a fairly complete picture of GI crime in Kanagawa (and an incomplete picture of some other locales) from the beginning of the Occupation until October 4. They include a total of nine rape cases.[73]

In addition to the internal Japanese reports on GI crime, there are also the reports submitted by the Japanese government to the Americans. In the early Occupation period, the Japanese Central Liaison Office (CLO) sent reports of American crime to GHQ. The CLO was the organ set up to transact all business between the Japanese central government and MacArthur's headquarters. It took the Home Ministry reports, rendered particular cases into English, and forwarded them to the Americans.[74] As was the case on the Japanese side, these reports also had wide circulation. Copies went to the commanders of the troops concerned, sometimes going through multiple levels of the chain of command. In addition, they were wired in the clear to G-3 Operations for action, and for information to the commander-in-chief, the chief of staff, G-2 Intelligence, and one other recipient.[75] However, one particularly shocking allegation of a gang rape by twenty-seven American soldiers apparently did not go through normal channels. Instead, the CLO sent it directly to the Supreme Commander.[76]

Copies of many of these reports are available in the U.S. National Archives. In addition, much of the correspondence between the CLO and MacArthur's command has been collected and edited by Takemae Eiji into reference works of several volumes.[77] The CLO correspondence serves to provide a reasonably complete English-language record of GI crime in the early Occupation period. This record largely corroborates the internal records of the Japanese government.

In its records of GI criminal activity between the opening of the Occupation and the end of September 1945, the volumes edited by Takemae list five rape cases, eleven attempted rapes, three women abducted (including two who escaped unharmed), and one attempted abduction.[78]

Finally, the CLO correspondence with GHQ gives the most definitive figures for GI crimes in the early Occupation in its missive number 342 from the Japanese government to GHQ, dated October 23, 1945. This report covers the total number of crimes committed by Allied servicemen up to the end of September 1945. It records that there were fourteen reported rapes and thirty more attempts.[79] These documents make clear that reports of rape during the early weeks of the Occupation were not nearly as common as is frequently alleged.

Another document at the U.S. National Archives also suggests how the misreading of primary materials has led to the propagation of the legend of mass rape during the Occupation. One of the most frequently cited figures is of 1,336 rapes reported during the first ten days of the Occupation in Kanagawa Prefecture. The figure appears in at least seven published academic accounts, including Takemae Eiji's *Inside GHQ: The Allied Occupation of Japan and Its Legacy* and John W. Dower's *Cultures of War*.[80] It has been incorporated into mainstream popular history with its appearance in Antony Beevor's *The Second World War* and has become something of an internet sensation, appearing on more than a hundred English-language and more than seventy Japanese-language websites.[81]

While at first blush this may appear to lend a certain credibility to the figure, on closer scrutiny what it actually reveals is a process of cascading mistakes followed by the incestuous amplification of the final result. The ultimate source for all of these claims is Yuki Tanaka's *Hidden Horrors:*

Japanese War Crimes in World War II.[82] This is evident because although sometimes the sourcing is poorly documented, undocumented, or indirect through multiple levels of citation, Tanaka's assertion contains three separate errors, all of which are duplicated in almost every account that includes this figure: (1) the correct number of incidents is not 1,336 but 1,326; (2) the period in question is actually twelve, not ten, days; (3), most important, *the number is not the figure for rapes, but for all incidents of any kind.*[83]

In order to establish this, one need only trace the provenance of Tanaka's claim. Tanaka cites Yamada Meiko's *Senryōgun Ianfu* (Comfort Women for the Occupation Army). Yamada, in turn, took her material from *Haisha no Okurimono* (Gifts from the Defeated) by Masayo Duus.[84] Duus' book was written for a popular audience and its sourcing is incomplete. The figure of 1,336 appears to have been taken from the following passage in Duus' work:

> With the advance of the occupation army, cases of rape and gang rape occurred in every part of Japan. The majority of these were by groups brandishing pistols so resistance was difficult. There were many incidents involving drunken soldiers. There were also many attempted rapes. From August 30 to September 10 the number of incidents involving the American Army was reported (from the Japanese Government to General Headquarters). Moreover, these were only the incidents from Kanagawa Prefecture.[85]

Duus provides no information for the source of these numbers other than that included in the text, but there is a communication from the Japanese government to GHQ on file in the National Archives that contains the exact figures cited by Duus.[86] Yamada must have made a minor transcription error, whereas in the statistical chart Duus provided (see Table 2) the total number of incidents is given as 1,326. Duus follows this information with an important caveat: "It is not clear how many of these incidents were cases of rape."[87] Yamada drops this qualification: "With the advance of the Occupation army, incidents of rape and gang rape occurred in every locale. From August 30 to September 10 the number of incidents in Kanagawa prefecture alone was 1,336."[88] The clear impression is that all of the "incidents" were rapes. That is certainly how Tanaka read it. He

TABLE 2 • Incidents Reported by Duus Masayo

Date	Number of Incidents
August 30	315
August 31	228
September 1	199
September 2	221
September 3	122
September 4	59
September 5	42
September 6	37
September 7	21
September 8	32
September 9	28
September 10	22
Total	1,326

plainly states, "There were 1,336 reported cases of rape of Japanese women by U.S. soldiers."[89]

In addition, while both Duus and Yamada record that the period in question was August 30–September 10, Tanaka adds the erroneous detail that this twelve-day period was actually ten days.[90] At the time he wrote *Hidden Horrors*, no one else had yet made this mistake. From that time forward, it is nearly ubiquitous. Thus, even where the chain of citations that led to this claim is unclear, there can be little doubt that Tanaka is the ultimate source.

This naturally leads to the question of how many of the 1,326 incidents cited in the original document were rape cases. Although Duus does not cite the document by name, her description of it makes clear that it was most likely a letter from Lieutenant General Arisue Seizō to GHQ sent on September 15, 1945. This letter contains every figure Duus cited. It makes no suggestion of mass rape by American military personnel. In fact, ironically, the letter was sent to note the Japanese government's satisfaction with the measures the U.S. forces were taking to police their personnel. Arisue wrote, "We believe it is a matter of mutual congratulation to be able to inform you that, as a result of sincere and adequate steps taken by you, there has been a distinct decrease in the number of reports of unfortunate incidents which have frequently taken place during the early part of the occupation of the Allied Forces." Moreover, while it may be technically correct that it was unclear how many of these "incidents" were rape, one could reasonably conclude from the letter that very few were: "In regard to the nature of these incidents, the classification would run in the order of looting of Arms, [sic] robbing of articles, appropriation of automobiles, robbing money and others. The total amount of damages are more than 420 rifles, 65 revolvers and 170 automobiles."[91] At least so far as Arisue was concerned, there were not enough cases of rape to even warrant mention. In fact, the best available records for Kanagawa Prefecture during the twelve-day period in question state that the number of rapes reported to the Japanese police in the area was actually seven, just over one-half of 1 percent (around 0.5234 percent) of what many writers allege.[92]

In short, there was a great deal of documentation generated about GI behavior during the early Occupation. An abundance of this documentation survives and is accessible. It includes press reports, recollections of witnesses, police histories, voluminous police records, many of which specifically focused on the issue of rape and Japanese government correspondence with GHQ. These documents make clear that there was a significant amount of petty theft, armed robbery, souvenir hunting, carjacking, and joyriding. This crime spree was aggravated by GHQ's decision to reverse its currency policy. Nevertheless, during this time, there was, relatively speaking, very little rape. The documentary evidence about GI crime in the early Occupation is copious and the conclusion to be drawn from it is clear: there was no mass rape of Japanese women by American soldiers during this time.

GI CRIME DURING THE REMAINDER OF THE OCCUPATION

After the initial phases of the Occupation, there is far less information on GI crime. GHQ imposed press censorship and so after September 18,

1945, the media no longer provides a window into American criminality. Moreover, the Japanese government seems to have to some degree lost interest after the initial period went relatively smoothly, and there are fewer records on the Japanese side. In addition, during the Occupation and the years immediately following it, SCAP dissolved the organs of domestic surveillance. The Kempeitai ended its existence in November 1945, and the Tokkō followed soon thereafter. Prefectural police departments are not required to maintain records before 1965, and many do not. Those that do maintain records sometimes restrict access to them.[93]

In addition, the reporting of crime became routinized to the point that, with some exceptions, beginning in early 1946, many reports about misconduct of Allied troops no longer include detailed information on cases and simply note that there is a statistical chart enclosed, but these enclosures do not appear in the edited volumes. Communications directly between the CLO and GHQ began to concentrate on other matters, and the reporting of GI crimes assumed a lower profile, with organs of the two governments working together to collect and distribute information on GI crime directly between one another at a subordinate level. As a result, I have to date been unable to discover any comprehensive source that covers the whole of the Occupation period.

Nevertheless, there is enough surviving information to present a picture in which one may place a high degree of confidence. By early 1946 Kanagawa Prefecture and GHQ had set up a system of information exchange that was likely standard for other prefectures as well. In the center of this information exchange was GHQ's Public Safety Division (PSD).

Many of PSD's records are included in the SCAP/GHQ records in the National Archives (Records Group 331). However, these records predate a major reform and standardization of the army's record-keeping practices. As a result, the SCAP records are not organized in a regular way. In fact, when the U.S. Army sought to compile statistics on rape in the Far Eastern Command in March 1950, the investigators could find no information prior to 1947.[94] Nevertheless, there are still numerous sources that cover the subject. There are reports on GI crime from the Central Liaison Office of the Japanese government, Japanese police reports, and Eighth Army provost marshal reports. These sources are not always consistent, however, and sometimes they obscure as much as they enlighten. The task of forming a coherent picture is complicated by the fact that the Japanese police went through major reorganizations in the early postwar period, one during the Occupation and others afterward.[95] After the first of these reorganizations, there were two major police organizations that collected data on crimes, the National Rural Police and the Metropolitan Police.[96] Both of these organizations submitted monthly reports to GHQ, and these figures were then tabulated and put into another report recording the grand totals for the country at large. It is not always clear from the documents which of these three reports one is reading. Examples of all three are in the Public Safety Division records, and some are not clearly labeled. Sometimes reports refer to "rapes" as including "attempted rape," and sometimes they do not. Complicating matters is the fact that the provost marshal, which had the responsibility of prosecuting criminal GIs, kept its own records. Where information is available from both sources, they often do not agree. This may be partially explained by the fact that Japanese records for crimes by Occupation personnel included crimes committed by the British Commonwealth Occupation Forces as well as those committed by the Eighth Army, whereas the provost marshal's records sometimes included these figures (e.g., in nationwide tallies) but not always (e.g., in tallying cases brought and cleared). Furthermore, criminals arrested directly by MPs would not necessarily generate a report by Japanese police. Finally, one group of statistics refers to "sex offenses" that had been "investigated" rather than "rapes" that had been "reported." Put simply, apples-to-apples comparisons of these data are impossible.

This limitation notwithstanding, the data provide enough information that, when combined with Japanese police records for the early Occupation, they allow one to derive a reasonable idea of the scale of GI crime through the whole of the Occupation. The overall picture does not differ significantly from that of its opening phase. If one uses Japanese police records for August 1945, the summary figure provided by the Japanese police for the first year of the Occupation (286 cases from September 1945 through August 1946), then assumes that in the months when multiple figures are available (e.g., from the Japanese police and the Eighth Army's provost marshal) the higher figure is correct, then counts all figures that include attempted rape as rape when the latter figure is unavailable, and finally assumes that the figures for the six months for which no data has yet been discovered (May–June 1951 and January–April 1952) have approximately the same average number of cases as the ten months of 1951 for which data is available, then one arrives at a figure of about 1,082 reported cases of rape for the whole of the Occupation, an average of about 183 cases per year.

Another source of information about rape during the Occupation comes from a report on the subject in the records of the Far East Command. According to this report, in 1947 there were 144 reported rapes and 77 arrests. In 1948 there were 140 reports with 83 arrests. In 1949 there were 171 reports with 146 arrests, of which 104 went to court martial and 53 resulted in conviction (for the whole of the Far East Command).[97] These numbers are on the same scale of those in the Public Safety Division records, but they are not in complete accord. For example, the crime statistics reported to the Eighth Army Headquarters during 1947 reported a total of 195 cases of rape, as opposed to the 144 cited in the later review by the Far Eastern Command. One reason for this discrepancy might involve the way accusations of rape were understood by those compiling the Far Eastern Command's 1950 review. The document contains references to reports of rape for the month of January 1950 and separates them into two categories: "Actual" and "Unfounded." In January, "Actual" was adjudged the appropriate category in thirteen of sixteen cases, for a rate of about 80 percent. A similar standard applied the cases of 1947 would account for much of the discrepancy.

Whatever the cause of this discrepancy, the statistics are in agreement on the scale of crime, if not the exact number of cases. Whether one chooses to use the figures submitted by the Japanese or those recorded by the Americans, at the time or after the fact, what is undeniable is that there is no reliable documentary evidence that even remotely suggests that there was mass sexual violence during the Occupation. If one assumes that the highest possible figures from the documentary base are the correct figures, then the rate of rape during the Occupation as a whole was about the same as what occurs in an average midsized American city every year.[98] In other words, sexual violence, like all violence in all times and places, was certainly a problem, and one that should not be trivialized.

Each one of these cases was a life-changing trauma for the victim. In one particularly egregious case, a ten-year-old girl was playing with her younger brothers near the Toranomon gate to the Imperial Palace when two Americans in a car abducted her and then both raped her before releasing her and giving her ¥300. The "doctor's preliminary report stated that she was badly torn and lost considerable blood." In fact, one of the most damning pieces of evidence against the culprits is that one of them had blood on his trousers that matched the girl's blood type and neither of theirs. There was also a considerable amount of blood pooled in the back seat, where a blood-soaked undershirt was also found. All of the blood matched the girl's blood type. Investigators also identified her fingerprint on the car. They also got the suspects to submit to a lie-detector test, which one took before the other spontaneously confessed to everything.[99]

Heinous as this crime was, we know about it precisely because Occupation authorities took it very seriously. They liaised with Japanese police, identified that these men were likely the same two who had been involved in an earlier disturbance at a teahouse, used that information to identify the vehicle that they used, called in forensic examiners to dust for fingerprints and determine blood type, got someone to administer a lie-detector test, and extracted a complete confession from one of the subjects. The final sentence of the report is "Investigation is continuing."[100] In other words, authorities were taking no chances. Though at the time of writing I have yet to discover the disposition of the case, the continuing investigation likely means that they were aiming to get a guilty verdict on violation of the 92nd Article of War, Murder-Rape. This would carry a mandatory sentence of death or life in prison.

The seriousness with which American authorities treated sexual violence was undoubtedly one reason that the rate of sexual violence during the Occupation was low, especially in comparison to that of other occupying armies in the mid-twentieth century.

▲ THE BEHAVIOR OF AMERICAN OCCUPATION TROOPS IN CONTEXT

Existing documentation makes clear that there was no mass rape of Japanese women by American servicemen during the Occupation. However, that is a different thing from saying that there was no rape at all. Rape did occur. The crime was not epidemic, and its scale was not even close to what is alleged in many sources. The numbers, however, were not trivial. As indicated above, given the size of the Occupation and its duration, the rate of rape was roughly equivalent to that of many contemporary American cities. There are, of course, problems comparing the rate of *reported* rapes in Japan in the 1940s and 1950s with the *reported* rate in America in the 2000s. For one, the rate in the United States in the 2000s would be expected to reflect a rise in reporting after a relative lessening of the stigma of rape victims. In addition, the definition of the crime of rape was generally narrower in the past. Such caveats notwithstanding, it is clear that rape was neither widespread nor common during the Occupation. This becomes even clearer when the behavior of American servicemen is compared with that of other occupying armies during and after World War II.

Comparable documentation does not exist in most cases for some of the exact reasons that the incidence of rape was relatively low in American-occupied Japan. In Japan, policing never broke down, so transgressors were reported and often punished. In many other theaters and regions, these conditions did not apply, so the picture presented is necessarily murkier. However, published sources make possible at least a qualitative comparison.

The most frequent point of comparison is with the soldiers of Imperial Japan. Japanese supporters of the mass rape legend often assert that the Japanese and American militaries were essentially no different in their treatment of women.[101] Such assertions cannot withstand even cursory scrutiny. While mass rape was not a problem in American-occupied Japan, it was certainly a problem in Japanese-occupied Asia, most conspicuously in China, for which sources are relatively abundant.

Nevertheless, much of the information about rape by Japanese soldiers remains anecdotal. The conditions that allow mass rape to occur make it very difficult to quantify. Policing of troops is often inadequate, ineffective, or altogether absent. Members of the occupying army often share a hatred for the conquered enemy, so officers and military police turn a blind eye to crime or even participate in it themselves. In addition, post hoc recollections by survivors are often colored by the terrors they witnessed, and rumors are repeated as fact. Nevertheless, there is a good deal of reliable contemporary evidence that mass rape was widespread in China. The most abundant evidence comes from the episode that is also the most notorious, "the Rape of Nanjing."

The number of women raped during the Nanjing atrocity remains both uncertain and controversial. However, it is indisputable that Japanese soldiers treated Chinese women as spoils of war. The International Military Tribunal for the Far East found that "approximately 20,000 cases of rape occurred within the city during the first month of the Occupation."[102] The basis for this conclusion remains obscure, but contemporaneous evidence makes clear that the number of victims was very large. The writings of Westerners who remained in the city provide ample testimony to this fact. On December 15, 1937, two days after the city fell, Robert O. Wilson, an American doctor and the only surgeon available to treat the victims of the Japanese military, wrote to his family, "I could go on for pages telling of cases of rape and brutality almost beyond belief."[103] Three days later, he described the city as a "modern Dante's inferno, written in huge letters with blood and rape. Murder by the wholesale and rape by the thousands of cases. There seems to be no stop to the ferocity, lust and atavism of the brutes."[104] On December 17, German businessman and Nazi Party member John Rabe recorded in his diary, "Last night up to 1,000 women are said to have been raped, about 100 girls at Ginling Girls College alone. You hear of nothing but rape. If husbands or brothers intervene, they're shot."[105] On December 19, 1937, the Rev. James M. McCallum, an American missionary, wrote in his diary, "Never have I heard or read such brutality. Rape! Rape! Rape! We estimate at least 1,000 cases a night, and many by day.... Women are being carried off every morning, afternoon and evening."[106]

Under the leadership of Rabe, some Westerners set up a so-called Safety Zone for refugees. This was supposed to be an area in which Chinese civilians were protected. Through the establishment of the Safety Zone,

Rabe and his colleagues saved untold numbers of civilians. Nevertheless, Japanese soldiers routinely violated the integrity of the zone, sometimes murdering people, or taking them away to almost certain death. They also frequently raped women.

Rabe and his associates submitted regular reports to the Japanese consul general in Nanjing detailing misconduct by Japanese troops. They submitted a total of 444 reports, of which 395 have been located. Of the surviving 395 complaints against Japanese troops, 124 of them are about rape.[107] These included girls as young as twelve and women over sixty, including one who was raped more than ten times.[108] Another twenty-eight concern attempted rape.[109] Fifty-eight others concern Japanese soldiers demanding young women.[110] Refusals were often met with violence.[111] Fourteen more of the reports are about abductions of women.[112] There were at least three large-scale organized roundups involving trucks. One was still empty, another had about ten women in it, and the third had twenty.[113] One abduction was carried out by a Japanese MP.[114] There are also seven cases of attempted abduction.[115]

Altogether, some 234 of the 395 surviving reports involve sexual violence or intended sexual violence. Many of the attacks were horrific. Some of the rape cases involve a single victim. Others involve multiple women, "many" women, "several" women, "thirty" women, "about thirty" women, and "more than thirty women."[116] The majority involve multiple perpetrators. Some of them involve so many perpetrators that the reports resort to quantifying the time that a woman was continuously violated rather than the number of men who raped her.[117] In four cases women were enslaved so that their ordeals persisted for days or even weeks.[118] After this, some women were murdered.[119] One woman over the age of sixty was raped and then murdered by means of a bayonet thrust into her vagina.[120] Some women were abducted and did not return.[121] Two women were simply raped to death.[122] Another was raped so violently that her fate hung in the balance.[123] Two more, including a twelve-year-old girl, were raped to the point of disability.[124] Women were raped before their husbands or, in one case, her mother.[125] One seventeen-year-old who was nine months pregnant was raped, inducing labor. The child was born healthy, but the mother was understandably "hysterical."[126] One woman was forced to "throw away her baby" by three soldiers who raped her.[127]

The situation was so bad that those witnessing it became inured and their language became warped. One man complained that his daughter was "raped badly."[128] In another case, Dr. Wilson, after his initial treatment of a fourteen-year-old whose ordeal was so grievous that she was going to require extensive surgery, noted in his report that her "body was not yet built for raping."[129] Of course, no woman should be considered "built for raping," and there is no such thing as being lightly raped, but in the "modern Dante's inferno," such formulations had a perverted logic to them. In short, the "Rape of Nanjing" was indeed about rape. Worse still, evidence suggests that it was exceptional primarily in that it was recorded in as much detail as it was.

Documentation on rapes committed by Japanese military personnel in other areas is less abundant. Moreover, in response to the atrocities at Nanjing, Japanese authorities expanded their "comfort woman" system to sate the carnal urges of their soldiers and reduce the incidence of rape.[130] In addition, the Imperial Japanese Army, concerned that rape was undermining Japan's position, tried to stop loose talk. One directive from an Army Ministry undersecretary issued in February 1939 included examples. One soldier said, "At XX [location censored in original text] we took four people captive—parents and daughters. We played with the daughters as if they were whores and killed the parents because they kept on telling us to release the daughters. We had our kicks until the unit was ordered to leave; then we killed the daughters." "One company commander hinted that rape was OK, saying 'Make sure no problems arise later on; after you're finished either pay them off or kill them outright.'" "No one cared about rapes at the front; some guys even shot at MPs who caught them in the act."[131]

Despite claims to the contrary, the behavior of American troops in Japan and Japanese troops in China was radically different.[132] While rape was treated as a serious crime by the U.S. Army in Japan, it was a matter of course for the IJA in China. The differences in scale and cruelty were so great as to make the two essentially incomparable. Indeed, shortly after the Occupation began, Hosokawa Morisada, secretary and son-in-law of

Prince Konoe Fumimaro (as well as father of later prime minister Hosokawa Morihiro), made exactly this point, writing that the sexual violence committed by American troops was like the weight of a single hair compared to that of nine cattle when considered in light of Japanese actions in China.[133]

The Soviet Red Army during World War II also engaged in mass rape. For reasons similar to those enumerated above in the Japanese case, the Soviet case also makes a reliable estimate very difficult. However, as in the Japanese case, what is known makes very clear that mass rape was a massive problem. The Red Army's rampage through Eastern Europe became so notorious that Communist partisans complained that frequent rape was undermining their position among their countrymen.[134] In the aftermath of the conflict there was a wave of abortions throughout Europe, largely necessitated by widespread rape.[135] According to the diary of Marta Hillers, published anonymously as *A Woman in Berlin*, after the Soviets captured the German capital, rape became so commonplace that women unknown to each other spontaneously shared their ordeals with one another while waiting in line for water.[136] Later she wrote, "Slowly but surely we're starting to view all the raping with a sense of humor—gallows humor."[137]

One Russian captain in World War II revealed the prevalent mentality when he declared, "I have fucked old women and young but what I liked most was fucking small girls in front of their mothers, when the girls were crying, '*Mutti! Mutti!*' . . . I had gonorrhea but I did not bother about it. But now I have syphilis. I have had enough of fucking."[138]

The record of Americans in Japan even compares favorably to that of their countrymen in Germany, though mass rape like that described above in the cases of the Japanese and Soviet armies did not take place in Germany either. Normal policing of troops was maintained. Record-keeping continued throughout the seizure and occupation of German lands. A thorough analysis is beyond the scope of this book. A brief quantitative comparison is possible, but even here the comparison is complicated. Unlike in the home islands of Japan, in Germany the American troops occupied areas only after they had conquered them. Thus, the passions of combat undoubtedly played a role. As the conflict neared its end, reports of rape by American soldiers increased dramatically, falling off almost equally dramatically as resistance ended. There were 18 reported cases in January, 31 in February, 402 in March, and 501 in April. The Germans surrendered unconditionally on May 8, 1945, and the rape rate began to fall. In May there were 241 reported cases; in June and July there were 63 and 45, respectively, and this rate remained more or less the same for the rest of the year.[139] Although the surrender did not occur until May 8, the American troops did relatively little fighting in the first days of May, and that month may thus be considered the first month of nearly pure occupation duty. Assuming that half of the approximately 3 million U.S. personnel in Europe were in Germany at this time, then the rate of rape was significantly higher than it was in Japan. However, considering the rapid falloff in June, it was approximately comparable to the rate of rape in the first month of occupation in Japan.

In summary, sexual violence against Japanese women was a problem throughout the Occupation, as it is a problem everywhere at all times. Yet tales of widespread sexual violence during the Occupation find no substantiation in surviving records. On the contrary, those records indicate that Americans occupying Japan committed much less sexual violence than some other World War II armies did. Tales of mass rape during the Occupation can reasonably be adjudged unfounded.

CHAPTER 2

"THIS DEGRADING SLAVERY"

GHQ AND PROSTITUTION

The perpetration of mass rape comprises only part, if the most significant part, of the legends about the maltreatment and sexual exploitation of Japanese women during the Occupation. Another set of legends, mostly intertwined with those of widespread sexual violence, has grown up around a supposed moral turpitude of the U.S. military when it came to the issue of prostitution. It is easy to understand why. American servicemen patronized Japanese prostitutes throughout the Occupation. In the lean postwar years, Americans had far more disposable income than the average Japanese man and thus could afford to pay more for sexual services than Japanese men did.[1] In addition, American policies toward prostitution had the unintended effect of pushing prostitutes from brothels in restricted districts to the streets of large cities. For many Japanese, the image of prostitutes soliciting American servicemen came to symbolize Japan's postwar plight.

This association led to the creation of numerous tales alleging that the U.S. military was directly involved in postwar Japanese prostitution because the sexual satisfaction of its troops was its top priority. Recently such tales have become common in academic treatments of the period.[2] Such treatments attempt to explain American actions with reference to a single variable. In fact, a number of factors influenced GHQ's approach to the issue. These included GHQ's overall policy toward women, the control of venereal disease, the degree of autonomy that should be afforded to the democratically elected Japanese government during the Occupation, the maintenance of public order, and the prestige and popularity of GHQ. Often these considerations came into conflict. Approaches changed as one or another factor gained precedence in the minds of Occupation officials. The result was that American policy on prostitution often appeared to be, and indeed often was, inconsistent. The largest apparent inconsistency stemmed from a distinction between varieties of prostitution. This difference was of cardinal importance to policymakers in GHQ. To many interested Japanese it seemed at best intellectually abstruse and at worst both wrong-headed and pernicious. The distinction was between the system of licensed prostitution as it had been practiced in Imperial Japan and prostitution as a general social phenomenon.[3] GHQ banned licensed prostitution outright shortly after learning how it functioned. As for prostitution in general, however, the Americans left the matter to the discretion of the Japanese people and government. The apparent contradiction in these decisions has led many to accuse GHQ of hypocrisy, cynical self-interest, and sexual opportunism.

The actual story is more nuanced and is best understood in terms of the struggle at the heart of the American project to remake Japan. Many in GHQ, especially the decision-makers at or close to the top of its hierarchy, saw their mission in Japan in not just military but also quasi-religious terms. MacArthur believed his job was to create a new Japan in the image of America. He once declared, "My major advisors now have boiled down to almost two men—George Washington and Abraham Lincoln."[4] Even allowing for MacArthur's penchant for melodramatic overstatement, this was an extraordinary assertion of cultural arrogance. While MacArthur's subordinates often leavened the project with a healthy dose of European-style social democracy, there can be little doubt that the thrust of many Occupation reforms was to make Japan more like America. GHQ wanted the new state to function more as a guarantor of individual liberty than as a defender of social order. Many Japanese desired just the opposite. GHQ's involvement in the issue of prostitution must be understood in terms of this fundamental difference.

THE ABOLITION OF LICENSED PROSTITUTION IN JAPAN

Organized and regulated prostitution had a long history in Japan. Shortly after the foundation of the Tokugawa Shogunate in 1600, government officials codified prostitution into a system that anticipated its early twentieth-century form.[5] In contrast to the situation in the West, there was less stigma surrounding prostitution. Artists and writers openly celebrated it. Commercial guides to red-light districts were published as early as the seventeenth century. One of these, produced in 1770 and attributed to the pioneering woodblock print artist (Suzuki) Harunobu, featured images of 166 women and a haiku poem for each. Rutherford Alcock, the first British diplomatic representative to Japan, wrote of his surprise on a visit to Sensōji, the oldest temple in Tokyo (then Edo), that the temple was adorned with portraits of what his guide called "all of the most celebrated courtesans, or public women in [Edo]."[6] Francis Hall, an American who served as the Japanese correspondent of the *New York Tribune*, also commented on this practice.[7]

Many Japanese felt that prostitution, as it had been traditionally practiced, was a national custom that deserved preservation. When Occupation officials sounded Japanese out on their attitudes, they found them to be largely neutral or favorably disposed toward prostitution. One American wrote, "While the Japanese practice monogamy in that they marry only one wife, there is no condemnation of a husband who seeks sexual entertainment at a geisha house, or at a house of prostitution. The practice is widespread and enjoyed in openly without suffering loss of social standing."[8]

Moreover, it was not just the customers but also the sex workers who suffered no real loss of social standing. While there was some social stigma attached to prostitution and it was largely seen as a profession for women

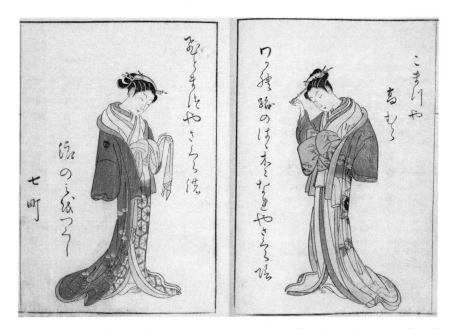

FIGURE 4 • Image from *Yoshiwara Bijin Awase* (Beauties of Yoshiwara), 1770; attributed to Suzuki Harunobu (Library of Congress)

of lower classes, a woman's former involvement in prostitution did not prevent her from finding a marriage partner. According to a survey of 304 former prostitutes who left the profession between 1931 and 1933, nearly half married into or above their own class.[9] Similarly, American ethnographers studying the village of Sue in Kyūshū in the early 1930s found that women who had left to work as prostitutes were able to reintegrate into the village when they returned.[10] This had been the pattern for centuries. Engelbert Kaempfer, a German physician and naturalist who was in Japan from 1690 to 1692, wrote, "If these prostitutes marry honest people, they pass as honest women among the commoners, since they are not responsible for their profession and furthermore have been well educated."[11]

Prostitutes were able to rejoin their communities in part because Japanese regarded self-sacrifice and filial piety as being among the highest virtues. There was an idealized vision of prostitutes that portrayed them as embodying both. They served society by providing an outlet for the passions of men, passions that otherwise might find expression in violent outbursts and the violation of nonprofessional women.[12] It was generally understood that women in the profession were dutifully assisting their families. In 1896 Itō Hirobumi, Japan's first prime minister, discussing the situation with an English reporter, explained that a prostitute worked "from a lofty desire to help her poor parents or relations; and when she forsakes the life, by good conduct she is readmitted to society." An official in prewar Japan asserted that one of the great strengths of their system was that the Home Ministry's registration procedures screened out any women who personally desired to be prostitutes.[13]

The esteem of officialdom must, however, have been cold comfort to the women and girls ensnared in the system. In the words of historian Sheldon Garon, their lives were "dangerously insecure." They were far more likely than women in the general population to take their own lives, and many did so with their lovers.[14] Their lot had no doubt vastly improved since the Edo period (1600–1868). In a span of fewer than sixty years, between 1743 and 1801, more than 20,000 women working in the Yoshiwara prostitution district of Edo (present-day Tokyo) died, apparently without family and lacking funds for a proper burial—approximately one woman a day for almost six decades. Their bodies were then simply dumped at Jōkanji, a local temple.[15] The district occupied an area of only about eighteen acres and housed about three thousand prostitutes.[16]

Hōdoji, a temple in Kyoto, served a similar purpose. In Nara, Shōnenji performed the same function for the Kitsuji Yūkaku, a prostitution area that dated to the eighth century. In fact, prostitution districts around Japan usually have some sort of temple or shrine to console the spirits of those who passed on without family or friends to see that they got a proper burial. Many of these sites remain a part of Japan's urban landscape.

Well into the modern era, brothel owners displayed women behind an iron grating in an order that reflected their status within the house. This practice was abandoned in the larger cities in 1916.[17]

Despite improvements to their conditions, as long as licensed prostitutes were in debt, they were essentially captives of the brothel owners, with no option but to continue working in the sex industry.[18] Historian Yoshimi

FIGURE 5 • Statue of Kanon, the Bodhisattva of Compassion, in the Tobita Prostitution District of Osaka (Photo by author)

FIGURE 6 • Prostitutes on display behind bars in the Yoshiwara district of Tokyo, ca. 1900. Within the brothel the prostitutes were arranged in a formal hierarchy that was reflected in their position on display, with the high-ranking prostitutes seated in the center and lower ranks consigned to the edges. (Haeckel Brothers)

Yoshiaki, who has done extensive work on the notorious "comfort woman" system of military prostitutes and sex slaves set up in territories Japan occupied during World War II, declared, "The licensed prostitution system was in reality a system of sexual slavery that amounted to traffic in people, the sale of sex and restraints on freedom."[19] In fact, Yoshimi and other scholars, including his frequent foil Hata Ikuhiko, have characterized the comfort woman system as a "natural" logical extension of the domestic licensed prostitution system.[20]

When the Americans arrived in Japan, they were unaware of these aspects of the licensed prostitution system. Indeed, they were largely ignorant of both the history and the current state of prostitution in Japan more generally. Because of their concerns with venereal disease, officials of the Public Health and Welfare Section (PHW) of GHQ sought as much information as they could get, dispatching personnel to visit prostitution districts.[21] They also recruited Japanese informants, including both doctors who dealt with public health or with venereal disease and police officials who handled prostitution.[22]

One thing they wanted to know was the size of the sex industry. According to the estimate of Dr. Ishibashi, a venereal disease specialist at the Health Ministry's Bureau of Infectious Disease, before the war there had been 100,000 women employed as registered licensed prostitutes, around 100,000 others working as unregistered prostitutes, and 80,000 geisha, whose work sometimes included prostitution, especially among the lower-end geisha.[23] Another estimate put the total number of women working as geisha, public prostitutes, and private prostitutes at the end of the war at 150,000, although it was admitted that this estimate was "not accurate" and did not include street prostitutes.[24] The number of women engaged in sex work in the home islands had rapidly decreased after so many young men went away to fight. It then increased markedly near the end of the war as young women employed in armaments industries lost their jobs when American bombing destroyed the factories. These women were turned out into the streets to fend for themselves. Many turned to prostitution and were soon competing over a shrinking number of customers as conscription took ever more men out of the civilian population. As the brothels filled, desperate young women turned to streetwalking, a social phenomenon that had long been suppressed in Japan.[25] While exact figures are elusive, it is clear that a very large number of women participated in sex work at the end of the war and continued to do so through the lean years of the Occupation. Many of them would serve Allied troops.

Clearly, PHW needed some way to keep venereal disease under control, and it soon discovered a possible means. In Japan, "public prostitutes [that is, licensed prostitutes]," were "permitted to operate only in fixed houses and subject to periodic examination and compulsory treatment."[26] At first, PHW officials saw this system as a good means of controlling disease. As the system had largely broken down in the chaos of the war's final stages, they urged that it be reinstated forthwith.[27] However, the more they learned about it, the more they soured on it. They found both the medical inspections and the treatment regimens unsatisfactory.

More importantly, they also learned that the system relied on human trafficking. On December 5, 1945, Lt. Col. James H. Gordon, head of the venereal disease division of PHW, and Lt. Col. H. H. MacDonald of PHW met with Dr. Yosano Hikaru, chief of the Preventive Medicine Section of the Tokyo Sanitation Board, and Dr. Ishibashi, a venereal disease specialist at the Health Ministry's Bureau of Infectious Disease. They discussed various aspects of the venereal disease problem and "the advisability of abrogating the regulations for control of licensed prostitutes."[28] PHW's Japanese informants left little doubt about the nature of the system. The regulations made "it possible for the girl to be enslaved against her will." Once she had been "established in a house, the girl, at least until very recent times, was virtually a prisoner." The sex workers lived in a walled-off district "under strict police supervision" and were not allowed to leave.

FIGURE 7 • Police station just inside the remnant of the entryway into Tobita prostitution district in Osaka and the wall separating the district from the outside world (Photo by author)

The women "were usually kept in locked premises and those who escaped were hunted down by specially hired hoodlums, beaten and brought back." The proprietors of these places were politically influential, did not scruple at the "bribing of police," and would readily use influence or bribery to "prevent the loss of a girl."

The situation had gotten better in recent years, as the need for labor in war industries had helped to alleviate rural poverty. Moreover, the position of rural farmers had vastly improved after the war. There was already public condemnation of the system, with women's organizations "particularly militant in demands for reform." Their efforts contributed to the abolition of licensed prostitution in fifteen of Japan's rural prefectures. The Japanese informants then stated their belief that

> in urban districts the practice of enslaving girls, while much less prevalent than in the past, still exists and that the following corrective measures should be taken:
> (1) Entire abrogation of the law, to include all of Japan.
> (2) Invalidation and outlawing of all contracts by which the parents or head of a family may be financially benefited and all contracts by which a girl may be brought into such existence without her consent.
> (3) Provision of a penalty much more severe than the present 3 months or 100 yen for anyone who obstructs or hinders the effort of any woman to abandon such existence.

Finally, they suggested that GHQ write a directive along these lines and discuss it with them at a later date.[29] PHW followed up by meeting with other experts on the subject, including private citizens and police.[30] In a December 11, 1945, meeting with Takanori Shakutoku, chief of the Peace Section of the Metropolitan Police Board, and a Mr. Itoga of the same section, MacDonald suggested the steps recommended by Yosano and Ishibashi. The policemen backed abrogation of the licensed prostitution law and the implementation of a harsher penalty for forcing women into prostitution. However, they balked at the nullification and outlawing of indenture contracts. They worried that such a measure would "cause probably some hardship" among poor families who had no other means of income.[31] The reservations of the police notwithstanding, PHW composed a draft directive outlawing licensed prostitution, nullifying contracts and imposing prison sentences of two to ten years and/or fines of ¥2,000–10,000 for any individual found guilty of causing any woman to engage in the practice of prostitution against her will, or of hindering, delaying, or obstructing the effort of any woman to abandon the practice.[32]

On January 7, 1946, MacDonald prepared a memorandum for the record and submitted it along with a proposed order to be made to the Japanese government. While the memo does offer a somewhat dubious assertion about the measure's usefulness in battling venereal disease, the bulk of it is concerned with human rights.[33] Brig. Gen. Kermit (Ken) R. Dyke, chief of the Civil Information and Education Section (CIE), praised the proposal as "commendable" and averred, "Such action should receive wide and enthusiastic support not only in Japan but throughout the civilized world." Dyke was normally a fairly activist liberal who had had a hand in abolishing State Shintō, breaking up the Tokkō (Special Higher Police), getting the emperor to renounce his divinity, and purging ultranationalists from schools and the media. Nevertheless, he expressed reservations about GHQ's authority, specifically questioning the proposal's foundation in the Potsdam Declaration.[34] The directive was amended to eliminate reference to the Potsdam Declaration and remove the specific penal provisions. On January 15, 1946, GHQ issued a preliminary order to the Japanese government.[35] About a week later, on January 21, GHQ issued the amended directive as SCAPIN 642. It directed the Japanese government to abolish licensed prostitution, declaring it to be "in contravention of the ideals of democracy and inconsistent with the development of individual freedom throughout the nation." It also ordered the abrogation of all "laws ordinances and other enactments which directly or indirectly authorize or permit the existence of licensed prostitution in Japan." Finally, it directed the Japanese government to "nullify all contracts and agreements" that effectively bound women to prostitution.[36]

A good deal of recent analysis of this decision has sought to explain it, or rather to explain it away, as something motivated by ulterior motives—the

FIGURE 8 • Japanese prostitutes in Yoshiwara celebrate the news of GHQ's directive liberating them from servitude. (*Kyodo News*)

control of venereal disease, a public relations move by GHQ, or even an attempt to appease Japanese women's groups.[37] None of these suggestions can adequately account for GHQ's actions. Where the control of venereal disease was concerned, PHW's early moves made clear that they thought a reinstatement of the system would have been a more effective strategy. The abolition of licensed prostitution made control of venereal disease more difficult, not easier. As for using the measure as a means to improve the image of the Occupation, it would have to be judged a total failure. It neither kept stories about prostitution out of the American press nor curried favor with the Japanese people. In fact, it had quite the opposite effect. Finally, while women's groups had campaigned against prostitution well before the end of the war and played a role in getting licensed prostitution outlawed in many prefectures, they played no significant role in GHQ's decision. PHW, with whom they had no contact at this time, initiated the move. Why, then, did GHQ decide to abolish licensed prostitution? In this case, the simplest explanation turns out to be the best.

GHQ abolished licensed prostitution for the very reasons that it claimed: the system was antidemocratic and was baneful to the development of individual freedom. Where sex slavery was concerned, GHQ objected to slavery, not sex. GHQ's internal memoranda, the personal journal entries of GHQ personnel, and the interactions of American officials and Japanese interested in the prostitution problem clearly demonstrate their priorities.

In August 1946, GHQ drafted a memorandum to local military commanders explaining the meaning of SCAPIN 642 (misidentified as SCAPIN 643). It leaves no doubt about the Occupation's intentions. GHQ had no patience for niceties about whether a business was or was not technically licensed prostitution. It did not care about prostitution per se so long as the decision to undertake the profession was not made under duress. It considered financial obligation of any kind, whether incurred at the beginning of a contract or undertaken to proprietors since that point, to be duress and declared all such obligations null and void. The cardinal issues were the volition and autonomy of the women involved. The directive includes these points:

2. *The primary consideration of the directive above is to forbid and to prevent the enslavement of women in prostitution.* It applies not only to women who are recognized prostitutes but equally well to other women such as waitresses, geisha, or dance hall hostesses who may be forced to prostitute themselves against their will. . . .

3. . . . . The engaging of individuals, of their own free will and accord, in the practice of prostitution as a source of livelihood is not forbidden by this directive.

4. No individual will be made, against her will and consent freely given, to engage in prostitution. Consent, once given, may be withdrawn at any time, for any reason, and no penalty of any sort shall attach to the individual for withdrawal of consent.

5. All contracts, agreements, and debts incurred as a result thereof, binding any woman in prostitution, that are now in existence are null and void. All contracts, agreements and debts which hereinafter may be entered into, shall be null and void.

6. All obligations to pay money, or to render services shall be considered to have extinguished and fully satisfied. Under this provision the debt shall be considered to have been fully paid, whether the debt in question is the original debt, or any debt incurred since the original debt, for such things as clothes, food or housing. *The primary consideration is that no woman shall be bound in prostitution to repay any debt*, regardless of the source of the debt. [Emphasis added][38]

Later, on October 10, 1946, the Japanese GG Association, identified as a group "made up of the employers and managers of geisha girls throughout Japan," met in Tokyo and asked PHW legal adviser Joseph V. Zaccone for guidance on the legal implications of the abolition order. Zaccone was clear that the question

of whether or not the police will tolerate "Gay Areas" is one for them to decide. However, *SCAP will not sit idly by and allow women to be bought and sold into prostitution.* Contracts binding women into prostitution are void. The debts contracted thereunder are void, and all the parties thereto are liable to prosecution for violation of a SCAP directive. The terms of the directive apply not only to girls who are held in prostitution in "Gay Areas," but *girls who are made to prostitute themselves against their will anywhere,* whether in dance halls, beer halls, restaurants, or geisha houses. [Emphasis added][39]

For PHW, the essential issue was volition. Involuntary prostitution was its chief concern. The same concern dominated the thinking of Occupation officials outside PHW. According to the recollection of Alfred C. Oppler of SCAP's Government Section (GS), which had no responsibility for venereal disease, the subject of prostitution and its possible prohibition came up on August 20, 1946, in a meeting between Oppler, GS deputy chief Col. Charles Kades, and Cdr. Alfred Hussey. Oppler argued against the move, as he thought it would "impose puritan morality on this oriental nation." Nevertheless, he was adamant that the Americans should "act severely against forced prostitution."[40]

The emphasis on free will and autonomy remained GHQ's bedrock position throughout subsequent debates on prostitution. This dedication to liberal principle was consistent with the Occupation's goals. Most members of the Occupation regarded it as axiomatic that involuntary prostitution was anathema to personal liberty and basic human decency and thus licensed prostitution had to end. To people who believed the ideal role of government began (although not necessarily ended) with the guarantee of individual liberty to its citizens, this was obvious.

To many Japanese, however, the government's first duty was to serve as the guardian of social order. To them, GHQ's decree was wrong-headed mischief that did palpable harm. Even people with relatively liberal outlooks supported the licensed prostitution system, regarding it as a positive good that helped to ensure order. GS member and later the section's deputy chief, Justin Williams, recalled that when he was interviewing an expert on discrimination against minorities and women in Japan, the latter man suddenly launched into a defense of Japan's licensed prostitution system. He complained that the GIs' high demand for women was ruining many of the country's good girls, telling of how a girl who had worked in their employ for two years had asked for her release so that she could go work in a nightclub for much higher pay. The thought of paying her more apparently never occurred to him.[41]

This was not an isolated case. Though the Americans had certainly been right that many women had been coerced into the licensed houses, it seems that many others were there of their own volition. Others, no doubt, had grown accustomed to the life and the work and had no other way to support themselves. Numerous women either did not wish to leave the profession or could not afford to. As a result, prostitution became far more visible, moving from designated brothels in specific walled-off districts to parks, train stations, and the streets of the city—wherever there were potential customers. Looking back on the move, Zaccone wrote that the abolition of licensed prostitution "unloosed a horde of 'street-walkers' and 'angels of the night' on the streets."[42]

The streetwalkers, or *panpan* as they came to be known, put commercial sexuality out in the open, a development offensive to most Japanese. A survey conducted in 1949 noted that 77 percent of respondents in the Kantō area (in and around Tokyo) supported legislation outlawing streetwalking, but 70 percent opposed similar legislation aimed at organized houses of prostitution.[43] One woman asserted, "Organized prostitutes don't go out so much, they don't run loose in the streets. They are not as harmful as the pan-pan girls."[44] The survey's summary of attitudes noted, "The *pan-pan* girl, with her brazen painted face and manners, her frizzy hair, her garish Western clothes, is unfamiliar, obtrusive, conspicuous, an eyesore, a disorderly element."[45] Letters to the Supreme Commander echoed this sentiment. One writer complained about "the streetwalkers, because they are too radical a departure from Japanese customs."[46]

Women walking the streets were aware of society's scorn. A Japanese police report of July 1950 describes a group of prostitutes who organized for the purpose of escaping their vocations, appealing to the public to treat them with sympathy. On May 15, 1950, they distributed a flyer to passersby in the Tokyo districts of Yūraku-chō and Hibiya.

What a Swan Would Be.
We are a flock of the lost sheep born from the social evils produced by the postwar confusion. Is it our self-defending appeal if we should say there was no alternative for us but to find our way to live in our own body when the war had deprived us of our parents, brothers and husbands, making us homeless and foodless?

Five years have passed since then amid the disorder and confusion. During these periods of time, we were chased by the police, put into the prison, and how often did we pledge to ourselves to go into a new life, looking at the moon through the bars of the jail weeping and thinking of our past happy days when we were all innocent girls?

But on returning to the world, the only things that came to meet us were cold eyes and we were again obliged to go back to our old way not to be saved as ought to be.

We think, however this is no time for us to be content with what we are at our ease.

Though we may be ignorant itself, our sincere desire of rehabilitating ourselves have found its way to a heartrending cry which has made us intend to have our own association "Haukucho Kai."[47]

Whether they were sympathetic to these women or not, in the minds of most Japanese the major effect of the order abolishing licensed prostitution was to create chaos where there had once been order. They clearly preferred getting the women off the streets and back into the houses. Only about 3 percent of respondents to the 1949 survey mentioned concerns about the human rights of the women employed in brothels.[48] While this was of primary importance to GHQ, it clearly had little resonance with ordinary Japanese.

Japanese police were even less enthusiastic about abolition. Having worked together with proprietors to maintain order in prewar Japan, they had close ties with them and were loath to surrender control.[49] After learning of the impending order to end licensed prostitution, the authorities tried to mitigate its impact and only reluctantly cracked down on violators after its issuance.[50] The Japanese police treated GHQ's categorical imperative more as a guideline than an order. A May 1946 report from the Home Ministry's Police Affairs Bureau to the superintendent-general of the Metropolitan Police Board declared, "Efforts will be made to persuade the proprietors of brothels to abandon such contracts. . . . Efforts will be made to persuade and guide the proprietors of the business to voluntarily abandon all such contracts as are likely to be binding the freedom of the service girls against their will."[51] The translation of this order appears in GHQ's files with question marks prominently penciled next to the passages cited above. In November 1946 Zaccone summoned Katō Yozo of the Home Ministry's Police Bureau and asked him about this situation. Katō explained that "the Japanese courts have rendered decisions declaring such contracts invalid and that when employers are urged and led to dissolve contracts by their own free will the intent is to persuade employers to agree to annulments rather than to force action through the courts."[52]

Katō was not being entirely forthright. If the courts had ruled on the question, he provided no evidence of the fact. Moreover, in 1902 the Japanese Supreme Court rendered a decision that was essentially the opposite of what Katō had claimed. In *Ōkuma Kin v. Watanabe Mase*, the court decreed that a prostitute was free to quit her profession whenever she wanted but was responsible for repaying any debt that she had incurred.

In real terms this bound her to prostitution.[53] Whatever the case, police treated the debt as valid whether the sex worker desired emancipation or not. They went easy on proprietors and neglected to submit translations of their directives, as they had been ordered to do in SCAPIN 642. This led to official chastisement along with demands of compliance in SCAPIN 1183, issued on September 6, 1946.[54]

To remove any doubt about what sorts of directives it expected, GHQ issued a clarifying statement on the issue in November 1946. The statement, made "BY COMMAND OF THE SUPREME COMMANDER," was very clear: "The intention of the notification issued to the prefectural authorities by the Home Ministry is to nullify contracts which bind women to prostitution. The annulment of the contract carries with it the extinguishment of the debt."[55] The invocation of the Supreme Commander left no doubt of its importance. Nevertheless, GHQ had to issue another follow-up just two months later. The January 13, 1947, directive unambiguously stated that both contracts and debts were null and void: "It can be stated as a rule of law that upon a contract being annulled, all obligations imposed on parties to the contract are likewise annulled. Any attempt, therefore, to separate the debt from the contract, coupled with an assertion that the contract is void but the debt is valid is merely an attempt to circumvent the clear meaning of the directive."[56]

At almost the same time, GHQ ordered the Japanese government to issue an Imperial Ordinance that "prohibited involuntary prostitution, the sale of human beings and licensed prostitution."[57] The actual ordinance, Imperial Ordinance #9 of 1947, was a less sweeping directive that provided penalties of up to three years' imprisonment or a fine of up to ¥10,000 for forcing a woman into prostitution or one year and up to ¥5,000 fine for concluding a contract that bound her to the same.[58] Despite these efforts, women and girls continued to be sold into virtual slavery throughout the Occupation and beyond. The question was not settled definitively in Japan until 1955, when the Supreme Court finally ruled on the issue.[59]

Though GHQ would maintain the illegitimacy and illegality of all involuntary prostitution, ultimately it failed to completely eradicate the practice. There was little support from Japanese authorities or from the Japanese populace. Indeed, the link between the abolition of licensed prostitution and the proliferation of streetwalkers made it unpopular, significantly dampening American enthusiasm for a prohibition on prostitution more generally.

THE DEBATE OVER PROHIBITION: GHQ DECLINES TO ACT

Prostitution in Japan became a major issue for the Americans in part because of the actions taken by the Japanese government. In the eyes of Japanese officialdom, "one of the hallmarks of a relationship based on domination was that the males of the ruling or conquering nation marry females of the ruled or conquered nation."[60] Initially, however, it was not so much marriage that Japanese officials feared (though in time that would become a major concern as well) but rape. One of their top priorities was to see that Japanese women were not despoiled by the American conquerors, and they went to great lengths to prevent rape. Individual women and local governments took a variety of measures.[61] However, it was the extraordinary action initiated by the central government that would reverberate the longest in Japanese historical memory.

Officials in the Japanese government, reasoning that if sex were easily available to them, the Americans would commit fewer rapes, ordered the establishment of brothels. The origins of this idea are obscure and have, in the intervening years, become the subject of many legends. What is known for certain is that on August 18, 1945, just three days after Emperor Hirohito's "sacred decision" to accept the demands of the Potsdam Declaration, the Home Ministry ordered the various prefectural police departments to establish brothels for the Allies.[62]

The Americans refused the Japanese offer. Nevertheless, the Japanese police, assuming that American coolness was just pretense, proceeded with their plan. The Home Ministry's Police Affairs Bureau sent all prefectural police departments a missive that stated, "Even though GHQ superficially refuses recognition for this type of facility [brothels], it is nevertheless absolutely necessary for our defense."[63] Soon after the Americans landed, the brothels opened.

When confronted with the unconventional hospitality of their new hosts (and the abundance of less official prostitution), the commanders initially decided on a policy of laissez-faire. On September 11, 1945, just days after American troops had moved into Tokyo, Eighth Army commander Lt. Gen. Robert L. Eichelberger recorded the decision in his diary:

> Gen. Hall called in the afternoon and discussed the venereal disease situation. It was decided that no attempt would be made to control the usage of houses of prostitution but that strong pressure would be exerted on them through the Japanese police to maintain cleanliness and order. Our MP's will be stationed in the vicinity of these establishments for the purpose of maintaining control. However, the army will not become involved in any sanction or operation of individual establishments.[64]

This policy was short-lived. American public health officials from GHQ's PHW soon began studying prostitution in Japan and became alarmed. Before the war, Japanese authorities had struggled mightily to keep prostitution under strict state control. To the extent that prostitution was considered a social evil, it was a necessary evil and one the authorities were determined to keep both legal and under their control. Even in times of peace and good order, however, they had found this difficult.[65]

During the war, and especially in the chaos after the American bombing offensive, controls broke down almost completely as livelihoods and families were destroyed. Many desperate young women turned to prostitution.[66] Naturally, this situation was only exacerbated after the surrender and the sudden appearance of hundreds of thousands of single men who, by Japanese standards at least, were flush with money.

Officers of PHW, after learning something of the history of prostitution in Japan, but still unaware of its more sordid details, at first recommended the reestablishment of the licensed system in order to bring some order to the situation.[67] American attitudes changed abruptly after learning that the system relied on human trafficking. However, even before that they had discovered that the perceived advantages of such a system were largely illusory. They found both the inspection protocols and the methods of treatment to be completely inadequate.[68] They also determined that a staggering percentage of the prostitutes had venereal infections.[69]

American anxiety about this situation grew, and by mid-October the initial policy of laissez-faire had been reversed and commanders began placing brothels off-limits to GIs.[70] The Japanese reaction to this was intriguing, to say the least. Though enough time had passed since the landings of the Americans to see that fears of mass rape had been groundless, Japanese authorities were very anxious to get the off-limits orders rescinded. Possibly they sought to ingratiate themselves with the conquerors and procure a favorable peace. Possibly they sought a source of government revenue or even personal enrichment. Most likely, as historian Yukiko Koshiro has suggested, the whole policy of establishing brothels had from the outset been an "anti-fraternization project" with the aim of preserving the purity of the Japanese bloodline by preventing and controlling intercourse in both its social and sexual varieties. In other words, it was about stopping fraternization "whether in the form of dating, marriage, or childbearing."[71]

Whatever the case, it is clear that getting the Americans into brothels was a priority for a number of Japanese officials who seemed to believe they were performing a vital service to their nation and their communities. In Shinhotta, a town in Niigata Prefecture, officials collected about two yen from every household to raise a total of about ¥20,000 for the purpose of establishing a brothel for Americans troops. When the American commander discovered this plan, he ordered the town to return the money. Mayor Hara made a somewhat shamefaced explanation that the brothel plan had only been intended to express the town's welcome and show gratitude for the peaceful manner of the American advance into the area.[72]

In his memoir, Ikeda Hirohiko, chief of police in the city of Tsuchiura in Ibaraki Prefecture, recalled his struggles to establish a brothel for the GIs. Like many police officers around the country, he traveled to Yokohama to see the bordellos the Kanagawa police had already established for the Americans.[73] Upon his return, he set out to recruit women. Utilizing an old police dormitory and surplus bedding from the Imperial Navy, he had established a facility in time to welcome the Americans when they arrived on September 20. In early October the Americans insisted on blood tests (presumably testing for syphilis only) for all the women working at the new establishment. When sixteen of the twenty-six women tested positive, they placed the facility off-limits. Ikeda, who was quick to believe rumors, wrote that his "biggest worry" was that the Americans who had up to that point patiently "lined up and waited their turns" would present a danger to the area's women now that their place of outlet had suddenly been closed to them. Determined to prevent that, he scoured other areas of the country and, after collecting an additional ten healthy women, reopened at the end of the month. He established another brothel for Black GIs and a third for officers, which he says he did at the request of the Americans. Despite his best efforts, all three were declared off-limits in December and were not subsequently reopened.[74]

On October 17, Gordon and MacDonald held a conference with Takanori Shakutoku, chief of the Peace Section of the Metropolitan Police Board;[75] Ōtake Bungo, his subchief; and Dr. Yosano Hikaru. At the conference all of the Japanese attendees "were somewhat concerned over the 'off limits' orders affecting these areas and asked when they would be rescinded." Told that that would depend on the "thoroughness and efficiency" of their VD control regime, they suggested that "three best and cleanest districts" in Tokyo be opened on a provisional basis if the police made special efforts to identify and immediately remove all infected workers.[76]

Such efforts proved inadequate and venereal disease became a growing problem for American commanders. As discussed above, local commanders with the advice of PHW officials began placing brothels off-limits to their soldiers when they were found to have a large number of infected prostitutes. On December 14 or 15 (accounts vary), GHQ informed prefectural police departments that all brothels would thenceforth be off-limits to all American personnel.[77] Later, GHQ further tightened restrictions by ordering that because all brothels and similar establishments were off-limits to American personnel, any Japanese in such a place serving GIs would be subject to American military justice.[78]

Judging from contemporary cartoons, the order was honored as much in the breach as the observance. The resulting encounters with MPs became a subject of merriment, lampooned in the pages of the *Pacific Stars and Stripes*. Cartoonist James Schell's "Occupation Outbursts" shows an MP approaching an establishment while a winsome Japanese woman in a

"Naughty naughty!"

FIGURE 9 • "Tokyo Joe" cartoon from *Stars and Stripes* lampooning GIs' attempts to circumvent "off-limits" restrictions (Ed Doughty)

GI's garrison cap surrounded by large American combat boots left in the entryway insists, "There are no soldiers here." Schell's colleague, Ed Doughty, poked fun at soldiers' attempts to circumvent the order and the MPs charged with enforcing it.

Flouting of the off-limits order was not the only problem that American commanders and health officials had to deal with. As had happened with the abolition of licensed prostitution, the off-limits order had the effect of sending thousands of women to the streets, where they solicited openly. Though this trend had begun in the war's final stages, it accelerated as the Occupation took an increasingly strict attitude toward organized prostitution. The trend became so marked that in May 1946, prostitutes operating in organized houses availed themselves of one of the new freedoms of the postwar era by organizing a union to help them deal with the competition of proliferating streetwalkers.[79]

The problem was all too simple: both Japanese prostitutes and American servicemen had high rates of venereal infection, and they actively sought one another's company. As long as they continued to couple, the infections would pass back and forth between these populations. Because there was no law against prostitution in Japan, there were few legal means to curb the practice.

Local authorities, including Japanese police as well as American base commanders and MPs, often resorted to quasi-legal or extralegal means to harass and intimidate streetwalkers. After the passage of an anti–venereal disease law, the Japanese police abused the authority the law gave them to begin wholesale roundups of streetwalkers and sometimes women who happened to be unaccompanied on the streets in certain areas. Based on venereal disease laws, local ordinances, and their own convictions, Japanese police also raided hotels suspected of facilitating prostitution. In one operation in June 1950, forty-six Japanese police officers conducted raids on two Tokyo hotels, where they apprehended six women. When they investigated, they learned that of the six, five were actually the girlfriends of American military personnel. On the report submitted to GHQ's Public Safety Division (PSD), one American official wrote, "Stupid procedures being followed—a repetition of past illegal practices of police wherein innocent persons have been picked up & arrested."[80]

Not all Americans, however, were so scrupulous about the limits of police powers. American military police, whom GHQ had authorized to go along on raids by Japanese police only to ensure that no Americans interfered with the Japanese police in the discharge of their duties, often took it upon themselves to assist.[81] PHW admonished them that such actions were a violation of the women's human rights and had no legal basis. Nevertheless, some local commanders and MPs were more in sympathy with the Japanese police than with GHQ bureaucrats. In Kyoto, Maj. Gen. Joseph M. Swing was commander of I Corps. Swing would later earn notoriety as the chief of the Immigration and Naturalization Service, where he originated "Operation Wetback," which deported hundreds of thousands of Mexican immigrants, some of them U.S. citizens. He used a similar mentality in dealing with prostitution, ordering his MPs to arrest all "likely" women out on the streets after six in the evening. After three nights of mass arrests, Dr. John Glismann, a young public health official, threatened Swing with a military suit. Swing threw him out of his office, but the roundups stopped—at least for a time.[82]

Despite their run-ins with PSD and PHW officials, many MPs and commanders were more concerned with social order than with legal abstractions, and they took to clearing out streetwalkers on their own authority.[83] In Oita Prefecture, the MPs and their interpreters were out of control, reaching the point that "women refrain[ed] as much as possible from going outdoors even in daytime," according to a very politely worded objection from a local Japanese liaison official.[84] However, aside from antagonizing the civilian population, such roundups had little effect.[85]

Those charged with handling the problem grew increasingly exasperated and began calling for stronger measures. On November 6, 1946, the Americans drew up a draft SCAPIN (directive from the Supreme Commander to the Japanese government) requiring that the Japanese government "enact a law prohibiting prostitution and its allied activities and providing penalties therefor."[86] Just two weeks later, Maj. Gen. Thomas D. White, chief of staff of the Pacific Air Command, made a similar recommendation, albeit more obliquely, in a memo he sent to MacArthur. After asserting that in order to make progress in combating venereal disease in the ranks, it would be necessary to address "the broad basic problem" of venereal disease in the civilian population and especially "the large reservoir of venereal disease infection that exists in and is spread by commercial prostitutes." He pointedly added, "Prostitution as such is still legal in Japan."[87]

On December 26, 1946, Col. Crawford F. Sams, chief of PHW, backed banning prostitution, recommending, "In order to further reduce the venereal disease rate among occupation forces in Japan, to an acceptable level, it is considered necessary that legal steps be taken to suppress prostitution as such." He also suggested that the Japanese government be directed to enact "a law making the act of prostitution illegal."[88] Sams did not take this step lightly. He had a very no-nonsense approach to his job, which in his mind began and largely ended with public health concerns. He had little patience for moralism.

Once Sams advocated this approach, others voiced support. On January 4, Eichelberger sent a memo to MacArthur expressing his "enthusiastic concurrence," a formulation he used twice. He was clear about his frustration with the situation, and though he acknowledged that "the passage of such a law will not be a panacea," he argued that the best possible step would be for GHQ to declare "any phase of prostitution unlawful."[89] The following month, the staff medical officer of the Commander of Naval Forces in the Far East command, citing the continuing high rates of venereal disease, recommended "that the proposed plan for providing a legal basis for the suppression of prostitution should be adopted."[90] Health officials from the Navy and the Army Air Force, the top public health official in Japan, and the commander of the Eighth Army were now unanimous in advocating a total ban on prostitution.

While the prohibition campaign gathered momentum, Hiroshima Prefecture inadvertently spurred more support for a ban with the proposal of an entertainment tax on brothels. The prefecture and especially its atomic-bombed namesake capital city were strapped for funds to rebuild after the war.[91] A tax on a luxury expense that was, after all, perfectly legal must have seemed just the ticket. The prefecture's timing could hardly have been worse. With a consensus beginning to form around outlawing prostitution, the last thing many Occupation authorities wanted was another vested interest to overcome.

Feeling the wind at their backs, those in favor of outlawing prostitution no longer limited their arguments to technical issues. In addressing the Hiroshima plan, PHW's venereal disease consultant Oscar Elkins responded with extraordinary vigor, openly embracing the sort of moralism that Sams had largely eschewed.[92] Elkins bluntly condemned prostitution in uncompromising terms: "Commercial prostitution should always be exposed for what it is—a filthy racket bringing immense profits to the exploiters who feed parasitically on the degradation of young women. These gangsters and vice lords corrupt the police, the courts, other branches of government and constitute a social evil which threatens the kind of society we are trying to encourage the Japanese people to form." He went on to denounce the "medieval ideas" of some Japanese officials, lamenting the fact that some in SCAP were being "taken in" by them. "No government," he asserted, "which purports to be democratic, should ever find the solution to its problems, financial or otherwise, at the expense of its poorest, lowliest, or most exploited people." In closing, he recommended "the enactment of a law to prohibit prostitution and its allied activities."[93]

The Government and Legal Sections of GHQ reviewed Hiroshima's proposal. With obvious reluctance, analysts concluded "that from a strict legal point of view, the Japanese Government, under existing directives, could be allowed to collect the tax as proposed." They advised rejection anyway, fearing that approval would be taken as "an admission that prostitution is recognized as being in the same class as other legitimate amusement enterprises. To do this is also to give it an aura of respectability which it does not possess." "Also," they continued, "in view of the fact that action is pending to prohibit prostitution in Japan, sanction of the proposed tax measure would be imposing another hurdle to overcome in achieving the elimination of prostitution with all its attendant social and economic evils."[94] The following month SCAP's Government Section, Legal Section, and PHW all endorsed this view, approving a statement advising the rejection of the proposed tax and denouncing prostitution as "this degrading slavery."[95] Moral issues were now clearly a factor.

Taking a stand against a revenue scheme in a provincial prefecture was one thing, however, and using a SCAPIN to prohibit prostitution altogether was, it turned out, quite another. When the idea went to Government Section (GS) for endorsement, it hit a snag. GS chief Courtney Whitney "strongly concur[red] in the necessity for immediate action to promote a legal basis for the attack on this problem," but then asserted, "The channels of informal approach have not been fully explored and [thus GS] recommends that the proposed action be undertaken through such channels."[96] In other words, GS believed that though legal prostitution was a problem, it was a Japanese problem and required a Japanese solution; GHQ should not try to solve the problem by fiat.

The proposal then went to the G-2 intelligence section, which oversaw American policing in Japan. G-2 head Brig. Gen. Charles Willoughby's response was a study in bureaucratic doublespeak. Though he began by declaring, "I concur in Govt Section's view," he then made clear that he meant GS's reservations and not the general idea of taking legal action against prostitution. Paying lip service to controlling venereal disease, he proceeded to enumerate every conceivable reason that GHQ should take no legal action against prostitution. Willoughby argued, "We should not be so simple as to believe that the passage of a law solves the problem in a country where public sentiment in general is non-committal or in favor of prostitution." He then asserted, "A law making prostitution a crime has never anywhere in the ancient or modern world stamped out or seriously approached the eradication of venereal infection." Moreover, such a law would "appear to be duplicating the Prohibition [of alcohol] Law [in the United States]," which would likewise corrupt the courts, politics, and law enforcement while also inviting a "flood of professional bondsmen and other known illegal practices that are parasites to prostitution." Finally, he recommended a vigorous campaign of education and legislation aimed "primarily at *prostitution coupled with venereal infection*" (emphasis in original).[97] This was nothing more than an intensification and formal codification of the measures already in place.

Government Section, on the other hand, had been sincere in both its reservations and its desire to see Japanese action on the issue. While GHQ debated its policy toward prostitution, a new coalition cabinet assumed power under the Christian Socialist Katayama Tetsu. Katayama's cabinet proved to be the most cooperative that GS ever dealt with. Perhaps encouraged by the new cabinet's attitude, Alfred Hussey, one of GS's top men, met with the incoming health and welfare minister, Hitotsumatsu Sadayoshi, on July 3, 1947. In line with GS's plan to use "the channels of informal approach," Hussey urged Hitotsumatsu to take measures to eliminate commercial prostitution. In response, "the Minister agreed that something should be done but felt that a program of education was necessary in order to secure the support of public opinion. He recommended that in the meantime the Japanese Government undertake segregation of prostitutes in districts and enforced treatment."[98] In other words, Hitotsumatsu urged return to the status quo antebellum. This was out of the question so far as the Americans were concerned.

In 1948, growing resentment of streetwalkers, particularly those around American military bases, led the Ashida government to introduce an anti-prostitution bill to the Diet.[99] The bill was a severe measure that essentially filled the earlier desiderata of American officials, making "any phase of prostitution unlawful."[100]

It provoked immediate resistance. On May 28, 1948, a group of Diet members including future prime minister Nakasone Yasuhiro submitted a petition to GHQ urging that prostitution remain legal.[101] Indeed, according to GHQ's informants, the cabinet itself opposed the bill but was "under the impression that this Headquarters [GHQ] desires or sponsors it."[102] It was very likely true that at the time of Hussey's meeting with Hitotsumatsu the previous year, GHQ did desire such a bill and would have given it full backing. Now that GHQ officials had considered the problem from a more practical standpoint, however, their ardor had cooled considerably. The possible harm to American prestige and popularity, the difficulty of enforcement, and questions about a ban's actual effects on the venereal disease situation had all worked to undermine support for prohibition. By the time the antiprostitution bill was submitted to the Diet, MacArthur had decided that SCAP would take no position publicly.[103]

> Neither the Cabinet nor the Diet should be left in the belief that this Headquarters is pushing or even favoring the proposed legislation. Unless the contrary is stated unambiguously, SCAP will be severely criticized as attempting to impose American moral standards on a nation whose sexual mores are based on essentially different Oriental traditions. . . . After involuntary prostitution has been outlawed, the occupation is concerned only with the health aspect of the problem. . . . The decisive question is whether the Japanese really and sincerely want this law.[104]

The Americans suspected that the Japanese did not. Col. (or Mr.) Alva C. Carpenter, head of GHQ's Legal Section, reported that the section's contacts had informed them "that unless considerable pressure is exercised by SCAP, the bill will be rejected by an overwhelming majority of the Diet."[105] The Diet then did what legislatures are wont to do when faced with difficult decisions: they decided the problem needed more study, including a public opinion survey. The Japanese government conducted just such a survey, and SCAP's Civil Information and Education Section (CIE) released a report on the survey's findings at the end of June 1949.[106]

The survey found that the Japanese people (as represented by the citizens of the Kantō region and the city of Sendai) regarded prostitution much the way GHQ had two years earlier: "Many people favor the abolition as an ideal, but feel that practically and realistically there are too many difficulties and that immediate attempts at abolition would either fail completely or bring about even worse consequences than the continued existence of prostitution."[107] As to the question of what practical steps should be taken, the respondents largely shared the attitudes of Japanese authorities, believing prostitution a necessary evil. The most common view was that the biggest problems stemmed from two major factors: the chaos created by postwar social and economic conditions and GHQ's abolition of licensed prostitution. A very small minority were sympathetic to the idea that prostitution should be so regulated as to be more accommodating of women's rights, but most Japanese simply did not understand GHQ's approach. They preferred to get prostitutes indoors, off the streets and out of sight, working in brothels segregated from the general population in recognized red-light districts. They did not regard prohibition, or at least the anticipated consequences of prohibition, as desirable.[108]

With the survey clearly militating against passage, the Diet shelved the bill indefinitely. There would be no more major efforts at the national level to prohibit prostitution for the remainder of the Occupation. Local American commanders used military police to round up women who were in violation of local prostitution ordinances, who were suspected of violating the Venereal Disease Control Law, or who simply struck them the wrong way. However, GHQ never again pushed for a national ban. Over time, it became increasingly clear that Willoughby's analysis was essentially correct. A blanket ban on prostitution did not enjoy popular support, and Japanese officials were opposed to it. The Americans contented themselves with outlawing involuntary prostitution and indentured sex slavery with SCAPIN 642. Most probably would not have gone so far as the Economic and Science Section official who blithely argued that in view of the promulgation of SCAPIN 642, "prostitution carried on in established amusement places may be presumed voluntary."[109] Trafficking continued. American officials took violations seriously and investigated them, mandating that any debts incurred were invalid.[110] Nevertheless, many, perhaps most, Americans tended to act as if these cases were aberrations even when there was ample reason to conclude that they were not.

CONCLUSION

Perhaps the fairest judgment that can be rendered on the Occupation's attempts to liberate Japanese women from "degrading slavery" would be, to borrow a formulation: they meant well—feebly. Damning as that faint praise may seem, it is nevertheless praise of a sort. For all their shortcomings in dealing with the issue of prostitution, officials in GHQ certainly did not direct a collaborationist government to set up a nationwide system of brothels for their troops. Nor did they connive in the enslavement of women to work in any such system. Moreover, GHQ took decisive and immediate action in an attempt to end the most egregious abuses of Japanese prostitution: human trafficking and involuntary sexual servitude.

Most Americans who dealt with the issue of prostitution favored a blanket prohibition on grounds of both public health and morality; however, in the end they seem to have concluded that Willoughby was probably correct. Banning prostitution was a fool's errand as long as the majority of the populace and of the elite still perceived it in neutral or even positive terms.

Even with the benefit of hindsight, it is hard to argue with that conclusion. After a campaign by Japanese women's groups through which, in the words of historian Sheldon Garon, "prostitution became bound up with deep-seated Japanese anxieties about racial contamination and racial subordination" to American forces and in which the rights of the women

FIGURE 10 • Brothels line both sides of a street in the Tobita prostitution district in Osaka. One hundred fifty-nine establishments, including at least one genuine dining facility, belong to the local Tobita Restaurant Association. (Photo by author)

involved were at best an afterthought, the Japanese government passed an antiprostitution law in 1956 that came into effect between April 1, 1957, and April 1, 1958.[111]

Though technically illegal, prostitution has been practiced openly throughout the postwar era, and the Japanese sex industry is one of the world's largest and most sophisticated. Very much in accordance with the preferences expressed by Japanese some seven decades ago, streetwalking is rare, but sexual services are available in big cities and resort towns in well-defined segregated areas.

Though brothels and similar establishments recruit openly, if euphemistically, and many of the women involved can be presumed to be there voluntarily, human trafficking and debt bondage remain major problems. In 2018 Japan became the last G7 nation to be recognized by the U.S. State Department as fully compliant with the minimum standards for the elimination of trafficking. However, authorities still tend to treat such crimes with lenience, and a 2018 State Department report noted that Japanese officials "continued to prosecute traffickers under laws carrying lesser sentences, which courts often suspended in lieu of incarceration. Many suspected cases of child sex trafficking and forced labor were addressed with administrative penalties or loss of business licenses rather than through criminal investigations and proceedings."[112] A recent case supports this judgment. In 2019, a Japanese court convicted Ogawa Yūtarō of ensnaring two women in debt bondage through fraudulent means and then pressuring them to join the sex industry to pay off their "debts." Moreover, the group he led was highly organized and had allegedly coerced hundreds of women into prostitution. Though Ogawa was the ringleader and was reported to have made nearly ¥100 million off the racket, he got a suspended sentence of two and a half years.[113]

GHQ's handling of the prostitution issue was at times ham-fisted, hypocritical, contradictory, and ineffective. It could even be counterproductive. However, its early recognition of the plight of women ensnared in the licensed prostitution system and its concrete actions to ban involuntary prostitution and debt bondage deserve both recognition and commendation. In the seven decades since it regained sovereignty, Japan's democratic government has neither successfully suppressed prostitution nor adequately reformed the practice to eliminate the most egregious social evils attendant to it. It seems unreasonable to expect GHQ to have done so in a tenth of that time during a period of widespread economic hardship when prostitution was widely supported and popular Japanese consciousness of human rights was still in its infancy.

CHAPTER 3

PHW'S WAR ON VENEREAL DISEASE

On February 27, 1953, Socialist firebrand Fujiwara Michiko addressed the Diet, denouncing the baneful influence of American troops on Japan's social and moral fabric. She lambasted them for introducing an entirely new type of venereal disease, the Sasebō disease, so-named for its outbreak near the town of Sasebō, which housed a major U.S. military base. In responding to the charge, Minister of State Yamagata Katsumi explained that the disease, a bacterial infection related to soft chancre, had a long history in Japan. The Americans regarded it as a form of soft chancre. The Japanese medical authorities did not agree. Though the infection was certainly sexually transmitted, it was not, in their experience, pathogenic. In any event, the classification was a medical debate and not the result of lascivious Americans spreading unknown sexual corruptions among the innocent women of Japan.[1]

In many ways, Fujiwara's mischaracterization anticipated the treatment of venereal disease in the present historiography of the Occupation. American authorities became aware of the presence of an existing sexually transmitted infection in the population and raised the issue with Japanese authorities. In the popular mind, the Americans thus became associated with the problem and in time, with the assistance of propagandists, unscrupulous politicians, and sensationalist writers, came to be identified as its source.

Such narratives are superficially plausible because they contain some truth. The large-scale American fraternization with Japanese women and especially with Japanese prostitutes certainly did not help matters. The rate of infection among GIs increased rapidly after their arrival in Japan and was high throughout the Occupation.[2] This was something that Crawford F. Sams, GHQ's point man on public health matters, frankly acknowledged, writing, "People of foreign lands sometimes need to be protected from our soldiers as far as the venereal diseases are concerned."[3] The spread of infection in American ranks made the problem urgent. This in turn often led base commanders and military police to make clumsy and authoritarian efforts to quash VD. These efforts sometimes negated the more measured and medically sound approaches taken by the professionals at GHQ's Public Health and Welfare Section (PHW). Moreover, they gave an appearance—sometimes accurately—of alarm, frustration, and an inability to impose discipline.

Propagandists then spun tales of oversexed GIs flooding Japan with malignant microbes of every sort and, through their phenomenal patronage of Japanese prostitutes—whom American commanders demanded the Japanese provide—spreading these diseases among themselves to the point that venereal infection was on the verge of incapacitating the entire Occupation force. Too late, the Americans realized their error and made clumsy efforts to control the trade in flesh. In the end, they blamed the women they had previously lured or even coerced into prostitution. In this telling, the primary mission of American medical authorities was to ensure a steady supply of clean women to sate the lusts of their troops.[4] Their efforts, however, were largely for naught, as the conquerors were well-nigh insatiable, spreading infection beyond any hope of control. In many versions of the story, when their commanders placed houses of prostitution off-limits, American servicemen resorted to mass rape.[5] Thus, the Americans were not only unable to quash venereal disease in their own ranks; they also, as Dietwoman Fujiwara suggested, even spread it to a previously unsullied Japanese population as well.

Many historians have subsequently adopted this basic narrative as their own. Some have reinforced it with cherry-picked or misrepresented documentary evidence.[6] In recent years, it has become something like the standard interpretation.[7] Despite the kernels of truth to be found here and there, for the most part this story, like those about GHQ's handling of the issue of prostitution, comes close to inverting reality. In fact, when the Americans arrived, venereal disease had long been endemic in Japan, infecting a significant portion of its population for centuries. When the Americans left, largely due to the efforts of PHW, venereal disease in Japan was on its way to virtual extinction.

THE HISTORY OF VENEREAL DISEASE IN JAPAN

The first documented outbreaks of syphilis were in the Kansai region of western Japan in 1512, only seventeen years after the first occurrence in Europe.[8] According to Suzuki Tadao, a paleopathologist and paleoepidemiologist, the disease spread in Japan with "dreadful speed," even considering its rapid spread elsewhere in the world.[9] Like many other peoples around the world, Japanese named the disease for a foreign nation, dubbing it the "Ryūkyū pox."[10]

Syphilis arrived when Japan was in a period of continuous civil war known as the Warring States period (1467–1600). The disorder and internecine violence became so serious that China suspended all trade relations just eleven years later. Political chaos persisted for nearly a century after the outbreak of syphilis, coming to an end only with the victory of Tokugawa Ieyasu in the Battle of Sekigahara in 1600.

However, the peace that followed actually exacerbated the spread of disease. Eschewing the old imperial capital of Kyoto, Ieyasu established the seat of his new government in Edo (now Tokyo), the little castle town in eastern Japan that had served as his headquarters. The subsequent long period of peace would be named for this town, which grew to be the largest city in the world in a little over a century.

However, Edo's growth was not organic. Although it would soon develop a rich urban culture, it was, after all, the stronghold of a warlord. As such, both the city's layout and the composition of its population developed according to the dictates of security. From the beginning, Edo was overwhelmingly male and would long remain so. It took more than two centuries for the sex ratio to become roughly even.[11] Unsurprisingly, a large sex industry developed to cater to this massive excess of males. Throughout the Edo period there were numerous officially recognized houses served by what were called public prostitutes. Moreover, despite the unceasing efforts of authorities, clandestine prostitution thrived as well.[12]

Later, the shogunate would set up a formalized system of hostage taking, in which the wives and families of all feudal lords resided in Edo at all times, while the lords themselves were required to live in Edo every other year and return to their home domains in the odd years. When they traveled between the two, they had large retinues of retainers accompanying them, most of whom left their own families in their home domains. These unaccompanied men and the many single warriors who served them naturally availed themselves of the services available in the pleasure quarters of both the metropolis itself and the many stations along the way.[13] By the time of the third Shōgun, Iemitsu, Japan was already annually importing (as part of its very limited external trade) 450 tons of *Sankirai*, a Chinese medicine believed to be effective against syphilis.[14]

Engelbert Kaempfer was a German physician who went to Japan between 1690 and 1692. One of the things that struck him was the pervasiveness and widespread acceptance of prostitution. Some towns, he noted, were known as "the Japanese whore mart or mills" because of the ubiquity of prostitutes in the inns, and "Japanese rarely pass through these towns without sleeping with this riffraff and generally discover to their dismay that they have returned home with an unwanted souvenir."[15] These men then distributed their souvenirs in both the capital and their home domains. A century and a half later, Otto Mohnike, another German physician, made much the same trek as Kaempfer had. He wrote that the main road from Kyoto to Tokyo was, "with the exception of some mountainous areas, almost literally one uninterrupted chain of hotels, resting places, inns, and brothels."[16]

Though exact figures on the prevalence of the disease are impossible to extract from the historical record, evidence suggests that it was very common. The results of a study done on skulls exhumed from nine locations in Edo (present-day Tokyo) concluded that, with a 95 percent confidence level, between 39.4 percent and 69.7 percent of the capital's entire adult population was infected.[17] While at first blush, this figure may seem extreme, it comports with contemporary testimony. Matsumoto Ryojun, a pioneer in introducing scientific epidemiology to Japan, conducted a study on prostitutes in Nagasaki in 1860 and concluded, "Syphilis may infect about 95 percent of the people among the humbler classes."[18] In 2020, excavation work in what is now the central business district of Osaka unearthed the remains of more than 1,500 people from a burial site used from the late Edo period to the turn of the twentieth century. Nearly 30 percent of those remains had bone lesions consistent with syphilis, an extraordinarily high number when one considers that such lesions appear only in a limited number of advanced cases.[19]

Widespread in the general population, the disease was nearly universal among the women sold into the flesh trade. Prostitutes who exhibited the hair loss associated with secondary syphilis were called *toya*, or molting birds, and after they recovered were considered to be among the most desirable women in the profession, as they were presumed to be infertile and also erroneously thought to be immune.[20] In fact, syphilis remains infectious during at least the first year after infection, and infected people can relapse without serious or readily observable symptoms. As a result, customers often actively sought liaisons with women who had a good chance of infecting them. In 1867, the last year of the Edo period, William Willis, an Irish-born physician who became attached to the British legation in Japan and later advised the new Japanese government, wrote a report on prostitution in Japan. According to Willis, the group of sex workers most desired were those who, after a period of training in various arts, were just beginning to serve customers. They were usually about fifteen years old.[21] Thus, the two most sought-after groups consisted of women known to have been infected and those just beginning to ply the trade, a situation almost guaranteed to make infection nearly ubiquitous.

Indications are that it was. According to Willis, "One third of all prostitutes die before the terms of their offices expires [sic] of syphilitic and other diseases."[22] Willis also noted that it was believed that about 10 percent of the prostitutes in Edo and "at least twice as large a percentage" in Yokohama were suffering from "syphilis in its various forms." Here it should be recalled that Willis wrote before the development of any blood tests, so his estimate was likely based only on symptomatic cases. The real number was almost certainly many times higher. In addition, he estimated that by age thirty, one-third of all males in larger towns had suffered from syphilis.[23]

More rigorous investigation showed that Willis' estimates were actually conservative. Willis wrote just as authorities, on the advice of foreign doctors, were introducing a regular regime of health inspections for prostitutes.[24] Inspections of prostitutes at Yokohama commenced right around the time that Willis wrote his report, and the results were sobering: in 1867, the infection rate was 90 percent.[25]

Exacerbating the situation was the fatalistic attitude of many Japanese toward disease. They considered disease a part of life, no more preventable than death itself. Japanese historian of pathology Tatsukawa Shōji noted that because Japanese lacked experience with communicable diseases like the bubonic plague, they were not as fearful of contagions as Europeans were.[26] With regard to syphilis specifically, some discouraged any sort of treatment whatsoever. Willis described a folk belief that the disease was "an effort of nature to throw out the internal disease to the surface" and, as such, attempts to rid the body of infection were "mischievous," so the disease was the "cause of many deaths."[27] Some prostitutes protested violently against control measures, believing that inspection was a disgrace that would ruin subsequent marriage prospects.[28] Others even took poison to avoid the "special disgrace" of being (superficially) cured of their disease.[29]

Japanese authorities never took any steps to directly confront the problem of venereal disease on their own initiative.[30] Willis drew up a list of proposed regulations of prostitution to reduce the risk of venereal disease.[31] British representatives pushed these proposals energetically until the government established an inspection and quarantine regime in Yokohama.[32] The measures instituted largely prefigured the approach the new Meiji government would later institutionalize in 1900.

Nevertheless, the steps advocated by Willis and others were rudimentary and reflected the limits of mid- to late nineteenth-century medicine. Though these doubtless helped restrict the spread of disease, the effect was likely minor. During the Occupation, PHW would pronounce such steps "wholly inadequate to prevent the spread of venereal disease in the civilian population."[33] Moreover, the near-singular focus on prostitutes and the continuing reliance on visual inspection after the development of more accurate serological testing rendered the efforts of Japanese authorities largely ineffective.[34] Another problem with the program was that it did not gather any data, so there are no reliable records of the extent of detected infection even in the limited population it examined.

Irrespective of these shortcomings, the regulation of prostitution was a significant step forward in recognizing venereal disease as a public health threat. More steps came as Japan, in its Westernizing efforts, imitated trends in Western medicine. In the early twentieth century one Western trend, especially in Germany, Japan's foremost model in this field, was the scientific investigation of sexuality.[35] Though this new trend produced a lot of pseudo-scientific claptrap in both the West and Japan, it also led to a mania for testing and record-keeping. These records provide the first rough idea of the prevalence of venereal disease in Japan in the first half of the twentieth century.

In 1906, August Paul von Wassermann, Julius Citron, and Albert Neisser at the Robert Koch Institute for Infectious diseases developed a test for syphilis antibodies. The test is far from 100 percent accurate. It cannot detect primary syphilis and produces both false negatives and false positives. It also reacts to antibodies for other ailments including malaria and tuberculosis; the latter was fairly widespread in the Japanese population at the time.[36] After its introduction, the test was used widely. According to statistics compiled by Yamamoto Shunichi, a professor emeritus at the University of Tokyo Medical School, in 1926 a number of mass tests indicated very high levels of infection. Some 20 percent of manual laborers in Kōbe, 22 percent of the employees of the Nagoya City Railroad, 20 percent of Tokyo slum dwellers, and 10 percent of people admitted to the hospital in Tokyo had positive Wasserman reactions. In 1937, the year of the outbreak of war with China, 12 percent of the people who came in for health consultations in the city of Tokyo, between 11 and 13 percent of Tokyo factory workers, 20 percent of company employees in Kōbe, and 32 percent of the employees of the South Manchuria railroad had positive Wassermann reactions.[37]

The results of these investigations clearly show that though the problem was not as severe as evidence suggests it was during the Edo period, it was still a major public health menace. Awareness of this menace, though still limited, grew throughout the prewar period. A small but growing number of physicians became concerned. Their alarm grew as Japanese society became saturated with expansionist and pronatalist norms. Disease and its effects on both the country's strength and prestige became worries of patriotically minded people. Kanō Jigorō, the educator and martial artist who founded judo, warned that "youths, from time to time, become a slave of their baser passions" and that a "momentary indiscretion can lead to a lifetime suffering from an unforeseen disease" that would not only bring misfortune on the youth's family but would also cost the state in lost productivity and fertility. In order to avoid such calamity, it was necessary that youths learn discipline to put them at ease in both body and mind.[38]

Efforts like Kanō's might have had some effect, but it is clear that indiscretion, momentary or otherwise, was far more common than self-discipline. A survey conducted in the early 1920s indicated that the majority of boys became sexually active before the age of eighteen. Moreover, about one-third of college- or high school–educated men reported that their first sexual experience was with a prostitute. Among those with only a junior high school education, the fraction was almost one-half.[39]

When these men later married, they spread infections to their brides. This became a major concern for advocates of women's rights, eugenicists, and pronatalists, groups that increasingly overlapped in the interwar period.

In 1919 the New Woman Association, under the leadership of such women's movement pioneers as Ichikawa Fusae, Hiratsuka Raichō, and Oku Mumeo, strongly advocated a eugenic law that would require men (but not women) to submit a certificate attesting to their sexual health before marriage.[40] In 1939 Takeuchi Shigeyo, a physician and the vice president of the pronatalist Eugenic Marriage Popularization Society, advocated an exchange of health certificates before marriage, claiming that statistics indicated that 20 percent of married women were infected with syphilis, and expressing her suspicion that many of these women had been infected by their husbands.[41] Though Takeuchi may have been judging from a self-selecting sample, evidence suggests that she was right about the cause if not the extent of the problem. In Wasserman tests conducted in 1943 unmarried and married men had positive reaction rates of 8.9 percent and 13.9 percent, respectively. The corresponding numbers for women were 1.7 percent and 9.4 percent.[42]

In March 1941, officials in the Japanese government's Health and Welfare Ministry published a pamphlet with even more alarming numbers. The authors estimated that one in three cases of male infertility and half of female infertility were the result of gonorrhea. Extrapolating from data on syphilis blood tests, they estimated that fully 10 percent of the adult population of the nation, including 60 percent of prostitutes, had the disease. More alarming still, they estimated that 3 percent of children were afflicted. Though reliable data was lacking, their best estimate was that when other venereal diseases were factored in, "it can probably be said that more than 20 percent of our nation's people are suffering from venereal disease."[43]

Though venereal diseases were far more common throughout the world in the days before antibiotics were widely available, these were still very high figures. In comparison, a 1941 study on serological tests of nearly 1.9 million men aged twenty-one to thirty-five inducted into the U.S. military found that the infection rate for syphilis in this group was 4.53 percent. After adjustment for various factors, the authors estimated a rate of 4.77 percent for this demographic within the society at large.[44] A later study extrapolating from this data concluded that the overall rate in the general population was about 2.4 percent, just under a quarter of the estimate for Japan.[45]

The Japanese situation likely grew worse between the government study and the end of the war. During that time Japanese servicemen had ready access to sex workers who served them under various degrees of duress.[46] These brothels, at first euphemistically and now notoriously known as "comfort stations," inevitably became a major source of infection. With millions of young men returning home, venereal disease rates could only be expected to grow.

THE AMERICANS ARRIVE: PHW IN JAPAN

At first the arrival of the Americans only complicated the situation. The U.S. military was already dealing with a rise in the rate of venereal disease in its ranks. After the partial reconquest of the Philippines, there had been a good deal of fraternizing with Filipino women.[47] These troops were then introduced to an environment that was even more sexualized. As I explained in chapter 2, with government encouragement Japanese police and entrepreneurs established brothels and encouraged GIs to use them.[48] One official in GHQ's Public Health and Welfare Section (PHW) complained, "Since the arrival of the occupation forces they [the brothel owners] have made extraordinary efforts to attract soldier patronage."[49] Easy access to recreational sex meant that venereal disease control would be challenging. Though concerned, top commanders initially decided on a policy of laissez-faire, relying on "Japanese police to maintain cleanliness and order."[50]

Medical authorities were more proactive. Prostitutes, it seemed, were everywhere.[51] GIs soon began patronizing them enthusiastically. By the end of September, American medical personnel had set up prophylactic stations in four of the major prostitution areas in Tokyo and were fast exhausting their supplies, running through "7,000–10,000 pros a week."[52] They concluded "that venereal diseases would constitute one of the major health hazards facing the occupational forces."[53] GHQ assigned responsibility for controlling VD to its Public Health and Welfare Section, which it formally established with General Order Number 7 on October 2, 1945. Its chief was Col. (later Brig. Gen.) Crawford F. Sams.[54] Sams conceived his mission broadly, later writing of "the health of the Japanese people, which was my responsibility."[55]

This responsibility proved to be vast, and PHW soon confronted, in the words of historian Richard B. Frank, "a medical textbook list of lethal infectious diseases in an environment primed for epidemics."[56] On staff visits around Japan, personnel of the Preventive Disease Division repeatedly encountered diseases such as smallpox, typhus, diphtheria, typhoid fever, and epidemic meningitis.[57] Understaffed and chronically overworked, PHW never had more than 150 people. In 1948 it had just 92 employees, including 22 Japanese staff.[58] Nevertheless, their dedication and the highly effective leadership of their chief enabled them to pull off several minor miracles in the field of public health. However, the overall situation was so serious that despite their efforts some 650,000 people contracted communicable diseases in the first three years of the Occupation. Of these, nearly 100,000 perished.[59]

Despite this situation, through aggressive programs of mass vaccination, public sanitation, the establishment of more than eight hundred public health centers across the country, the importation of medicine, the transfer of technology, the establishment of domestic sources of manufacture, and most famously mass disinfection with a nationwide program of dusting with DDT, PHW had a massive impact. Working in close cooperation with Japanese authorities and medical personnel, they quashed incipient epidemics, including outbreaks of typhus and smallpox, and later established a nationwide vaccination program.[60] Initiated in 1948 with American medicines and technology, the program mandated vaccines for smallpox, diphtheria, typhoid fever, paratyphus, pertussis, tuberculosis, eruptive typhus, cholera, pest (plague), scarlet fever, influenza, and Weil's disease (leptospirosis).[61]

PHW and their Japanese partners also pioneered a campaign against tuberculosis, which introduced the just-developed antibiotic streptomycin.[62] This effort actually got a year's head start in the Kyoto area, where Dr. John Glismann, reflecting the results-first ethic of American public health officials, started a treatment program using $200,000 worth of the drug that had been seized on the black market by the Criminal Investigation Division.[63] PHW's campaign put this disease, the number one killer in Japan

FIGURE 11 • Members of the Public Health and Welfare Section. PHW Chief Crawford Sams is in the front row, sixth from the right. In the same row, Chief of Nursing Maj. Grace Alt is the third from the right; legal adviser J. V. Zaccone is the first on the left; and Maj. P. E. M. Bourland, who served twice as chief of the Venereal Disease Control Branch, is third from the left. (Hoover Institution Archives)

(excluding enemy action) from 1920 to 1948, on the path to extinction.[64] Eiji Takemae, generally recognized as the dean of Occupation historians, estimated that these programs may have saved as many as 3 million lives.[65]

But the most consequential campaign PHW spearheaded during the Occupation was the food relief program. The specter of famine hung over the Occupation through 1948. Japan, which had relied on its conquests for food, has never attained food self-sufficiency since the loss of its empire. For years it did not have the means of exchange to offset that shortcoming. At one point during July and August 1946, GHQ was providing the equivalent of all of the nutrition consumed by the entire population of Tokyo. This would lead Occupation authorities to estimate that food relief meant that "more than eleven million Japanese escaped possible starvation." Though it is unclear exactly what escaping "possible starvation" meant, and what fraction of that number would have died, it is beyond dispute that a very large number of Japanese survived because of the aid program PHW managed. In its efforts to combat malnutrition PHW also introduced a pilot school lunch program and, after demonstrating its effectiveness, successfully lobbied the Japanese government to extend the program to the entire country. Due to its popularity, it survived post-Occupation efforts to economize and continues to the present day.[66]

In the midst of all this, PHW tackled Japan's massive venereal disease problem. Given the severity of its other problems, it is remarkable that PHW appreciated the threat posed by venereal disease at all. Perhaps because the problem directly affected the health and prestige of the Occupation forces, the effort did not get short shrift. From its inception PHW had a branch dedicated to VD control.[67] From October 1945 to December 1949, four men served as head of the Venereal Disease Control Branch (VDCB). Lt. Col. James H. Gordon was the first chief, from October 1945 to March 1946. Major P. E. M. Bourland served as the second and fourth chief, from March 1946 to September 1946 and from October 1947 to December 1947. Dr. Oscar M. Elkins was the third chief, from September 1946 to October 1947. Finally, Dr. Isamu Nieda served from December 1947 to December 1949.[68] The day after its formation, PHW officials had two meetings with experts on venereal disease and prostitution.[69] In one of these meetings, VDCB chief Gordon spoke to Dr. Yosano Hikaru, head of the Preventive Medicine Section at the Tokyo Preventive Health Department, and Dr. Fukai of the Yoshiwara city hospital, which specialized in treating prostitutes for venereal disease. The Americans got a rude awakening. Dr. Fukai estimated that "about 50%" of the women working as prostitutes in Yoshiwara and Senju had "a history of syphilis." More disturbing, he estimated that 40 percent of women coming into prostitution from the countryside had syphilis. Summing up the conference, Gordon wrote, "The present organization and functioning of the program of venereal disease control is wholly inadequate to prevent the spread of venereal disease in the civilian population. The most pressing needs are for modern drugs and competent personnel of all types."[70]

Nevertheless, PHW's more urgent concern was the frequency of infection among prostitutes. Two days later, PHW chief Col. Crawford Sams concluded, "It is apparent from preliminary conferences and observation that a serious situation exists in connection with prostitution activities and prevalence of the venereal diseases in the indigenous populations of Japan and Korea."[71] PHW compiled all of the information it could on prostitution, interrogating Japanese sources about the varieties of prostitution, particularly the licensed prostitution system, the approximate number of women involved in prostitution, its place in contemporary Japanese society, and its history back to the early Edo period.[72]

They soon determined that a staggering percentage of prostitutes had venereal infections. An inspection of 1,210 prostitutes in Tokyo on October 4, 1945, found that 373 of them, or more than 30 percent, were infected with some form of venereal disease, mostly gonorrhea. Of these only fifteen cases were syphilis, detected by inspection only. In Yokohama, the more accurate Kahn serological test for syphilis was done on 200 of 988 known prostitutes. Of these some 51 percent tested positive.[73] PHW chief Colonel Sams reported to MacArthur's chief of staff that sample surveys indicated that between 50 percent and 80 percent of prostitutes were infected with venereal diseases, approximately in line with what Japan's Health Ministry had estimated four years earlier.[74]

Shortly thereafter, Japanese authorities, who seemed uniformly anxious to get Americans into the brothels, reported a significant drop in the rate of infection among Tokyo prostitutes. Occupation medical authorities suspected that their counterparts were cooking the books: "The rapid reduction in prevalence of VD is hardly credible in view of the lack of adequate treatment and facilities."[75] Capt. Irving Richmon soon confirmed these suspicions by reexamining women previously checked by the Tokyo Health Department: his results were very different. In Tokyo's Shinjuku district he found that twenty-three of twenty-six women were infected with gonorrhea, as opposed to the three women reported by the health department. In the Shinagawa area, 96 percent of women tested were positive. These cases were treated with penicillin, but this could have done little to mollify the Americans' anxieties. In the margins Oscar Elkins, a PHW consultant on venereal diseases who would later serve as VDCB chief, scrawled a handwritten note: "This is more like the true state of affairs."[76] Summing up the situation years later, VDCB chief Isamu Nieda wrote, "Positive serological tests for syphilis were found in 50 to 70% of these individuals [prostitutes], gonorrhea in 15 to 30% and chancroid in 2 to 5%. Since it was anticipated that the majority of contacts of Occupation personnel would involve this group, it was imperative that measures be adopted to reduce this large reservoir of infection."[77]

Initially, PHW concentrated on this "reservoir." In apparent response to a request from Tokyo medical authorities for anti–venereal disease medicines to treat prostitutes, PHW provisionally released limited stocks of Eighth Army supplies. The supplies were strictly for use "in the treatment of individuals who represent a potential source of venereal disease to personnel of the occupational forces, that is, women infected with gonorrhea, chancroid, lymphogranulom[a] ve[n]ereum or early syphilis."[78] As late as November of the following year, a local health official felt constrained to prioritize treatment facilities in areas with high troop concentrations at the expense of other areas with larger populations.[79]

This early focus on prostitutes and their GI patrons gave rise to a number of urban legends, most prominently accusations that PHW essentially acted as panderers for American troops.[80] In reality, these measures are better understood as a prioritization of scarce resources in stopgap measures. They were only the opening moves in what would become an ambitious large-scale and long-term campaign to, in the words of Dr. Isamu Nieda, writing when he served as chief of the branch, "reduce the venereal disease rate in Japan down to an irreduc[i]ble minimum."[81]

GHQ'S VENEREAL DISEASE CONTROL CAMPAIGN

In its efforts to eradicate venereal disease in Japan, PHW encountered countless obstacles. These included indifference and ignorance on the part of both the general public and Japanese medical and government authorities; a tendency on the part of these authorities to prioritize control of sexuality over control and treatment of infection;[82] a lack of medical supplies;[83] widespread prostitution;[84] the enthusiastic patronage of prostitutes by GIs;[85] the connivance or even encouragement of some of their officers in this patronage;[86] the meddling of moralists;[87] misguided direction from the War Department in Washington;[88] the often counterproductive efforts at suppression of prostitution by local commanders, American military police, and especially the Japanese police;[89] improper treatment regimens that evidently resulted in the emergence of drug-resistant strains of disease;[90] and, finally, the poor overall health and pervasive want of a generally malnourished and immiserated population.[91] Despite these hindrances, PHW succeeded in introducing procedures, bureaucratic machinery, and, most consequentially, medicines that would ultimately quash endemic VD in Japan.

Success was ultimately achieved partly because Sams focused on results. He accepted that mistakes were part of every solution, and he was unafraid to either make or admit them.[92] He cared little for taboos or sensitivities. An example of his style can be glimpsed in one of the measures he recommended for narcotics control. After the Communist victory in the Chinese Civil War, Sams learned that the Communists had attained five hundred tons of opium. Sams unsuccessfully advocated that the U.S. government buy the lot, disregarding the fact that it would be directly funding an adversary. In Sams' view, the drug would be worth more on the black market, so the Communists would obtain more money in the long run, and it would come at the expense of public health in Japan, the United States, and elsewhere.[93] A similar attitude inspired PHW's handling of a problem that had a direct bearing on VD control. When the War Department refused assistance in establishing domestic sources of penicillin production, PHW essentially resorted to industrial espionage to transfer a key lifesaving technology to Japan (detailed later in this chapter). On the problem of VD, Sams later recalled that in countries (including Japan) where prostitution was legal, the steps taken to keep infection rates low "were quite different from those which would be acceptable in this country, but they did work."[94]

By this vague statement, Sams apparently meant eschewing moralism in public health policy. In the anti-VD campaign this meant a relative lack of emphasis on suppressing prostitution, a tactic that had been enthusiastically embraced in the United States in recent decades and that Sams "consider[ed] to be a comparatively ineffective means of controlling venereal disease in a large population."[95] Sams was very much a pragmatist who well understood that preaching and cultural presumption more often led to resentment and resistance than to reform. He later wrote, "The control of venereal disease,

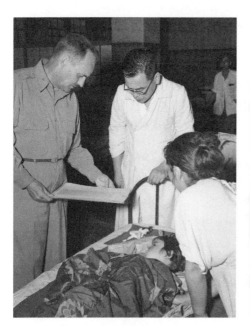 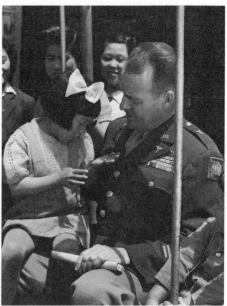

FIGURES 12, 13 • PHW Chief Crawford Sams (*left*) overseeing encephalitis research, August 31, 1948; (*right*) Chief Sams with Japanese children, 1951 (Hoover Institution Archives)

particularly in foreign countries, must be adapted to the moral and cultural mores of those countries, and we can go far astray in our attempts to impose on others our moral concepts. Conversely, we can frequently learn from other people."[96] As discussed in the previous chapter, this initially meant that PHW embraced the licensed prostitution system and attempted to reinstate it. However, after discovering that the inspection protocols were little more than a ritual that wasted both time and resources and, more importantly, that the system relied on human trafficking, PHW immediately moved to abolish it. This would be neither their last misstep nor their last course correction. However, in the end, PHW, working in cooperation with Japanese authorities and medical professionals, succeeded.

At first the situation was bleak. Venereal disease was endemic and widespread. Prostitution was deeply entrenched and protected by powerful vested interests.[97] Worse, the existing infrastructure for VD control was ineffective, wrong-headed, and often counterproductive.[98] The biggest problems, however, were the ignorance and indifference of most Japanese officials and medical personnel in responsible positions. There was a widespread belief that venereal diseases were "maladies entirely confined to prostitutes."[99] Apathy went right to the top. On October 16, officials of the Health Ministry, including Minister Ashida Hitoshi, met with Lt. Col. H. H. MacDonald of PHW to discuss VD. Ashida, a normally punctilious diarist and conscientious public servant, did not even bother to record the event in his journal.[100]

Shortly after its creation, PHW established a nationwide network of officials to oversee efforts to combat communicable diseases. It directed the Japanese Ministry of Health and Welfare to appoint a venereal disease control officer in every prefecture. The PHW personnel gathered information and oversaw the local governments' efforts.

At first they were dismayed. Personnel throughout Japan complained of indifference and of the exclusive focus on women, primarily prostitutes, as the source of infection. In an early 1947 summary of reports one official noted, "It is traditional for the physicians here to consider the problem of venereal disease entirely in the light of the control of prostitution." Another complained, "Aside from the prostitutes and Geisha girls I believe the only people being treated are those that present themselves to the local physician." A third reported, "The main problem lies in the fact that the treatment of V.D. has been limited to licensed prostitutes and geisha girls, records have been incomplete, and there has been no attempt made on contact tracing." Another noted that there were "no public venereal disease clinics open to male patients." One PHW official despaired, "The calibre of the work done is tragic, both in diagnosis and treatment."[101]

Such judgments, while largely accurate, were also expressions of frustration. They were too sweeping and also out of step with Sams' philosophy. He regarded "sympathetic understanding and tolerance of peoples of other lands" as a vital asset in developing a public health program. He also had a disdain amounting to "intolerance" for Americans who were "unwilling to concede that anything developed in another country can in any sense equal, and certainly cannot be superior to, ideas or things made in America."[102] Within the Japanese medical community there was both expertise on venereal disease and zeal for a program of eradication. Indeed, Salvarsan, the first effective modern antisyphilitic drug, was developed by a Japanese scientist working in a German laboratory. In addition, Japanese doctors had developed their own serological tests for syphilis. Early in the Occupation, American and Japanese lab personnel conducted tests for syphilis and compared the sensitivity and accuracy of the tests used by Americans (Kahn and Kolmer tests) with those used by Japanese (Murata and Kitasato tests). They determined that the Japanese tests were reliable.[103] Had there not been such expertise and, more importantly, enthusiasm on the Japanese side, PHW's anti-VD program would likely have ended in failure. The problem was less cultural than it was structural. Simply put, the wrong people were in charge.

Like bureaucracies everywhere, the Japanese Ministry of Health ossified and began valuing stability over achievement. Dr. Ichikawa Tokuji, a urologist and longtime campaigner against venereal disease, put the matter in terms that would likely resonate with would-be reformers anywhere: it was hard to attract "outstanding men" because salaries were too low and experts often found themselves subordinate to bureaucrats lacking technical skill and specialized knowledge.[104] Nevertheless, hard and impossible were different things.

Ichikawa was himself the head of the Japanese Association for the Control of Venereal Diseases (JACVD), a group that had been founded in 1905 as the Nihon Karyūbyō Yobōkai (Japanese Society for the Prevention of Venereal Disease) and is still in operation today as the Sei no Kenkō Igaku Zaidan (Japanese Foundation for Sexual Health Medicine). One prominent member of the group, Dr. Takano Rokurō, had written a book about venereal diseases in 1942 that largely anticipated all the later complaints and frustrations of PHW's prefectural officials.[105] Four members of this group met with a medical officer attached to the Office of the Chief Surgeon. He found them to be "by far the most proficient in their field" and "anxious to take an active part in civic venereal disease control." He felt that if they could be placed in responsible positions, the "whole problem would be materially benefitted."[106]

Lt. Col. James Gordon, the chief of the Venereal Disease Control Branch, met with Ichikawa October 27, 1945, to learn about the JACVD.[107] Gordon also met with Dr. Tōyama Ikuzō, Ichikawa's colleague at the JACVD, twice in December. In late January, Tōyama mailed Gordon a letter outlining a program that he had been urging on the government at "every available opportunity" and whose adoption he had advocated "several times in the Diet." Though the government approved his suggestions, "they have not been put into practice."[108] He would have better luck with PHW. Although the Americans did not agree with all of Toyama's suggestions, on one point they were in complete agreement: "It is evident from past experience that it is impossible to control or eliminate Venereal Diseases by previous unenthusiastic methods."[109]

Nevertheless, there was disagreement, including controversy about one of PHW's first actions. There was neither reliable data on the extent of VD in the general population nor any mechanism to control its spread outside the population of licensed prostitutes. Venereal diseases were not even covered by Japan's infectious disease control law. GHQ ordered this situation remedied with SCAPIN 153 on October 16, 1945. It directed the Japanese government to include syphilis, gonorrhea, and chancroid as infectious diseases. GHQ also ordered the reporting of all cases "by name, age, sex and full address of the individual concerned."[110] Tōyama advised against the reporting provision, fearing it would cause infected individuals to hide their condition or to seek treatment from quacks.[111] This disagreement was characteristic of Japanese reluctance to engage in rigorous contact tracing. PHW believed contact tracing was imperative.

GHQ pursued the identification of infected individuals aggressively. Because of this goal, the new order included a highly resented provision, which specifically "[brought] under the examination, treatment and health provisions of these laws, ordinances, and regulations all individuals whose occupations or activities subject them to serious hazard of venereal disease."[112] This rather elastic requirement led to draconian policies that infringed on the rights of a large number of people, almost exclusively young women. Health authorities conducted a number of tests that humiliated women and served little practical purpose. One report from a provincial PHW official noted, "Routine examination of restaurant girls brings about some special problems. There are a few restaurants in town which claim to be nothing more than restaurants. Periodically, there are tear-stained faces in the Military Government offices, as these periodical examinations are thought to be embarrassing and degrading by the women." The official admitted that "some of the better restaurants" had no history of infection but argued, "We cannot make exceptions."[113]

Clearly Tōyama's anxieties were well founded. Nevertheless, it was clear that PHW did not want for energy. PHW personnel also learned that enthusiasm was not an American monopoly. Over time they developed working relationships with their Japanese counterparts. Even among all the complaints of 1946, there were bright spots. While one officer denounced the procedures in some clinics as "mid-Victorian quackery," he allowed that others practiced "almost complete adherence to the principles" outlined by PHW.[114] Another boasted of the use of radio broadcasts and newspaper articles in local media "in very simple language that the ordinary Japanese can easily understand" as part of their effort to "enlighten the public."[115] Obviously, such a campaign involved the active cooperation of Japanese at multiple levels.

Even as local health officials were compiling their largely critical reports, PHW and the Japanese Ministry of Health and Welfare put together a three-day training seminar at which half the time was to be taken up by Ministry officials and half by PHW's venereal disease consultant. Every prefecture had a Japanese venereal disease control officer (VDCO) who liaised with a PHW prefectural official. They held the seminar late in 1946, and every Japanese prefectural VDCO except that of Aomori Prefecture attended.[116] Together with its new Japanese partners, PHW was, however slowly, winning in the war on indifference.

Material want was another serious challenge. Scarcity plagued the anti-VD campaign. One report noted that there was no organic medium in which to culture test samples because "culture nutrients apparently are used to feed people rather than microbes."[117] In such circumstances, VD neither was nor probably should have been the top priority. The lack of food, which remained a problem through 1948, hampered anti-VD efforts in other ways as well. In mid-1946, PHW officers discovered that women who had been quarantined for treatment of venereal disease were stealing away from hospitals. However, nothing could be done, as hunger motivated their truancy: the hospitals were not feeding them enough.[118] Shortly before his prefectural officers reported in, Elkins himself noted, "Housing and food for in-patients are inadequate and constitute the chief difficulties in detaining patients for adequate treatment."[119]

Shortages of medicine were another problem. Worse, where VD was concerned, scarce medicines were often worse than no medicines at all. The lack of "modern drugs" noted by Gordon in his initial meeting with Japanese authorities persisted. One of the biggest developments in mid-twentieth-century medicine was the advent of antibiotics. These drugs revolutionized medicine and the treatment of venereal disease. After a brief lag, treatment in Japan would, thanks to the efforts of PHW, ultimately progress in tandem with antibiotic treatments developed in the United States. In the early years, however, there was simply not enough medicine to go around.

Shortages likely contributed to bad practices on the part of Japanese medical personnel. Whether because of ignorance, limited medical supplies, or both, Japanese often continued treatment "until the patient becomes symptom free only."[120] This was common. One PHW official observed, "There is no such thing as complete treatment here in . . . prefecture." Another noted that "in general syphilis is called 'cured' on the basis of one negative blood test." A third complained, "Syphilitics are all inadequately treated." Incomplete treatment was probably partly due to the scarcity of supplies and partly due to what one official termed "a profound lack of knowledge concerning these diseases and the basic concepts of bacteriological theories of transmission." Of course, treating patients only until they are symptom-free is a textbook method of creating antibiotic-resistant strains in the population. There was a similar problem with the treatment of gonorrhea with sulfathiazole.[121] Later, Japanese physicians would indeed encounter resistance to antibiotics in many of their patients, and researchers would blame the problem on this kind of partial treatment.[122]

In order to deal with medication shortages, GHQ began large-scale importation of new anti–venereal disease drugs such as Mapharsen and bismuth subsalicylate until domestic production of these drugs began in 1947. In addition, mass production of sulfadiazine and of sulfathiazole began in 1946.[123]

GHQ also requested that the War Department provide technical information for the mass production of penicillin, but the department refused on the grounds that it was a "secret process of manufacture."[124] This was in stark contrast to the case with streptomycin, a much newer drug that had been shown to be effective against tuberculosis. Samples of that medicine were sent to Japan, and mass production soon began. It helped to virtually eliminate tuberculosis, which had been the number one killer in Japan for decades.[125]

PHW managed to avoid the consequences of this ill-advised decision by directly procuring the services of one Dr. Foster, a penicillin production expert. Foster gave Japanese manufacturers guidance in methods of submerged deep-tank mass production. This led to a massive growth in Japanese penicillin production that allowed the drug to be used effectively against gonorrhea, but at the end of 1949 the supply was still insufficient to "permit generalized usage in the treatment of syphilis."[126]

However, before the problem of shortages was solved, PHW expanded its program within the limits of their resources. By 1947, PHW's VDCB officers were touring the country, visiting every prefecture to check the progress of the anti-VD campaign, finding out which suggested or even mandated steps were being followed, answering questions about the program, and encouraging greater efforts.[127] They held meetings with local medical authorities and clinicians, explained the VD control program, emphasized the health department's responsibility to the public, and urged coordination of the public and government agencies.[128]

After such conferences, the PHW people checked the hospitals and clinics to get an idea of the value of care and gathered information on local infection rates. From 1947, relationships between PHW and local governments grew closer and more collegial, though a hierarchical element remained as long as PHW controlled the supplies and affected the funding. Sometimes there were bureaucratic snafus. In one case a model hospital run by a Dr. Ashida in Fukuchiyama, Kyoto Prefecture, was disqualified as the host of a pilot project for a new penicillin therapy. Local health authorities had performed so well that the area no longer had a suitable level of infection to check the efficacy of the new method.[129]

At the national level, PHW cooperated with the Health and Welfare Ministry in a public education campaign. This included directing government funding toward the production of movies and filmstrips to raise awareness. While the mass appeal of some of these efforts, with titles like *Guard against Venereal Disease Danger, A Thing That Will Ruin Japan,* or *Flowers of the Poisonous Plant, Chap. 1: Oecological Study of the Spirochete,* is certainly questionable, the campaign was associated with at least one event of interest in film history. One of the movies it sponsored was *Shizukanaru Kettō* (The Silent Duel), a film by Kurosawa Akira about a

FIGURE 14 • Poster from *Shizukanaru Kettō* (The Silent Duel), a Kurosawa Akira film about a doctor infected with syphilis, produced in part with government funding as part of a PHW public awareness campaign (Daiei Pictures)

surgeon infected with syphilis by a patient during an operation in a war zone.[130] Boasting the second collaboration between the film maestro and frequent future stars Shimura Takashi and Mifune Toshirō, the film, though one of Kurosawa's less celebrated efforts, undoubtedly made a significant contribution to postwar Japanese cinema. However, with a plot centered on a stoic doctor who attempts to treat himself in secret while rejecting his love interest for her own good, its contribution to public health is dubious. It clearly sent the wrong message.

Nevertheless, the effort reflected PHW's holistic approach to its mission. In the view of PHW chief Sams, "There are four basic elements to a nationwide program that has its objective the health of the people: public health or preventive medicine; medical care; welfare; and social security. No one of these elements should dominate the others, as occurs in many governmental organizations."[131]

Looking at the problem from the perspective of welfare, PHW pursued rehabilitation as a strategy to reduce the number of women working as prostitutes. VDCB chief Isamu Nieda advocated shutting down the largely vacant hospitals for prostitutes and replacing them with rehabilitation centers.[132] PHW also took on a welfare services adviser, Marta Green, who was charged with overseeing rehabilitation, among other duties. Green was indefatigable. She met with advocates of a ban on prostitution.[133] She followed trends in rehabilitation, followed and reported on media coverage of rehabilitation centers, and went all over Japan inspecting various homes for young women.[134] She coordinated with private charities in the United States to provide clothing for the women in the facilities.[135] She oversaw and negotiated minimum standards for rehabilitation homes with the Japanese Ministry of Health and Welfare.[136] She also met and consulted with prefectural officials and the directors of seventeen rehabilitation centers from around Japan. She found a wide variation in their quality as well as in the quality of people who established and ran them. One, run by Catholic nuns, was well kept and clean but overly focused on discipline.[137] She found the operators of another to be well meaning but lacking in training: "They are trying to provide a home atmosphere and doing much with kind treatment and pleasant surroundings to help the girls attain self-respect and a desire for a normal productive way of life."[138] Another institution was run-down, and the vocational training was limited to doing monotonous work that required no extensive training.[139] Others, though providing the women with employment, gave them only menial work at low wages and seemed to have been designed around the exploitation of this cheap source of labor.[140]

Green worked with her colleagues in other SCAP sections and Japanese officials in the Labor Ministry to help the women in the centers. She consulted with GHQ's Economic and Scientific Section (ESS) to inquire about job placement, with the Japanese Labor Ministry to find out about standards in women's company dormitories to see how the rehab centers measured up, and with the Civil Information and Education Section (CIE) to set up a training course of home economics and domestic science.[141] After visiting the institutions, consulting with her colleagues at GHQ, and working with officials at the Welfare Ministry, Green met with the directors of these rehabilitation homes and discussed with them a proposed list of minimum requirements to be met by the homes. Rather than attempting to impose an unrealistic ideal by fiat, she worked with them to reach a consensus on standards they could reasonably expect to meet.[142]

The quality of the rehabilitation programs varied considerably, and none measured up to the level of care, training, and recreational opportunities envisioned by Green. The major problem was funding. The Japanese government budgeted ¥16 million for the homes, whereas Green estimated that it would take at least ¥21 million to run them effectively. Nevertheless, by 1950 the rehabilitation homes had admitted 7,815 girls and women, providing them with, at minimum, food and shelter during the time of their stay.[143]

How much did efforts like these affect the venereal disease situation? It is impossible to know, for the very simple reason that there was no attempt at accurate record-keeping until PHW's program began. At first blush, PHW records seem to indicate a steadily worsening situation from 1946 until 1948.[144] This may have been due to a spread of the disease or to improvements in reporting. It was probably a combination of the two, but the effect of the latter factor is clearly demonstrated by the fact that when, in 1949, overall rates of venereal disease began to decline, PHW's VD control branch chief was unsure whether the decrease was due to genuine improvements or to a "slackening of effort" in testing and reporting.[145] The uncertainty continued into the next year, when the chief of the Preventive Medicine Subsection wrote, regarding an apparent increase in venereal disease rates in Osaka, "It is difficult to know whether this high reported rate is because of, or in spite of, intense anti–venereal disease activity."[146] However, it is clear that in most (though not all) places for which data is available, the reported rate of infection in the general population had decreased from 1948 to 1949.[147] If one compares the data gathered in 1949 with the fragmentary data available for prewar Japan, the impression is one of a VD situation that was quite serious but had nevertheless improved dramatically. One Japanese study cited in 1945 concluded, "The average positive rate of syphilis serum reaction with the general public is 7 to 8%," figures slightly lower than but on the same order as the 10 percent estimate cited in the 1941 Ministry of Health study.[148] In a mass serological exam in which 8,500 tests were carried out in Ibaraki Prefecture between February and July 1948, it was learned that 9 percent of prisoners, 5 percent of coal mine workers, 5 percent of factory workers, and 40 percent of prostitutes tested positive for VD.[149] Mass testing in Niigata conducted from 1947 to 1948 discovered a syphilis infection rate of 3.06 percent.[150] Mass testing conducted on factory workers in Matsuyama, Ehime Prefecture, in October 1948 revealed an infection rate of 4.4 percent.[151] These numbers suggest an overall decline, but they cannot be considered conclusive. However, it is beyond dispute is that venereal disease rates continued to fall in subsequent years and soon plummeted to the "irreduc[i]ble minimum," to which PHW aspired.

CONCLUSIONS

The narrative that Americans first introduced VD into Japan and then spread it among themselves until it nearly incapacitated them because of their excessive patronage of prostitutes cannot withstand scrutiny. When the Americans arrived, venereal disease was endemic in Japan. When the Occupation ended, it was being brought under control for the first time since its introduction some four centuries prior. This was not a coincidence.

During its time in Japan, PHW, working with Japanese medical authorities, initiated programs and introduced methods and medications that revolutionized Japanese health care. Writing on the situation at the end of 1949, PHW's VD Control Branch chief, Isamu Nieda, noted the cooperation of the various Japanese authorities involved in the anti-VD campaign and predicted steady improvement, though he believed it would be several years before it could be demonstrated statistically.[152] In fact, Nieda was unduly pessimistic. By November 1953 the improvement was already so conspicuous that Socialist Dietwoman Miyano Tamayo asked Yosano Hikaru, chief of the preventive medicine section at the Tokyo Preventive Health Department, what had caused it. Yosano answered that the changes in treatment and testing regimens since the end of the war had been responsible.[153] These changes had, of course, been initiated by PHW. The biggest of them was the introduction of penicillin therapy, a revolution made possible by PHW's transfer of technology in defiance of the spirit if not the letter of the War Department's direction.[154]

In other words, PHW's anti-VD campaign was yet another success for the section. It certainly involved missteps including authoritarian overreach, but in the end, in Sams' words, it "did work." Moreover, the success was not trivial. In 1941 the Health and Welfare Ministry estimated that some 3 percent of the entire population was cursed with syphilis from birth. In 1949, after years of the anti-VD campaign, a study by the Japanese Association of Obstetricians and Gynecologists identified syphilis as the cause of 5,492 deaths in Japan, including 1,146 infant deaths.[155] Assuming comparable numbers in the previous three years, then syphilis alone was responsible for between 13 and 15 percent of all deaths from communicable diseases.[156] It would, like tuberculosis, smallpox, typhus, diphtheria, and many other diseases, soon be responsible for almost none.

PHW's anti-VD campaign was just one of the ways that Sams addressed his responsibility: "the health of the Japanese people." As a result of PHW's efforts, the U.S. military probably saved more Japanese lives than it took, a considerable achievement in light of the unprecedented levels of indiscriminate violence it unleashed at the end of the war. Moreover, Japanese lived longer and healthier lives. In 1955, the first year for which figures entirely after the Occupation are available, newborn Japanese boys could expect to live an average of more than sixteen years longer than those who were born in 1935–36, the last year for which data is available before the outbreak of full-scale war in China (63.6 vs. 46.92 years). Japanese girls could expect more than eighteen more years of life (67.75 vs 49.63 years). As Japan's Ministry of Health Labor and Welfare put it, "The improvements in Japanese life expectancies were remarkable."[157] A significant part of this increase was due to the quashing of venereal disease, especially syphilis.

If, as many critics allege, this was done from self-interest, then that self-interest was also impressively enlightened. Those who would criticize PHW's efforts at combating venereal disease in Japan—and there are certainly ample grounds for criticism—should at least contextualize those efforts. This means acknowledging that whatever its shortcomings, PHW's anti-VD campaign was an integral part of one of the greatest practical humanitarian accomplishments in the history of the world.

CHAPTER 4

"HOT AND FORCING VIOLATION"

WAR, RAPE, AND THE HUMAN PSYCHE

The behavior of the American troops during the Occupation was far better than most Japanese had feared. Many remembered this well into their elderly years. Nevertheless, the psychic environment in the postwar years was ripe for a myth of mass rape to take root. The reasons for this were manifold. First, the incidence of rape in war is so high as to create a strong association between the two deep in the human psyche. This association is frequently employed by propagandists seeking to elicit a ferocious last-ditch resistance. The use of these fears was widespread in word-of-mouth and printed propaganda in Japan. In addition, Japan's understanding and conduct of war served to reinforce the instinctive fears of humans under attack. Finally, in the years after the war, a large number of Japanese had limited access to mass media and, after years of wartime experience, their trust in it had decreased. As a result, rumors, especially in the early weeks and months of the Occupation, spread quickly and the impression they left sometimes survived direct experience that contradicted their purport. Each of these factors will be examined in turn.

Rape and war are deeply entwined in the collective unconscious. The connection has been made countless times in literature and art and has been acted out in the real world with such appalling regularity that, were it not for the inherent horrors of the subject, it would have long ago grown tedious. The abduction or rape of women attendant to warfare is depicted as something like standard operating procedure in the Homeric epics; one classicist has gone so far as to assert that all the conflicts in the *Iliad* and *Odyssey* stemmed from a shortage of women.[1] Rape in war is presented as a matter of course in the Bible.[2] In Shakespeare's *Henry V* the king obtained the surrender of Harfleur in part by threatening to set his troops loose on the town, subjecting its "pure maidens" to "hot and forcing violation."[3]

Moreover, it is clear that this is a case of art imitating life not just in bygone ages but in living memory and the present day. Sexual violence has been endemic in wars of the twentieth and twenty-first centuries alike. Indeed, the very state of war seems to act on the minds of men in a way that predisposes them to sexual violence. The philosopher J. Glenn Gray, recalling his experiences in World War II, described the predatory sexual appetites excited by battle: "The conquest of the sexual partner thus becomes very like the conquest of the enemy, who has forfeited any right to human status or equality."[4] In 1971, during Bangladesh's war for independence from Pakistan, the soldiers of what was then West Pakistan routinely killed the men and raped the women. According to the estimate of one doctor who attended to the women afterward, more than 100,000 Bangladeshi women were raped.[5] In recent years, mass rape has been reported in Bosnia, Darfur, and the Congo region, where it has been integrated as both a motive for and a weapon in the conflict.[6] Mass rape has been called a "significant weapon of war" in the ongoing conflict in Syria.[7]

Rape is so prevalent in war that some studies of hunter-gatherer societies indicate that the desire for sexual conquest, and its attendant reproductive advantages, may itself be one of the primary causes of war in these societies.[8] Archeological excavation of prehistoric massacre sites often unearth a disproportionately low number of remains of females of reproductive age.[9] In more recent times, there have been reports that ISIS (the Islamic State of Iraq and Syria) turned the enslavement and rape of enemy women into a form of worship and used the sexual opportunities such beliefs legitimate as a recruiting tool "to lure men from deeply conservative Muslim societies, where casual sex is taboo and dating is forbidden."[10]

War rape may have evolutionary roots. As a strategy for reproduction, it can be shockingly successful. One recent study found that some 8 percent of all men in Central Asia are descendants of Genghis Khan.[11] A chilling report of wartime rape in Bosnia concluded that reproductive advantage was among the conscious motives in constructing a system of rape camps, noting there was "little doubt that the intention is deliberately to make women pregnant and then to detain them until pregnancy is far enough advanced to make termination impossible."[12]

However, the phenomenon of war rape is too complex to attribute to a single cause. War rape contains elements of sadism that, though often present in peacetime rape, become so prevalent that they seem to be unconnected or even detrimental to reproductive success. It includes a disproportionate number of victims who are obviously prepubescent or postmenopausal.[13] Peacetime rape is, on average, far less violent than rapes that occur in warfare. In peacetime about 4 percent of rape victims sustain serious injury, and less than one in five hundred is murdered.[14] In war rape, by contrast, extreme violence is common. In Syria there were reports of "women and young girls being kidnapped, raped, tortured and killed."[15] During the My Lai massacre, a number of American soldiers from Charlie Company became "double veterans," those who had the experience of raping a woman before murdering her: "Many women were raped and sodomized, mutilated, and had their vaginas ripped open with knives or bayonets. One woman was killed when the muzzle of a gun was inserted into her vagina and the trigger was pulled."[16] Still more recently, when Ukrainian forces recaptured Buka in the ongoing Russian invasion of Ukraine, investigators found ample evidence that many women had been raped before they were murdered.[17] During the Rape of Manila, Servillano Aquino witnessed Japanese marines attempt to rape a fourteen-year-old girl who had been dead for more than ten hours. They abandoned the attempt only because rigor mortis prevented them from parting her legs.[18] Obviously such atrocities confer no direct reproductive benefit to their perpetrators.

They might, however, provide a military advantage. Mass rape—especially, but not only, in traditional societies—produces such psychic trauma in both the victimized women and their male relatives that it can break up families and destroy communities. In Iraq, rape was "rampant as an instrument of war during the vicious sectarian reprisals of the mid-2000s." In the Syrian civil war, rape was likewise weaponized.[19] Many refugees fled the country precisely because of the fear of pervasive sexual violence. One said resignedly, "We surrendered to the reality of rape."[20] The orgy of sadism that is war rape is effective as a military weapon. It can be nothing more subtle than cruelty for its own sake.

However, whether war rape is an evolved reproductive strategy or a terror tactic to demoralize the enemy is a question that is largely academic for the victims or those who love them, and it should come as no surprise that the fear of marauding rapists is as instinctive a response to aggression as the sexual urge itself is to the attacking soldier. When faced with a hostile group, women often fear rape first and foremost. Although this fear can often be adaptive, it can also sometimes lead to ridiculous extremes of virginitiphobia, an irrational fear of rape. When anti–Vietnam War activists held a protest outside the Pentagon in 1967, the secretaries inside the office-fortress, surrounded by a ring of soldiers and federal marshals, were reportedly terrified that somehow the peace protestors would overwhelm the defenders, penetrate the perimeter, force entry into the building, and rape them.[21]

While this fear may be paralyzing to some, it can be a source of great motivation to others. As an attack on the community and by extension on the masculinity of the men who regard it as their duty to protect it, the fear of mass rape is a powerful psychological tool to build solidarity among those men. It helps them to repel invaders. Historically, the fear that their mates, mothers, and sisters will be forcibly taken from them, that they will fail their loved ones in their hour of most desperate need—that they will, when tested, prove to be something less than a man—has been a potent motivator.

Military and political leaders and propagandists have long exploited this (often altogether justified) fear to unite their men and infuse them with passion. In the so-called Boston Massacre of 1770, British soldiers fired on an unruly mob of colonists that had been taunting and assaulting them with hand-thrown missiles. As early as 1772 colonial agitators spun yarns of "our beauteous virgins exposed to all the insolence of unbridled passion."[22] After tensions between the British and their American subjects broke into open hostilities, reports of widespread rape of American women by British soldiers were crucial to undermining British General William Howe's strategy of reconciliation.[23]

Patriotic Chinese accounts of the Opium War recounted fictional battlefield glory of Chinese militias as well as accounts of how, after the Chinese people's valor was undermined by corrupt Qing officials, British and Commonwealth troops or, as they were styled, "white and black barbarians" went on expeditions of mass rape every night and thus drove hundreds of Chinese women to suicide.[24]

D. W. Griffith's racist epic *Birth of a Nation*, which helped inspire the rebirth of the Ku Klux Klan in the United States, depicted Black Union soldiers as predatory beasts. In one of the movie's more famous scenes, Flora, a young southern White woman, throws herself from a cliff to prevent being violated by Gus, "a renegade negro."

In the time between the world wars, the German government led a campaign to discredit the Allied Occupation of the Rhineland by sponsoring and publishing fabricated reports of mass rape of German women by French colonial troops.[25] Though this campaign denouncing the "Black Horror on the Rhine" largely failed in its main objectives, it succeeded in providing Nazi propagandists, including Alfred Rosenberg and Adolf Hitler, with another grievance to wield against the Versailles settlement.[26] Due to the efforts of these agitators, many Germans regarded the story as established truth. When the Japanese army was making itself notorious for sexual violence during the Rape of Nanjing, Paul Scharffenberg, the chancellor of the Nanjing office of the German embassy, wrote of the invaders, "I'm quite sure that like the Negroes in 1918 they were promised: If you hold out, you'll each get a pretty girl in Nanking."[27]

Indeed, the campaign was so successful that Nazis again attempted to employ it in France during World War II. In June 1940, after the fall of Chartres, the German invaders captured Jean Moulin, who administered the city as a prefect. They demanded he attest that French colonial troops from Senegal had raped and murdered French women. Moulin steadfastly refused despite repeated torture. Once, between sessions, he found a piece of broken glass and cut his throat because he knew he was at his limit and in danger of yielding. To him, being party to such a libel against men who had fought for his country was a fate worse than death. Incredibly, a German doctor treated his grievous wounds and foiled his suicide, but Moulin never betrayed the colonial troops.[28]

The Chinese Communist Party used a single rape case as the keystone in a campaign to turn Chinese nationalism from anti-Japanese to anti-American and thus anti-Kuomintang during the Chinese Civil War.[29] More recently, the intelligence organs of the Muammar Gadhafi regime in Libya, in what may have been an episode of projection propaganda, spread tales of rebel forces carrying Viagra into battle so they could more effectively rape women in the territories they conquered.[30]

The visceral fear of mass rape at the hands of invaders is so potent that propagandists make great efforts to exploit it. Even if the women of a particular nation face no plausible danger, attempts are made to identify with women who do. An American anti-German poster of World War I enjoined the American people to "remember Belgium" with a depiction of a conflagration in the background and the silhouette of a German soldier dragging a young girl off to her fate. Such imaginative leaps of sympathy, however, are not always needed. The terror of mass rape is so powerful that propagandists understand that they can freely employ its image even when the threat invoked is patently absurd. One of the most-remembered World War I posters depicts a beastly ape in a Prussian helmet arriving on the shores of America. In one hand he carries a club labeled "Kultur," and in the other a helpless woman, her dress torn open to the waist.

Propagandists employed similar themes in World War II. Shortly after the Pearl Harbor attack, American painter Thomas Hart Benton sought, in his words, "to wake up the Middle West to the grimness of our national

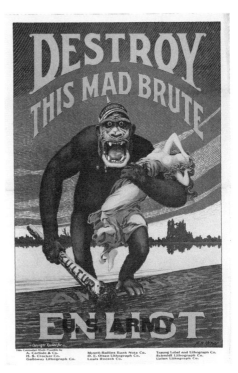

FIGURES 15, 16 • World War I propaganda posters by Ellsworth Young (*left*) and Harry R. Hopps (*right*) (Library of Congress)

situation" and produced a series of works collectively known as *The Year of Peril*. One of them, *Invasion*, depicts a Japanese attack on an American farm, in which a blond woman is raped while her husband and children are murdered by the invaders.[31] Other anti-Japanese propaganda invoked the image of a sneaky, vermin-like Japanese slinking off with a nude white woman over his shoulder. Another depicts a snarling, beastly Japanese seizing a woman from behind, his hand inside the collar of her shirt. It urges the viewer to "keep this horror from *your* home" (emphasis in original).

For the men of a conquered nation who fail to protect the women, defeat is perceived as an emasculating insult. The loss of women to an enemy is such a singular dishonor that any such episode, no matter how peripheral, can be used to goad men into a belligerent response. The Trojan War of Homer's *Iliad* was fought over the abduction of a single woman. Whether

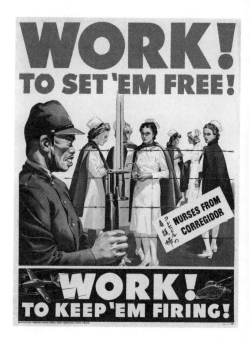

FIGURE 17 (*left*) • World War II American propaganda poster: "Keep This Horror from Your Home" (NARA)

FIGURE 18 (*right*) • General Motors poster featuring nurses captured at the surrender of Corregidor being guarded by a bestial Japanese (NARA)

that detail was legendary or not, it at least rang true enough to the ancient Greeks to be a plausible foundation of their greatest epic. In World War II, the very few white nurses seized by the Japanese military in its conquest of Asia became the theme of another anti-Japanese broadside, as illustrated by figure 18.[32]

"A RELATIONSHIP BASED ON DOMINATION": JAPANESE UNDERSTANDINGS OF SEX AND WAR IN THE MID-TWENTIETH CENTURY

In mid-twentieth-century Japan, the women of foreign nations were often considered to be legitimate spoils of war. A wartime study of the Japanese Health and Welfare Ministry put the matter bluntly: "The fundamental principle of a relationship based on domination is that the males of the ruling or conquering nation marry females of the ruled or conquered nation."[33] The idea that conquest naturally conferred sexual privilege extended to the farthest reaches of rural Japan. In his classic study *A Japanese Village*, John Embree described a carnival-like greeting given to young men returning to the village of Sue from military training. The women dressed as soldiers and tramps and, so disguised, engaged in behaviors they associated with men and soldiers, one of which was to "try to rape the young schoolgirls."[34]

This close association, at least of the behavior of armies at midcentury, seems commonsensical even in contemporary Japan. As recently as 2012, NHK, Japan's public broadcaster, aired a drama about Yoshida Shigeru, Japan's most consequential postwar prime minister. The first episode in the series depicts a probably legendary meeting held by former prime minister Prince Konoye Fumimarō in which Konoe explains the necessity of setting up brothels for the conquering army. Turning to future prime minister Ikeda Hayato, Konoye chides his junior for his apparent naïveté in the ways of war, intoning very seriously, "Ikeda-kun, the occupation of a country means that its women will be violated."[35]

The strength of the link between sex and war in the minds of many wartime Japanese is also evident in the work of their propagandists. In leaflets aimed at inducing American troops to surrender, they included photographs of dark-featured women reclining on a bed or posing nude, with the clear implication that fighting was not necessary to get sex.

However, the clearest evidence of the intimate association of sex and war in the minds of many wartime Japanese is in the way the Imperial armed forces conducted themselves in conquered territories. As described in chapter 1, mass rape was common in territories occupied by the Japanese army. Many in Japan assumed this was just the way occupying armies behaved and lived in terror of what would happen to the women of Japan if their homeland should ever fall to an invader.

RUMORS AND WARTIME IMAGES OF THE AMERICAN ENEMY

Prior to the arrival of American forces most Japanese expected their country to be subject to mass rape. Japan's government, and especially its army, wanted to convince Americans of the futility of attacking the home islands.[36] One way they sought to do this was to present them with a populace that adamantly refused to surrender, and the easiest way to do that was to convince civilians and soldiers alike that surrender was simply not an option.[37] According to historian Handō Kazutoshi, Japanese leaders at every level created and disseminated rumors of enemy depravity in order to raise the fighting spirit of the populace.[38]

Such rumors spread throughout the empire with the approach of American forces. In early December 1945, one Tokyo woman recalled government propaganda that the men would all be killed and the women would be sacrificed to the Black soldiers.[39] In the Caroline Islands, the Japanese military warned women they would be raped when the Americans came.[40] Sixty-one years after the events, Eiko Goldwater, a resident of Saipan at the time of the American invasion, recalled with terror the stories spread by Japanese soldiers. All of the men would be killed, and the women would be raped. After they were raped, they would be stripped stark naked and strung up with their arms and legs spread as ornaments on American battleships. Then they would be taken to America, where they would again be raped until they were finally murdered, with their naked bodies left exposed for all and sundry to see their dishonor.[41] Such stories doubtless contributed to an atmosphere in which hundreds of civilians leapt to their deaths in one of history's most notorious mass suicides.

Fears of rapacious Americans were not confined to civilians. They also inspired the fighting spirit of Japanese military men—or at least made it easier for them to accept their fates. Naval aviator Lt. Seki Yukio, who was selected to lead the first kamikaze attack of the war, spoke with Dōmei journalist Onoda Masashi on the eve of his fateful mission. According to Onoda's later account, Seki was not particularly eager to give his life and in fact thought the mission a waste of his talent and training. Seki also said that he was not going to sacrifice himself for either the Japanese empire or the emperor; rather, he would meet his death to protect his wife: "If Japan were defeated, who knows what the Americans would do to my wife? I am going to die to protect her."[42] Japan was defeated, of course, and Seki's wife, Mariko, was never attacked but did remarry.[43]

Fears of sexual atrocity also drove one of the most-commemorated grievous episodes of the enormous tragedy that was the Battle of Okinawa. In March 1945, in anticipation of the coming American invasion, the Japanese army impressed teachers and students from two Okinawa girls' high schools into military service and formed them into the Himeyuri Nursing Corps. Forced into frontline duty, these girls and their teachers were in harm's way throughout the bloodiest and most violent stages of the battle. Nevertheless, the majority, some 180 of them, survived their ordeals until June 18, just four days before the end of organized resistance on the island. Nishihira Hideo, the teacher who served as the leader of their unit, then told the girls to disperse, warning them against being taken alive by the Americans. They were to flee and avoid becoming prisoners at all costs, not even stopping or slowing their pace to aid others who had been wounded or were falling behind.[44]

Nishihira's warning served to reinforce the greatest fears of many of the girls. A tabloid paper that had been printed near the front lines and distributed among the people carried rumors very much like those that had terrified Eiko Goldwater on Saipan. The girls and women would all be raped repeatedly by the Americans, and then they would be tied as trophies to the American warships from which their lamentations would carry across the seas.[45] In order to avoid this fate, the girls of the Himeyuri corps took great risks to avoid capture, and many paid with their lives. Others, despairing of eluding the Americans, killed themselves with hand grenades. In the end only ninety-nine students and five teachers survived.[46]

Elsewhere there were rumors that any men who surrendered to the Americans would be run down by tanks, while women would find themselves reduced to the mere playthings of the foreign troops.[47] Such rumors were widely believed. It is estimated that more than 100,000 civilians perished during the Okinawa campaign. Thousands of them died in terror of an inhuman foe, taking their own lives or dying violently at the hands of trusted loved ones who believed themselves to be agents of mercy.[48] Many simply refused to surrender. In one instance American interpreters twice entered a cave where a large number of civilians had taken refuge. They pleaded in vain for the Okinawans to surrender. Rather than submit, eighty-two killed one another in a ghastly spectacle of collective self-immolation. One woman killed her own daughter with a kitchen knife after the eighteen-year-old begged her to do the deed while "she was still pure."[49]

Rumors of the kind that helped inspire these horrors were common in the home islands as well. In at least one case it steeled a young woman with the kind of courage that comes only to those who have abandoned hope. Hara Yuriko was a servant in the official residence of Prime Minister Suzuki Kantarō when, on the morning of August 15, 1945, nationalist extremists stormed the building in an attempt to prevent surrender. She mustered the courage to face down the insurgent leader even as he "put the point of his sword against her breast and demanded to speak to the Prime Minister." She reasoned that it was better to thus die honorably than to face the inevitable disgrace of rape by American soldiers.[50]

On hearing the shocking news of the surrender, Handō, then a fifteen-year-old schoolboy impressed into labor at a factory, returned home terrified of the cruel fate awaiting him and all he knew and loved. His teachers and the cranky "old militarist" at the factory had been continually filling his head with horror stories. Handō believed that all the women would be enslaved and defiled by the Americans, while he and all the boys and men would be shipped off to be worked to death as slaves for the Americans at some South Seas island or in California. He told his father of his fears. His father snapped at him, calling him a fool and asking him where exactly the Americans were going to procure the shipping capacity to carry off every single living Japanese and whether he thought American women were really going to let their men keep Japanese sex slaves. It was an eye-opening experience for the young Handō, and he began to think more skeptically.[51] Handō's experience, however, was atypical. Considering the time, he was lucky to have a father at all, let alone one who was not only present but also judicious and persuasive. Elsewhere rumors ran unchecked.

In Okayama Prefecture police recorded a rumor that the troops that were to occupy their area were particularly short-tempered and vicious and that they would castrate all the men and rape the women.[52] People in Yamagata believed that after castration the men would be enslaved at hard labor, while the women would be forced to work in brothels for the pleasure of the GIs.[53] Rumors involving rape, murder, emasculation, slavery, and other horrors circulated throughout the country.[54] Ten years after the war, cartoonist Hattori Michio caught the mood of the time with a drawing of downcast Japanese officers, their hands over their crotches, and a young soldier looking on with evident relief. The caption read, "Officers, rumors said, would be castrated by the Americans. I was never so thankful for being a buck private."[55]

The prevalence of these stories is reflected by the frequency with which they appeared in the reports of the Tokkō (Special Higher Police). Rumors of mass rape were already circulating five days before the Americans had even landed.[56] One rumor had it that the Americans would impose a sexual levy, forcing the town committee to supply them with women from each household.[57] On September 15, police arrested one Onizawa Yoshio, a plasterer from Itabashi, and fined him ten yen for telling people he had seen GIs in a truck abduct two Japanese girls from a streetcar stop. The next day, police in Aoyama took Matsui Kikuji, an unemployed woman, into custody and dressed her down for telling people that she had personally witnessed a member of the Kempeitai (Japanese military police) kill an American soldier who was trying to abduct a Japanese woman.[58]

Groundless rumors were so prevalent that after the Occupation began, one Tokkō report noted matter-of-factly that "the violence and rape that were the subject of rumor has not taken place."[59] More evidence of widespread rumors can be seen in Japanese press reports. For example, on August 19, the *Asahi Shimbun* carried an article written to assure its readers that despite the many rumors about the barbarity of American troops, there was no reason to expect rape or attacks on civilians. It cited the relatively restrained and disciplined behavior of American troops in Germany as evidence that there was no need for alarm.[60]

Nevertheless, panic, both official and unofficial, was the rule in the days before the Americans landed. In Fukuoka a special train to evacuate women to the countryside ran for three days. Those left behind cut their hair, blackened their faces, and did everything they could to make themselves less attractive.[61] In Okayama young women were escorted to a cave complex that had been prepared for a last-ditch defense in the anticipated battle for the home islands.[62] On August 17, an intelligence officer of an air unit stationed in Gifu created a panic by claiming that all the women would be raped. Hearing this, the mayor of Gifu City ordered the evacuation of all women aged fifteen to twenty-five years old, telling them to go into the mountains.[63] A later report had it that all the women from eighteen to thirty were sent to remote regions with nothing more than a sake bottle filled with rice.[64] Even after the landings, when it became clear that there was no need for the kind of alarm that had swept the country, many women remained in hiding. In Muroto City in Kōchi Prefecture, the situation was so serious that the chief of police had to personally go into the mountains to persuade the town's young women that it was safe to go home.[65] The Americans soon noticed the tension in the air. Gen. William Chase, commander of the First Cavalry Division, noted that "the women had all disappeared and kept under cover for a week or two."[66] Four days after the surrender, Father Patrick Barn, an American Catholic priest who had been resident in Japan during the war, wrote an article for publication in the *Asahi Shimbun*. In it he sought to reassure Japanese civilians that American troops were well disciplined and that they had nothing to worry about.[67]

Much of this dread originated in knowledge of the way that Japan's own servicemen had behaved in foreign lands. The persistence of rumors among the general population often was the result of the anxieties of people who had personally observed or even participated in Japanese atrocities abroad. Loose talk about the widespread sexual violence perpetrated by soldiers in China had long been a concern of the army. As I discussed in chapter 1, a 1939 report sought to restrict the careless remarks of returning soldiers but seemed to be considerably less concerned with cutting down on actual rape.[68] Despite the attention of the authorities, tongues continued to wag. In June 1941, writer Nagai Kafū recorded a rumor about a soldier who, sometime after returning from China, learned that during his absence both his wife and mother had been raped during a robbery. The man broke down and began confessing to everyone in the neighborhood that while in Hankou he and his comrades had raped two girls in front of their parents and then murdered the entire family by throwing them alive into a garden well.[69]

In his account of the Hiroshima bombing and its aftermath, Dr. Hachiya Michihiko related an exchange he had with Dr. Akiyama, a junior colleague of his. While they were waiting for the arrival of the Allied troops, the younger man was insistent that he, Hachiya, and Hachiya's wife should all leave the city. When Hachiya refused, Akiyama repeatedly begged to be allowed to at least take the older man's wife. He insisted that she was "in danger" and said, "I know what I am talking about." Hachiya relates that "Dr. Akiyama, who had been in China, was afraid the same thing would happen to us that he had seen in North China."[70] Those who were most adamantly opposed to surrender were those who had served with the Japanese army in China. One twenty-five-year-old nurse who had been with the army on the continent was so terrified of the coming ordeal that she called her family together in a cave and injected all of them with poison.[71]

The combination of deliberate propaganda and careless rumors begun by China veterans proved a remarkably potent combination and the fear of American soldiers persisted well into the Occupation. Even after ordinary citizens had had ample opportunity to observe and interact with relatively well-disciplined GIs, many proved reluctant to abandon wartime notions. Some simply refused to credit the evidence of their senses. For example, Yamamoto Kumatarō, a farmer from Iwate Prefecture, testified to police that "even though they have been good-tempered, they get on my nerves every time I see them. I want them to go back as soon as possible. This good behavior must be some sort of a trick."[72] Yamamoto's feelings were not uncommon. Tokkō reports detail persistent rumors that the good behavior of American troops was highly unusual and due only to the luck of the draw. Many believed that though the particular group that was currently on duty in a given area happened to be a good bunch, the unit that would come to replace them was notoriously full of bad characters.[73]

Press reports echoed these sentiments. They are full of alleged encounters with nameless American servicemen or officers who voice concerns that seem suspiciously consistent with those of the Japanese reading public.[74] In one such report in the *Asahi Shimbun* on September 12, 1945, a journalist claimed to have interviewed an unnamed American soldier. Clearly reflecting the concerns of many of the *Asahi*'s readers, the journalist specifically asked whether the next group of GIs would be as well behaved as the current batch. The "soldier" responded that he "doesn't know how it will go when the gang that doesn't have sufficient training" came in to replace him and his fellows.[75]

Fear of sexual atrocity had extraordinary staying power. While many Japanese greeted the unexpectedly good behavior of American troops with relief, there were many others who remained suspicious, convinced that their situation was somehow both exceptional and temporary. Such attitudes are evident even in many of the official prefectural police histories, which assert that GI crime, including mass rape, was rampant, but it just so happened that there was no such crime in their own particular prefecture. "The advance of the American army into Hokkaidō was more tranquil than in other locales."[76] The Yamagata history notes, "From what we heard afterward, it seems that the troops that came at this time were model soldiers. The people of our prefecture were truly blessed."[77] Shimane was apparently similarly privileged: "Fortunately the unit that came to our area was composed of disciplined stalwarts who had served in the New Guinea and Solomon campaigns. Just as General Willoughby assured us, they were gentlemanly and caused no trouble."[78]

Regardless of the behavior of the actual Americans in their midst it is clear that some Japanese, like the Iwate farmer, were clearly looking for any pretext to nurse a grievance. Such people would not have had to look far, because there was one conspicuous facet of the Occupation that many found both distasteful and humiliating: the American treatment of Japanese women and children, whether at levels of national policy or in casual encounters between GIs and civilians. That is the subject of the next chapter.

CHAPTER 5

"THE ABSURDITY OF HISTORY"

THE AMERICAN OCCUPATION AS A DENIAL OF TRADITIONAL JAPANESE MASCULINITY

The relatively good behavior of the Americans, while initially appreciated, could not entirely overcome the resentment of defeat. Many Japanese, like the Iwate farmer who believed that the benign treatment of civilians by GIs was "some sort of trick," were looking for reasons to hold a grudge against them. For Japanese men and many Japanese women, it would not be difficult to find such reasons. To them, the Occupation came to seem a denial of, or even assault on, traditional Japanese notions of masculinity.

Though notions of what is truly masculine, what makes a man a man, vary from culture to culture, there are some basic elements common to all. These can be summed up as the three Ps of manhood, the actions men are expected to perform to demonstrate their masculinity, "three criteria of performance": protection, provision, and procreation.[1] The actions and policies of Americans during the Occupation challenged Japanese men in all three areas. These challenges came in the shape of high policy and everyday interaction. They came from high and low, from MacArthur at the top to buck privates at the bottom. They came in at least five major ways.

The first and most obvious challenge was the Americans' very presence. They were only there because Japanese men had manifestly failed in their role as protectors. The second major challenge came in the form of SCAP's restructuring of relations between the sexes. In the implementation of a new constitution and new laws for the country, SCAP enforced an entirely new relationship between men and women. In doing so they presumed to be the true protectors of Japanese women. Third, the Americans also robbed Japanese men of the control over women's sexuality, which had historically and traditionally been theirs. They overthrew a system of explicit patriarchal privilege and replaced it, at least in formal legal terms, with complete equality between the sexes. Fourth, the American military and government also took on Japanese men's roles as providers, giving food and material aid to the country. Symbolically the rank and file did this in more direct ways, showering Japanese children and women with gifts of chocolate, chewing gum, and candy. They often did so in a way that was easygoing and cheerful, unintentionally mocking a traditional Japanese image of men as stern, serious people charged with the business of protection and provision. Finally, in probably the unkindest cut of all from the perspective of Japanese men, they claimed Japanese women as consorts and mates. They cavorted with them openly and expressed both their affections and desires publicly in ways that many Japanese found alien, awkward, and offensive.[2] According to the American consulate, some 11,000 American military men registered marriages with Japanese women by December 24, 1952.[3] Later studies indicated that unions (of any sort) between American men and Japanese women probably produced about 5,000 children.[4] All of these perceived slights contributed to an atmosphere of resentment that would further prepare the psychological ground in which myths of mass rape and sexual predation would take root in the years after the Occupation.

GHQ'S SEXUAL REVOLUTION

Aside from the inevitable cardinal insult of occupying Japan's sacred homeland, the American action most resented by Japanese men was the imposition of a new social order based on the formal political, social, and economic equality of the sexes. For many Japanese men, women's suffrage remained a black mark on the Occupation even decades later.[5] GHQ overthrew well-established social norms that had undergirded Japanese society since soon after its emergence into the modern world. The basic unit of this society was the household under the control of a single male head. In its place the Americans established a new polity that had the individual as its fundamental unit. As if being defeated were not bad enough, now Japanese men had to endure Americans presuming to mandate how they could treat the women they regarded as their own. Along with the changes to the emperor's status, the changes in women's position were those that encountered the most protracted and stubborn resistance from the champions of the ancien régime. As political scientist Susan Pharr noted, "Japanese leaders made a persistent effort to dilute, omit, or change the intent of SCAP's women's rights provisions."[6]

It was not just Japanese leaders that took exception. The supposedly destructive changes that would result from female suffrage were widely condemned.[7] It was feared that exposure to politics would addle women's brains and turn them into something both unfeminine and un-Japanese. Even relatively liberal or progressive men found the changes frightening. During debates on the new constitution, the right-wing Socialist leader Nishio Suehiro confronted feminist Katō Shizue about the changes, which she supported. "You're a terrible person!" Nishio berated her. "You're trying to tear down the family system!"[8] When interviewed by Japanese Home Ministry bureaucrats, Christian Socialist (and later prime minister) Katayama Tetsu lamented the change even while he dismissed its practical significance, saying women would just vote with their husbands and that Japan was not yet ready for such a change.[9]

Most American planners believed, or at least feared, that Katayama was right, and they were reluctant to tackle something as fundamental as relations between the sexes. According to MacArthur's partly fictionalized account of his own life, he had decided on his own authority that women would be enfranchised.[10] While the Supreme Commander had a penchant for claiming credit for reforms ordered by Washington, in this case his recollection was largely accurate. Washington's initial postsurrender instructions contained no reference to the position of women.[11] In fact, no document from the State War Navy Coordinating Committee, the precursor to the National Security Council and the body responsible for giving MacArthur his marching orders, even mentioned the position of women in Japan.[12] The closest it came was in its instructions to MacArthur concerning the drafting of a new constitution. It ordered that elections should be "based upon a wide representative suffrage."[13] Brigadier Courtney Whitney later corroborated MacArthur's account, writing that MacArthur had announced to his intimates while they were en route to Japan from Manila on August 30, 1945, that women's suffrage was one of his key goals for the Occupation.[14]

GHQ was proactive not just in effecting reform, but in including Japanese women's rights activists in the process. Katō Shizue remembered that one day "just after they had established GHQ at Hibiya," a jeep arrived at her house. U.S. Army Capt. Tarō Tsukamoto informed her and her husband Kanjū that GHQ would like to confer with them informally. They wished to discuss the labor problem with Kanjū and women's issues with Shizue. To the best of her recollection, this was "around October."[15]

Whatever the exact date of this visit, it is beyond dispute that on October 11, 1945, MacArthur met with newly inaugurated prime minister Shidehara Kijurō. The Supreme Commander made clear that he expected the new government to enact legislation that would fundamentally reform the Japanese polity. The first thing on his list was the enfranchisement of women.[16] MacArthur's stated reason for giving support to women's suffrage was strategic. He believed that female domesticity would have a pacifying effect on the Japanese electorate by "making government directly subservient to the well-being of the home."[17]

Nevertheless, the early visit to Katō suggests that GHQ was at least open to more fundamental changes. American policy went from this relatively modest and practical goal to a far more radical and sweeping reform partly because fate had placed an extraordinary young woman in a pivotal position. This, along with the fact that MacArthur had never met a bold dramatic action he didn't like, led to one of the most extraordinarily rapid and fundamental transformations of women's formal status in world history. The young woman most directly responsible for these changes was Beate Sirota. Sirota, just twenty-two years old at the time GHQ decided to take on the task of writing a new constitution for Japan, had lived in Japan longer than she had anywhere else. An Austrian Jew by birth, she had moved to Japan at the age of five when her father, a concert pianist, was hired as the head of the Piano Department of the Japanese Imperial Academy of Music in Tokyo.[18] Hailing from the polyglot metropolis of Vienna and possessed of a natural talent for languages, Sirota, according to her own later account, learned Japanese (at least to a five-year-old's level) in just three months.[19]

Living in Japan for the next ten years, she further mastered the language and witnessed firsthand the legal disabilities under which women in Japan lived. Sirota and her family associated with relatively cosmopolitan Japanese, and their social circle had no shortage of bright, talented women. Japanese custom kept these women in positions of inferiority. Sirota left Japan to study at Mills College in the United States in 1939. She earned a degree in modern languages while concurrently working for the U.S. government monitoring Japanese radio broadcasts.[20] She worked for a time at the Office of War Information and became a U.S. citizen in January 1945. Having had no contact with her parents since the outbreak of war, Sirota traveled to Washington, where she secured a job as a translator for GHQ so she could return to Japan to look for them. She arrived on December 24, 1945. Six weeks later she was assigned the task of writing the women's rights sections of a new constitution.[21]

Both thrilled and intimidated by the task before her, Sirota set to work restructuring Japanese society at its most fundamental level.[22] In a 1999 interview, Sirota, who by that point was living under her married name, Gordon, gave a rather blunt description of the position of women in prewar Japan: "Japanese women were historically treated like chattel; they were property to be bought and sold on a whim."[23] While in practical terms this was an exaggeration and Sirota knew it, in strictly formal legal terms it was essentially correct—especially where young women were concerned.[24] Sirota had the opportunity to eliminate the legal handicaps under which Japanese women had operated, and she was determined to do so within the text of the constitution. Sirota and her Government Section colleagues ensured that women's suffrage was enshrined in the new national charter. In addition, in Article 24 they explicitly guaranteed the equal rights of women in marriages and within the family, for the first time requiring "mutual consent" for marriage.

Conservatives tried to mitigate these radical statements of equality by qualifying them into irrelevance. Among other things, they had proposed amending Article 24 to explicitly keep the family as the basis of society, prefacing the article with this declaration: "The state guarantees to protect the family in its constitution and authority as the necessary basis of social order and as indispensable to the welfare of the nation." In addition, they attempted to insert passages promising to "safeguard the institution of marriage and protecting women from having to work outside the home."[25] This, of course, was exactly contrary to the intent of the original Government Section draft. GHQ did not permit the changes.

The new structure of the family, based on the dignity and autonomy of the individual, became one of the points about the new constitution that GHQ emphasized to the Japanese public. The head of the household in Imperial Japan, as was pointed out in a GHQ-sponsored pamphlet about the new constitution (see figure 19), was the father.[26] Among his recognized exclusive privileges were the disposal of household assets, participation in public life, control of his wife, and the decision about his children's marriage partners. GHQ's reforms stripped household heads of the ability to decide their children's marriage partners and reformed the husband's former privileges to be rights equally enjoyed by his wife.

Along with the abolition of licensed prostitution discussed in chapter 2, these changes formally stripped Japanese men of the control they had exercised over women's sexuality. Before the Occupation a man was legally entitled to sexual exclusivity from his wife, while she could not expect the same from him. Adultery was a crime for women, but not for men except

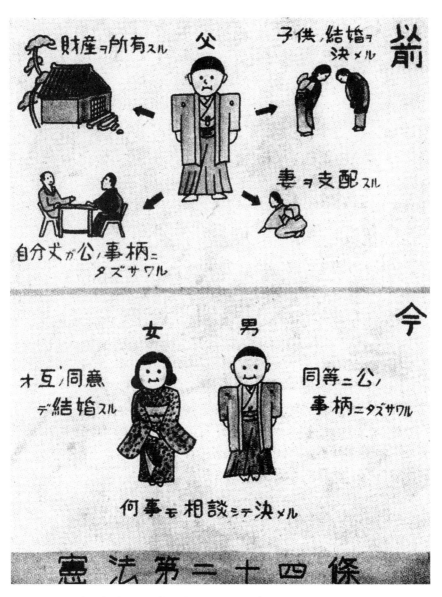

FIGURE 19 • The changes in the relative status of women and men under the new constitution as illustrated in a pamphlet produced by GHQ (Image reproduced courtesy of Michiyo Morioka, from her book *An American Artist in Japan • Francis Blakemore, 1906–1997* [Seattle: Marquand Books, 2007], 88)

under special circumstances.[27] Moreover, a woman could be compelled to become legal mother to her husband's illegitimate offspring if he recognized the child.[28] Laws like these had to be amended in light of the new constitutional equality. In fact, the Japanese government had to make so many fundamental changes to its civil code that there was no time to properly alter it before the new constitution came into effect. Instead, it was necessary to enact temporary legislation mandating wholesale negation of much of the existing civil code, including "provisions which, on the ground of the individual being a wife or mother, restrict legal capacity, etc."[29] SCAPIN 642 also eliminated the ability of household heads to sell daughters into prostitution. In short, GHQ's changes in the status of women eliminated patriarchal control over Japanese women's sexuality and assigned it to the women themselves. These changes engendered deep resentment.

THE GENTLE CONQUERORS: GIS AS AN ALTERNATE MODEL OF MASCULINITY

During World War II, many Japanese viewed Americans and their British allies as savage, subhuman animals. *Kichikubeei*, "American and British fiends," was a standard epithet. Fears of wholesale massacre, mutilation, and rape were rampant.[30] In short, the bar GIs had to clear to make a relatively good impression on Japanese civilians was extraordinarily low. In the early days of the Occupation many Japanese were undoubtedly relieved to just not be physically attacked. The behavior and temperament of the American servicemen was not only better than they had expected; it was better than they had dared hope. For the most part, the Americans were well disciplined but also open and relaxed. The model of masculinity they presented was completely alien.

In the early and mid-twentieth century, the Japanese ideal of manhood centered on the military man. The military quite consciously instilled its recruits with a sense of superiority to their civilian neighbors.[31] The military not only considered itself beyond civilian control institutionally; it even asserted that all of its members were above any civilian authority.[32] Military men were accustomed to privilege when they were in uniform among the civilian population, skipping to the front of lines while their inferiors waited patiently. Their training was a brutal and sadomasochistic regimen that emphasized resignation to the whims of superiors and the complete denial of self.[33] They were indoctrinated in a cult of *bushidō*, a martial tradition largely invented by peacetime samurai and modern ideologues, piecing together an invented tradition of national glory in martial discipline and obedience.[34] Stoicism and self-immolation, divorced from context and celebrated for their own sake, were the cardinal virtues.[35] Death in battle was the ultimate glory, surrender the ultimate shame.[36] The Japanese military and the society that both produced and emulated it created an ideal of masculinity in which men were expected to be dutiful, selfless, stern, and authoritarian. Ideally these qualities would be tempered by half-concealed generosity of spirit and kindness of heart, demonstrated by the occasional indulgence of subordinates, inferiors, and, in particular, small children, but solemnity was the rule.

Superficially, at least, the contrast to American soldiers could scarcely have been greater. The GIs were disciplined and military in bearing, to be sure, but they appeared relaxed and cheerful.[37] They seemed at least as happy to have survived the war as they were to have won it. They were full of a joie de vivre that was the very antithesis of the mid-twentieth-century understanding of *bushidō*. Many Japanese no doubt—certainly the military men—would have been wont to dismiss them as frivolous were it not for the circumstances responsible for their presence. They were, after all, victors and conquerors. For years, the rigor of Japanese life, the contumelies of the Japanese military and, to a lesser extent, of Japanese men, had been justified as necessities for handling the serious business of security. Yet Japan's military had been beaten. It had surrendered—unconditionally—to this army of cheerful men with springs in their steps and smiles on their faces.

From MacArthur on down, the Americans who arrived in Japan impressed the Japanese with an aura of confident optimism. The Supreme Commander embodied this spirit, quite self-consciously, from the moment he first appeared in Japan. Recalling his iconic deplaning at Atsugi airbase, lounge singer Peggy Hayama recalled, "The sight of MacArthur stepping off the plane at Astugi Field was very impressive. With that pipe in his teeth, it was like the director had just yelled 'action' and he makes his appearance—just like a movie star."[38] The image was burned into the Japanese consciousness and remains a symbol of both Japan's defeat and its subsequent renewal, though not all were favorably impressed. Fuchida Mitsuo, the naval aviator who had led the attack on Pearl Harbor, recalled that upon seeing MacArthur make his entrance, he found himself "trying to suppress my urge to give him a double-slap on his face."[39] No doubt many shared his sentiment.

Though few could match MacArthur for dramatic flair, ordinary servicemen did their best to project confidence and authority, and in large part they succeeded. Chief Yeoman Harold Hopper, USN, recalling his first days in the country, said that he and his fellow sailors would walk the streets, and at first only the older people would come out. They would greet each other and move on: "We were being seen."[40] And seen they were.

Ultranationalist firebrand Ishihara Shintarō recalled those early days with some bitterness: "Swaggering GIs often walked down the street as if they owned it. To a child's mind, the sense of Americans as the enemy

FIGURE 20 • MacArthur arrives at Atsugi, August 30, 1945. (U.S. Army)

didn't disappear overnight."[41] Others had a more positive impression. Nearly seventy years after the fact, retired publisher Itō Bungaku recalled seeing the well-fed, well-equipped Americans. They were "tremendously good looking," walking around in polished leather boots at a time when most Japanese wore *geta* (wooden sandals) or footwear made of cloth. With their pressed pants and tall statures, they were objects of the young boy's admiration, something that he would aspire to be.[42]

The well-fed, well-equipped Americans formed quite a contrast to the defeated Japanese servicemen, most of whom were undernourished, unwashed, wearing threadbare uniforms—often their only clothes—and sometimes disfigured or maimed.[43] Many young boys aspired to be like the victors rather than the defeated. In the traditional Japanese *shichi-go-san* ceremony, which celebrates children reaching certain points in their childhood (three and seven years for girls, three and five years for boys), it had been popular for boys to go in replica uniforms of Japanese army and navy personnel during the war.[44] During the Occupation, however, their objects of aspiration became American soldiers, and replicas of their uniforms were worn by little boys as they celebrated their milestones.[45]

Americans did far more than simply be seen. They also interacted with everyday Japanese, and their relative modesty when compared to the men of the Japanese military made a good and reasonably long-lived impression. Recall from chapter 1 Yamada Futarō's friend, Old Man Saitō, who remarked that from the way Americans behaved, it was hard to know who had won the war, and Nagai Kafū's observation that they were "far and away more genial than Japanese military men."[46] In her autobiography, Christian women's activist Kawai Michi wrote that the first troops into Tokyo were well disciplined, courteous, kind to children and the poor, and so solicitous toward the welfare of elderly women as to make them almost uncomfortable. Like Nagai and Old Man Saitō, she made a special point of noting that they were rarely haughty or condescending.[47]

Many Japanese men, particularly those in authority, had a different experience. Government Section member Harry E. Wildes recalled, "Many Occupationnaires believed sincerely that while the women of Japan were lovely gentle creatures, the men were of an entirely different race."[48] The

FIGURE 21 • Little boys wearing GI-style garrison caps to *shichi-go-san* ceremonies at Atsuta Shrine in Nagoya in 1946 (*Mainichi Shimbun*, Mainichi Photobank)

Americans went out of their way to make absolutely sure Japanese men understood that they had lost the war and there was, so to speak, a new sheriff in town.

This was especially true with policemen, with whom Americans clashed from the first day in the country.[49] While Americans gradually began to treat Japanese police as partners in keeping order, they constantly reminded them that they were junior partners who were helping to maintain an American order. Japanese police lived in constant anxiety of demotion, dismissal, or disciplinary action at the whim of the conquerors. They were required to salute all Allied military officers and their cars when they passed, an order they naturally resented and resisted despite continued American insistence.[50] Americans expected obedience from the Japanese. According to later police recollections, some American officers would even brandish their weapons to enforce compliance. In one case, an American officer struck a Japanese policeman with a riding crop and then kicked him.[51]

Americans also dictated how Japanese police were to interact with civilians. The highest-profile case of American intervention was in Shikoku. In the Japanese military it had been common for officers and NCOs to discipline their subordinates by ritual corporal punishment. In one such ritual, the offending subordinate was forced to stand at attention and brace himself while the superior beat him about the face and head. This ritual had been incorporated into civilian life, and Japanese police used it to discipline youths they considered wayward. On learning of this, Maj. Gen. Kenneth F. Cramer ordered all Shikoku police to cease and desist immediately on pain of arrest by the American military.[52]

Through actions such as these Americans undermined the prestige of Japanese masculine authority and made very clear to Japanese men that their grasp on their prerogatives was both tenuous and conditional on American pleasure. While GIs and American authorities did not hesitate to lord it over Japanese men, they were far less severe with women and children. Used to playing subordinate roles, women and children presented no real challenge to American supremacy, so Americans could afford to be, and often were, kind toward them. Whether in high politics, as with the constitution, or in daily interaction, as with the order to Shikoku police, Americans presumed to be the champions of Japanese women and children. With the notable exception of the treatment of suspected *panpan* by military police, Americans were generally respectful and deferential toward women, sometimes consciously playing the gallant.[53] Toward children, their attitude was usually one of avuncular indulgence. Generally more approachable than Japanese authority figures, many GIs attracted children, and soon Japanese children happily interacting with servicemen became a common theme of American photographers.

One of the most common themes was GIs giving candy to Japanese children. Scenes of Americans showering groups of young children with confectionary delights warmed the hearts of many Americans and convinced them that the American mission in Japan was both noble and

FIGURE 22 • A GI distributes candy to Japanese children in Koga city, Ibaraki Prefecture, shortly after the Americans first arrived in 1945. This scene was captured by film crews and later broadcast in *The Big Picture* episode on Japan. (U.S. Army)

generous. Indeed, they became a staple of American propaganda. One episode of *The Big Picture*, a television program produced by the U.S. Army between 1950 and 1975, focused on the U.S. military's role in Japan. Predictably, it featured a scene of a GI showering candy on eager Japanese children. The narrator of the film boasted, "The greatest unofficial ambassador of goodwill has been the American soldier."[54]

The GIs' kindness toward children initially had the effect of easing tensions, putting Japanese at ease and helping the Occupation to go smoothly. However, over time what the GIs and American propagandists deemed to be nothing more than simple kindness began to seem altogether different to some Japanese. As the shock of defeat wore off and the Occupation wore on, patriotic feeling, dormant for a time, began to stir. The GIs' supposed kindness began to seem more like condescending insult. To many women and especially men struggling to provide for their children, the sight of those kids clamoring for the indulgence of the foreign conqueror was hard to stomach. The envy they felt toward those who could so casually bestow a few moments' happiness on their children began to grow.

Indeed, even during the early Occupation, when many found GIs' treatment of children reassuring, there was still a good deal of ambivalence. This much is inadvertently revealed for a split second in *Our Far East Partner*, with a brief shot of adults looking on as the GI distributes candy. Their postures seem to indicate as much resignation as relief. One Japanese man appears openly hostile, standing with arms akimbo as he watches. Among a certain group of Japanese, the giving of candy to children came to be among one of the most vehemently resented actions commonly taken by GIs.

By 1953, the leftist teachers' union Nikkyōso had begun to list distribution of candy to Japanese children among their complaints about American bases and the U.S.-Japan security treaty. In their national convention, a report of the situation near military bases told of a child going to get candy from an American serviceman and then returning to school with a self-satisfied expression. Seeing this, one of the teachers broke down in tears while yelling at the student. It was clear that sympathy was meant to lie with the teacher rather than the student.[55] Historian Matsushima Eiichi denounced American chocolate, along with Coca-Cola and the *panpan*, as symbols of Japan's descent into a colonized state.[56]

Others opposed to the American military presence in Japan took up the same theme. Shimizu Ikutarō was a sociologist and pundit who first made his name as a leftist before undergoing a *tenkō* conversion experience and becoming vocal rightist. In his earlier incarnation he edited a volume called *Kichi no Ko* (Children of the Base-Towns), a collection of essays purportedly written by children living in base towns about their experiences with Americans. In his introduction Shimizu reveals his thoughts on the essays:

> Possibly readers will be most distraught by images of children pestering American soldiers for chocolate or chewing gum. No matter how

you look at it, these children cannot be considered anything but beggars. When I read the essays portraying these children, I could hardly hold back my tears. True, Japan's children are poor, but they are poor not just in material things but in spirit as well. If they were not poor in spirit but had the ideals of peace and independence engraved in their hearts, then no matter how much they lacked materially, they would not be found playing the beggar.[57]

Later he opined that the children of base towns were "themselves, however indirectly, parasites living off the bases."[58] This sort of venom directed at children was nothing but the flip side of a wounded sense of patriotism and masculinity. Thousands of hungry Japanese children had obviously not gotten the memo about engraving the ideals of "peace and independence" in their hearts and were perfectly happy to indulge in the largesse of American troops. In doing so they had made their elders feel that the Americans had, at least in a symbolic way, supplanted Japanese men as providers. While this cut a great many Japanese patriots and men to the quick, it paled into insignificance compared to the feeling of humiliation and rage caused by American encroachment into another preserve of traditional masculinity.

GIS AND JAPANESE WOMEN

As discussed in chapter 2, when faced with the prospect of American occupation, Japanese authorities sought to recruit and organize women to provide sexual services for the conquerors. Part of this was, as many testified, because they desired to prevent widespread sexual violence. However, even when many police had themselves already noted that the Americans had, on the whole, been well behaved and well disciplined, they continued their efforts to get the Americans into brothels. Many have noted that the women that had been recruited for these brothels had been seen as a breakwater meant to hold back the waves of Americans' bestial passions. However, others have suggested that it was also a way to prevent more conventional relationships from developing between GIs and Japanese women.

To the frustration of Japanese officials, these plans came to naught. On November 10, 1945, Kanagawa Prefectural Assembly member Takahashi

Nagaharu (Chōji) addressed the assembly decrying the money the prefecture's people had spent in the summer evacuating women to the countryside to protect them from American men. When they returned, he claimed that everyone could see they were now proactively seeking American company. It had reached the point that they were inviting these foreigners into their homes.[59] Policemen who had spent the late summer setting up brothels to protect women from anticipated violence experienced similar frustrations. With the coming of autumn, the women approached the Americans of their own accord and eventually gave birth to mixed-race children.[60]

Americans and their informal relationships with Japanese women presented conservatives with a real challenge. Japanese officialdom had long seen the control of youthful sexuality as part of their purview. When unmarried young women and young men began associating freely during the relatively liberal times of the 1920s and early 1930s in Tokyo's café culture, authorities reacted by mounting "morals campaigns" to stop the free intermingling of the sexes. This culture, with its modern girls (*moga*) and modern boys (*mobo*), had been associated with what were perceived as decadent Western influences. Students were forbidden to enter these dens of sin.[61]

American actions challenged sexual control. The order to ban licensed prostitution led to many prostitutes plying their trade on the streets. This trend was further exacerbated by the order placing all brothels off-limits to American service personnel nationwide. Many of these women naturally gravitated to young men with money. And in postwar Japan, a very large number of these men were GIs. Adding to the chaos was that this unregulated mixing of the sexes extended beyond the realm of the purely carnal, and many friendly and romantic liaisons began.

American artist Frances Baker (later Blakemore), who had been employed at SCAP's Civil Information and Education Section and who led the team that produced the pamphlet about the new constitution excerpted earlier, published a book of prints about life in occupied Japan. One of them depicts a castle moat on a moonlit night. All three couples enjoying the evening are interracial, and two of the men are in uniform.

This scene reflected an everyday reality. GIs with Japanese women was a common sight, all too common for many Japanese males. It often hurt

FIGURE 23 • "Newcomers learn that pretty faces are not confined to certain races." This print by Frances Baker (later Frances Blakemore) points toward the prevalence of interracial romance. (Estate of Frances Blakemore, courtesy of Cascadia Art Museum, Edmonds, WA)

their pride, and that injury was compounded by the perceived attitudes of many Japanese women. Sociologist Yamomoto Akira was just twelve years old at the time of surrender. He later recalled with bitterness, "When Japanese women, escorted by American soldiers, would come waltzing out [of the PX], their eyes would happen to fall on a Japanese man, whom they looked at as if he were not even human." He found it "unimaginable" that many of these same women had previously worked in munitions plants making weapons for the Japanese military with cloth bands tied around their heads that read "kamikaze." It was, he wrote, an image "burned in memory," one he would never forget.[62]

Demographic and economic considerations virtually guaranteed that such encounters would be frequent. During the war, while millions of young Japanese men were away at the front, those who were left at home benefited from a terribly skewed sex ratio. In his journal, Japanese novelist Nagai Kafū

FIGURE 24 • "Swearing off cigarettes prompts one to think, 'Is she inspired by virtue or inspired by mink.'" This print by Frances Blakemore notes the openly opportunistic nature of many relationships between GIs and Japanese women. (Estate of Frances Blakemore, courtesy of Cascadia Art Museum, Edmonds, WA)

recorded a conversation that he had with a taxi driver in which the ratio became a topic of discussion even before the war with America began. "We haven't got enough rice, tobacco or gasoline," the driver lamented. "The only thing of which there is no shortage is women."[63] Similarly, Yamada Fūtarō recalled a conversation he had with a factory owner on August 18, 1945, in the anxious interval between the surrender and the beginning of the Occupation. The man was nonchalant about the possibility of rape, noting that Japan had a surfeit of women and thus had plenty of prostitutes to sate the foreigners. His biggest worry was that once the Americans discovered how wonderful Japanese women were, they wouldn't want to return to their own women and that the Occupation would thus drag on forever.[64]

According to the 1950 census (understandably, no census was carried out in 1945) there were 11,161,212 Japanese women between the ages of 25 and 44 (who would have been between 20 and 39 in 1945). There were only 9,757,091 men, meaning that there were 1,404,121 more women than men, for a sex ratio of more than 114 women for every 100 men. For the 25–29 cohort (the survivors of those 20–24 in 1945) the disparity is even worse, with 542,324 more women than men, for a sex ratio of 119 to 100.[65] In addition, a substantial number of the surviving men had been severely wounded in the war. In 1947, GHQ's Public Health and Welfare Section designated 325,000 of them, including more than 93,000 amputees, as physically disabled and thus eligible for public assistance. These men were unable to provide for themselves, let alone others.[66]

Even those who were healthy and able-bodied often had no way to support themselves, and those who did manage to hold on to a woman sometimes had to endure the humiliation of relying on her attractiveness to Allied servicemen for their own support. In the early correspondence from the CLO to GHQ was a report about a Japanese man who had held three American servicemen at pistol point, accusing them of short-changing him after they had procured the services of his common-law wife, who was working as a prostitute.[67] A Japanese police report submitted to GHQ in 1950 recorded that almost 10 percent of prostitutes surveyed were currently married. Another 15 percent were widows living with their children. An additional 18 percent were still living with their families.[68]

In the early postwar years, relying on a Japanese man for sustenance was a risky bet. The postwar baby boom is ample evidence that despite the odds, it was a wager that millions of young Japanese women were eager to make. Nevertheless, they could not all be winners, and they did have other options, which many of them chose to exercise. As a result, sex-starved GIs often found it easy to satisfy their carnal desires. Former Occupation official Faubion Bowers recalled that "sex was about the only thing the GIs had. They had been in jungles. They had been on islands. And suddenly there were women. And for a bar of chocolate when you're hungry . . . There's *nothing* these girls wouldn't do."[69] The apparent ease with which American soldiers often obtained the women that Japanese men had regarded as their own aggravated the sense of grievance. Compounding the wound to masculine pride was the shameless and insensitive way Americans capitalized on their sexual fortunes.

Not only did the Americans carry on with Japanese women, but they often did so brazenly and in semipublic venues with little or no regard for Japanese sensitivities or even basic propriety. Bowers recalled that "the moat around the imperial palace was so filled with used condoms that it had to be cleaned out once a week with big wire scoops."[70] One anonymous Japanese wrote to MacArthur complaining that the Americans in the area and the "'pom-pom' girls carry on boisterously. They are not embarrassed at all when seen in the act of copulation."[71] Others complained of neighbors running brothels or renting out rooms in ordinary Japanese neighborhoods for prostitutes and GIs to carry on their assignations. One Japanese complained that the constant noise made by the Americans in one such place kept him or her up all night.[72] Japan became almost synonymous with easy sex and prostitution in the minds of many Americans.[73]

Resentment of the GIs and their Japanese girlfriends was omnipresent. One anonymous letter addressed to MacArthur complained about an American soldier who took his girlfriend to the Sakeya Hotel at Hatake Hot Springs every Friday and warned that "the young men of the locale are threatening to burn the hotel if this affair continues."[74] Such tensions could lead to tragedy. In one case an American on a drinking binge smuggled a .45 pistol off the base when he went for a midnight stroll with a young Japanese woman. She complained to him "that Japanese men sometimes beat Japanese girls for going out with U.S. troops." Just at that moment an unfortunate Japanese man happened by on a bicycle. The enraged GI drew the gun and shot the man dead.[75]

Many Japanese men resented not only the Americans fraternizing with Japanese women, but also the fact that the Occupation had upset the relations between the sexes that had obtained before defeat. Takami Jun gave voice to this sense of dual grievances in his diary. On October 20, 1945, he recounted an incident earlier that day when he had seen a group of female station employees enthusiastically flirting with a GI, and he ended the passage by writing that he "shuddered to think that these wretched sluts have the right to vote."[76]

Others seemed to share the attitude of the elites who first conceived brothels for the conquerors. They didn't begrudge the Americans their due as conquerors but resented them when they took it too far. The historical novelist Yoshimura Akira recalled that in his youth during the Occupation it did not bother him so much to see Americans together with unattractive women who were overly made up, but it pained him greatly to see "pretty, well-bred, inexperienced, and pure-looking women walking happily arm-in-arm with American soldiers." Thinking that they probably had a sexual relationship, he became bitter about the changes that had come over women since defeat.[77]

Sometimes American men rubbed salt in the wounds of Japanese masculine pride, putting Japanese men into what the Americans regarded as the proper place. Christian women's activist Kawai Michi recounted an episode in which a "well-built and stern-looking" GI boarded a train to discover that the passengers were not measuring up to his idea of chivalry. Gesticulating wildly, he managed to convey his displeasure as he forced the men to stand and then indicated to the women that they should take a seat. After doing so, he looked around the carriage at the new arrangement with evident pleasure.[78] In other cases, Americans could not lay claim to enforcing some sense of chivalry: their actions were purely malicious. One poor Japanese man had the unfortunate experience of having three American soldiers throw rocks at him while their Japanese dates simply watched as he had to flee.[79]

Harada Hiroshi, a policeman from Tokyo had a chance to see the new hierarchy from a unique vantage point. Having studied English, Harada was given the opportunity to patrol the capital together with an American MP. As such, he was afforded the deference reserved for these privileged people from GI and Japanese alike. Nevertheless, as a Japanese man he was pained to see GIs in uniforms, some strolling with their "gorgeous" families and others walking arm in arm with gaudily made-up "ladies of the evening," while Japanese men in contrast presented an image that was "the picture of wretchedness."[80]

In an attempt to reduce tensions, Eighth Army commander Robert Eichelberger forbade public displays of affection between GIs and Japanese women: "The sight of our soldiers walking along the streets with their arms around Japanese girls is equally repugnant to Americans at home and to those in the occupation areas as well as to most Japanese." Violation was to be treated as disorderly conduct, and offenders were to be immediately incarcerated until they received a request for their release "presented in person by the company commander."[81]

Some local commanders either encouraged or connived in an extraordinary amount of harassment of Japanese women in relationships with GIs. In Kyoto, squads of military police together with groups of Japanese civil police conducted raids on the residences of local women. One of the criteria for choosing a home to raid was that "girls who at one time or another associated with GIs lived there." In these raids, conducted between the hours

"Who's fraternizing?"

FIGURE 25 • "Tokyo Joe" cartoon by Ed Doughty lampooning the often lackluster and ineffective attempts GIs made to conceal relationships with Japanese women (Ed Doughty)

of 12:45 a.m. and 2:00 a.m. by self-styled vice squads, "entry in most cases was effected by kicking in the door." Japanese police performed this task while the MPs looked on with approval. The police had no warrants. MPs then selected the women to be hauled off for further harassment and VD checks.[82] The local provost marshal put an immediate stop to the practice on receipt of a complaint by John D. Glismann, the local public health officer in Kyoto, but evidence suggests that Kyoto was exceptional only in the degree of harassment endured by women consorting with Americans.[83]

In the eyes of a number of base commanders, Japanese women who dated Americans were functionally equivalent to prostitutes. Some required any woman dating an American to submit to weekly checks for gonorrhea and monthly checks for syphilis and to have these test results printed on a card, much as prostitutes had been required to do by the Japanese government early in the Occupation. The health information, along with the woman's photograph, address, and the name of her American boyfriend, had to be carried on an "only one" pass, in effect a GI girlfriend license. The Occupation authorities at Yonago Air Base in Tottori and, for a time, in the Hiroshima area issued such passes.[84]

While treating Japanese women consorting with Americans as prostitutes was common among Occupation authorities, it was nearly universal among Japanese. Women with GIs were seen not just as prostitutes but as war booty. Defeat and interracial sex were intimately tied in the minds of many and remained so for decades afterward. Peggy Hayama was a lounge singer who got her start performing for GIs in officers' clubs during the Occupation. Recalling those days some fifty years after the end of the war, she talked about the large numbers of women with GIs and how that affected her: "I often rode the bus with prostitutes. I didn't think they were bad women. They were doing all they could to survive. But when I saw those girls dancing with the GIs, cheek dancing, I thought, well, we are all part of the same industry. I said to myself, 'We really did lose the war, didn't we?'"[85]

Hayama's self-awareness and empathy toward the women with Americans was exceptional. However, her use of the word "prostitutes" (most likely *panpan*) to describe women who were, after all, only dancing was somewhat typical. Indeed, right up to the present day, Japanese books about

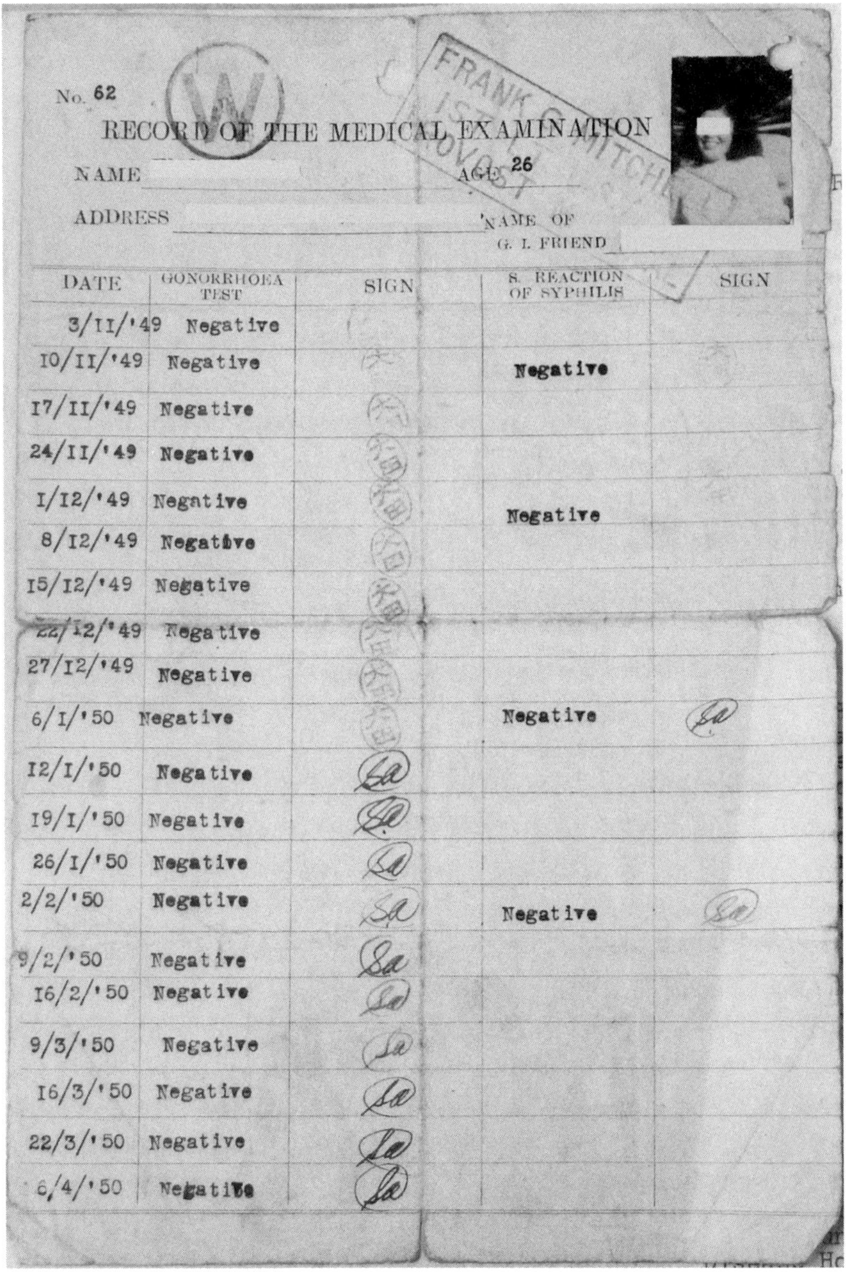

No. 62					
RECORD OF THE MEDICAL EXAMINATION					
NAME			AGE 26		
ADDRESS			NAME OF G. I. FRIEND		
DATE	GONORRHOEA TEST	SIGN	S. REACTION OF SYPHILIS	SIGN	
3/11/'49	Negative				
10/11/'49	Negative		Negative		
17/11/'49	Negative				
24/11/'49	Negative				
1/12/'49	Negative		Negative		
8/12/'49	Negative				
15/12/'49	Negative				
22/12/'49	Negative				
27/12/'49	Negative				
6/1/'50	Negative		Negative	𝒮𝒶	
12/1/'50	Negative	𝒮𝒶			
19/1/'50	Negative	𝒮𝒶			
26/1/'50	Negative	𝒮𝒶			
2/2/'50	Negative	𝒮𝒶	Negative	𝒮𝒶	
9/2/'50	Negative	𝒮𝒶			
16/2/'50	Negative	𝒮𝒶			
9/3/'50	Negative	𝒮𝒶			
16/3/'50	Negative	𝒮𝒶			
22/3/'50	Negative	𝒮𝒶			
6/4/'50	Negative	𝒮𝒶			

FIGURE 26 • "Only One" pass issued by Occupation authorities in Tottori (NARA document; photo by author) prostitution or sexual violence during the Occupation feature pictures of Japanese women dancing with American servicemen.[86] Many Japanese, especially conservatives and men, manifested their resentments in the attitudes they expressed not toward the Americans but, rather, toward their companions; and the most common way of doing so was to regard and call any woman with an American a *panpan*. This was a tendency shared by officials and everyday men and women, and it was strongest among those who most resented such relationships.

Women who consorted with or married Americans were frequently denounced in the press as "traitors," "disgraces," and, of course, *panpan*.[87] One girl of seventeen married an American soldier, who was himself only eighteen, and was walking hand in hand with him when the couple were accosted by several Japanese men denouncing her as a *panpan*. The men, it turned out had chosen the wrong couple to harass: the soldier grabbed one of men, dragged him off to the police station, and forced him to apologize to his bride while on his knees.[88]

Other Japanese men with either less courage or more wisdom waited until the Americans had left. Police were particularly eager to arrest women who were in the company of GIs. According to an interview one young woman gave in 1949, she had a date with a foreign (probably American) soldier whom she hoped to marry. Afterward he took her to the station and dropped her off. Shortly after they parted, a policeman appeared and hauled her off to the police station and then forced her to go to the hospital and undergo a VD examination.[89]

Another young woman interviewed at about the same time said she was arrested after a chance encounter with a foreign (probably American) soldier on the street. The soldier approached her and asked her where she was going. She replied that she was going home. He then asked her where she lived. She replied, "Kyoto." Then he got on a bus. A plainclothes policeman who saw the interaction confronted her. She protested that she did not even know the man. The policeman countered that she should not have adopted an attitude that would cause an American to accost her. He said he had caught her in the act and hauled off her off to Kawabata police station to await transport for the inevitable VD examination.[90]

The above examples were taken from an academic work on "prostitution" done by some Kyoto area professors and their graduate students. They limited their analysis to subjects whom they called *onrii*, from the English for "only one"—that is, a so-called prostitute who had only one customer and was not necessarily remunerated. Their attitude toward both the women and their relationship is perhaps best understood in light of the fact that they titled their work *Gaishō* (*Street Prostitutes*).[91] As Chazono Toshimi, a researcher on postwar prostitution, has pointed out, this work would actually have been better labeled an investigation of the lives of GIs' girlfriends.[92] To many Japanese men, and not a few women, there was no such thing as a legitimate relationship between Japanese women and American men. Noted women's activist Ichikawa Fusae wrote approvingly of women who had emigrated to the United States, as the action had resulted in Japan ridding itself of ten thousand *panpan*.[93]

For these people, the sight of Japanese women with American men was simply an outrage. It even affected some who never had personal experience with GIs and Japanese women. In 1997, a group of so-called war brides (a formulation to which they generally object, as they feel it degrades them to the status of war booty) gathered for a convention of overseas Japanese. Hayashi Kaori, a writer who accompanied some of the women, attended as well. After the opening ceremony, a group of them were waiting for a bus. A man in his fifties who had the appearance of a bureaucrat came upon them and violently pushed them aside as if they were "something filthy." Hayashi recalled that she had never seen a look of such contempt on the face of any human being.[94]

At about the same time, renowned ultranationalist Ishihara Shintarō recalled his experience with defeat and occupation: "You saw so many GIs with prostitutes everywhere. As a male, I had such a feeling of humiliation—No, more than that—maybe a reluctance to believe, a sense of the absurdity of history. I still remember that feeling."[95] That reluctance to believe would soon find expression in a myth of mass rape and sexual predation in the literature of the immediate post-Occupation period. Some of this was overtly fictional, and some was presented as fact. These latter works would eventually have a profound effect on how the Occupation was perceived.

CHAPTER 6

PANPAN LITERATURE

PUNISHMENT, PORNOGRAPHY, PROPAGANDA, AND THE FOUNDATIONS OF A LEGEND

In 2005, when the American Film Institute chose the greatest heroes from the first century of motion pictures, the place of honor went to Atticus Finch, the defense attorney in the film *To Kill a Mockingbird*.[1] Though Gregory Peck's character placed higher than such cinematic stalwarts as Indiana Jones and James Bond, there was one respect in which he could not measure up to his literary counterpart. The movie and the book both centered around the story of Tom Robinson, a young Black man accused of rape after he was caught in a compromising position with Mayella Ewell, a young White woman. In both versions of the story, Mayella's father catches her in *flagrante delicto* attempting to seduce Tom. However, in the book, Finch had both the courage and the impertinence to put the matter in the plainest but also the most provocative way possible. Addressing Mayella, he asked whether what her father saw was "the crime of rape, or the best defense to it."[2] The idea that a White woman would willingly pursue a Black man was not only too much for the all-White, all-male jury in the novel; it was also apparently deemed too much for the sensibilities of American moviegoers of the 1960s.

In the wake of the Occupation, many Japanese, confronted with the reality of frequent consensual relations between GIs and Japanese women, experienced the same "reluctance to believe" that Ishihara described. They, like the jury in *To Kill a Mockingbird*, sought to pass judgment on American servicemen not so much for any actual crime as for flagrant violation of their sense of propriety and threatened contamination of their nation's racial purity. To many Japanese men, the Americans, with their hypocritical sermonizing about women's rights, their chivalric deference to women, the material gifts they bestowed so casually, and the fundamentally unserious nature of their courtship, were nothing more than crass sexual opportunists poaching women who were not rightfully theirs. They had expropriated control of Japanese women's sexuality and then had seized it for themselves. Their very presence was an attack on Japanese sexual morality itself. To these men, the Americans were nothing if not rapists.[3]

The niche for narratives playing to this aggrieved masculinity was enormous, and entrepreneurs, both commercial and political, exploited it relentlessly and with great success. Reviewing the written fiction of the time, Michael S. Molasky, a scholar of Occupation-era literature, wrote, "With remarkable consistency, male writers from both mainland Japan and Okinawa have articulated their humiliating experience of defeat and occupation in terms of the sexual violation of women."[4]

GHQ enacted a wide-ranging sexual revolution as part of its reform agenda. Where there had once been a firm order of patriarchal control of sexuality extending to marriage, prostitution, and courtship, there was now a system of at least formal equality between the sexes based on the sexual autonomy of the individual. However, the idea of individual rights was slow to take hold among ordinary Japanese. According to a government survey carried out in 1950, some 13 percent of Tokyo residents had never even heard the term "human rights." In rural areas, the number reached 45 percent.[5]

While the elevation in women's status was in practice often little more than a hazy abstraction, the changes it wrought were constant irritations to many men. Throughout the country women became more assertive. Many also began relationships with Americans. In the eyes of many Japanese all of these women, GI girlfriends and streetwalkers alike, were *panpan* and were an affront to Japan's once discreet and orderly sexual relations. Unlike the captive prostitutes of the public licensed system, these women were sexual free agents, and they often flaunted both their sexuality and their relative material wealth.[6] They became ubiquitous as a symbol of postwar Japan and its straitened circumstances.[7] Resentment of GIs with Japanese women was commonplace, and when Occupation-era censorship ended, *panpan* stories exploded onto the publishing scene.

Though the emergence of such stories was probably inevitable, it was by no means foreordained that they would become a cultural phenomenon, let alone that they would distort perceptions of the Occupation for decades afterward. An extraordinary confluence of events in Japanese leftist political circles and publishing groups thrust these writings to the forefront of social consciousness and created the foundation of the myth of mass rape.

In January 1950, the Cominform's official news organ carried an anonymous letter. Though unsigned, it was widely understood to be the work of Josef Stalin, and its impact was profound. It criticized the Japanese Communist Party (JCP) for its strategy of peaceful revolution and set off an internal struggle within the party. The impressionist faction led by Tokuda Kyūichi eventually prevailed. The results for the party were a disaster. They went from holding thirty-five seats in the Diet to holding none. An official history of the party later castigated the episode as disastrous "adventurism."[8] However, the reckoning would be some time in coming. In the interim the party sought to arm itself for the violent overthrow of the democratically elected government and to undermine the greatest obstacle to its assumption of power: the U.S. military.[9] To accomplish this, the party emphasized the need to mobilize Japanese women for the coming struggle.[10] Rape propaganda would figure prominently in the subsequent anti-American campaign.

On March 24, after consolidating much of the party behind him, Tokuda called for a unified national front against American imperialism.

Denouncing the United States as a neocolonial bully bent on using the Japanese people as cannon fodder in future wars of aggression in Asia, he called on all true patriots to unite in order to overthrow the treacherous conservative Yoshida government and expel the foreign interlopers whose interests it served. National solidarity was a prerequisite for true independence and the restoration of the country's spirit, now sullied by defeat and occupation.[11] In their anti-American campaign, Tokuda and his allies were ready to exploit any source of resentment against the occupiers. The relations between American troops and Japanese women was an obvious choice. Tokuda himself played on this theme when he denounced government policies as "forcing the Japanese people to adopt the character of a supine prostitute."[12]

In 1951, after internal squabbling, the JCP came together to announce a new program. The party officially rejected "the idea that the liberation and democratic growth and expansion of JAPAN can be attained through peaceful means." In the coming struggle, the party would need to lead the establishment of a new "racial democratic system" that would throw off the oppressor by raising the consciousness of the average Japanese about the "slavery-like oppression of the Occupation policies." However, with the economy booming, this was no easy task, so the Communists made an appeal on something that, while not true, felt that way to so many: "Women are forced even to become prostitutes."[13]

Communists and their allies stressed this theme constantly, often using exactly these words.[14] The JCP's closest associates in their "national front," the left-wing Socialists, were particularly fond of it. On February 27, 1953, Socialist Dietwoman Fujiwara Michiko addressed the House of Councilors and vehemently denounced the disorderly and lascivious atmosphere around American bases. Citing an article from the previous summer's *Asahi Shimbun*, she asserted that the problem was even becoming a big issue in the United States and that Senator O'Hara had been grilling Defense Secretary Robert Lovett about it.[15] As it turns out, there was no one by the name of O'Hara in the Senate. The Senate was not even in session on the date of the alleged exchange. In reality, O'Hara was a House member who had sent an inquiry to Lovett, to which the Pentagon responded months later, stating that the legal status of prostitution was outside the purview of the American forces in Japan. The response was carried in an article in the *Asahi* which occupied all of about four square inches.[16] In the United States, it made nary a ripple. Nevertheless, Fujiwara, a member of the body responsible for making Japanese laws, in an address to that very body, demanded to know why the United States had not outlawed prostitution.

In the same address Fujiwara asserted that there were 1,878 cases of "outrage" by American soldiers between May 1 and the end of the year.[17] Actually, the number she cited was the total number of allegations lodged against all UN forces, associated personnel, and their dependents for any crime whatsoever during that period.[18] The number of rape allegations against American servicemen during that period was twenty-two.[19]

During the same period, the number of rape allegations against Korean residents of Japan was sixty-nine.[20] The number of Japanese nationals accused of the same crime was 2,735.[21] Thus, the average Japanese woman was 124 times more likely to be raped by a Japanese man than by an American soldier. Moreover, assuming that 90 percent of the reported rape cases against Japanese men were committed by males between the ages of fifteen and forty-nine, the rape rate for this demographic was approximately 11.67 per 100,000, while that for male Korean residents of Japan was about 23 per 100,000. The comparable figure for American servicemen was about 8.46.[22]

In other words, judging from police reports, there was no single group of young men from whom Japanese women had less to fear during the very time Fujiwara railed about. But such details mattered little in the charged atmosphere of the early 1950s. With the outbreak of the Korean War, many on the left began denouncing American servicemen not only as crass sexual opportunists but also as violent criminals. The myth of mass rape was born.

One of the earliest examples of such narratives surfaced shortly after a GI was murdered in a Korean neighborhood. A propaganda flyer justified the killing on the grounds of the "barbarous conducts" of the GIs, which were supposedly "beyond description," including violence, robbery, and, of course, rape. Anticipating a theme that would later be a staple of leftist atrocity propaganda, it alleged that these acts were undertaken "in despair" by Americans who did not want to go to the Korean front.[23]

American Harry E. Wildes, who had worked as a teacher in prewar Tokyo and had subsequently served in the Occupation, noticed that Communist newspapers like *Akahata* had been thundering against Americans, claiming that American soldiers were raping Japanese girls and corrupting Japanese schoolchildren.[24] By the time Japan regained its sovereignty in April 1952, tales of American violence had grown in the recounting and were projected back to the beginning of the Occupation. Mass rape was presented as ubiquitous from the time the first Americans landed. By October, Hessel Tiltman, longtime Far Eastern correspondent for the *Manchester Guardian*, warned readers of the *Washington Post* that due to tales of mass rape and other imaginary atrocities, anti-American sentiment was "seething in Japan."[25]

On March 6, 1953, *Akahata* carried an article sure to stoke the flames of nationalism. Americans, they claimed, forced four thousand women who worked at the Tachikawa base to undergo a VD test, and 60 percent were positive. Moreover, it claimed that American servicemen and members of the Japanese Safety Security Force were gang-raping women and infecting them with VD.[26] There can be little doubt that this article, published the day after Stalin's death, received a great deal of attention.

In September of that year, Richard L.-G. Deverall, an AFL labor activist and former chief of labor education for GHQ, warned of "rotten pornography" produced by Communists to stir up anti-American feelings.[27] Tiltman, too, warned of a campaign of "malicious lies" to discredit American forces, with "less reputable Japanese publications" seeking to cash in on "lurid stories purportedly written by the Japanese 'victims' of alleged American rapes."[28]

Tiltman's article caught the interest of the Japanese Foreign Ministry, which translated and reported on it but took no further action.[29] This may have been due to a complacency that Japanese officials seemed to share with their American counterparts. The latter drove Wildes almost to distraction with their apathy. He denounced the "lethargy in organizing counterpropaganda" and later lamented that *Akahata*'s charges had entered the mainstream. "We sat idly by" while the "mass media are hammering out anti-American themes, representing our boys in Japan as dope addicts, lechers, sadists, criminals, and degenerates."[30]

Certainly, both the United States and its Japanese allies were entirely too blasé in confronting what Wildes characterized as "this wave of Communist propaganda."[31] It cannot be said for certain exactly what "less reputable Japanese publications" Tiltman was referring to, but several publications and writers were highly influential in constructing the myth of mass rape. None of these sources is reliable. Some are proven frauds. Others are just plain ridiculous. The most consequential of them will be examined in detail below.

▲ KANZAKI KIYOSHI

The first major writer of *panpan* propaganda, Kanzaki Kiyoshi, would become synonymous with agitation against prostitution, miscegenation, and the U.S.-Japan military alliance, causes he invariably linked.[32] During Kanzaki's activism against prostitution, he testified before the Diet and even served on investigative committees.[33] He is most often identified by scholars citing his work as a literary critic or social activist. As the Occupation began, however, he was neither. His activism on the prostitution issue brought him to prominence. Before he began writing on the subject, he was a frustrated literatus living off dreck well beneath his ambitions, if not his talents. Though he was a graduate of the elite Tokyo University and had been an intimate of the renowned but ill-fated writer Akutagawa Ryūnosuke, he had manifestly not lived up to his promise. At war's end Kanzaki, to the chagrin of some of his friends, was making his living writing pulp romances for teenage girls.[34]

After graduation, Kanzaki got a job as literature teacher at a girls' high school, where he worked for only two years. Kanzaki's son, Takeshi, wrote of his father's dismissal in a hagiography and collection of reminiscences about Kiyoshi. According to Takeshi, Kiyoshi was fired for his outspoken opposition to the school administration's mercenary embrace of the profit motive.[35]

At this point Kanzaki embarked on his literary career. Writing under the name Shimamoto Shizuo, he began contributing short stories to the monthly *Shōjo no Tomo*, a magazine for teenage girls. For several years Kanzaki, writing as Shimamoto, contributed to nearly every issue. However short his teaching career, Kanzaki put it to good use. The most common story pattern he produced was an intergenerational chaste romance between a high school teacher and an unruly student. Typically, this girl is wild, troublesome, and untamed. No other male teacher can reach her, but Kanzaki's teacher (usually named "Shimamoto," like his nom de plume) is somehow able to get through to her and make a real difference in her life. He is empathetic, young, and charismatic, not staid and stuffy like the others. Typically, he gains her trust and shows her the error of her ways and the true significance of the values that she so thoughtlessly flouts. In the end, the girl learns a valuable lesson and is back on track to, presumably, becoming a responsible member of society. All of this was made possible because of her teacher's unique ability to understand her urges to rebellion while simultaneously appreciating the importance of the values against which she rebelled.[36] This conceit would carry over into Kanzaki's writing on prostitution.

Politically, Kanzaki became strongly leftist after the war and had reportedly been attracted to leftist ideas in his youth as well.[37] During the war, however, Kanzaki drank deep from the cup of Japanese militarism. In his Shimamoto persona, he was fulsome in his praise for Japan's military and what he saw as its world-historical mission to liberate Asia from the yoke of Western imperialism.[38] He was particularly critical of Chiang Kai-shek for not understanding Japan's benevolent role.[39] His short stories constantly reaffirmed the value and importance of Japan's wartime gender roles, lauding the valor and intrepidity of its men, especially its military men, as well as the modesty and chastity of its women. He extolled the virtues of patriotism and self-sacrifice, penning inspirational stories about the sort of young women whose families quartered troops, or schoolgirls who went to Manchuria to distribute food and presents to the soldiers.[40] In the preface to a collection of short stories he wrote, "Now Japan's schoolgirls must move as one, facing this era of the great war gallantly, beautifully, and with gentle hearts. It is with dreams that this book will accompany thousands upon thousands of the nation's schoolgirls, their footsteps echoing as they march on the road to victory, that I conclude this preface and put down my pen."[41]

A corollary of Kanzaki's embrace of the militarist cause was a loathing and contempt for Japan's principal antagonist, the United States. In one of his stories, "The English Teacher," written in 1942, after the study of English had been downgraded to an elective, one student who rather likes English confesses to her teacher that she has an American sewing-pattern book and asks for help reading it. Her teacher flies into a chauvinistic anti-American rant, demanding that she destroy the book and reducing the girl to a tearful repentance. The teacher insists that the student cannot even allow herself to think of imitating "vain American women." At this point, Kanzaki inserts his own approving comments:

> Kasahara Sensei was completely right. In order to defeat America, we must fight them not only in the Pacific, but also in the realms of our culture and customs. At a time when our schoolgirls, burning with patriotic fervor, are sewing parachutes, packing our bombs with explosives and making magnificent contributions to our war effort, it is mortifying that some girls still dress as Americans and cannot rid themselves of their deplorable preoccupation with American movies and fashions. . . . That sound [of the student destroying the pattern book] was nothing less than the sound of a Japanese schoolgirl returning to her true form as a Japanese woman, unhesitatingly throwing off the influence of Americanism.[42]

Immediately after the war, Kanzaki published a book in his own name implicitly endorsing a far more radical anti-American resistance. In what one can only conclude was meant as an allegory for Japanese women, Kanzaki wrote of the fall of the Aizu domain in Japan's Bōshin Civil War, some seventy-eight years earlier. He extolled the magnificence of Aizu's women who committed suicide rather than allow themselves to be sullied by the hands of the victorious troops of the Imperial Japanese Army and thus won a glorious and eternal victory in death.[43] Despite the general air of panic, very few Japanese women drew inspiration from this example.

Worse, the Americans and Americanism were soon everywhere, and their arrival presaged the onset of hard times for Kanzaki. He published little new material for four years, had no regular job, and relied on recycled collections of his old Shimamoto stories to makes ends meet.[44] According to his own recollection, it was during this time that he watched well-fed and well-dressed Japanese women, oblivious to the noble example of Aizu's women, cavorting with Americans. It filled him with a deep sense of humiliation and resentment.[45] In this sense, he was no different from millions of Japanese men dealing with the realities of defeat and Occupation. Kanzaki, however, could do something: he could give expression to the shared feelings of the multitudes in his writings.

After the Occupation lifted its regime of pre-censorship in 1949, Kanzaki reemerged on the literary scene burning with self-righteous indignation. When he did, he wrote under his own name, retiring "Shimamoto" forever. He also quietly abandoned his support for militarism and embraced the ascendent political left. He discarded all but one of his wartime animosities, even becoming a member of the boards of both the Japan-Soviet Friendship Society and the Japan-China Friendship Society.[46] American intelligence judged both of these organizations to be Communist fronts. Of the latter, one analyst wrote, "The Japan-China Friendship Association (JCFA) is one of the major Communist-front organizations in Japan and a link between the Japan and Chinese Communist Parties (JCP, CCP)."[47] Indeed, according to *Minshu Shimbun*, a CCP-sponsored Japanese-language newspaper, some 2.4 billion yuan had been sent from China to the JCFA to support various friendly organizations and propaganda activities between July 1951 and February 1953.[48]

While Kanzaki had clearly reevaluated his position on China, he retained his wartime hatred of America. With the onset of the Cold War, Kanzaki became one of the chief proponents of a new nationalist anti-Americanism.[49] He spoke to grievances nursed by many Japanese men who were both nauseated and titillated by the apparently care-free and fun-filled relationships between GIs and the women Japanese men had formerly considered their exclusive property.[50] During the Occupation, anywhere Americans were, there were often Japanese women, and to many Japanese men, including Kanzaki and Ishihara, it was infuriating.[51] In Kanzaki's view, women consorting with Americans were not just whores but traitors. Kanzaki wrote of an incident that occurred during the May Day Riot of 1952, just days after the return of sovereignty. A mob, seeing an American soldier with a Japanese woman, attacked the couple, hurling stones at them. Kanzaki recalled the episode with evident approbation, denouncing the woman as a traitor to her country and celebrating the crowd's awakened national consciousness.[52] It was this spirit that animated Kanzaki's campaign against prostitution.

In April 1949 Kanzaki began writing articles on prostitution and its attendant evils and published in any venue that would have him. He clearly blamed the Occupation authorities and American troops for the situation. Kanzaki supported and sometimes collaborated with Socialist Dietwoman Fujiwara Michiko and became so noted for his advocacy that he was invited to testify before the Education Committee of the House of Councilors on the subject in 1957. There he railed against "Americanism," which he defined as the "delusion that sexual pleasure is life's greatest purpose."[53]

In his writings on prostitutes Kanzaki continually feigns a paternal concern, à la Shimamoto, for these poor fallen girls. Nevertheless, his desire to punish the women about whom he writes, literarily if not literally, is barely concealed. In one place he asserted that to American soldiers, Japanese women were nothing but "tools to satisfy their sexual needs."[54] Discussing the situation of the bases in Tachikawa, Chitose, and Kure, he claimed that most of the women who worked on the base had either been girlfriends of GIs when they got the job or quickly became so. After they were inevitably deserted, most fell into lives of prostitution and were, without exception, miserable creatures. This applied to all women with any connection to Americans, even those that worked as domestic servants, jobs that paid relatively well and were thus desirable to many women in postwar Japan.[55] His resentment toward the women he viewed as traitors is only surpassed by that which he evinces for their consorts, the American sexual interlopers. In his writings Americans are, without exception, either brutish satyrs, devilishly charming forked-tongued lotharios, or both.[56] In the service of promoting these themes there can be little doubt that Kanzaki put his experience with creative writing to good use.

Kanzaki's stories range from the improbable to the simply absurd. It is impossible to know what, if anything, that Kanzaki wrote on the subject is factual. However, it is very easy to establish that much of it is outrageously false.

In an anecdote that has been widely repeated, he has hundreds of American soldiers finding their way to a "comfort station" in Tokyo on August 28, the first day of the Occupation. The brothel had opened that very day and its employees were barely set up. The women were separated only by rudimentary curtains, but the GIs had no shame. They engaged in "animalistic sex" right in the hall, leaving the Japanese police and others involved in the operation in tears as they witnessed their defenseless women in the embrace of the bestial conquerors.[57]

It never happened.

On August 28 there were, aside from POWs, fewer than two hundred (mostly terrified) American troops in the country. Most of them were specialists working overtime to prepare for MacArthur's landing two days later.[58] None of them left Atsugi air base, which was completely surrounded by Japanese police. As darkness fell, the Americans all retired to their barracks, and the only activity from the camp was the patrolling of a small security detail.[59] The Americans did not enter Tokyo in force until September 8.[60]

Elsewhere Kanzaki alleges that even before the Americans had officially landed, an enterprising pimp from Kure arranged for a boat full of prostitutes to approach an Allied warship in the harbor, where, one can only assume, the sailors instantly forgot military discipline and wartime suspicions alike and, rather than gunning down the boat as a possible kamikaze, allowed it to approach. Then, suspecting no treachery, they welcomed the prostitutes aboard and ushered them into their quarters, where they must have enjoyed their services communally. Meanwhile, in Yokosuka a group of American sailors simply could no longer wait to get their hands on Japanese women, so before the landing they abandoned their stations (and, once again, military discipline and all of their fears of the enemy), commandeered boats of an unspecified kind from an unknown source, and came ashore in search of prostitutes.[61]

Kanzaki also, apparently following the lead of police bureaucrat Ōtake Bungo, claimed that the "comfort stations" established for Allied troops were created not in response to a well-documented August 18 directive from the Home Ministry but, rather, in response to a specific request from the

American military relayed through a group of intrepid American journalists who somehow made their way into Japan before August 23, five days prior to the arrival of the vanguard.[62] In fact, no newsmen accompanied the initial party that arrived on the 28th and would not be allowed in until the main body began its landings on the 30th.[63] In the same article, Kanzaki claimed that Americans approached Japanese civil police for assistance in procuring women because the latter wore armbands marked "CP," which the men naturally interpreted as "communicate party," which as everyone familiar with American English apparently knows, is a euphemism for "brothel barker" or "pimp."[64] In another article, Kanzaki claims that "GI," a formulation commonly used in internal SCAP correspondence, was actually a derogatory term in American slang for someone on the dole.[65]

Kanzaki titled one article "Kiiroi Benki," a term he claimed was a translation of "yellow stool," GI slang for Japanese women.[66] This claim is now common in writing on postwar prostitution.[67] One should first note that English for *benki* is not "stool" but "toilet" and that "stool" in any scatological sense is more likely to be used by doctors than soldiers. Moreover, according to dictionaries of Japanese slang, the association of prostitution and toilets had been current in Japan for more than three decades when Kanzaki wrote.[68] One officer of the IJA's Eleventh Army Signal Corps insisted that brothels were a necessity for men, as the sexual urge "is the same as hunger or the need to urinate, and soldiers merely thought of comfort stations as practically the same as latrines."[69] Brothel owners themselves used the word to describe their business as late as 1958, when they barged into Dietwoman Miyagi Tamayo's hotel room on the pretense of presenting her with a gift. They argued that she should stop her antiprostitution activities, as brothels were a biological requirement. "Our job is running public toilets for men. We provide a place for them to dispose of their sexual urges."[70]

Kanzaki repeatedly used *benki* and other such terms to denigrate Japanese women. Chazono Toshimi and Tanaka Masakazu, two scholars who have studied *panpan*, noted Kanzaki's extraordinary antipathy. Chazono denounced the "sexual violence of language" Kanzaki employed, while Tanaka asserted that "in his use of filthy language one can see Kanzaki's extremely contemptuous attitude toward women."[71] Chazono insightfully noted that Kanzaki's desire to monopolize and control Japanese women was the motive force in his work.[72] Certainly that conclusion makes sense in light of his earlier Shimamoto stories. In sum, the writings of Kanzaki Kiyoshi are better interpreted as expressions of personal frustration and antipathy than sober sociological studies.

KITABAYASHI YOSHIKO AND KITABAYASHI TŌMA

Beginning in 1952, Communist and left-leaning publishers began a concerted campaign of atrocity and rape propaganda against American forces. The JCP had originally welcomed the liberating Allies (almost exclusively American), hailing the Occupation as a "democratic revolution." In time this would be forgotten, and any initial friendly contacts between the left-leaning elements and the United States would be denounced, explained away, or forgotten.

One of the opening salvos in this new offensive was a piece by Kitabayashi Yoshiko. Kitabayashi was a colorful character. Born Suzuki Yoshi into an artisan's family, she was influenced by her sister Ito, who had run away to the United States. There Ito married a Japanese man, Niizuma Kan. She would later return and win election to the Diet. She also worked under Marxist firebrand Yamakawa Kikue in the Ministry of Labor's Women and Minors Bureau. In the meantime, to escape a life of domesticity (at that point she was the only daughter in the household), Yoshi studied Western typing at the YWCA. Afterward she found work in Tokyo, where she took up residence.

For some time she associated with Comintern circles, where she met Kikue and her husband, an equally committed Marxist, on the eve of the foundation of the Japanese Communist Party. Shortly thereafter, the Great Kantō Earthquake struck (September 1, 1923) and Yoshi had to make her way to Akabane, where Ito, who had returned to Japan in 1918, had taken up residence. The two began working together to advance women's issues.

In March 1934 Yoshi, now calling herself Yoshiko, wed Shimizu Kinsaku, whom she had known since childhood. Shimizu wrote under the name Kitabayashi Tōma. Taking his pen name as their family name, Yoshiko would endure decades of Tōma's philandering and hard living before he was finally debilitated by a stroke; he spent the last eight years of his life as an invalid in her care.[73] Tōma associated with a literary crowd. His best friend would become the editor of a Socialist newspaper. He wrote sensationalist fiction featuring prostitution, murder, rape, and suicide, usually including something to do with foreigners and often youths of mixed race.[74]

Love is a mystery beyond words, and why Yoshiko, a self-professed "child of the revolution," and ne'er-do-well man about town Tōma decided to tie the knot defied the understanding of most of their associates, but they did, and remained together to Tōma's dying day. What is of more substance is that between them, the pair had skills and information that made them ideally suited to play key roles in the anti-American campaign of the political left in the early 1950s.

During the war, Tōma worked as a correspondent in the Southern Area (mostly Burma) with other writers, including Takami Jun and Shimizu Ikutarō (who would later become a leading figure in the anti-base movement).[75] While there, Tōma penned a treatise on how to write effective propaganda, noting in particular the effectiveness of rape propaganda. In Tōma's view, it was almost impossible to defend against accusations of mass rape, as countries denying them only found themselves identified ever more with sexual violence.[76]

After the war, Yoshiko found work as typist for the Central Liaison Office, the government agency that handled correspondence with GHQ in the opening days of the Occupation. As discussed in chapter 1, this correspondence included crime reports. A piece published under Yoshiko's name in the magazine *Fuji* includes stories that, unlike much of the *panpan* literature that would form the backbone of postwar myths, are clearly based on actual reports.[77]

In some ways these are the most obscene lies of all. The stories in Kitabayashi's article are clearly embellished and include many details that she could not have gleaned from any reports. They also include an eroticization of sexual violence that is typical of men's writing, and specifically of Tōma's work. Thus, actual rape victims had their ordeals twisted into propaganda and mass entertainment spiced up with invented salacious details and wholly fabricated elements of gothic romance. Over the next few years, these women got to relive these horrors repeatedly as they were publicized first in a magazine and then in a nationwide bestseller hawked by left-wing politicians throughout the country.

Kitabayashi's piece also pioneered a conceit that would become a staple of *panpan* literature: the pretended insider's view of the legendary dens of iniquity that were American military bases in Japan. Another section of the article includes accounts from time she allegedly spent working at a base, and these are almost certainly pure invention. They include the type of rape-themed horror porn that would typify later examples of this genre. The real irony is that although Kitabayashi's tales of her work on the base are hardly credible, after her time at the CLO she did in fact work for the Americans. They recruited her to write a Japanese-language radio script explaining the newly recognized rights of Japanese women, ensuring that these rights could be explained in a native Japanese female voice.[78]

Kitabayashi's spurious article would later be rewritten and included in *Zoku Nippon no Teisō*, a sequel to the most consequential example of *panpan* literature produced at this time.

NIPPON NO TEISŌ AND THE MYSTERY OF MIZUNO HIROSHI

Nippon no Teisō, or *The Chastity of Japan*, first published in March 1953 at just about the time *Akahata* was carrying lurid tales of rape on American bases, was heavily promoted in a nationwide advertising campaign. Subtitled *Journals of Women Raped by the Foreign Troops*, it was undoubtedly the kind of book Tiltman had in mind when he denounced the campaign of "malicious lies" defaming American servicemen.

It certainly alarmed Deverall. Its publication was one reason he wrote his book trying to raise awareness of the rising tide of anti-Americanism in Japan. The book was so patently ridiculous that Deverall's entire refutation of it consisted of two pages of commentary and thirty-three of a translated excerpt.[79] To the American reader, Deverall was confident that that was all that was necessary. However, he was also savvy enough to know that the book contained enough details—"the forced physical examinations of Japanese women, the lush *machiai* parties given many Americans by Japanese contractors for the American Army, the dance hall racket"—to provide just enough verisimilitude for resentful Japanese. In Deverall's words, "This book fires paper bullets. And the bullets are aimed one way: *America.* That is the real significance of *The Chastity of Japan.*"[80]

Molasky, however, saw nothing realistic in the book. The writing, with its eroticized sexual violation, bore such a strong resemblance to the fiction penned by Japanese men that he concluded that the book was not, as was claimed, an edited collection of first-person accounts by Japanese women but, rather, the work of a single male author.[81] He later confirmed his suspicions with Hihara Shigenori, who had once worked at the book's now-defunct publishing house, Sōjusha. Hihara acknowledged that the supposed editor of the book, "Mizuno Hiroshi," was in fact its sole author. According to Hihara, Mizuno was affiliated with the Japan Communist Party (JCP), had been living in Yokosuka, and claimed familiarity with "the panpan situation." Mizuno wrote the book "as part of a broader indictment of American imperialism." Sōjusha had its own close ties with the JCP and approved of the idea of using the work as an attack on American imperialism but was anxious about its pornographic nature. However, after obtaining the JCP's approval, Sōjusha released *The Chastity of Japan* under their imprimatur.[82]

Hihara's story differs in some places from other accounts of the book's genesis. According to Deverall, the publisher was in financial difficulties until it undertook to publish *Nippon no Teisō.* However, it still managed to pull off a nationwide publicity campaign and enlist the enthusiastic assistance of the Japan Teachers' Union to make sure "that it reached every village and hamlet in the country."[83] This would have been well beyond Sōjusha's means. It seems likely that both Sōjusha and the JCP were more proactive than Hihara suggested.

According to Nakiri Tetuso, the president of Sōjusha at the time, the idea for the book was his own. In an interview published in *Chosha to Shuppansha* (Author and Publisher), he described the genesis of the project. He said that he had read the original version of *Nippon no Teisō* when it appeared as a novel in *Jinmin Bungaku.*[84]

Jinmin Bungaku was a short-lived left-wing literary magazine established in 1950. Founded in the wake of the divisive Cominform Criticism that had roiled the JCP, the journal's purpose was to be part of a cultural offensive aimed at mobilizing the masses and the laboring class behind the struggle against the democratically elected Japanese government and its American allies.[85] The impetus behind the magazine's foundation originated with Nuyama Hiroshi (aka Nishizawa Takaji), leader of the JCP's Cultural Division. Nuyama was also the son-in-law of the party chairman and leader of its radical impressionist faction, Tokuda Kyūichi.[86] One of the magazine's editors, Kobayashi Masaru, was a JCP member who was later imprisoned for his role in an attack with Molotov cocktails in front Tokyo's Shinjuku station on June 25, 1952.[87] The journal was dedicated to tapping the literary potential of the masses and aggressively recruited first-time writers. As a result, its pages repeatedly carried self-criticism, promises to do better, and requests for patience on the most uncomradely grounds that its stories were only the works of uneducated workers, after all.[88]

In any event, it is not clear exactly what story Nakiri was referring to.[89] *Jinmin Bungaku* carried no story credited to Mizuno prior to the publication of *Nippon no Teisō*. Nor did it carry any portion of the novel written under another name. Kuroi Senji, who would later go on to win several prestigious literary awards, did contribute two stories about *panpan*, writing under the name Kashii Toshie.[90] One of these, "Izukoe," features rape by a GI and some of the other elements that would become standard in *panpan* literature.[91] According to Nakiri, the story he read was true to the magazine's reputation, and he did not think much of it. Later, he read the same story presented as fact in a flyer at an employment office outside Ikebukuro in Tokyo. He thought to himself, "That's it!"[92] Such stories published as actual victim testimonies would have much more appeal. The result was a runaway sensation that seems to have gone to Nakiri's head. Just two years after he had foisted this hoax on the world, he was brazenly boasting about it.

Whatever the actual details of its origins, it is beyond dispute that *Nippon no Teisō* was a total fabrication with a definite political agenda. Nevertheless, in the psychic environment of post-Occupation Japan it was received uncritically by a large number of readers and had an impact on domestic politics, particularly on questions of defense and security. From the middle of March 1953, the month of *Nippon no Teisō*'s release, the Communist

FIGURE 27 • Women attend an anti-base rally in Uchinada, June 13, 1953. (*Asahi Shimbun*)

Party launched an ultimately successful propaganda campaign against Hayashiya Kamejirō, a minister in the Yoshida government who was trying to negotiate an agreement between the residents of the area around Uchinada, Ishikawa Prefecture and the U.S. military, which planned to build a base there. In the campaign they distributed *Akahata* and propaganda leaflets, with the intention of terrorizing women.[93] They also distributed pornographic photographs supposedly depicting American soldiers raping Japanese women, threatening that "this will be happening to your daughters before you know it!"[94] They claimed that "Uchinada will become a *panpan* town." This had the intended effect, and women became deeply involved in the campaign.[95]

An allied labor union, the Hokuriku Tetsudō railway workers' union, purchased copies of *Nippon no Teisō* and another anti-base hoax, *Kichi no Ko*, to distribute to youth and women's groups in the area.[96] According to Uchiyama Mitsuo, the leader of the railway workers' union at that time, *Nippon no Teisō* circulated among the young people, going "from pocket to pocket."[97]

Nippon no Teisō became required reading for anyone on the left side of the political spectrum. In an annual retrospective on the labor movement's activities, the monthly magazine *Chūō Kōron* noted the wide distribution of *Nippon no Teisō*.[98] Samejima Tsuruko, a reader of *Shin Josei*, a Communist magazine aimed at women, described how she and her comrades pooled funds to purchase a copy of *Nippon no Teisō*, which they all read.[99] In a leaflet distributed in the former Imperial Japanese Navy base town of Maizuru, residents were told the terrible consequences awaiting them if the U.S. military moved in—already amply documented in *Nippon no Teisō* and *Kichi no Ko*.[100] The phrase *Nippon no Teisō* became a stock phrase in the anti-base movement, always as something being corrupted by Americans or their lackeys in the Yoshida government.[101]

Shin Josei carried one of the four "testimonies" from *Nippon no Teisō* in its June 1953 issue, along with the enraged commentary of prominent, if credulous, women's activists Hiratsuka Raichō, Kamichika Ichiko, and Kubushiro Ochimi.[102] This in turn inspired a torrent of outraged letters from readers.[103]

Yamazaki Yasuo, author of the 1955 book *Chosha to Shuppansha* described *Nippon no Teisō* as "the bible of the anti-base movement," a book constantly cited in speeches of left-wing politicians and agitators.[104] As part of the campaign to bring the good news of Japan's purity to the world at large, *Nippon no Teisō* was translated into Mandarin in April 1954 and into Esperanto in August.[105]

Despite the efforts of men like Tiltman, Deverall, Wilde, and a number of skeptical Japanese, it is clear that all too many of the paper bullets Deverall described found their marks. *Nippon no Teisō* was a publishing sensation. By December, it was already in its nineteenth printing.

Amazingly, despite the hullabaloo, Mizuno Hiroshi, the "editor" and actual author, never revealed himself. There was no lecture circuit; there were no book signings or other promotions. He appears to be lost in the mists of time. In 1982, when the editor of the publishing house Tōgosha wished to reissue *Nippon no Teisō*, he claims that he could not locate Mizuno and had to approve the publication on his own authority.[106]

One person who did know the identity of Mizuno was Kanzaki Kiyoshi. In a discussion published in the August 1953 issue of *Shin Josei*, these two maestros of agitprop horror porn sat down to discuss their "insights" on the *panpan* issue. They focused in particular how so many Japanese women were being sullied in mind, body, and spirit while working on U.S. bases in Japan.[107] Kanzaki asserted that the really horrible stuff was going on inside the bases.[108] Mizuno offered the juicy tidbit that according to "the officer in charge of personnel" on the base in 1948, fully 89 percent of the women working at Tachikawa airbase were no longer virgins.[109] Many of them, after a week of hearing jazz music, had addled brains. For eight pages, Mizuno and Kanzaki engage in dueling yarns about the debauched and corrupted women working for the Americans. For the women working on the bases, these lies and others like them were devastating. Some five decades later, city officials in Kure matter-of-factly stated that no woman would admit to having worked on a base at those times because of the vicious rumors that had circulated about female base employees.[110] As to the identity of Mizuno, some possibilities are suggested by the publication of its sequel, *Zoku Nippon no Teisō*.

ZOKU NIPPON NO TEISŌ AND GOTŌ BEN (TSUTOMU)

The financial and political success of *Nippon no Teisō* inspired Sōjusha to produce a sequel, unimaginatively titled *Zoku Nippon no Teisō* (The Chastity of Japan: A Sequel). This one, however, was not written or edited by "Mizuno Hiroshi." Rather, Sōjusha entrusted it to a young writer called Gotō Tsutomu. At first glance, Gotō was an odd choice. According to Gotō's account, he had graduated from Tōhoku University the same month that *Nippon no Teisō* was released. His only published works to date had been pornographic stories, on the profits of which he had paid his room and board at college.[111]

Stranger still, the book Gotō "edited" did include at least one genuine contribution from someone else, *Kizu wa Iezu*, by Kitabayashi Yoshiko. Kitabayashi Tōma, the advocate of rape propaganda, would seem to have been a leading candidate as the real "Mizuno Hiroshi." He had a talent for the kind of eroticized rape porn that makes up most of the stories in *Zoku Nippon no Teisō*. The Kitabayashis had deep connections with left-wing Socialists, and most importantly, Yoshiko's *Kizu wa Iezu*, which shows all the signs of having been a joint collaboration, made up the final fifth of *Zoku Nippon no Teisō*. Moreover, these were important books.

FIGURE 28 • Copies of *Nippon no Teisō* and *Zoku Nippon no Teisō*, inscribed by Socialist representative Nakazaki Toshi to no particular recipient (Photo by author)

Both *Nippon no Teisō* and *Zoku Nippon no Teisō*, became staples of not just the Communists but also the Socialists. Purchased in bulk and distributed in various campaigns against bases, the alliance with the United States, and prostitution, they had a profound impact on Japanese politics and have ever since affected the way that the Occupation has been perceived.

The success of the books and Yoshiko's involvement in the project almost led to a career in politics. She had had a long-standing relationship with Suzuki Mosaburō, chairman of the left-wing Socialists, and he called on her in 1954. Asukata Ichio, a local Diet representative from the left-wing Socialists and a middle school acquaintance of Tōma, arranged the meeting. Asukata would later become mayor of Yokohama and chairman of the Socialist Party. Suzuki, Asukata, and the Kitabayashis dined together. Upon Suzuki's departure, Asukata urged Yoshiko to run for the Kanagawa Prefectural Assembly as a left-wing Socialist on the strength of the popularity of her essay among the younger generation. Ultimately, she declined the offer because of the warnings she received from fortune tellers.[112]

With one-fifth of the text already prepared, and Tōma clearly an experienced writer in the genre, why would Sōjusha have gone with an unknown kid? It could have been a matter of timing. With *Nippon no Teisō* a runaway bestseller, Sōjusha was apparently looking to strike while the iron was hot, and Gotō had a reputation for working fast.[113] Molasky learned that Sōjusha "provided Gotō with a pile of data and asked him to write a sequel.

As is often the case in Japan, he was placed in a hotel room for a week and wrote the entire book during that time."[114] Contrary to assertions Gotō made about his involvement, he certainly had no time to do any original research.[115] A close reading of his book makes clear that whatever the value of the materials he got, the final product is a pastiche of lies ranging from embellishments to outright inventions.[116]

If Sōjusha did in fact feed him this information, it was probably unnecessary. Gotō was fast, and his imagination was boundless. In the years that followed, Gotō invented many more tales of American lechery.[117] In the sensationalist magazine *Shinsō*, Gotō related an episode allegedly from the Battle of Iwo Jima. A Captain Martin of the Sixth Marines rallied his men with the following rousing harangue: "You braves! After Jap just broken here, nobody can't impede your road to Tokyo! Tokyo, many girls of peach are waiting to be conquered. Jap girls all given you! Now go for break!" It seems that just the very thought of girls of peach drove these men to superhuman efforts. The Sixth Marines carried the battle and annihilated the Japanese garrison, which was no small achievement, considering that they were on Saipan at the time. When they were finished, they took up a battle cry that soon spread to the entire U.S. military in the Pacific: "Jap girls of peach are all ours!"[118]

Risible as stories like these are, they are also disturbing. The Americans in these stories are all monsters, but they are monsters with one literary purpose: the violent sexual conquest and degradation of Japanese women. Gotō's writing spoke to something dark within the postwar Japanese male psyche. His work is saturated with misogynistic violence and contempt toward Japanese women. While Kanzaki's writings were typified by a certain violence of language toward women, Gotō far surpassed him in this respect. If one thing can be said to tie all of Gotō's *panpan* and GI stories together, it is an almost visceral antipathy toward Japanese women and girls. Hardly a woman appears in Gotō's work who is not raped, beaten, abused, abandoned, forced into prostitution, infected with venereal disease, driven to suicide, or just outright murdered. Rarely are these women lucky enough to suffer only one of these fates. Dreadful misfortune befalls any woman foolish enough to be involved with an American. In one story Gotō related the fates of women who had married GIs and moved to America. There, Gotō asserts, according to an "unofficial survey" done by the "United States immigration authorities," 8,300 of these 9,000 women were abandoned by their husbands and ended up working in brothels that catered exclusively to Black and Chinese men. Every last one of them.[119]

Zoku Nippon no Teisō was the first book Gotō published under the name Gotō Tsutomu. He would later go by "Gotō Ben" ("Ben" is an alternative reading of the character for "Tsutomu"). It was the beginning of a very long and prolific career of sensationalism and invention. In fact, he is better known to readers in Japan for his books about the prophesies of Nostradamus, of which he has published at least thirteen.[120] In one of them Gotō confidently predicted that the world would end in July 1999.[121] Gotō also broke the story that Japan had actually developed the atomic bomb before the United States but lost the war nevertheless because the country was forbidden to use such a weapon by its august and humane sovereign, even after the Americans had deployed it against Japan.[122] He also detailed how human civilization was initially founded by extraterrestrials.[123] Another of Gotō's subjects was Adolf Hitler, of whom he wrote admiringly. In Gotō's telling, the Nazi dictator was a great prophet whose writings and utterances provided the key to understanding world history, especially the role played by the nefarious Jews. Gotō returned to this subject and revised his writings as recently as 2015.[124]

His end-of-the-world prophesy affected the actions of multiple cults, including Aum Shinrikyō, the doomsday sect that carried out sarin gas attacks in Matsumoto and Tokyo in 1994 and 1995, respectively.[125] His Japanese *Wikipedia* entry lists him as a "pornowriter and SF writer" whose main works include "Jewish Conspiracy Theories, Anti-American-theories, and Prophecy-research." While earlier writers might have been forgiven for overlooking some of his more questionable assertions, they are not exactly well-kept secrets anymore.[126]

Gotō was an unscrupulous sensationalist and a neo-Nazi crackpot. Worse, this is obvious from the first pages of the very source many scholars cite so frequently. In the third paragraph of his introduction to *Kuroi Haru*, a reissued and slightly altered version of *Zoku Nippon no Teisō*, he writes

FIGURE 29 • Gotō Ben's last book on Hitler's "prophesy" of doomsday and beyond, 「ヒトラーの終末予言側近に語った２０３９年」 (Hitler's Prophesy of the End • The Year 2039 as Revealed to His Intimates) (Shōdensha—used by permission)

of the secret plan of the "elite group of Jews who controlled American leaders" to "completely annihilate" the Japanese people by means of atomic weapons.[127]

However, Gotō may have had something besides his rapid pen and febrile imagination to recommend him for the project of *Zoku Nippon no Teisō*. He may well have written the original. In the preface to a later work, *Tokyo no Teisō* (The Chastity of Tokyo), Gotō wrote that he had penned an earlier work, which he identified as *Nippon no Teisō*, not *Zoku Nippon no Teisō*, based on the journals of women—the ostensible genesis of *Nippon no Teisō* but not of its sequel.[128] He made a similar claim in *Kinjirareta Chitai* (The Forbidden Zone).[129] In addition, *Sengo Zankoku Monogatari* (Story of Postwar Cruelty), one of the countless reissues of *Nippon no Teisō* and *Zoku Nippon no Teisō*, is actually a hybrid of the two, including parts of *Zoku Nippon no Teisō*, and the "testimony" of "Ono Toshiko," from the original. The work is credited to Gotō as editor, with no mention of "Mizuno." Finally, *Sengo Zankoku Monogatari* became the basis for a 1968 film by the same name. Its screenplay is credited to Gotō and "Ono," again with no mention of Mizuno.

In short, it seems likely that the "bible" of the anti-American postwar left was written by the same man who composed the bible of Aum Shinrikyō.

▲ THE RAA AND HASHIMOTO YOSHIO'S *HYAKUOKUEN NO BAISHUN SHIJŌ* (THE TEN-BILLION YEN PROSTITUTION MARKET)

By 1958, thanks largely to Gotō's creative talents and the relentless flogging of his works by the anti-American left, the Recreation and Amusement Association (RAA) grew in the popular imagination into something far larger than it actually was. In reality, the RAA was but one of many organizations that sprang up across the country in response to the Home Ministry's August 18, 1945, directive to prefectural police departments to organize brothels for the Occupation troops. Only three days after this order went out, Lt. Gen. Kawabe Torashirō, just back from a trip to MacArthur's headquarters in the Philippines, bluntly advised against the measure.[130]

Nevertheless, the Home Ministry did not rescind the order, and all over Japan local police, working with their long-standing contacts in the prostitution industry, proceeded apace. The RAA was one such collaboration in Tokyo. The RAA also organized less explicitly sexual entertainment venues such as beer halls, cabarets, and dancing halls. In fact, the Oasis of Ginza, one of the RAA's most notorious establishments in postwar legends, was not a brothel but a dance hall. Moreover, many RAA dance halls catered to Japanese customers during the midday hours.[131] After GHQ placed all brothels off-limits, the RAA's brothels either diversified or went out of business.

In Gotō's expansive imagination, however, the RAA was something far larger and more sinister: a government agency in all but name, with deep, corrupt ties to officials and police. It employed as many as 70,000 women in a nationwide network of prostitution and human trafficking.[132]

It was only a matter of time until someone decided to monetize this legend. That time came in 1958 with the publication of *Hyakuokuen no Baishun Shijō* (The Ten-Billion Yen Prostitution Market). Allegedly cowritten, compiled, and edited by Hashimoto Yoshio, an RAA employee, the book purports to be an exposé of horrors perpetrated by American personnel in the brothels of the RAA.[133] It consists of a collection of "testimonies" as well as Hashimoto's own recollections.

Published by Saikō Shinsha, whose other titles include *Furin no Seitai* (The Ecology of Infidelity), *Hadaka Nihonshi* (A Naked History of Japan), and *Nikutai no Junrei* (Pilgrimage of Flesh), it was clearly meant to cater more to prurient than political interests.[134] Nevertheless, its sensational stories were perfectly serviceable as agitprop and have been repeatedly used in that role ever since.

A cursory examination, however, reveals that Hashimoto's book is no more reliable than the works of Kanzaki or Gotō. One story in his book has it that in the middle of November, the Commander of the Pacific Fleet paid a visit to Tokyo. This commander was called Admiral R, because, one presumes, Fleet Adm. Chester William Nimitz liked to be called by the final letter of his first name. People also called him "General," because, one surmises, five-star admirals like it when people do that for some reason. Apparently, Nimitz (or rather, Admiral R) desired sexual entertainment. To this end he had Colonel Lee and his assistant, Captain Proud of the Far Eastern Air Force, arrange the matter with one Takagi Yoshio. One can only conclude that Nimitz relied on Army Air Forces personnel to arrange this liaison because they had been the first in Tokyo and thus had the contacts to get matters arranged. They must also have been very discreet as well, what with managing to occupy Tokyo without even being noticed by the population of the city, the American press, or the First Cavalry Division, which to this day remains under the impression that they were "first in Tokyo."[135]

FIGURE 30 • Maj. Gen. William C. Chase and Pfc. Paul Davis of the U.S. First Cavalry Division, September 8, 1945 (U.S. Army)

Another episode, reminiscent of scenes of organized mass sexual violence in *Zoku Nippon no Teisō*, has groups of Americans led by interpreter guides from the Hawaiian Nisei Unit "224th," routinely raping and plundering the women in the RAA dormitories whenever they got short of money. Of course, the Nisei 224th never existed, and the Nisei 442nd fought in Europe. Also, the requirement that interpreters be present for rape and pillage is not explained.[136]

In another story by Hashimoto, one Hatanaka Eizō joined the Akabane Kaikan, a dance hall run by the RAA, as a dance instructor "just after the war ended," but ended up quitting soon after an ugly run-in with a GI in November.[137] Miyoko, one of his students, hated Americans because her brother had been killed in the war. Nevertheless, in her desperation after the war she took a job as a dancer, but one of the men she had danced with was apparently not satisfied with just that. One night after drinking, he and three comrades broke into the dance hall after hours. An employee rushed to fetch Hatanaka. When he arrived, the drunken GI demanded that "Miyoko come here!" When Hatanaka tried to persuade him to leave, the GI struck him, sending him sprawling. The American then drew a pistol and would have shot Hatanaka had Miyoko not showed up at just that moment and sacrificed her virtue on his behalf. Dressed in nothing but a chemise, Miyoko tore the garment open and told the American brute that he could have her.[138]

The problem with this story is that, according to the RAA's in-house history (admittedly not always a reliable source), it did not even open the building in question until December 20, 1945. When it did, it was called the "Cabaret Akabane." Later it closed the dance hall and reopened it on August 18, 1948, as the "Akabane Kaikan," upgraded to include a café, cabaret, food service, and dance school.[139]

Hashimoto's work also includes another feature common to *panpan* literature, the inclusion of the terrible things the GIs say when interacting with their Japanese victims, rendered in English—just as the GIs said them. Thus, we hear of one American who most unchivalrously told a young Japanese woman, "Monkey very stink!"[140] Another, apparently feeling that he had been swindled, indignantly insisted, "You put me with fair promise!"[141] A third, losing his temper, burst out with the well-known American curse "Konfanda You!" One can only imagine how many confused Americans were left speechless when angry Japanese gave them a taste of their own medicine after reading Hashimoto's book.

Whoever wrote Hashimoto's book did so unburdened by the most basic knowledge of the U.S. military, its operations during the Occupation, or even, it seems, of the RAA. They seem likewise to have had no direct experience of real Americans except in the most superficial way. If Hashimoto did in fact write it himself, he concocted the stories and he put very little effort into doing so.

● KOBAYASHI DAIJIRŌ AND MURASE AKIRA'S *MINNA WA SHIRANAI KOKKA BAISHUN MEIREI* (THE STATE-ORDERED PROSTITUTION NO ONE KNOWS ABOUT)

Another frequently cited source on rape and prostitution during the Occupation era is *Minna wa Shiranai Kokka Baishun Meirei* (The State-Ordered Prostitution That No One Knows About). Published in 1961, the book purports to be an expose of the supposedly unknown world of prostitution during the Occupation, even though this "unknown world" had been at the center of a national debate and the subject of countless books, movies, and plays. Often cited as it were a sober scholarly investigation of prostitution, the book is nothing of the sort. It is based largely on a series of articles that Kobayshi Daijirō and Murase Akira wrote for the *Naigai Taimusu* over a period of about five weeks in early 1961.[142] The *Naigai Taimusu* was a "sports" paper that was best known for its coverage of *fūzoku* adult establishments, that is to say cabarets, strip shows, and brothels or their near equivalents.

Published without bylines under headlines like "The Violated Bud: 16-Year-Old Girl: At Some Point the Pain Became Pleasure," and featuring lurid tales of hypervirile Americans like the Black GI that copulated with a prostitute twenty times in a row, the articles were clearly meant to arouse and entertain rather than discuss a serious social issue.[143] Though Murase and Kobayashi toned it down when they published in book form, the articles are replete with the eroticization of rape common in *panpan* literature. Moreover, they appear next to writing about sports stars, tips for bets on horse and boat racing, and salacious pieces about adultery and revenge. The paper also published reviews of cabarets and brothels. Some of these advertised in the paper with photos of topless models, appearing alongside ads for quack venereal disease cures and penis enlargers. The paper was clearly aimed at young and middle-aged men, and it was assumed that their interest in the subject of prostitution was prurient.

Kobayashi and Murase's research was minimal. As they acknowledge, they relied extensively on Gotō, Kanzaki, and other dubious sources.[144] Any original work they did consisted largely of interviewing shady figures like Kaburagi Seiichi (see below) or politically connected brothel owners like Suzuki Akira and Yamaguchi Tomisaburō, both of whom ended up in prison on charges of bribery.[145] Unsurprisingly, these men portrayed themselves as patriots who had done a great service to their country by helping to slake the sexual thirsts of libidinous Americans.[146] *Minna wa Shiranai* is mostly salacious gossip and downright nonsense, but many writers treat it as a reputable source. Though Kobayashi and Murase are often referenced, their work, like those of Kanzaki, Mizuno, Gotō, and Hashimoto, is best regarded as fiction.

KABURAGI SEIICHI AND HIROKU: SHINCHŪGUN IAN SAKUSEN (SECRET RECORD OF THE COMFORT OPERATIONS FOR THE OCCUPYING TROOPS)

Kaburagi Seiichi is another extensively cited "authority" on the subject of postwar prostitution and rape. His 1972 "memoir," *Hiroku: Shinchūgun Ian Sakusen* (Secret Record of the Comfort Operations for the Occupying Troops), remains highly influential. Some scholars cite it as a genuine inside account. Kaburagi claims to have served as the chief of the information section for the RAA. Calling on his experiences in this capacity, he gave numerous interviews on postwar interracial prostitution.[147] Though the book published under his name purports to be a "memoir," it is in fact simply a minimally reworked version of the 1957 book *Onna no Bōhatei* (Female Floodwalls), supposedly written by Tanaka Kimiko, an RAA prostitute.[148] The book also includes a new introduction, parts of which are clearly cribbed from Kobayashi and Murase.[149] With scenes like the one in which an experienced madam instructs new recruits on sexual positions and advises them how to satisfy the deviant Americans, the book is clearly intended to arouse something other than the social conscience.[150] Like *Nippon no Teisō*, *Onna no Bōhatei*, with its relentless series of sex scenes, struck Molasky as the work of a man. Again he confirmed his suspicions, this time in a conversation with the publisher's son, Itō Bungaku.[151] Molasky's interest was primarily literary, so he did not follow it up further to confirm his hunch.

To the historian, however, the work's general acceptance as a legitimate source requires more investigation, and such investigation makes clear that neither Kaburagi nor his book can be trusted at all. While Mizuno and Gotō were content to invent their narratives, Kaburagi's creativity extended to his own biography. He claimed that in 1957 he was the president of the Nihon Nyūsu Eigasha, but that company changed its name in 1946 to Nihon Eigasha. In 1951 it was reorganized under the aegis of Tōhō and became Nihon Eigashinsha, which functioned until its dissolution in 2009, whereupon its archives became the property of Tōhō Sutera. According to Koizumi Katsurō, custodian of the archive, there was no record of any Kaburagi Seiichi having ever worked there. Moreover, employees who had entered the company as early as 1960 had never heard of Kaburagi, a fairly uncommon and memorable name.[152] Kaburagi's profile said that he had been an editor at *Bungei Shunjū*. However, as with Nihon Eigashinsha, *Bungei Shunjū* had neither record nor recollection of anyone by that name.[153] Kaburagi claims to have graduated from Keiō Gijuku University, and though Keiō, citing "privacy" concerns, would neither confirm nor deny that such a person ever attended their school, they did, unprompted, reveal that his name is not in a list of notable graduates.[154] This may have been because Kaburagi did have one prominent association with Keiō: in 1978 he was involved in a scam soliciting donations for a hospital that Keiō was supposedly going to build. The university ended up taking out advertisements in five national newspapers to warn people about the swindle. According to an article in the *Shūkan Posuto*, Kaburagi had been falsely claiming to be an alumnus of Keiō as part of the scam.[155] Kaburagi also claims to have been a manager of the Shinjuku Musashinokan theater, but like his other alleged places of employment, the theater has neither record nor recollection of anyone by that name ever having worked there.[156] In short, nothing in Kaburagi's "profile" can be confirmed, most of it is doubtful, and much is demonstrably false. To put it bluntly, Kaburagi was a con man.

Moreover, a study of his writings on postwar prostitution makes clear that they were just another of his rackets. He cannot even keep his story straight, contradicting himself in the two versions of the introduction that serve as his memoir. In the first, he claims the book was written by Tanaka Kimiko, a woman he had never even met. In the second, he claims to have known her quite well.[157] In the first, he asserted that the RAA had a total workforce of about 1,800, including dancers, singers, waitresses, and prostitutes. In the second he asserts the organization employed 70,000 prostitutes.[158] Kaburagi even contradicts himself within a single work, reporting first that Tanaka's husband was killed in the Korean War and later that she was expecting him home at any minute.[159] According to both versions, Tanaka became pregnant while working as a prostitute at the RAA (whose brothels were disbanded in 1946), but somehow her lover is killed in the Korean War (which began in 1950) *before* she gives birth.[160] When asked about Kaburagi, Itō was unaware that the book originally published by his company, Dainishobō, had been revised and reissued under a different title, or whether a man named Kaburagi ever even existed.[161]

Considering the number of people who have interviewed him, it is certain that Kaburagi, or at least someone using that name, did exist. In fact, he is listed as an employee in an RAA company history.[162] In addition, writer Inoue Setsuko tracked him down in the hospital near the end of his life, and Kaburagi told her that he was in fact the author of *Onna no Bōhatei.*[163] Kaburagi's work, like the man himself, simply cannot be trusted.

To state the matter plainly, the works of Kanzaki, Mizuno, Gotō, Hashimoto, Kobayashi and Murase, and Kaburagi are worthless as historical resources. The problem of these bogus sources is further exacerbated by the immense popularity of *Nippon no Teisō*, which was, thanks to the active promotion of both the Communist and Socialist Parties, a publishing sensation. It spawned many imitations and became the first in what Molasky has called "a long line of titillating panpan publications during the 1950s," many of which enjoyed great success.[164] Gotō's and Kaburagi's works are the most obvious examples, but there are countless others. For example, *Minna ga Miteiru Mae de* (*In Front of Everyone's Eyes*), a book by erotic novelist Fujiwara Shinji and purporting to be a true exposé of life in base towns, was put out by Masu Shobō, on August 15, 1955, the tenth anniversary of Japan's surrender. It went through thirty-six more printings in the next thirty-six days, and writer and publisher had a sequel ready for press by November 20.[165] As it became clear that *panpan* literature was, in the words of comedian Tom Lehrer, "a market they can't glut," other writers and publishers jumped on the bandwagon, all of them promoting outrageous and incredible stories.

Many in the genre would not even qualify as good fiction. They suffer from internal inconsistencies; impossible timelines; first-person "testimonies" that slip into the omniscient viewpoint;[166] GIs who suddenly lose their command of the English present progressive as they approach climax ("I come now!");[167] violent, sex-crazed Americans brutes who somehow manage to articulate their evil passions in Japanese;[168] Americans fearing deterioration of their eyesight from sex with Japanese women;[169] Americans with names like "Barbary," "Chart," "Hebin," "Cheridan," or the aforementioned "Captain Proud";[170] mixed-race children whose fathers' recessive genes magically become dominant;[171] a suspiciously large number of Americans who resemble movie stars (James Cagney, Bing Crosby, and Alan Ladd);[172] and first-person "testimonials" from women who had supposedly died from their ordeals.[173] The transparent fraudulence and poor quality of these books notwithstanding, they met with wild success. In addition to many prima facie absurdities, some contain transparent plagiarism of earlier hoaxes.[174] In responding to skepticism regarding previous works of his, one author admitted in *two* subsequent works that he could not attest to the truth of his work.[175] In another the "editor" and actual author tries to explain away inconsistencies and absurdities in his story as the result of the "mental instability" of the "women" whose stories he purports to tell.[176] Some stories border on pornographic self-parody. In one episode it was alleged that a group of female American personnel from the WAC kidnapped a Japanese police officer, confined him for three days, and continually forced themselves on the hapless lawman.[177] One presumes that readers could not help but sympathize with his misfortune.

Despite their patent absurdity, such works feature prominently in journalistic and scholarly accounts of sexual relations between Japanese women and American servicemen during the Occupation.[178] Even the official Kanagawa Prefectural Police History, an otherwise generally reliable source, excerpts Gotō for more than a full page.[179] Numerous sources claim that there were 70,000 women working as prostitutes exclusively for the Occupation forces; one source asserts that there were as many as 150,000 and that these women served a minimum of fifteen customers a day and sometimes as many as sixty.[180] This would imply that the average American stationed in Japan procured the services of prostitutes somewhere between 2.65 times and 22.7 times *every day*,[181] all while somewhere between 25 and as many as 85 percent of them were suffering from at least one venereal disease. The 70,000 figure, like so many others, first appeared in Gotō's *Zoku Nippon no Teisō*. Gotō's figure was then repeated by Kaburagi, among others, and has subsequently been incorporated into the literature so thoroughly that any researcher who does not consider the implications is bound to regard it as an established fact.[182] Indeed, Hirai Kazuko has done exactly that, referring to the 70,000 figure as "commonly accepted."[183]

The nearly ubiquitous and uncritical citation of these sources has led to their acceptance as authentic even though they were never really believed even by the people who promoted them most vigorously. Ironically their bluff was called by their own primary mythmaker. In two of the innumerable reissues and mashups of *Nippon no Teisō* and *Zoku Nippon no Teisō*, Gotō asserted that he and a group of interpreters who had worked on American bases stood ready to testify to the horrors that they had witnessed at any time.[184] Despite their incessant flogging of the issue over the previous dozen years, left-wing legislators never took Gotō up on his offer.

Likely, the rising generation of Japanese scholars will regard these books as reliable primary resources. Between 2004 and 2010 the academic publisher Fuji compiled a thirty-six-volume reference set on the problem of postwar sexual violence. Its volumes incorporate genuine primary sources on sexual violence right next to works by Kanzaki, Mizuno, Gotō, and Kaburagi; two obvious frauds by erotic novelist Fujiwara Shinji; and other highly dubious works.[185] The *panpan* literature of the 1950s, both fraudulent and fictional, still influences popular memory of the American Occupation. Part of that was due to the success of a deliberate smear campaign by leftist elements in Japan, but a good deal of it was simply because these stories served as an effective and emotionally resonant metaphor for America's conquest, occupation, and continuing diplomatic dominance.

Most of these books are simply manifestations of their authors' desires to punish Japanese women for consorting with American men, literary equivalents of shearing women to mark them as outcasts. This practice, carried out widely in Europe after the war, is something that Kanzaki specifically cited with an approbation suggesting envy. He treated the "cruel fate" of Chinese women who consorted with Japanese soldiers the same way.[186] *Panpan* literature is saturated with a spirit of mob violence. That so many scholars have helped to legitimize this misogynistic garbage is nothing short of scandalous.

That scandal is the subject of the next chapter.

CHAPTER 7

A NEW GENERATION OF MYTHMAKERS

For many years after the Occupation, most people viewed GI conduct as good, or even exemplary. Indeed, the contrast between the savagery many Japanese expected and the restraint and good cheer actual American servicemen was cited as a reason for the smooth occupation. To be sure, tales of American bloodlust and sexual violence had always enjoyed an audience in Japan, but few gave them credence.

The writers and purveyors of these tales attest to this fact with their constant need to affirm that the stories are true. Publishing at a time when virtually their entire reading audience had had extended firsthand experience with the Occupation, they incessantly enjoined them, in essence, not to believe their lying memories.[1] One gets the feeling that, among the elite at least, these books were circulated with a nod and a wink. Their fraudulence was an open secret.[2] The currency of these tales was largely limited to cynical sensationalists, easy marks, and anti-American agitators. As recently as 1995, participants from both sides vividly recalled both the fear of violence and the profound relief at its relative absence in the Occupation's opening days.

That began to change almost immediately afterward, and stories of bloody-minded American rapists rampaging through the streets of Japan entered the mainstream of Occupation historiography. A number of scholars have contributed to this change.

YUKI TANAKA

The most significant figure in this transformation has been Yuki Tanaka. The first major claim put forth by Tanaka and subsequently repeated by many writers is the grossly inflated figure of 1,336 reported rapes in Kanagawa Prefecture during the first ten days of the Occupation. As discussed in chapter 1, there were actually seven reports of rape in Kanagawa during this time. For his extraordinary figure Tanaka had relied exclusively on Yamada Meiko's *Senryōgun Ianfu* (*Comfort Women for the Occupation Army*), a popular work that is both poorly researched and highly tendentious.

Historian Roger Brown cast doubt on Tanaka's figure when he pointed out some of the problems with Yamada's work, particularly her misreading of her own source material, in a post to H-Japan in 2004.[3] Tanaka responded to Brown as follows:

> Shortly after the book was published, I became aware that the statistical information I obtained through Yamada's book was somewhat dubious. In a deliberate effort to amend this situation, I made sure that I used mainly original sources in Chapter 5 ("Sexual Violence Committed by the Allied Occupation Forces Against Japanese Women: 1945–1946") of my latest book, *Japan's Comfort Women*. Here, I used various police reports, reports compiled by the Kempei-Tai, Tokko Police, the Central Liaison Office, etc. I therefore believe that what I described in this chapter represents a more accurate account of the situation at the time. I also made extensive use of testimonies by rape victims, so that we could understand the horror and pain that these women had experienced.[4]

While Tanaka acknowledges that his writing included "somewhat dubious" information, his "deliberate effort to amend this situation" did not involve any acknowledgment of his earlier mistake. This was a consequential delinquency. Well after the publication of *Japan's Comfort Women* in 2002, scholars continued citing his ridiculous figure. John W. Dower, who wrote the foreword to *Hidden Horrors* and contributed a blurb for *Japan's Comfort Women*, would have been saved some embarrassment by an explicit acknowledgment of the mistake. He cited Tanaka as his source when he repeated the 1,336 figure in 2010.[5] Likewise, Antony Beevor, writing in 2012, gave the same figure, again citing Tanaka.[6] Worse, Tanaka himself, despite admitting that his source was "somewhat dubious," produced a revised edition of *Hidden Horrors* in 2018 in which he repeated the claim without amendment despite making numerous other changes.[7] He then republished the chapter containing this falsehood as an article in the online *Asia-Pacific Journal: Japan Focus* at the end of 2019.[8]

Moreover, if one scrutinizes *Japan's Comfort Women*, it becomes clear that this latter effort did not make amends for his earlier (and subsequent) erroneous statement. Instead, it exacerbated the situation. This is most obvious in Tanaka's use of what he claims are "testimonies of rape victims." In reality, these accounts *do not include a single genuine victim testimony*. Rather, they are the violent pornographic fantasies of male writers. Tanaka quotes almost exclusively from the agitprop and exploitation fiction works masquerading as exposés discussed in the previous chapter.

Tanaka begins his discussion of "victim testimony" by asserting that "the most reliable" sources on the subject "are *Nippon no Teisō* (Japan's Virtue) published in 1947 [*sic*], and *Kuroi Haru* (Black Spring) [an altered reissue of *Zoku Nippon no Teisō*], published in 1953 [*sic*—actually, it was published under this title only in 1985]."[9] Both of these works are transparently fraudulent. The latter is the work of a notorious charlatan and neo-Nazi. Likely the former is as well. Worse, that is made obvious in the introduction of the very work Tanaka deems one of the "most reliable" on his subject: its third paragraph rails about the "elite group of Jews manipulating the American leadership" to use several dozen atomic bombs to achieve the "total annihilation of the Japanese race."[10]

Despite this anti-Semitic nonsense, Tanaka, who is himself married to a Jewish woman, treats Gotō as a reliable authority. Indeed, it seems that Tanaka mistakes Gotō for someone else altogether. Tanaka calls him "Itsushima Tsutomu," which is an alternative reading of the characters of Gotō's name, but one that Gotō himself did not use. Tanaka identifies Gotō (or "Itsushima") as the editor of the book, whereas *Kuroi Haru* (as opposed to earlier versions of the book under different titles) clearly identifies Gotō as the author. Elsewhere Tanaka credulously repeats Gotō's claim that he worked as an interpreter for the Occupation forces. However, in 1980 Gotō admitted that he was unable to carry on basic conversations in English with a Canadian acquaintance "from Seattle."[11] Tanaka also credits the absurd claim that "Itsushima" conducted a survey of five hundred prostitutes specializing in services for GIs in 1949, when Gotō was just nineteen years old.[12]

Nevertheless, Tanaka treats Gotō as if he were a mature and respected social scientist with unrivaled access to cooperative prostitutes, rape victims, and informers from the ranks of Japanese employed by the Occupation. Gotō is Tanaka's source for what he identifies as the "testimony of one of the rape victims."[13] In the episode, as Gotō relates it, a group of high school–age girls were working at an arsenal in Kure, a naval base town just outside Hiroshima, when the war ended. They had all been orphaned by the atomic bombing. To add to their misery, the bombing killed everyone who could release them from service. As such, they "became slaves."

As Gotō tells the story, on September 14, 1945, they learned they had been impressed into service as prostitutes for the Occupation troops. Then, members of the British Commonwealth Occupation Force (BCOF) rounded them up and forced them into the back of a truck at gunpoint. After being driven around, one girl tried to escape, whereupon the BCOF men cut her down with machine guns. They took the others to a building, training machine guns on them the whole time. There the soldiers raped the girls until they lost consciousness. When they came to, they were forced back into the truck and driven elsewhere at high speeds. During their trip, they hit something and heard a scream, but the truck did not even slow down. Finally, they were taken to another building, where they were all gang-raped once again. In the midst of this ordeal, one of the victims committed suicide by biting her tongue and drowning in her own blood. Afterward, at a brothel set up for the Occupation troops, they underwent medical examinations, which determined that every single one of them had contracted venereal disease.[14]

There are numerous problems with this horrific story, beginning with the casual murders committed by the BCOF men and the highly improbable honor suicide achieved by the girl who bit her own tongue while she was being raped, a detail that seems medically improbable but is consistent with traditional Japanese melodrama. More significantly, according to the official history of the Hiroshima Prefectural Police Department, no such incident occurred: "After landing, all the units [of the occupying forces] proceeded to their assigned stations by automobile. To the relief of the [Japanese police] escort detail, there were none of the kind of untoward incidents that were initially feared."[15] In fact, there was not a single report of rape by an Allied serviceman in Hiroshima Prefecture during the entire first month of the Occupation.[16] The extreme violence of Gotō's story is both implausible and flatly contradicted by a far more reliable source. Nevertheless, that is not the biggest problem with this story.

The biggest problem is that of timing. Gotō was no historian, and this is reflected in his sloppiness with dates. On September 14, 1945, there were no BCOF troops anywhere in Japan. They announced their participation in the Allied Occupation only on January 31, 1946, and the main body landed on February 21, 1946.[17] In fact, there were no occupying troops of any kind in Hiroshima on September 14. The first Americans, an advance party of six people, arrived on September 26. Troops arrived in force on September 30.[18] Finally, the first "comfort facilities" (brothels) did not open until October 7.[19] The story is an obvious fabrication.

Unlike Gotō, Tanaka is a historian, and there is evidence that he was aware of all these facts. In *Japan's Comfort Women* he duly noted all of them: the Americans' October arrival, the early 1946 arrival of the BCOF, and the brothels opening on October 7.[20] In other words, at the time he wrote Tanaka demonstrated sufficient knowledge to adjudge the story false. Nevertheless, he presented it as true. Worse, Tanaka's retelling differs significantly from his source material. He has omitted the casual murder, the hit-and-run killing, and the gruesome honor-suicide, by far the most sensational and incredible parts of the story. In addition, where Gotō wrote of attacks by the BCOF, in Tanaka's portrayal the perpetrators are "a number of GIs" and "a different group of GIs."[21] Finally, Tanaka describes the time of the attack only as "one day."[22]

To summarize:

1. Gotō's story is incredible and contains sensational details that should clearly invite skepticism.
2. In Tanaka's presentation, the least credible details have been eliminated.
3. Gotō's story contains details that are demonstrably false.
4. Tanaka demonstrates awareness of the historical facts that contradict the story's details.
5. In Tanaka's presentation the demonstrably false details have been altered or omitted.

This is not the only time that Tanaka's presentation serves to effectively obscure falsehood in his source material. Tanaka, like others, also relays the story told by both Kanzaki and Kaburagi about the sex-obsessed GIs lining up for miles to wait on the poor unprepared novices at the brothel named Komachien. This story, as presented by Kanzaki and Kaburagi, is full of both absurdities and demonstrable falsehoods.

In the former category is Kanzaki's attribution of supernatural sexual instincts to American servicemen. Kanzaki speculates about how the Americans found their way to the Komachien brothel: "One can only surmise that they developed an extraordinary sense of smell by which they could sniff out the scent of a woman's body."[23] As to the questions of how these olfactory superpowers managed this feat through the walls of the building, or how they managed to detect and distinguish a woman's particular body odor over the stench of their own bodies after a full day in the August heat, or why they did not detect any of the other tens if not hundreds of thousands of women along the circuitous route on uncharted and bomb-damaged roads from Atsugi Air Base, a distance of thirty kilometers (eighteen miles) as the crow flies, Kanzaki offers no explanation.

Kaburagi's version is hardly more credible. In it, the reader learns that MacArthur's GHQ had a special section, sent with the advance team on August 28. In Kaburagi's telling, the duty of this organization was to see to the sexual needs of its servicemen, or, more precisely, as he made clear, servicepeople. Kaburagi wrote of the considerable "consternation" caused by the presence of women in the American ranks. This was not due to any fear of censure from the women but, rather, because he and others preparing "comfort facilities" had only considered the needs of men. "As one would expect from America, where women are so powerful, we had nothing but trouble in trying to handle the demands for comfort facilities from the women's units and this led to several peculiar episodes."[24] One sympathizes with the plight of Kaburagi and his fellows as they struggled to find patriotic young men willing to shoulder this onerous burden for the sake of their country—a burden which, one surmises, was quite beyond the capacity of the scores of thousands of young American men in the Occupation.

Quite aside from such incredible claims both accounts are plagued with demonstrable falsehoods. In Kaburagi's telling, MacArthur landed at Atsugi on August 28.[25] In Kanzaki's account, he deplaned on August 29.[26] In reality, MacArthur arrived on August 30, another fact of which Tanaka has demonstrated awareness.[27] Kanzaki reports that the first unit to arrive in Japan was the Tenth Airborne Division, which has never existed. Kaburagi has it that one of the first units was the First Division, which was in Europe. (The First *Calvary* Division, a completely different unit, did participate in the Occupation.) Kaburagi also asserted that on August 28 "an endless line of four or five hundred" GIs were outside the Komachien brothel in Tokyo's Ōmori district clamoring to be let in, even though there were fewer than two hundred in the country, all of whom were confined to Atsugi air base and completely surrounded by Japanese police. Finally, he combines demonstrable falsehood with absurdity when he claims that after the initial landings, the GIs set off in the direction of Kyoto, some 330 kilometers (200 miles) away, a locale the Americans, quite reasonably, chose to approach after a separate landing at the much closer beaches of Wakayama.[28]

Despite these obvious problems, Tanaka treats these as reliable accounts. Tanaka goes on to note that the first brothel to open was Komachien "in the Ōmori district of the Keihin area"; that it opened on August 28, the date of an alleged ceremony for the RAA before the "Royal Palace"; and that several GIs made their way there that evening. According to Tanaka, "It is probable they found the comfort station on the way from Atsugi to Kanagawa prefecture, where they had to inspect the port facilities of Yokosuka in preparation for the landing of US marines a few days later. The selection of the site—on the highway linking Tokyo, Yokohama and Yokosuka—was a deft business decision by the RAA."[29]

The presentation of this material eliminates much of the demonstrable falsehood, error, and absurdity from Kaburagi and Kanzaki's accounts, but it also introduces demonstrable falsehood, error, and absurdity absent in the original source material. In Tanaka's telling, there is no mention of the troublesome and demanding American women and the GIs who had extraordinary noses for women are replaced by mundane port-inspectors dispatched from Atsugi. Rather than Kaburagi's "four or five hundred," we are presented with a vague but more modest-sounding "some GIs." However, while superficially more plausible than either Kanzaki's or Kaburagi's tales, Tanaka's version is, like them, both demonstrably false and absurd. It cannot withstand geographic or historical scrutiny.

The first problem with Tanaka's story is his claim that the GIs who found the brothel were probably "on the way from Atsugi to Kanagawa prefecture, where they had to inspect the port facilities of Yokosuka in preparation for the landing of US marines a few days later." Atsugi is in Kanagawa Prefecture. One can no more be on the way from Atsugi to Kanagawa Prefecture than one can be on the way from San Francisco to California. It also strains credulity that marines would depend on army men to inspect port facilities, that they should require such facilities to come ashore, or that the army would run such an errand for the marines many miles deep in enemy territory. Indeed, they did not, nor did they need to. The Fourth Marines came ashore at Futtsu Saki and Yokosuka in the customary fashion, over the beaches.

FIGURE 31 • Marines come ashore at Yokosuka, August 30, 1945. (U.S. Marine Corps, NARA Photo 127-N-133859)

Naval vessels began docking an hour later, after the marines themselves had secured the Yokosuka Naval base. The first time anyone from Atsugi ventured near was when the Eleventh Airborne Division effected patrol contact with the Fourth Marines on the afternoon of August 30.[30] Aside from these facts, a glance at a map makes clear that Tanaka's account is geographically implausible.

Even if soldiers had ventured overland to inspect port facilities, they would have gone nowhere near Tokyo. The location of the Komachien brothel (in the neighborhood of the present-day Shinagawa aquarium and Haneda Airport) is not on any conceivable path between Atsugi and Yokosuka. Moreover, the American plan as recorded by Eighth Army commander Lt. Gen. Robert Eichelberger, called for a landing at Atsugi, followed by an advance to a relay point between Fujisawa and Kamakura. Seaborne landings were to be conducted at Yokosuka. Allied commanders

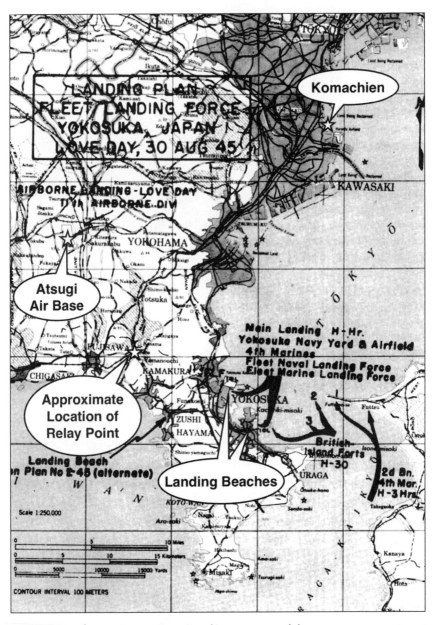

MAP 1 • Map of operations on Love Day (August 30, 1945) (Adapted from Charles R. Smith, *Securing the Surrender: Marines in the Occupation of Japan*, Marines in World War II Commemorative Series [Washington, DC: History and Museums Division, Headquarters Marine Corps, 1997], 7)

specifically avoided Tokyo because they thought the extent of destruction there would render its facilities inadequate and its population hostile. Eichelberger told his staff, "I look forward to a city considerably devastated by war with the remaining population under poor control, the public parks filled with homeless, and all suburban areas and the remaining people in a nasty mood."[31] Finally, the road between Tokyo and Yokohama was a bombed-out ruin. Soon after landing in Yokohama, PHW Chief Crawford Sams traveled that road to investigate a rumored outbreak of cholera in the capital. The best speed he could make was five miles an hour.[32] According to historian and Occupation veteran Stanley Falk, it was not until 1948 that one could travel the road in an ordinary sedan.[33]

To summarize:

1. Kanzaki's and Kaburagi's stories are incredible and contain sensational details that should clearly invite skepticism.
2. In Tanaka's presentation, the least credible details of these accounts are not mentioned.
3. Kaburagi's and Kanzaki's stories contain details that are demonstrably false.
4. Tanaka demonstrates awareness of the facts that contradict the story's details.
5. In Tanaka's presentation the demonstrably false details have been altered or omitted.
6. Tanaka's presentation contains additional demonstrably false details that were not present in his source material and that, superficially at least, render the telling more plausible.

These examples are neither isolated nor exceptional. Tanaka employs *panpan* literature freely. He uses Gotō as his sole source for two groundless and absurdly sensational stories of organized sexual atrocity. In one, a group of GIs in three trucks approached a hospital, and at the sound of a whistle about fifty of them "invaded and raped 17 nurses, 20 nursing assistants and more than 40 female patients" and "murdered a two-day-old baby and two Japanese men who tried to intervene."[34] In another, a group of between thirty and sixty U.S. servicemen surrounded a block in Nagoya, cut the telephone lines, and "intruded into a number of houses simultaneously, raping many girls and women between the ages of 10 and 55 years."[35] Both of these stories, indirectly citing Tanaka, feature prominently in the article "Rape during the Occupation of Japan" in Wikipedia.[36] Altogether, in a total of 195 notes in two chapters, Tanaka either directly or indirectly cites the fraudulent sources detailed in the previous chapter no fewer than 56 times.[37] This includes a staggering 17 out of 19 notes in the section he titles "Testimonies of Victims of Sexual Violence Committed by the Occupation Troops," to which he alluded in his response to Roger Brown's H-Japan post.[38]

Incredibly, these are not his most problematic citations. Those come in references to official police histories and government records. Tanaka tracked down a wealth of valuable sources from both the Japanese and American governments. However, Tanaka's presentation of them gives very strong false impressions. For example, citing the official history of the Hiroshima Prefectural Police, Tanaka asserts that there were 263 reports of GI crimes between October and December 1945, of which 84 were rape. For 1946 Tanaka claims that 303 of 800 crime reports were rape cases—"the single most common crime."[39]

In fact, the Hiroshima Prefectural Police history states that between October and December 1945 the number of rape cases reported was 14, not 84. Eighty-four was the number of robberies.[40] Similarly, the figure given for rape in 1946 was 23, not 303. Again, 303 is the number of reported robberies.[41] It is difficult to see how Tanaka misread these figures, particularly as the numbers for 1945 appear on the very pages in which the history plainly states, "The Occupation troops did not engage in the sort of lawless activity that had been anticipated" and specifically notes, "In particular there were relatively few of the kinds of sexual crimes that had initially been feared."[42] Tanaka's presentation of this material nearly inverts reality.

However, this pales in significance compared to Tanaka's misrepresentation of one of the most important documents he discusses, a memorandum from GHQ's Public Health and Welfare Section (PHW). In this document, Lt. Col. Hugh McDonald, chief of the Legal Subsection of PHW, described "the practice of procuring girls" to serve in brothels. Tanaka cites McDonald thus:

> "The girl is impressed into contracting by the desperate financial straits of her parents and their urging, occasionally supplemented by her own willingness to make such a sacrifice to help her family.
>
> . . .
>
> "It is the belief of our informants, however, that in urban districts the practice of enslaving girls, while much less prevalent than in the past, still exists . . ." [Tanaka's ellipsis]

Tanaka then implies that GHQ knew human trafficking was used to support brothels that had been set up for its troops and cared nothing about the women who were trafficked:

> Yet, for most of the staff of the PHW Section, whatever their thoughts on the plight of the women, their most important task was quickly to reduce a high VD rate among the Japanese sex workers.
>
> . . . For them, the main concern was the health of their own men and not the health and welfare of the Japanese "service women."[43]

Both of these suppositions are false. The document described not the brothels that Japanese police had organized for the Occupation troops but, rather, Japan's decades-old licensed prostitution system. (See chapter 2.) It had nothing to do with prostitutes serving GIs. Tanaka himself noted this fact only two pages later.[44] Even more troubling is Tanaka's assertion that the welfare of the Japanese women did not concern GHQ. In 2007, this interpretation made headlines around the world when the late AP journalist Eric Talmadge wrote an article relying almost entirely on Tanaka's book and an interview with Tanaka himself. In it, Talmadge declared, "An Associated Press review of historical documents and records—some never before translated into English—shows American authorities permitted the official brothel system to operate despite internal reports that women were being coerced into prostitution." Talmadge clearly did very little, if any, reviewing of actual documents. He did quote the same document Tanaka did, but he placed a period where Tanaka admitted an ellipsis.[45] In this difference lies much significance, for Tanaka's elision was crucial. Tanaka's quote, in fact, stops midsentence. The original passage reads:

> It is the belief of our informants, however, that in urban districts the practice of enslaving girls, while much less prevalent than in the past, still exists *and that the following corrective measures should be taken*:
>
> (1) Entire abrogation of the law, to include all of Japan.
> (2) Invalidation and outlawing of all contracts by which the parents or head of a family may be financially benefited and all contracts by which a girl may be brought into such existence without her consent.
> (3) Provision of a penalty much more severe than the present 3 months or 100 yen for anyone who obstructs or hinders the effort of any woman to abandon such existence. [Emphasis added][46]

As described in chapter 2, MacDonald acted on these suggestions, and they formed the basis of the first draft of GHQ's order to abolish licensed prostitution. In other words, the victims described in the document were not serving American troops. Furthermore, American authorities did not turn a blind eye to their plight. On the contrary, very soon after GHQ learned that some of the women in Japan's licensed brothels had been enslaved, it took peremptory action to outlaw the whole system. Moreover, this action, which came weeks before the new constitution was drafted, marked the first time in Japanese history that any law, ordinance, or order recognized a woman's right to be sovereign of her own sexuality. GHQ was not indifferent to the rights of women. It respected them in a way that was unprecedented in Japanese history. Once again, this is nearly the polar opposite of Tanaka's presentation.

Such misrepresentations are legion. Some documents have no relation to Tanaka's assertions. For example, he claims one letter to GHQ from the CLO "complains that many of the low-paid Japanese employees of the occupation forces, in jobs like telephone operators, contracted VD from GIs."[47] The document does not even discuss civilian employees of the Occupation, let alone suggest that they contracted VD from GIs.

Tanaka repeatedly puts scare quotes around his own formulations in contexts that make them appear to be drawn from documents cited. Only when one has traced down the actual documents does one learn that "service women" is how Tanaka himself describes Japanese prostitutes and that the words appear in none of the American documents he cites, even though he persistently puts them in quotes.[48] Tanaka also writes, "Despite their knowledge of the factors related to the spread of the diseases, both the staff of PHW Section and the military chaplains shared the same belief that the source of 'evil VD' was the Japanese women." Here again, "evil VD" is Tanaka's formulation.[49] The same is true of "shameless Japanese women."[50]

The examples above are representative, but far from exhaustive. To paraphrase Oscar Wilde, Tanaka's writing on this subject is both true and significant. Unfortunately, the true parts are not significant and the significant parts are not true. In short, Tanaka's work is untrustworthy and pernicious and has exercised an outsize and unambiguously baneful influence on the fields of Occupation studies and military sexual violence. Unwary readers come away not only knowing less than they did prior to exposure but also laboring under the delusion that they know more.

◢ JOHN W. DOWER

John W. Dower's *Embracing Defeat* was a publishing sensation. Winner of numerous awards, including the Pulitzer and Bancroft Prizes, it provided many readers with their first exposure to Occupation history. It is a singularly influential work. Although the section of this work that deals with prostitution and sexual violence makes up a very small part of the whole, it has powerfully shaped popular and scholarly perception of these issues. However, Dower's coverage of these subjects is almost wholly dependent on dubious or fraudulent sources.

Dower's selection of sources is poor, and his scrutiny of them is insufficient. Out of a total of sixty-one citations from the twenty-seven notes in this section, exactly two of them involve primary sources, and both discuss rumors prior to the American arrival.[51] Of his remaining citations, only nineteen are from sources predating 1974.[52] Seven of these are from a 1974 collection of Kanzaki Kiyoshi's earlier *panpan* writings.[53] Another is erroneous and is actually from 1974.[54] Four are quotations or reprints in later publications.[55] One is meant to provide anecdotal support for a preposterous statistic.[56] Four come from a sensationalist "exposé" penned by an access journalist.[57] Finally, there are two citations from a single page in an almanac published by the Asahi newspaper publishing company.[58]

This is a rickety foundation upon which to build a historical narrative, and unsurprisingly it collapses almost immediately under the weight of decades of accumulated myths. Dower headlines his section on prostitution with two stories taken from popular sources. The second of these is a radio broadcast of an interview with a nineteen-year-old prostitute, identified as "Rakuchō no Otoki." This is a highly problematic source toward which Dower exhibits extraordinary credulity.

Dower uncritically accepts that the story comes from a broadcast of an interview with a young street prostitute captured on hidden microphone by national broadcaster NHK.[59] This should have raised suspicion. How did NHK record a broadcast-quality interview by means of a hidden microphone? In 1947 there was no app for that. Less than two years earlier NHK had produced the most important recording in its history, Emperor Hirohito's surrender message. That recording, done with the active cooperation of its subject and considerable time and effort devoted to producing studio-like conditions, is noticeably inferior to the interview with Otoki.[60] A quarter century later, Richard Nixon, then the most powerful man in the world, installed a secret microphone system in the Oval Office, and its recordings were full of indistinct words.[61] It is simply not credible that NHK successfully produced a broadcast-quality recording in a noisy outdoor urban environment in 1947. As early as 1956 one journalist naively marveled that they could accomplish it with such ancient technology.[62] In 1947 NHK produced recordings by means of platters mounted on old-fashioned turntables that had to be mounted on a stable, level surface. Encouraged by GHQ's Civil Information and Education (CIE) section to do "man on the street" interviews as part of democratizing the media, NHK had a large van to accommodate this equipment. This was then hooked up to a microphone that was approximately the size of a miniature toy football by a very long cord to interviewer Fujikura Shūichi. Fujikura later wrote that he concealed the microphone in the sleeve of his trench coat and then walked with the cord trailing behind him, in one case through heavy pedestrian traffic in rush hour.[63] Fujikura's misadventures with this getup became something of dramatic conceit or even a running gag of these programs and later recollections. He related one incident in which he was discovered and attacked.[64] In the program featuring Otoki, she directly asks him about the cord and whether he planned to use it to tie her and her friends up and take them away.[65] This was not serious investigative journalism. It was more like something out of *Mad* magazine's "Spy vs. Spy." At the end of the interview, Fujikura abandons pretense altogether and signs off, noting that he is standing there *with* the girls whom he claims to have just surreptitiously recorded.[66]

Worse than Dower's choice to treat this account seriously is that his retelling of it is inaccurate. This is understandable, as there was no Wayback Machine in 1947 and subsequent accounts of the interview were thus derived from memories of the broadcast. A partial transcript of the original recording became available only in 2021.[67] Furthermore, in the time after the interview Otoki became a minor celebrity, giving interviews to numerous media outlets, and later accounts no doubt reflect these interviews as well.[68] It is unclear where Dower got his ideas, because his citations for this story are erroneous. They have nothing at all to do with Otoki.[69] Whatever his source, clearly derived from Fujikura's later embellishment, it misled him badly.[70] Dower writes that Otoki "was identified as a leader among the prostitutes in that area."[71] In fact, in the interview Otoki identifies the group not as prostitutes but, rather, as a group of no-good girls—in her description, "female hooligans" (女の愚連隊). She freely admitted that they engaged in petty crime, and some were involved in prostitution, but she specifically denied being involved in it herself.[72]

Dower then presents an extended quotation purporting to be from the interview that has absolutely no intersection whatsoever with the actual transcript. Neither does it accurately convey the tenor of the conversation. Dower's mystery source notes that Otoki's "voice becomes tearful," but according to Ozaki Yoshimitsu, who transcribed the recording, it remained matter-of-fact throughout.[73] Far from the desperate, destitute outcasts presented by Dower, Otoki describes the girls as predominantly "middle class." Most, she said, faced no financial hardship but were there because of friction with their families.[74] Fujikura clearly wanted to present Otoki and the other girls in the area as prostitutes. He himself later frankly acknowledged that he regularly posed leading questions designed to get answers that made for good radio.[75] Otoki's story, as presented by Dower, is nothing more than an urban legend.

In fact, Dower himself seems on some level to understand this, for he calls the story a "parable," which usually connotes an invented tale. He also refers to this story and another one about a letter allegedly submitted to the *Mainichi* newspaper as "sentimentalized images."[76] One could argue that this is Dower's way of giving more sophisticated readers a wink and a nod to let them know that these tales were meant more as a metaphoric expression of the zeitgeist than as strictly factual accounts.

On closer examination, however, this is better explained as part of a pattern in which Dower uses distancing language that has the effect of enhancing his narrative with material from dodgy sources without fully endorsing the sources themselves. Thus, key parts of the story include language like the following: "Ikeda Hayato . . . *was later quoted* as saying that 'a hundred million yen is cheap for protecting chastity.'"[77] "Some, *it is said*, were even barefoot."[78] "The local police chief *is said* to have wept."[79] "*By one estimate*, R.A.A. women engaged between fifteen and sixty GIs a day."[80] "There were soon thirty-three [brothels serving U.S. troops] *by one count*" (all emphasis added).[81] The most outrageous example comes in a mind-boggling footnote about rape by American soldiers. Dower is totally incoherent on this subject. After asserting, "The incidence of rape remained relatively low given the huge size of the occupation force—much as the government had hoped," Dower provides the following footnote: "According to one calculation, the number of rapes and assaults on Japanese women amounted to around 40 *daily* while the R.A.A. was in operation and then rose to 330 a day after it was terminated in early 1946; Yoshimi, 198" (emphasis in original).[82] One hardly knows where to begin. Is Dower actually suggesting that 40, let alone 330, rapes a day is a "relatively low" incidence? If so, why did he italicize the word "daily"? Is he conversely letting sophisticated readers know that some writers have put forth sensational figures in defiance of the actual facts? If it is the latter, he clearly underestimated the sophistication required to divine his meaning. One would be hard pressed to find a more sophisticated reader than writer and literary critic Ian Buruma. Yet Buruma, citing Dower and employing his language, wrote in *Year Zero*, "According to one estimate, forty women were raped every day in the latter half of 1945, which is probably an underestimation, since many cases would not have been reported."[83] Dower's note has brought this figure into general acceptance. It features prominently in Wikipedia entries on the subject in English, Japanese, French, and Italian.[84] Buruma's citation of Dower is also cited as if it constitutes independent corroboration, in English, Japanese, and French.[85]

Dower's source for this figure, Yoshimi Kaneko's *Baishō no Shakaishi* (A Social History of Prostitution), illustrates why his reliance on latter-day sources is so problematic. Yoshimi's work, written in 1992, incorporates the works of Kaburagi, Hashimoto, and Kobayashi and Murase. Her source for the outrageous statistic quoted by Dower is Kobayashi and Murase.[86] They got the figure from Gotō.[87] In such manner, many of the tales that originally appeared in the works described and debunked in the previous chapter have, through complex genealogies of citation, retelling, and recombinant evolution, lost many of their more obvious pornographic edges and acquired superficially respectable pedigrees. They have become inextricably entangled in mainstream academic literature. That Dower's writing exacerbates this problem is evident from his explanatory note on his sources: "The most widely cited author dealing with prostitution in postwar Japan is Kanzaki Kiyoshi, whose various findings are summarized in his *Baishun: Ketteiban Kanzaki Repōto*. . . . Some of the data in this valuable 'report' must be used with care."[88] This is certainly a bold approach to a suspect source. However, Dower's "care" clearly did not involve effective corroboration or even basic fact-checking.

In the pages that follow, Dower directly cites Kanzaki on five additional occasions.[89] Like Tanaka, he relates Kanzaki's story of several hundred GIs finding their way to Komachien as soon as it opened. Like Tanaka, he makes no reference to their supposed olfactory superpowers. Unlike Tanaka, Dower is either unaware or unconcerned that the story is chronologically impossible. In short, his scrutiny consisted of omitting Kanzaki's most sensational claims and corroborating the story with Yoshimi Kaneko's *Baishō no Shakaishi*. Yoshimi excerpted Kaburagi.[90] Dower also neglected to mention one of Kanzaki's more revolting comments. On the concluding page of the very section Dower recommended to his readers, Kanzaki, the former girls' schoolteacher, wrote that it mattered not at all whether Japanese women had engaged in consensual prostitution or whether they had been raped.[91] One would think it mattered to the women. It should have mattered to Dower as well.

Nor is Kanzaki the only rogue from the gallery to grace Dower's pages. Hashimoto, Kaburagi, Kobayashi and Murase, and Gotō—in fact, the whole gang—contribute to his story via intermediaries. For example, Dower writes, "One naïve recruit to the R.A.A. later recalled the terror of her first day, when she was called on to service twenty-three American soldiers."[92] Dower cites an article by Makabe Hiroshi for this tidbit.[93] Makabe in turn cites an article from the magazine *Ushio*, in which the story is presented as the testimony of Yoshikawa Yukiko or Sachiko (the kanji can be read either way), allegedly a former employee of the RAA.[94]

However, the story is transparently plagiarized from Kaburagi, where the testimony comes from Tanaka Kimiko and the dominant emotion is not terror but a thoroughgoing physical exhaustion tinged with no small measure of pride as Kimiko learns from her astonished and admiring madam of the vast number of conquerors she has sated. After a well-earned bath break, she discovers that word of her mad bed skills has spread and that the tall, muscular MP assigned to watch the brothel is demanding his own turn with the now-legendary sexual dynamo. Seeing no alternative, Kimiko relents and in his hard, masculine embrace learns for the first time the true meaning of physical love. It is but the beginning of yet another literal orgy of patriotic devotion and self-sacrifice as she gentles the riled, violent spirits of warrior after warrior until she learns that she has served a total of no fewer than thirty-nine of the brutes—a new record! Not bad for the first day on the job. This goes on for seven pages.[95]

Dower, of course, did not directly employ this tumescent tale, but his near-total dependence on latter-day popular sources guarantees that this sort of pulp permeates and in fact dominates his account. Dower also ultimately relies on such sources to shape his understanding of GHQ's approach to venereal disease, and it goes just about as well as one would imagine. After an unsupported, and in fact insupportable, claim that GHQ had "acknowledged that their major motivation" in abolishing licensed prostitution was "an alarming rise in venereal disease among the troops," Dower writes, "By the time the prohibition went into effect a few months later, 90 percent of the R.A.A. women tested positive for infection. Around the same time, syphilis was detected in 70 percent of the members of a single unit of the U.S. Eighth Army and gonorrhea in 50 percent."[96]

In support of this extraordinary claim, Dower cites a virtual smorgasbord of sources, but every one of them is either unreliable, irrelevant, or both. First up is a two-page article in a popular nineteen-volume retrospective on the years of Emperor Hirohito's reign. The article was so important that its author is not even named. It notes, "it is said that" medical authorities of the Eighth Army tested prostitutes in Yokohama and found that 50 percent of them had syphilis and 70 percent had gonorrhea.[97] Though this does contain the 50 and 70 percent figures noted by Dower, they are for prostitutes, not GIs, and the figures for gonorrhea and syphilis are reversed. Second is Yoshimi Kaneko's *Baishō no Shakaishi*. Yoshimi writes that the "infection rate" of "one unit in the US military" was 68 percent. Yoshimi provides no citation, but investigation reveals that her source is Kobayshi and Murase.[98] Kobayashi and Murase got their information from Gotō.[99] Another citation of Yoshimi is nothing but a tangential reference to statistics regarding women arrested for streetwalking in May 1947. Their VD rate was nowhere near 90 percent; they did not work for the RAA, and the connection between these 1947 figures and Dower's assertion about statistics in 1946 is totally obscure.[100] Then there is an article by freelance journalist Takahashi Kazuo that discusses streetwalker roundups. The relevance to Dower's assertions is again totally obscure.[101] Next up is Kanzaki, who at last provides some information that supports Dower's claim. According to Kanzaki, a report of the Tokyo Hygiene Department stated that 90 percent of RAA prostitutes were infected with venereal disease, and a survey of the American First Division showed that 70 percent of American soldiers were infected with venereal disease. Setting aside for a moment the veracity of this claim, it is irrelevant. The First Division was not even in Japan.[102] Though he does not state it, Kanzaki's information clearly comes from Kaburagi, whose ignorance of the U.S. military he repeats.[103] Kaburagi's information appears to be a distortion of a claim put forth by Kobayashi and Murase, who cite the Tokyo Hygiene Department as submitting a report to GHQ stating that 90 percent of RAA prostitutes were infected with venereal disease and that after one division of *marines* were examined in the passive voice by agents unknown, 70 percent of them were diagnosed with venereal disease.[104] At this point, the reader can probably guess the ultimate destination on this well-trodden path: neo-Nazi and sensationalist crackpot Gotō Tsutomu's *Zoku Nippon no Teisō*.[105]

Dower's reliance on *panpan* literature and sources derived from it distorts his understanding of prostitution in Japan at a fundamental level. This is revealed in Dower's comments on GHQ's decision to ban licensed prostitution (see chapter 2): "Ending formal public prostitution did not, of course, mean the end of prostitution itself. The trade simply was carried out more privately—and venereal disease naturally remained difficult to control."[106]

Here Dower seems to have no idea what "public prostitution" meant or why GHQ banned it. He suggests that "public prostitution" meant simply prostitution carried on openly as opposed to "carried on more privately." In reality, what Dower translated as "public prostitution" can also be rendered as "licensed prostitution," which was a legal designation for a system that relied on debt bondage and indentured servitude.[107] The primary reason for the order, as PHW's legal adviser J. V. Zaccone put it, was that "SCAP will not sit idly by and allow women to be bought and sold into prostitution." The problem was neither the venue nor the degree of discretion. Its purpose was to emancipate girls and women "who are made to prostitute themselves against their will anywhere, whether in dance halls, beer halls, restaurants, or geisha houses."[108]

The narratives flogged in *panpan* literature sometimes seem to have impaired Dower's judgment. Of *panpan* Dower wrote, "Some panpan serviced only Japanese customers; others, much more numerous, serviced

Americans. The distinction was rigidly observed in certain *shima*, and panpan who transgressed either turf or race could be subjected to abuse or even torture by other prostitutes." Dower's evidence for these assertions is not even dubious. It is nonexistent. He makes no reference to any source whatsoever.

His first claim, that many more women served Americans than Japanese, is a prima facie absurdity. The average American man in Japan certainly had more disposable income and, according to one survey, paid about twice as much as Japanese clients.[109] Nevertheless, they were not millionaires, nor were they omnipresent. During the Occupation there was a maximum of 354,675 American troops in Japan and an average of 164,000. By contrast, according to Japanese census figures from 1950 there were an estimated 11,222,000 Japanese men between the ages of twenty-three and forty-four in 1950 (making the same men between eighteen and thirty-nine in 1945).[110] In other words, there was a minimum of 31 Japanese men in this age group and during the entire Occupation an average of more than 68 of them for every Allied serviceman. The idea that the prostitutes serving the latter group were "much more numerous" than those serving the former does not merit serious consideration, but the trope of Americans as satyric supermen was constantly flogged in *panpan* literature. It became so dominant in the postwar popular imagination that at one point during a Diet interpellation in 1952, Hara Chōei, deputy chief prosecutor in Niigata, found it necessary to inform legislators of the obvious fact that most patrons of Japanese prostitutes were in fact Japanese.[111]

As for Dower's second claim, it is extraordinary and thus requires extraordinary evidence. Again, Dower provides none. Though it is certainly not outside the realm of possibility, I have never seen credible reports of women torturing one another over poached clientele. However, violent altercations between prostitutes were a feature of *panpan* literature and cinema, where they served roughly the same dramatic function as mud-wrestling scenes in American cinema. The sensationalist and best-selling novel *Nikutai no Mon* (Gates of Flesh) by Tamura Tajirō contains some famous scenes featuring behavior very much like that Dower describes.[112] Ironically, Michael Molasky, a scholar of Occupation-era literature, remarked on how profoundly this sensationalist novel had influenced popular perceptions of prostitution, particularly on the question of violence between the women involved, noting that it "provided a perfect example of how fiction can shape social knowledge and acquire the status of truth."[113] The same could be said of almost the entirety of Dower's coverage of this subject.

In sum, Dower's writing on prostitution during the Occupation of Japan has some value as an introduction to how the problem was understood in the Japanese popular imagination in the postwar years. This, however, should be the contribution of folklorists, not historians.

TAKEMAE EIJI

Eiji was the dean of historians of the Occupation era. His transgressions are neither as extensive as Dower's nor even close to being as egregious as Tanaka's. Nevertheless, they bear enumeration due to Takemae's immense prestige. As Takemae tells the story, GIs frequently committed "gang rapes and other sex atrocities," and American military commander Robert Eichelberger ruthlessly crushed the one attempt at organized resistance to these outrages.[114] Incredibly, the only source he gives for this story is Eichelberger's memoir. Unsurprisingly, Eichelberger tells the story differently. According to the general, citizens in Yamata became annoyed by the visits of off-duty GIs and formed a vigilante association: "Unarmed GIs were set upon and assaulted—to warn them and their comrades that they were not welcome in Yamata during their off-duty hours. The climax of this campaign of terrorism came when two Americans, returning to their barracks, were seized and beaten for two hours." In response, Eichelberger ordered a show of force and had the ringleaders arrested and sentenced to long prison terms.[115] Were the abducted men guilty of gang rape or other sex atrocities? Eichelberger certainly does not indicate that, and Takemae provides no evidence that they were. What is worse, if there was ever a historian who could have done so, it was Takemae.

It was he, after all, who collated and edited much of the massive correspondence between the Japanese government's Central Liaison Office and General Headquarters. Thus, he has sufficient evidence to write of the misbehavior of American troops in the opening days of the Occupation. In fact, the first chapter of this book relies greatly on the volumes Takemae edited. Thus, he is also in a position to know that his repetition of Tanaka's ridiculous claims about there being 1,336 reports of rape in Kanagawa in the first ten days of the Occupation was utterly without foundation. Similarly, he should have known that the claims of frequent "gang rapes and other sex atrocities" preceding the abduction of unarmed GIs was completely spurious. This is all the more ridiculous as Takemae himself cited a news report detailing a completely incongruous total of 9 cases of rape in the first week of the Occupation in the Yokohama area immediately before giving the 1,336 figure for "ten" days in Kanagawa (the prefecture whose largest city is Yokohoma). The level of cognitive dissonance in these sentences would seem hard to exceed, but Takemae seems game to try. In note 33 on page 579 of his book, Takemae incredibly cites one of the innumerable reissues of *The Chastity of Japan, Shi ni Nozonde Uttaeru* (Our Dying Words Accuse), as if it were a factual account of the lives of prostitutes during the Occupation immediately after citing the very chapter of Molasky's book, which established that it was a politically motivated hoax.[116] In fact, it was from this bizarre footnote that I first learned of both works.

Takemae Eiji was a pioneering scholar of Occupation studies. Although his work does have a left-wing bias, it is on the whole not only generally reliable but also the best place to begin one's research. His coverage of this subject, however, has done him no credit whatsoever.

HAYASHI HIROFUMI

Hayashi Hirofumi is a prominent scholar of sexual violence and exploitation by military forces. He has written many works on this subject, and unlike the scholars discussed above, he does not cite any *panpan* literature. Hayashi has also done prodigious research in archives around the world. He scoured the National Archives in the United States for documents relevant to GHQ's handling of prostitution and venereal disease, reproduced them, and compiled them into a set of nine volumes published by Sōtensha between 2016 and 2017.

In collecting this information, Hayashi has performed a valuable service. Researchers at many institutions now have access to a wealth of documentary material. Indeed, many of the documents I consulted in writing chapters 2 and 3 are now available in this excellent collection. Moreover, Hayashi did not merely collect these documents; he actively engaged with them. As anyone who has worked with the GHQ/SCAP records at the National Archives can attest, they are kind of a mess. Documents are filed in a haphazard way. Moreover, sometimes they are out of order, with some clerk having numbered them so that page 2 of a given document has a different and nonsequential document number from page 1. Hayashi's collection corrects these mistakes.[117]

Hayashi's attention to the documentary record has clearly paid dividends. He is far better informed than most of his colleagues and has clearly rejected some of the biases that have long infected this field. Hayashi is one of the few writers on prostitution during the Occupation that has accurately noted that concern for human rights was behind GHQ's decision to ban licensed prostitution.[118] Hayashi is also one of the very few scholars to present reasonable figures based on documentary evidence for the level of sexual violence perpetrated by American servicemen during the Occupation and has done this based on documents he discovered in locations I myself have not yet investigated.[119]

Despite this, Hayashi's understanding of sexual violence and exploitation has evidently been deeply influenced by the narratives common to the *panpan* literature of the early postwar period. Hayashi writes of GHQ's "proactive" embrace of the prostitution facilities set up by the Japanese police.[120] Throughout his writing, he refers to all prostitution aimed at Allied troops as "the RAA." This is reflects neither the documentation nor the reality; rather, it derives from the narratives of *panpan* literature. The adoption of "RAA" as shorthand for "prostitution for Americans" is something that became common in *panpan* literature after Gotō Tsutomu's *Zoku Nippon no Teisō*. This English-language acronym, so reminiscent of the alphabet organizations introduced by the Americans (GHQ, SCAP, PHW, ESS, CIE, GS) and alien to previous Japanese experience, conjures an image of Occupation authority. No doubt this was the primary reason Gotō seized on this organization and ascribed to it a power, reach, and significance it never had. To use "RAA" in this manner is to treat folklore as history.

Panpan literature appears to have exerted a direct effect on Hayashi's writing in his presentation of a 1954 incident in the Diet. Socialist Diet-woman Tokano Satoko asked Izeki Yūjirō of the Foreign Ministry what the United States was doing about the problem of prostitution near its bases. Izeki replied that the United States had been doing all that it could and that prostitution in Japan was clearly causing controversies in the United States. Moreover, venereal disease rates were one way that a commander's performance was measured. Generally speaking, the United States attempted to place brothel areas off-limits, and the result was that American actions taken to suppress prostitution sometimes had the effect of creating a de facto red-light district in the remaining areas, as proprietors moved businesses to attract American clientele.[121] Hayashi somehow twisted this response into proof that the United States was using its power to assume control over prostitution in Japan for the entertainment of its troops.[122] Though Hayashi never cites him, Kanzaki Kiyoshi made a virtually identical argument in 1954.[123]

Another of Hayashi's arguments reflecting *panpan* stories is that PHW chief Crawford F. Sams was instrumental in constructing GHQ's "pro-prostitution policy."[124] No such policy ever existed, but Hayashi's argument that GHQ's attitude was one of "official recognition" (公認) is nearly identical to the argument made by Gotō in *Zoku Nippon no Teisō*, even employing the same term.[125] Furthermore, this, like so many other Gotō inventions, is pure nonsense. Worse, in order to ascertain its fictional status Hayashi need only to have looked at page 290 in volume 7 of his own document collection. There one can see Sams' statement from December 26, 1946: "It is recommended that the memorandum to the Imperial Japanese Government directing the enactment of a law making the act of prostitution illegal be approved."[126] As chapter 2 illustrated, the story was far more complicated than this single document in isolation would suggest. Nevertheless, this document alone is sufficient to make nonsense of Hayashi's narrative, and it is in the collection he himself compiled. Hayashi is selective about which documents he employs.

A similar problem exists with Hayashi's contention that the Americans solely blamed Japanese women, particularly prostitutes, as possible sources of infection.[127] In fact, the United States was well aware that its own troops were contributing to the problem.[128] U.S. military leaders made prodigious efforts to restrain them. Indeed, the bulk of the final two hundred pages of documents in volume 8 of Hayashi's collection are devoted to this topic.[129] PHW also understood that venereal disease was widespread in the Japanese population generally and was frustrated that Japanese medical personnel often regarded VD as a problem confined to prostitutes. Once again, there is copious evidence of this in Hayashi's own document collection.[130]

Hayashi also asserts that the American military had no respect for the human rights of women involved in prostitution and regarded them as equivalent to an "enemy."[131] While his assertion is certainly true of some MPs and local base commanders, it is just plain wrong to ascribe such an attitude to the Occupation force as a whole. Documentation attesting to this basic fact comprises virtually the entirety of volume 7, the largest volume in Hayashi's collection.[132]

Hayashi is not only selective in which documents he consults; he is also parsimonious in his footnotes. Most of Hayashi's archival citations are nearly opaque, consisting only of a records group and a box number. In the case of the GHQ/SCAP records at the U.S. National Archives and Records Administration, these are not standard document boxes, but cubic-foot storage boxes. They contain an immense number of documents. In fact, in his collection Hayashi devotes five entire volumes and part of a sixth (vols. 4–9) totaling more than 1,700 pages to documents from a single one of these boxes (box 9370). Hayashi often merely describes documents, sometimes inaccurately. Sometimes he provides neither date nor the title. In one article, he informs the reader, "Anything not footnoted in this paper comes from this box [9370]."[133]

Worse, if one manages to track down Hayashi's documents, they do not always say what Hayashi claims. One example comes in what Hayashi touts as his seminal work on the subject. Hayashi himself translated the article's title into English as "The US Military's Pro-prostitution Policy in Japan during the U.S. Occupation and in the 1950s."[134] In this article Hayashi writes, "Brigadier General [George] Rice of the 8th Army suggested that while the 8th Army would probably put houses of prostitution off-limits, the Japanese side might do them the favor of establishing 'amusement houses,' where it could be possible to have sexual relations with the hostesses."[135] If it were true, this would show that Occupation medical officers actively evaded army policy in order to provide sexual services for GIs. This is Hayashi's central thesis, so such a document would be a momentous discovery. Oddly, however, Hayashi provides no evidence whatsoever. In place of a citation, he simply rants about how nefarious Crawford Sams was.[136]

When one finds and peruses the actual document, it becomes clear that Hayashi's description can most charitably be described as "inspired by real events." Rice did attend a meeting on the subject of venereal disease on October 21, 1945. He did discuss houses of amusement where prostitution might be carried on. There real events end and inspiration takes over. According to the minutes taken by Lt. Col. James Gordon, head of PHW's VD control branch,

> General Rice pointed out that the demand for recreational and amuse-ment outlets for military personnel will greatly exceed the Army's ability to supply them, especially when the winter closes down outdoor sports. He expressed the opinion that the 8th Army would adopt a policy of placing off-limits all houses of prostitution. He envisages the possibility, however, that Japanese might establish "houses of amusement" which might or might not feature the opportunity for sexual congress with the hostesses as a part of the stock in trade. All females working in such establishments should be subjected to registration and weekly health examinations by competent Japanese physicians according to standards approved and checked by medical officer [sic] of the Army.[137]

In other words, Rice was expressing not hopes but fears. While one can certainly object to Rice's proposed countermeasures and deplore his readiness to infringe on the rights of women, it is clear that he regarded the possible creation of "houses of amusement" as something to be wary of. It was not, as Hayashi suggests, a development he desired. In other words, the "U.S. mili-tary's pro-prostitution policy in Japan" is a creation of Hayashi's imagination.

In sum, despite the enormous amount of archival research he has under-taken, Hayashi's writings on GHQ's handling of prostitution during the

Occupation are deeply influenced by the decades-old legends of *panpan* literature. Moreover, his use of primary resources can be biased in selection, opaque in citation, and inaccurate in presentation, thus rendering his citations largely ornamental.

◖ OTHER WRITERS

Tanaka, Dower, Takemae, and Hayashi are the most influential writers whose works either incorporate or have been shaped by *panpan* literature. Due to the influence of these writers as well as the direct and continuing influence of many *panpan* books and their cumulative effect on the popular imagination over many years, a great many other writers on the subjects of sexual violence and exploitation during the Occupation employ the conceits and stories of this literature as well.

In his 2018 book *Sanitizing Sex*, Robert Kramm cites Kanzaki, Gotō (whom he, apparently following Tanaka, calls "Itsushima"), and Kobayashi and Murase. He cites Gotō for the Hiroshima maidens story but, apparently unaware of the impossibilities involved, leaves the original details unaltered.[138] Citing Dower, he also repeats the unsupported claim about territorial violence between prostitutes.[139] Fujime Yuki cites Gotō for her assertion that Americans raped 3,500 Japanese women during the first month of the Occupation.[140] In addition, though she does not cite him, she adopts Gotō's narrative and language about the RAA and even uses his figures for the number of prostitutes employed.[141] In addition, she cites Kanzaki a number of times.[142] She also invents some whoppers of her own.[143] Hirai Kazuko draws extensively from Kanzaki, Kobayashi and Murase, and Kaburagi.[144] She even explicitly argues against mainstream historical sources and in favor of what she calls reportage, specifically Kaburagi and Kobayashi and Murase.[145] In a footnote she also explicitly endorses Kanzaki.[146]

In addition to these writers, many others have employed the fraudulent sources discussed in the previous chapter. Included in this group are Hayakawa Noriyo, Sugiyama Akiko, Tanaka Masakazu, Furukubo Sakura, Makabe Hiroshi, Takahashi Kazuo, Kishi Kensuke, Murakami Katsuhiko, and Shibata Hideaki.[147] In addition, there are writers who do not provide notes but include *panpan* literature in their bibliographies and use these works extensively. Yamada Meiko and Inoue Setsuko are in this category.[148] The stories and tropes of *panpan* literature have become so thoroughly embedded in the historiography of these subjects that even the most skeptical of readers will find their ideas influenced by these writings. Indeed, I have on multiple occasions come to the sinking realization that one or another commonly accepted "fact" about the subjects has no firm basis in any reliable source. This tendency is exacerbated by the facility with which metaphors of sexual violation and domination come to the minds of those who object to Japan's postwar relationship with the United States. That is the topic of the next and final chapter.

CONCLUSION

"THE GENIUS OF AN ENRAGED PEOPLE"

On August 15, 2019, NHK, Japan's national broadcaster, televised a remarkable ceremony. A new emperor and empress approached a wooden monument inscribed with the phrase "souls of the war dead" for the first time. As the clock moved toward twelve noon precisely, a series of tones marked the countdown. At the appointed time there was a moment of silence, after which the emperor read a prayer for peace and for the consolation of the souls of the departed. Ironically, this essentially secular ceremony is arguably the most important role of the high priest of the Shintō religion. In his constitutional role as "the symbol of the State and the unity of the People," he represents a people that are rarely so united as they are at that moment every year. In that moment they commemorate the passing of a shared aspiration and all those who gave their lives in its ultimately vain pursuit.

Part commemoration and part reenactment, the ceremony recalled the most dramatic moment in modern Japanese history, when NHK carried another special broadcast, beginning at precisely noon on the same date in 1945. In that broadcast the present monarch's grandfather, for the first time, addressed his subjects by radio. His message was for the living, and it was couched in the convoluted language of the imperial court, but it contained a phrase that stuck in the minds of many and made the purport of the message clear: Japan would have to "bear the unbearable and endure the unendurable." He had just, in effect, announced the passing of the Japanese Empire. For many Japanese, the empire had represented, a dream common to peoples around the world, described by philosopher Karl Popper as "a paradise in which the tribal unity reveals itself as the unchanging reality."[1] The emperor;s broadcase represented the death of that dream in Japan. While the nation did endure and even thrive in subsequent decades, the empire was no more. Most painful of all, the sense of tribal unity would never be completely recovered.

On August 15, 1945, as they gathered among the rubble to hear the formal and slightly effeminate voice of their emperor, those who had fervently believed in that dream, and indeed many who only half-believed it, knew despair as only the forsaken children of a defeated god can. Japan had suffered a total defeat; its military had been forced to surrender unconditionally and would soon cease to exist. The country lay open to an enemy most Japanese had thitherto known only through the grotesque caricatures of wartime propaganda and that enemy's own apparently boundless capacity for industrialized pyromaniacal rage.

In the coming weeks, as legions of unimaginably well-equipped, well-fed, and incongruously cheerful Americans descended on the country, many Japanese wondered what had led their country to go to war in the first place. The sight of these strapping young conquerors fraternizing with young women and guilelessly indulging both the curiosity and appetites of Japanese children dispelled the worst of their fears. Over time, however, the sense of relief wore off.

At first the dominant emotion, aside from relief, was confusion. People had been fed so many stories of American savagery and brutality—some of them completely factual—that when they encountered the enemy for the first time, they simply could not believe what they were experiencing. The feelings of the Iwate farmer who believed "this good behavior must be some kind of trick," while certainly not universal, were probably not uncommon either. Some idea of the disorienting experience of defeat and occupation can be gleaned from a glance at the magazine *Nippon no Kodomo* (*Children of Japan*), before and after defeat. The magazine was aimed at children just beginning to learn to read. All of its characters, save those for "Japan" on its cover, and the names of its artists, are in the phonetic *kana* syllabaries, the first characters students of Japanese acquired. The cover of its April edition is illustrated with a group of small children. The little boy in the middle of the group is thrusting a bamboo spear into a straw target dummy, and

FIGURE 32 • Cover of *Nippon no Kodomo*, April 1945
(Kawame Teiji)

FIGURE 33 • Illustration from November 1945 issue of *Nippon no Kodomo* (Ōsawa Shōsuke—courtesy of Ōsawa Yasuo)

the caption reads, "Annihilate the Enemy!" Its pages carry illustrations of a B-29 going down in flames, a school group performing military exercises, and a two-page spread depicting a Special Attack (Kamikaze) Corps strike on an American aircraft carrier.

The November issue features a two-page spread of an idyllic scene in the Japanese countryside with a boy working in a field with his mother. Driving along the road is a jeep with American soldiers. Both the boy and the American in the passenger seat are waving. "'Hello.' 'Hello,' responds the chipper American soldier. Smiling, mother and I say 'goodbye.' A jeep runs along the road in our village."

In such circumstances, confusion should have been expected. Of course, both illustrations tell us more about the imperatives of propagandists than they do about the actual state of affairs. Nevertheless, in neither case were they far off the reality. As artist Yasuoka Akio recalled the shock, "It was like our whole value system was overturned in the middle of the night."[2] Before the surrender, Japanese were conditioned to fight to the last and to sacrifice their lives, whether that served any higher strategic purpose or not. On Saipan and Okinawa many of them, with a wide variation in the degree of volition, did just that. After their arrival, Americans—at least in the aggregate—were friendly and cheerful.

More importantly, by the standards of a mid-twentieth-century mass conscript force, the American military in Japan during the Occupation was well disciplined. When American troops first moved into Japan and order had not yet been established, there was a brief period of lawlessness during which many soldiers committed theft, robbery, and other crimes. This crime wave was exacerbated by the decision to allow Japan to maintain sovereignty over its currency, thus rendering the GIs' scrip worthless. However, even during this relatively chaotic time, violent crimes like rape and murder were rare. They were so rare, in fact, that numerous Japanese commented on the good behavior of American troops. Compared to many other armies during World War II, American troops in Occupied Japan comported themselves in an exemplary manner. However, in a conflict that included Nazi Germany and Josef Stalin's Soviet Union as well as Imperial Japan, the bar is bound to be extraordinarily low. While rape by American soldiers in Japan was relatively rare, it was certainly not unknown.

There can be little doubt that many Japanese girls and women suffered sexual violence at the hands of American troops, and something on the order of 1,100 of them reported rapes by Allied soldiers during the Occupation. Rape statistics are, of course, always burdened with the inaccuracies introduced by false accusations and nonreporting. There are examples of both in the documentary record.[3] Assuming the latter to be the larger problem, it is beyond dispute that a large number of Japanese women were raped by American servicemen. In addition, the fact that the United States was in Japan as an occupier seems to have contributed to American criminality. As Hessel Tiltman pointed out in one of his articles about the leftist campaign to discredit the United States, after the return of sovereignty the GI crime rate had dropped to about half what it was during the Occupation. While that certainly spoke well for the discipline enforced after the Occupation, it inevitably raises the question of why Americans had not behaved equally well before.[4] Similarly, Socialist Dietwoman Fujiwara Michiko's misleading speech before the Diet in which she accused Americans of 1,878 cases of "outrage" against Japanese women was in part so absurd because of the time period she chose to discuss.[5] The rape rate for that period would have been 33 cases per year, which was lower than the average annual rate during the Occupation and in fact lower even than the 37 cases reported during the single month of May 1946.[6] Though the number of soldiers was quite a bit higher in 1946, that still represents a considerable discrepancy. While sexual violence is a problem in all places and at all times, it was also more of a problem during the Occupation than it was after the return of sovereignty.

Nevertheless, the problem was nothing like what is alleged in many Japanese sources. The best sources available provide no evidence that mass rape occurred, and the most reliable figures available suggest that the actual rate of occurrence was well below 1 percent of that alleged in many recent works. Still, accounts of widespread sexual violence are common in Japanese presentations. One estimate quoted in numerous sources would yield a total of more than 700,000 rapes for the period as a whole. Though such figures are simply not credible, they are treated uncritically by many Japanese writers as well as by non-Japanese academics.

American servicemen also frequently availed themselves of the services of Japanese prostitutes, and the related problems of prostitution, sex slavery, venereal disease, and individual liberty greatly vexed GHQ. Their approach to prostitution was undertaken from a standpoint of individual liberty and sexual autonomy and appeared inconsistent and incoherent to many Japanese. Nevertheless, GHQ did not encourage or even connive in the establishment of brothels for its troops. As with rape, however, a number of legends about GHQ's involvement in prostitution have grown up in the intervening years.

Similarly, many legends have grown up around GHQ's approach to venereal diseases. Many tales about GHQ's handling of venereal diseases during the Occupation present it as a series of inept, ineffective measures rendered meaningless by the enormous sexual appetites of American servicemen. In fact, venereal disease was widespread in Japan before the Americans arrived. Despite many frustrations and a number of missteps, PHW ultimately succeeded in putting VD on the path to virtual eradication by about 1950, and by 1953 the decrease in infection rates was already conspicuous.

These facts are easily established by any reasonable investigation of the documentary record. Nevertheless, current literature on these subjects presents a very different picture. Much of it depicts American military personnel as vicious sexual predators, frequently raping Japanese women and forcing them into prostitution, while Occupation authorities condoned this behavior and even used their power to control a nationwide network of brothels and other "amusement centers" that were nothing but brothels by another name.

How did this happen?

There were a number of contributing factors. Some of these are common to the human condition and primal fears about conquering armies and what they do. In the case of Japan, these fears were exacerbated by wartime propaganda playing on these fears and the behavior of Japan's own military as well as by the general belief in mid-twentieth-century Japan that women were the natural spoils of victory. There were many Japanese who continued to believe well into the Occupation and even afterward that their particular essentially peaceful experience had been exceptional.

Moreover, as the Occupation dragged on there was a growing feeling of resentment toward Americans. No doubt many Japanese had initially felt something akin to what diplomat Kase Toshikazu described after MacArthur's grandiloquent exhibition of American magnanimity during the surrender ceremony on USS *Missouri*: "After all, we were not beaten on the battlefields by dint of superior arms. We were defeated by a nobler ideal. The real issue was moral—beyond all the powers of algebra to compute."[7] Many may have continued to feel that way had not so many Americans infused their initial generosity of spirit with large doses of chauvinistic self-righteous censure of all things Japanese.

In war crimes trials, in public proclamations, in education and propaganda, in their everyday dealings with Japanese officials and workaday

Japanese alike, many Americans adopted an air of superiority. Japanese heritage was the constant target of invidious comparisons. In 1954, Harry Emerson Wildes, formerly of GHQ's Government Section, lamented the tendency of Occupation officials to see "all things American as glistening white, all things Japanese as jet black or blood red." "Japanese customs," he argued, "may have differed from our own, but Japan has a right to do her own selecting."[8] Not only did Japan have that right, but it was inevitable that it would exercise that right after sovereignty returned. When it did, many found themselves longing for that sense of unity, purpose, and autonomy they had known before that fateful broadcast, now so solemnly recalled in the Japanese state's most national annual ritual. It was only natural that a desire to return to the status quo antebellum would emerge and many Japanese would grow nostalgic about the parts of their lives that had changed so drastically. Inevitably, for many Japanese men the thing that they grew to miss most was their sense of collective possession of Japanese women and the "sovereignty" over their households.[9]

Americans had destroyed this. SCAP not only elevated women's position; it also forcibly deprived Japanese men of the control they had traditionally enjoyed over their women's sexuality. To make matters worse, economic and demographic factors guaranteed that a very large number of young Japanese women exercised their newly recognized sexual autonomy by consorting with the personnel of the conquering military, a development that undoubtedly made American platitudes about justice and equality seem like cynical posturing. Many men (and not a few women) considered this an illegitimate appropriation of sexuality—that is, a sort of rape—on a national scale.

This was the hurt on which Kanzaki Kiyoshi capitalized when he wrote of the American assault on Japan's "sexual morality." This is why he could casually dismiss any difference between voluntary prostitution and rape.[10] In Kanzaki's view, one he shared with many of his readers, women's sexual autonomy was antithetical to this sexual morality, which was premised on fidelity to Japanese men and women's acceptance of those men's control over their lives and bodies. Kanzaki and other political agitators in concert with opportunistic publishers moved to mobilize this resentment with a flood of *panpan* publications in the 1950s. Over time many Japanese internalized the stories in these books, often presented as real accounts, as the literal truth. This view then became inextricably woven into Occupation historiography.

At first blush, it may seem far-fetched to suggest that abstract symbolism played such a central role in shaping perceptions of the postwar U.S.-Japan relationship. However, it is beyond dispute that critics of that relationship describe it using metaphors of rape and sexual domination with astonishing frequency.

Even before the Americans arrived, many Japanese framed the anticipated encounter in sexual terms.[11] Numerous scholars of Japanese literature and cinema have remarked on this tendency. Relations between GIs and Japanese *panpan* were transformed in nature to coercive and violent acts in which the women had no volition. Rape became so standard as to be a cliché.

In his book *"Minshu" to "Aikoku"* ("Democracy" and "Patriotism"), historian Oguma Eiji observed, "The '*panpan*' were a symbol of Japan's subordination to America."[12] Nothing symbolized defeat to many Japanese so much as the sight of American men with Japanese women. Moreover, it was widely assumed (by American authorities as well as by Japanese generally) that all women who consorted with Americans were, ipso facto, prostitutes. The idea that some Japanese women would willingly be with Americans for any motive save those that were pecuniary was not even entertained.[13] The idea that American men might willingly be with Japanese women for reasons other than to satisfy base sexual urges was likewise rejected.

When a drama called for expressing Japan's straitened circumstances after the war, the image of a *panpan* with an American served as convenient shorthand. In Takarazuka's 2007 drama about Shirasu Jirō, an intimate of Foreign Minister and Prime Minister Yoshida Shigeru during the Occupation, Japan's dire situation is portrayed in one of the opening scenes. Desperate Japanese attempt to eke out a hardscrabble existence among the bombed-out ruins while Yoshida wails to his daughter in a plaintive voice, "Isn't it wretched, Kazuko?" Standing in the center of this pathetic scene is a haughty GI, a Japanese woman at his side pleading with him to make her his mistress (*onrii*).

Shōsetsu Yoshida Shigeru was a 1986 film based on a novel depicting the process whereby Prime Minister Yoshida concluded the San Francisco Peace Treaty and the U.S.-Japan Security Treaty, thus restoring Japanese sovereignty. The first part of the film, depicting Japan during the Occupation, is shot entirely in black and white. After the successful conclusion of the treaties, the film depicts a now-independent Japan in full color. One of the first color scenes shows Yoshida strolling along a beach near his country villa. As if to remind him of the price his country had paid for its new quasi-independent status, a GI and his Japanese girlfriend embrace and then kiss as Yoshida looks on in evident displeasure.

Sexual violation, degradation, and emasculation were, and to a remarkable extent remain, the preferred metaphors for defeat and occupation. It is striking how often they have been invoked to criticize the United States or its allies in the Japanese government. Though this association was first exploited politically by leftists, it occurred to people across the political spectrum. After about a week's negotiation with GHQ over the American-authored draft constitution, Yoshida's aide, Shirasu Jirō, described his experience to an associate as akin to "being locked up and raped" and referred to the resulting constitution as nothing more than a "bastard half-breed."[14]

Nosaka Akiyuki, the writer best known in the West for *Hotaru no Haka* (Grave of the Fireflies), which was subsequently made into an animated film by Studio Ghibli, recalled GIs working with Japanese medical personnel in yet another of PHW's successful campaigns, this one to rid Japan of typhus and other infectious diseases by using DDT to delouse literally anyone they could get their hands on. In Nosaka's recollection, the DDT pump was like a horse's penis, violating him, intruding into his clothes, and leaving its humiliating and telltale white deposits all over his body.[15] Igarashi Yoshikuni, a historian at Vanderbilt University, extended the metaphor, noting that for Nosaka and many other Japanese, the experience was akin to a symbolic rape or castration.[16]

Those critical of a continuing international relationship in which the United States is clearly the senior partner favor conceits of sexual domination and subordination. From both the left and the right, for more than seven decades, critics of the United States and its security arrangements in Japan have presented their home country as an unfortunate woman (or emasculated man) in a relationship with a domineering, violent man. Metaphors of rape, prostitution, subservience, promiscuity, and pollution abound.

Such metaphors are a constant of the discourse about security arrangements. One writer, referring to the changes brought about by the Occupation reforms, lamented "the spiritual castration called 'democratization.'"[17] In the immediate postwar period, the scholar Maruyama Masao lamented the ethos of "naked egoism" that had seized Japan and asserted that in comparison to other Asian countries, where a spirit of nationalism was awakening the people, Japan had "the broken spirit of a helpless *pan-pan*."[18] In 1952 Takahashi Shinichi, an activist concerned with education policy, denounced the postwar education system as a *"panpan* education" that made Japanese forget pride in their history and culture.[19] Gotō Ben, who constantly presented American hegemony in terms of sexual domination, asserted that "security pact" was actually English slang for entering into a sexual relationship with another man's wife after obtaining his consent.[20] Objecting to the possible establishment of an American base in the town of Uchinada, Shimizu Ikutarō asserted that the village was now a "pure maiden" and should be kept that way rather than allowing itself to become like Yokohama and Yokosuka, which were "parasitic whores living off the American military."[21] As mentioned earlier, Tokuda Kyūichi described his countrymen as having been forced into the position of a "supine prostitute."

Critics of the United States are also fond of employing mixed-race children as a metaphor for products of the U.S.-Japan relationship. Usually depicted as the unwanted bastard offspring of unbridled lusts between inferior representatives of both races, these children have long been staples of anti-American propaganda.[22] Testifying before the Diet concerning the issue of rearmament, Kanzaki Kiyoshi referred to the recently founded Police Reserve, a body that would eventually evolve into Japan's Self-Defense Forces, as "the bastard mixed-race child of the Occupation." Kanzaki later used the phrase "mixed-race child" to describe the organizational structure of the new armed force, which had been based on an American model.

"Mixed-race child" was, in Kanzaki's mind, so self-evidently pejorative that he felt no need to provide any more argument than that.[23]

More recently figures such as the late nationalist firebrand Ishihara Shintarō could not seem to get enough of sexual metaphors. Ishihara is arguably best known for his stock phrase "the Japan that can say no," taken from a 1989 book he coauthored with then–Sony chief Morita Akio. The phrase that gave the book its title was actually taken from an essay by Morita, but in a singular act of unabashed plagiarism, Ishihara appropriated it and made it synonymous with himself.[24] Whatever the provenance of the phrase, Ishihara's explanation of its meaning is telling. When he was asked to describe what he meant by "the Japan that can say no," he described a situation in which America and Japan were married and Japan, as the wife, "can clearly say no when she wants to, unlike a mistress who can be discarded if she says no." Later he returned to the theme: "It's not the mistress is asking her master to have her registered officially so that she can formally become his wife. We are the wife, we must be recognized as such."[25]

Years later, when Japan's international position did not look as rosy, Ishihara lambasted the relationship between Japan and the United States in less flattering terms: "[The security alliance] is nothing more or less than a scheme by which America unilaterally rapes the very state itself. Japan has become like a teenage prostitute that America uses for its own gratification. What's worse is that instead of receiving money we are actually paying for this treatment. You can't call this anything but the apex of masochism."[26]

Later, in *Kokka Naru Genei*, meant to be his political memoir after his first retirement, he wrote,

> When I gave my retirement address to the Diet, I, without thinking much about it, compared this country to a eunuch, something with the form of a man but lacking masculine faculty. The reality is even more atrocious. America, out of an excessive fear of Japan, deliberately and completely demolished the true essence of our country. As a result, our former leaders, who came to loathe the idea of our country standing on its own two feet and treading its own path, reduced us to the condition of a concubine with bound feet.[27]

Shirai Satoshi, a sociologist and best-selling author who advocates a greater degree of autonomy in the bilateral relationship, wrote that "it was America that had castrated Japan."[28]

Another who favors sexual metaphors is comic book artist and right-wing activist Kobayashi Yoshinori. In one of his books, Kobayashi denounced pro-American Japanese intellectuals and diplomats who support Japan's security treaty, calling them "yellow cab-men," invoking a derogatory Japanese slang term he defines as "loose girls who are exclusively used by foreigners."[29] Castigating "weak-willed women who spread their legs because they are afraid of being disliked," he compares them to pro-American politicians who think that "being liked by White Americans" is the key to getting high status.[30]

Such metaphors have been a staple of cartoonists for years, presenting Japan or parts of it as fallen women or the victims of unwanted attention from America. A jarring and vulgar use of the theme can be seen in a 1969 cartoon by Mizuno Ryōtarō that depicts Okinawa as a woman being fondled by a U.S. servicemen as she sits astride his enormous erection, depicted as an artillery piece emerging from his loins. In the background Japanese men from the home islands fecklessly protest her mistreatment.[31]

Yasuoka Akio is a very talented artist who has worked in numerous media and genres in the course of a very long career. During the 1960s and '70s, he worked as a cartoonist and employed a somewhat subtler touch to depict Okinawa's plight as the last occupied area of Japan in 1969 during the twilight of American administration. A poignant image of a woman, naked but for an American flag, is captioned "Shōfu Okinawa," or "Okinawa, the prostitute." He recalled that of all his cartoons, it was the one of which he was the proudest, both making good use of his talents as an artist and political satirist and capturing the energy of the time. He also lamented that the energy of those days slowly ebbed as the ruling Liberal Democratic Party embraced the United States more tightly in the coming decades. "In truth," he said, "it should have been captioned 'Japan, the prostitute.'"[32]

Sexualized imagery is nearly ubiquitous in depictions of Japan's subordination to the United States in diplomatic and strategic affairs. It both reflects and reinforces the historical experiences of defeat, occupation, and

FIGURE 34 • "Shōfu Okinawa" by Yasuoka Akio, originally
published in *Shūkan Genron*, April 9, 1969 (Courtesy of Yasuoka Akio)

subordination in the Japanese popular imagination. It was a constant of the
panpan literature used in the anti-American struggles of the 1950s. However,
many of those works took the conceits a step further. Following Communist
propaganda themes, they presented these images of rape and sexual subjuga-
tion as literal truth. *Panpan* stories seeking to agitate against the alliance
with the United States, or simply to profit from more general resentments
against Americans by presenting stock villains in exploitation fiction, flooded
the market. In a short time, the association of American military men and
sexual violence dominated the Japanese popular consciousness and so

became a ready device to discredit American policy toward Japan. Thus, it should come as no surprise that those most responsible for embedding *panpan* literature into mainstream historiography are also political activists who agitate against the U.S.-Japan security alliance. To many of these scholars and writers, conceits of American sexual violence, domination, and exploitation affirm them in some of their most cherished beliefs.

John Dower was a charter member of the Committee of Concerned Asian Scholars (CCAS), who came together in the late 1960s to protest America's involvement in the Vietnam War. In their "Statement of Purpose," they made clear their belief that their scholarship had to serve what they regarded as proper political ends: "Those in the field of Asian studies bear responsibility for the consequences of their research and the political posture of their profession."[33] As to the question of the correct political posture, they spelled it out in October 1969 with their policy statement on Japan: "We oppose continuation of the U.S.-Japan security treaty, which has compromised Japanese independence by turning Japan into a bulwark of American empire in Asia and forcing her into a posture of hostility to China."[34]

In leading this opposition, Dower himself penned an explicit endorsement of the national-front tactics employed by the Communists and left-wing Socialists in their anti-American campaign of the 1950s, the very campaign that produced *Nippon no Teisō* and its sequel: "Since the closing years of the occupation, Japanese critics of the U.S.-Japan relationship have warned against becoming an American satellite. Over the years this slogan has gained rather than lost support, and present-day nationalistic sentiment may well constitute the greatest single factor underlying Japanese opposition to a continuing forced ideological alliance with the United States."[35]

Although that was more than half a century ago, Dower's attitude toward the U.S.-Japan alliance has not appreciably changed. In 2010, he wrote that "Okinawa remained a grotesquely militarized U.S. outpost."[36] In the same book, he repeated Tanaka's claim about 1,336 rapes being committed by U.S. servicemen in Kanagawa Prefecture in the first "ten days" of the Occupation.[37] In a 2019 discussion with Patrick Lawrence and Herbert Bix, he characterized the U.S.-Japan relationship as "egregious."[38] It is little wonder that he gave so little scrutiny to sources that reinforce his passions.

In other cases, some scholars remain under the influence of the conceits of *panpan* fiction even after they have been confronted with evidence that should have made it clear that certain stories are fraudulent or deeply flawed. Mark Selden was another charter member of the CCAS, and it seems that his desire to shape "the political posture of [his] profession" affected his judgment as well. Selden was the editor of Yuki Tanaka's 2002 book *Japan's Comfort Women*. In this book, Tanaka called *Nippon no Teisō* and *Kuroi Haru*, a later somewhat reworked version of *Zoku Nippon no Teisō*, the "most reliable" Japanese publications on sexual violence by GIs in the 1950s. While editors should not be held responsible for every outrageous thing that appears in books they edit—that is the primary responsibility of the authors—Selden should have known this was a problem. Just three years earlier he had been the editor of Michael Molasky's *The American Occupation of Japan and Okinawa: Literature and Memory*, in which Molasky established that the very book Tanaka said was one of the most reliable on the subject of rape and prostitution was, in fact, a hoax.

Of course, Selden was outdone by Takemae, who, as discussed in the previous chapter, cited both the very chapter in which Molasky established that *Nippon no Teisō* was a hoax and a reprint of *Nippon no Teisō*, treating the latter as if it were a factual account of Americans relating to Japanese women. In an essay published almost two decades after the Prague Spring, Takemae treated it as a matter of established fact that "the U.S. was an imperialist country," while appearing sympathetic to the suggestion that the Soviet Union was not.[39]

Yuki Tanaka has identified himself as an "activist" who has "long been involved" in the "anti–U.S. military bases" movement. He presents his understanding of the U.S.-Japan relationship in the following terms: "The Japanese government, always subservient to U.S. military power, continues to agree to U.S. demands eagerly."[40] On this point, at least, he and Kobayashi Yoshinori are in complete agreement. As such, it is little wonder that he eagerly subscribes to *panpan* narratives that depict the Japanese government as literally pandering to the lusts of Americans. It also goes some way to explaining why, after admitting he used a source that was "somewhat dubious" to charge Americans with 1,336 rapes in the first ten days of the

Occupation in Kanagawa Prefecture alone, he recycled that bogus charge not once but twice, the latest time in 2019.[41]

In an interview with the journal *Anpo Haki* (*Scrap the Security Treaty*) in 2012, Hayashi Hirofumi lamented the fact that most Japanese people supported the security treaty with the United States and favored maintaining the status quo. "I feel that overturning this sort of 'common sense' is a task we must accomplish."[42] How exactly should this common sense be overturned? Apparently one way is to depict PHW Chief Crawford Sams as little more than a pimp obsessed with providing clean Japanese women as sexual entertainment for American troops.

U.S. president George W. Bush invoked the Occupation of Japan, and particularly its advancement of the position of women in Japanese society, in defense of the Iraq War. In response Hirai Kazuko wrote that she was inspired to look into the question of whether the Occupation really did help women.[43] While Bush's comparison was facile to the point of simple-mindedness, Hirai's attempt at refutation excels it in absurdity. She concluded that scholars like Iokibe Makoto, a former president of the Japanese National Defense Academy, were sadly mistaken in their assertions that the Occupation was a success. In her telling, this was a male view of the Occupation. From a woman's perspective the Occupation was an abject failure on the grounds that the Americans engaged in such massive amounts of human trafficking and forced prostitution.[44] Ironically, in making this case Hirai relied on violent pornography written by men incensed at the changes that had come over Japanese women since the Americans forced recognition of their human rights. Indeed, journalist Ōya Sōichi, in a retrospective of the Occupation, stated that the biggest winners of the Occupation were Japanese women. And the biggest losers? That was easy: Japanese men.[45] So much for male perspectives. As for actual women, at the end of the Occupation the Japanese Labor Ministry had the radical idea to ask them what they thought. In a survey of 1,352 working women and 494 homemakers, the ministry asked the women whether their positions had improved since the end of the war. By a nearly six-to-one margin they replied that they had: 66.4 percent said their status had somewhat improved, 7.2 percent said that it had improved greatly, only 12.6 percent believed that it had not improved, and 13.8 percent said that they did not know.[46] Nevertheless, in Hirai's telling, these women, the majority of them single and living at the supposed epicenter of American sexual exploitation, just didn't know what they were talking about.

Some writers seem to find these narratives so appealing that they resort to downright conspiracist thinking in order to maintain their suspension of disbelief—or to attempt to get the reader to maintain theirs. Once someone enters this mindset, the lack of evidence is itself evidence. For example, after relating Gotō's story of the Hiroshima maidens, a story that he either knew or should have known to be impossible, Yuki Tanaka writes, "Very little information is available about the cases of high-school students who were deceived or forced to become comfort women [for the Allied soldiers]."[47] One can only wonder why.

Shibata Hideaki, in his 2022 book *Senryōki no Seibōryoku* (Sexual Violence during the Occupation), writes extensively about all the rape allegedly going on in that period. He then notes that Japanese keeping journals, like Yamada Futarō, did not note any mass rape and in fact on the contrary wrote that the Americans were very well behaved. Apparently this was because Yamada was "servile."[48] The same was true of Americans who wrote memoirs of the time. Harry Emerson Wildes insisted that there was very little crime.[49] He, naturally, was covering it up. Hardest of all for Shibata to reconcile himself with was the fact that Beate Sirota, the champion of the rights of women in Japan, wrote nothing whatsoever on the subject of all that rape. It was, in Shibata's eyes, very strange indeed.[50]

Something strange is obviously going on with accounts of mass rape and sexual exploitation during the American Occupation of Japan, but it has nothing to do with Beate Sirota. Edward Gibbon once observed, "The most incredible stories are the best adapted to the genius of an enraged people."[51] At the end of World War II, rage, suppressed though it may have been, was one of the few commodities Japan had in abundance. The resentment many Japanese felt about defeat in that conflict and their country's subsequent inability to emerge from the shadow of its conqueror provided an ample foundation of ire on which to build a number of legends. One of those legends was that GIs perpetrated mass rape and widespread sexual atrocity. The endurance of these legends and their close association with anti-American activists is ample proof that no small measure of resentments persists. Although these legends are mostly nonsense, the concerns and questions about U.S.-Japan relations that inspire them are not necessarily so easily dismissed. American policymakers would be wise to take note of the nationalist indignation that roils the spirits of Japanese across the political spectrum—but not to entertain the fantastic tales of sexual predation such indignation inspires. Such accounts are best regarded not as serious history but as metaphoric expressions of the experience of national humiliation. They are, in other words, incredible stories adapted to the genius of an enraged people.

APPENDIX

STATISTICAL CHART OF REPORTED RAPES

Table source note

Sources: **Column B,** "Shinchūgun no Fuhō Kōi Chikubetsu Hassei Jōkyō, Kugatsu Itsuka Genzai Shirabe," in *Shinchūgun ni Tai Suru [mama] Fuhō Kōi Shinpō Tsuzuri,* JNDL, MOJ 38, reel 13, 383035; **Column C,** "Offenses by Occupation against Japanese, September '45 to Aug. '46," NARA, RG 331, box 288, folder 5: "Offenses against Occupation [*sic*]"; **Column D,** "C.L.O. No. 342: Report on the Misconduct of American Soldiers up to the End of September," October 23, 1945, from CLO to SCAP, NARA, RG 331, GHQ/SCAP, box 408, folder 14-(1-2); **Column E,** "Table of Misconducts Committed by Allied Servicemen" (English; typed) for April–August 1946, December 1946, NARA, RG 331, GHQ/SCAP, box 290, folder 16; **Column F,** "Offenses by the Occupation Forces" (English; handwritten) for September–December 1946, November 1947, January–March 1948, and May–December 1948, NARA, RG 331, GHQ/SCAP, box 290, folder 16; **Column G,** "Rengōgun ni Yoru Fuhō Kōi" (Japanese; handwritten) for February–July 1946, August–October 1946, and June 1947, NARA, RG 331, GHQ/SCAP, box 290, folder 16; **Column H,** "US Occupational Troops [Offenses] against Japanese Nationals," Eighth Army Headquarters, for September 1946–August 1948, October–December 1948, NARA, RG 331, GHQ/SCAP, box 290, folder 17; **Column I,** "Table of Misconducts by Allied Servicemen during November, 1946," NARA, RG 331, GHQ/SCAP, box 502, folder 7 (1-2) 250-1, no. 1; **Column J,** "Provost Marshal Statistical Report" for August–November 1951, NARA, RG 331, GHQ/SCAP, box 351, folder 7 ("Crimes 000.5A"); **Column K,** "Rengōgun ni Yoru Mono," January–April, September, and December 1951, NARA, RG 331, box 351, folder 8 ("000.5B Crimes by Allied Pers."); **Column L,** "Alleged Misconduct of Occupational Troops against Japanese Nationals for the Month of April 1950," NARA, RG 331, GHQ/SCAP, box 263, folder 3; **Column M,** "Offenses against Japanese by Occupation," NARA, RG 331, GHQ/SCAP, box 362, folder 11; **Column N,** "Sex Offenses Investigated" section of graph titled "Major Crimes Investigated 1949," NARA, RG 338, entry A1 209, Eighth Army Records Annual Histories 1949, box 1582, folder 20.

A		B	C	D	E	F	G
Year	Month	Rapes Reported by Japanese Police 8/45	Rapes Reported by Japanese Police 9/45–8/46	Rapes Reported by Japanese Central Liason Office 8–9/45	Rapes Reported by Japanese Police 4–8/45 (English—Typed)	Rapes Reported by Japanese Police 9–12/46; 11/47; 1–3; 5–12/48 (English—Handwritten)	Rapes Reported by Japanese Police, 2–10/46 (Japanese—Handwritten)
1945	August	3					
	September			14 (Includes August)			
	October						
	November						
	December						
1946	January						
	February						61 (Includes Attempts)
	March						14
	April				16		16
	May				37		37
	June				31		29
	July		9/45–8/46		19		19
	August		286 Total		29		30
	September		Avg. 23.8/			17	17
	October		Month			18	12 (Not Including Tokyo)
	November					17	
	December				9	9	
1947	January						
	February						
	March						
	April						
	May						
	June						19
	July						
	August						
	September						

H	I	J	K	L	M	N
Rapes Reported by US Eighth Army Provost Marshal	Rapes Reported by Japanese Central Liaison Office, 11/46	Rapes Reported by US Eighth Army Provost Marshal 8–11/51	Rapes Reported by Japanese Police, 1–4, 9,12/51	Rapes Reported by US Eighth Army Provost Marshal, 4/50	Rapes Reported by Japanese Police 2–11/50; 7,8,10,11/51	Sex Crimes Investigated by 8th Army Judge Advocate General, 1–12/49
28						
20						
20	17					
12						
11						
15						
9						
14						
16						
21						
26						
29						
24						

A		B	C	D	E	F	G
Year	Month	Rapes Reported by Japanese Police 8/45	Rapes Reported by Japanese Police 9/45–8/46	Rapes Reported by Japanese Central Liason Office 8–9/45	Rapes Reported by Japanese Police 4–8/45 (English—Typed)	Rapes Reported by Japanese Police 9–12/46; 11/47; 1–3; 5–12/48 (English—Handwritten)	Rapes Reported by Japanese Police, 2–10/46 (Japanese—Handwritten)
	October						
	November					7	
	December						
1948	January					4	
	February					7	
	March					3	
	April						
	May					13	
	June					22	
	July					17	
	August					13	
	September					14	
	October					19	
	November					16	
	December					13	
1949	January						
	February						
	March						
	April						
	May						
	June						
	July						
	August						
	September						
	October						
	November						
	December						
1950	January						

H	I	J	K	L	M	N
Rapes Reported by US Eighth Army Provost Marshal	Rapes Reported by Japanese Central Liaison Office, 11/46	Rapes Reported by US Eighth Army Provost Marshal 8–11/51	Rapes Reported by Japanese Police, 1–4, 9,12/51	Rapes Reported by US Eighth Army Provost Marshal, 4/50	Rapes Reported by Japanese Police 2–11/50; 7,8,10,11/51	Sex Crimes Investigated by 8th Army Judge Advocate General, 1–12/49
16						
6						
8						
6						
9						
6						
11						
8						
21						
21						
9						
11 (+3 Tokyo)						
4 (2 Tokyo)						
5						
						7
						6
						10
						8
						5
						18
						23
						9
						7
						5
						7
						8
					9	

A		B	C	D	E	F	G
Year	Month	Rapes Reported by Japanese Police 8/45	Rapes Reported by Japanese Police 9/45–8/46	Rapes Reported by Japanese Central Liason Office 8–9/45	Rapes Reported by Japanese Police 4–8/45 (English—Typed)	Rapes Reported by Japanese Police 9–12/46; 11/47; 1–3; 5–12/48 (English—Handwritten)	Rapes Reported by Japanese Police, 2–10/46 (Japanese—Handwritten)
	February						
	March						
	April						
	May						
	June						
	July						
	August						
	September						
	October						
	November						
	December						
1951	January						
	February						
	March						
	April						
	May						
	June						
	July						
	August						
	September						
	October						
	November						
	December						
1952	January						
	February						
	March						
	April						

H	I	J	K	L	M	N
Rapes Reported by US Eighth Army Provost Marshal	Rapes Reported by Japanese Central Liaison Office, 11/46	Rapes Reported by US Eighth Army Provost Marshal 8–11/51	Rapes Reported by Japanese Police, 1–4, 9,12/51	Rapes Reported by US Eighth Army Provost Marshal, 4/50	Rapes Reported by Japanese Police 2–11/50; 7,8,10,11/51	Sex Crimes Investigated by 8th Army Judge Advocate General, 1–12/49
					7	
					13	
				5	16	
					18	
					9	
					17	
					11	
					9	
					8	
					3	
					1	
			8			
			6			
			9			
			10			
					2	
		11			9	
		10	7			
		6			2	
		5			2	
			4			

NOTES

INTRODUCTION

1. "Hate Speech Law Faces Uphill Battle as Snap Poll May Derail Debate," *Japan Times*, November 17, 2014, http://www.japantimes.co.jp/news/2014/11/17 /reference/hate-speech-law-faces-uphill-battle-snap-poll-may-derail-debate /#.VGny2azLd2k.
2. See the sign held by the man in the top right of the frame in figure 1. Unless otherwise stated, all translations are my own.
3. "Judgment of the International Military Tribunal of the Far East," excerpted in Timothy Brook, ed., *Documents on the Rape of Nanking* (Ann Arbor: University of Michigan Press, 1999), 259.
4. Yoshimi Yoshiaki, *Comfort Women*, trans. Suzanne O'Brien (New York: Columbia University Press, 2000), 49–51; Sarah Kovner, *Occupying Power* (Stanford, CA: Stanford University Press, 2012), 22.
5. See, for example, Mizuma Masanori, "Fūin Sareteita Senryōka no Beihei 'Nihonjin Fujoshi Ryōjoku Jiken' Fairu," *Sapio*, April 11, 2007.
6. Higashinakano Shūdō and Fujioka Nobukatsu, *"Za Reipu obu Nankin" no Kenkyū [Research on "The Rape of Nanking"]* (Tokyo: Shōdensha, 1999), 152.
7. "Takajin no Soko Made Itte Iinkai," *Yomiuri Terebi*, March 6, 2005.
8. Foreign Correspondents' Club of Japan, "Comfort Women Question and Answer," YouTube, August 6, 2015, https://www.youtube.com/watch?v =emQOr75GzvA (accessed March 27, 2016).
9. "Biito Takeshi no TV Takkuru," *Terebi Asahi*, May 27, 2013.
10. Erik Slavin, "Osaka Mayor: 'Wild Marines' Should Consider Using Prostitutes," *Stars and Stripes*, May 14, 2013, http://www.stripes.com/osaka-mayor-wild -marines-should-consider-using-prostitutes-1.220845 (accessed August 23, 2004).
11. "Head of Japan Broadcaster Says Fuss over Wartime Brothels 'Puzzling,'" *Reuters*, January 26, 2014, http://www.reuters.com/article/2014/01/26/japan -korea-comfortwomen-idUSL3N0L003U20140126.

12. Yuki Tanaka, *Hidden Horrors: Japanese War Crimes in World War II* (Boulder, CO: Westview, 1996), 103.

13. Fujime Yuki, *Sei no Rekishigaku* [*A History of Sexuality*] (1997; repr., Tokyo: Fuji Shuppan, 2015), 326.

14. John W. Dower, *Embracing Defeat* (New York: W. W. Norton and New Press, 1999), 579n16. Writers citing the "40 to 330 a day" figure include Kobayashi Daijiro and Murase Akira, *Minna wa Shiranai Kokka Baishun Meirei* (Tokyo: Yuzankaku Shuppan, 1992), 69. See also Inoue Setsuko, *Senryōgun Ianjo* (Tokyo: Shinpyoron, 1992), 105; Yoshimi Kaneko, *Baishun no Shakaishi* (Tokyo: Yuzankaku Shuppan, 1984), 198; John Lie, "The State as Pimp: Prostitution and the Patriarchal State in Japan in the 1940s," *Sociological Quarterly* 38, no. 2 (Spring 1997): 258; and Yuki Tanaka, *Japan's Comfort Women: Sexual Slavery and Prostitution during World War II and the US Occupation* (New York: Routledge, 2002), 163.

15. Thomas U. Berger, *War, Guilt, and World Politics after World War II* (New York: Cambridge University Press, 2012), 132; Ian Buruma, *Year Zero* (New York: Penguin Press, 2013), 38.

16. See, for example, Tanaka, *Japan's Comfort Women*, 128, 130, for allegations of MP misconduct.

17. For example, Yuki Tanaka claims that by March 25, 1946, a quarter of all GIs had a sexually transmitted disease. Tanaka, *Japan's Comfort Women*, 161–62.

18. Malcolm Potts and Thomas Hayden, *Sex and War* (Dallas: Benbella Books, 2008), 3.

19. See, for example, Hirai Kazuko, *Senryō to Jendaa* [*Gender and the Occupation of Japan*] (Tokyo: Yūshisha, 2014), 30; Hayakawa Noriyo, "Senryōgun Heishi no Ian to Baibaishunsei no Saihen" ["The Comfort of the Occupation Troops and the Reorganization of the Prostitution System"], in *Senryō to Sei* [*The Occupation and Sex*], ed. Keisen Jogakuen Daigaku Heiwa Bunka Kenkyūjo (Tokyo: Impakuto Shuppankai, 2007), 47; Arai Eiko, "Kiristo Kyōkai no 'Panpan' Gensetsu to Magudara no Maria," in *Senryō to Sei*, 154; Hayashi Hirofumi, "Amerika Gun no Seitaisaku no Rekishi—1950 Nendai Made," *Josei, Sensō, Jinken*, no. 7 (March 2005): http://www.geocities.jp/hhhirofumi/paper71.htm.

20. Hirai Kazuko, *Nihon Senryō to Jendaa*, 217.

21. Hirai, 223.

22. Eric Talmadge, "GIs Frequented Japan's 'Comfort Women,'" *Washington Post*, April 25, 2007. See also Yuki Tanaka, *Japan's Comfort Women*, 165–66.

23. Richard McGregor, *Asia's Reckoning* (New York: Viking, 2017), 193–94.

24. Sarah Kovner's *Occupying Power* (Stanford, CA: Stanford University Press, 2012) and Chazono Toshimi's *Panpan to wa Dare Nanoka* [*Who Were the*

Panpan?] (Tokyo: Impakuto Shuppankai, 2014) are notable exceptions to these trends.

25. Susan J. Pharr, "The Politics of Women's Rights," in *Democratizing Japan*, ed. Robert E. Ward and Sakamoto Yoshikazu (Honolulu: University of Hawai'i Press, 1987), 221–22.

CHAPTER 1. GI BEHAVIOR DURING THE OCCUPATION OF JAPAN AND IN COMPARATIVE PERSPECTIVE

1. Takemae Eiji, *Inside GHQ: The Allied Occupation of Japan and Its Legacy* (New York: Continuum, 2002), 39–40.
2. William C. Chase, *Front Line General* (Houston: Pacesetter Press, 1975), 126.
3. Norman H. Naimark, *The Russians in Germany* (Cambridge, MA: Harvard University Press, 1995), chap. 2; Harold James, *Europe Reborn* (Harlow, U.K.: Pearson, Longman, 2003), 30; Anonymous, *A Woman in Berlin*, trans. Philip Boehm (New York: Metropolitan Books / Henry Holt, 2005); Timothy Brook, ed., *Documents on the Rape of Nanking* (Ann Arbor: University of Michigan Press, 1999), 10–160 passim; Joseph R. Starr, Office of the Chief Historian, European Command, "Fraternization with the Germans" (Frankfurt-am-Main: Headquarters, European Command, August 1947), 81. See below for details.
4. Fujime Yuki, *Sei no Rekishigaku* (1997; repr., Tokyo: Fuji Shuppan, 2015), 326.
5. Takemae, *Inside GHQ*, 67, 72.
6. "Shinchūgun ni tai Suru [mama] Fuhō Kōi Shinpō Tsuzuri," Japanese National Archive (Kokuritsu Kōbun Shokan), Hensei, 3A, 15, 32-4, 383035.
7. See "Shinchūgun no Fuhō Kōi," reprinted in *Seibōryoku Mondai Shiryō Shūsei*, vol. 1 (Tokyo: Fujiya Shuppan, 2004), 9–10.
8. Robert Eichelberger, diary entry, September 2, 1945, in box 1, folder titled "Miscellaneous: Diary Photocopies: Diaries: July 23–October 20; October 24–December 4," Robert L. Eichelberger Papers, Rubenstein Library, Duke University, Durham, NC.
9. "Shinchūgun no Fuhō Kōi," reprinted in *Seibōryoku Mondai Shiryō Shūsei*, 1:9–10.
10. Eichelberger, diary entry, September 11, 1945.
11. "Shinchūgun no Fuhō Kōi," 1:9–10.
12. Takemae, *Inside GHQ*, 39–40.
13. "C.L.O. No. 342: Report on the Misconduct of Allied Soldiers up to the End of September," October 23, 1945, in National Archives and Records Administration, Archives II (NARA), RG 331, GHQ/SCAP, box 408, folder 14 (1-2).
14. See, for example, Hatoyama Ichirō's criticism of the American use of the atomic bomb in Hatoyama Ichirō, "Shintō Kessei no Kōsō," *Asahi Shimbun*, September 15, 1945, 1.

15. "Ichibu Beihei no Bōkō," *Asahi Shimbun*, September 2, 1945, 2.
16. The U.S. forces, not knowing what to anticipate did not send in many military police in the opening days of the Occupation. The shortage of these forces was so acute that even Eichelberger was obliged to rely on Japanese "gendarmes" (by which he probably meant *kenpei*) to provide for his personal security. See Robert L. Eichelberger, letter to Emmalina Eichelberger, August 31, 1945, Eichelberger Papers.
17. "Kanagawa no Jiko Zengen," *Asahi Shimbun*, September 7, 1945, 2.
18. "Fujoshi e no Bōkō wa Kaimu," *Asahi Shimbun*, September 11, 1945, 2.
19. Kanagawa Ken Keisatsushi Hensan Iinkai, ed., *Kanagawa Ken Keisatsushi*, vol. 3 (Yokohama: Kanagawa Keisatsu Honbu, 1974), 101.
20. Kōchi Ken Keisatsushi Hensan Iinkai, ed., *Kōchi Ken Keisatsushi Shōwa Hen* (Sagawa, Kochi: Sagawa Insatsusho, 1979), 103.
21. Shizuoka Ken Keisatsushi Hensan Iinkai, ed., *Shizuoka Ken Keisatsushi*, vol. 2 (Shizuoka: Shizuoka Keisatsu Honbu, 1979), 583.
22. Yamagata Ken Keisatsushi Hensan Iinkai, ed., *Yamagata Ken Keisatsushi*, vol. 2 (Yamagata: Tamiya Insatsusho, 1971), 897.
23. For additional examples see Wakayama Ken Keisatsushi Hensan Iinkai, ed., *Wakayama Ken Keisatsushi*, vol. 2 (Tokyo: Kawakita Insatsusho, 1992), 494; Ōsaka Fu Keisatsushi Hensan Iinkai, ed., *Ōsaka Fu Keisatsushi*, vol. 3 (Ōsaka: Ōsaka Fu Keisatsu Honbu, 1973), 24; Gifu Ken Keisatsushi Hensan Iinkai, ed., *Gifu Ken Keisatsushi*, vol. 2 (Tokyo: Daiichi Hōki Shuppan, 1982), 418–19; Kagawa Ken Keisatsushi Kenshū Iinkai, ed., *Kagawa Ken Keisatsushi* (Nagano: Tōkyō Horei Shuppan, 1957), 196; Shimane Ken Keisatsushi Hensan Iinkai, ed., *Shimane Ken Keisatsushi Shōwa Hen* (Toppan Insatsu, 1984), 442; Chiba Ken Keisatsushi Hensan Iinkai, ed., *Chiba Ken Keisatsushi*, vol. 2 (Tokyo: Tōkyō Horei Shuppan, 1987), 475, 483; Saitama Ken Keisatsushi Hensan Iinkai, ed., *Saitama Ken Keisatsushi* (Tokyo: Tōkyō Horei Shuppan, 1977), 632; Tottori Ken Keisatsushi Hensan Iinkai, ed., *Tottori Ken Keisatsushi*, vol. 1 (Tottori City: Yatani Insatsusho, 1981), 1077, 1095; Kyōtofu Keisatsushi Henshū Iinkai, ed., *Kyōtofu Keisatsushi*, vol. 3 (Kyōto: Kyōto Keisatsu Honbu, 1980), 578; Aomori Ken Keisatsushi Hensan Iinkai, ed., *Aomori Ken Keisatsushi*, vol. 2 (Hirosaki: Ono Insatsu, 1977), 685; Ehime Ken Keisatsushi Hensan Iinkai, ed., *Ehime Ken Keisatsushi*, vol. 12 (Imabari: Hara Insatsu, 1978), 564; Hiroshima Ken Keisatsu Henshū Iinkai, ed., *Shinpen Hiroshima Ken Keisatsushi* (Hiroshima: Kyōdō Insatsu Tōsho, 1974), 879, 884–85.
24. Yamada Fūtarō, *Senchūha Fusen Nikki* (Tokyo: Kōdansha, 2002), 503, 560.
25. Yamada Fūtarō, 639–42.

26. Nagai Kafū, *Danchōtei Nichijō* (Tokyo: Iwanami Shoten, 1987), 285.
27. Ishihara Shintarō interviewed in Spencer A. Sherman and Janice Fuhrman, *Occupied Japan: An Experiment in Democracy* (Oregon Public Broadcasting and Look East Productions, 1996).
28. Tottori Ken Keisatsushi Hensan Iinkai, ed., *Tottori Ken Keisatsushi*, vol. 1 (Tottori City: Yatani Insatsusho, 1981), 1075.
29. "Basic: Ltr, GHQ, AG 000.5 (12 Oct 45) GA, dtd 14 Oct 45, subj, 'Misconduct among Occupation Troops,'" RG 331, GHQ/SCAP, box 408, folder 14-(1-2).
30. "Shinchūgun no Fuhō Kōi," Japanese National Archive (Kokuritsu Kōbun Shokan), Hensei, 3A 15, 11-1 (hereafter cited as "JNA Hensei 3A 15, 11-1"), 0001.
31. See JNA Hensei 3A 15, 11-1, and "Rengōgun Shinchūgun ni Okeru Jiko Hassei Chōsahyō" Kokuritsu Kokkai Toshokan (Japanese National Diet Library, hereafter cited as JNDL), Ministry of Justice (MOJ) 6, reel 2, August 30, 1945–September 25, 1945; MOJ 6, reel 2, and MOJ 38, reel 13, 382940–3034; and the files, whose first part is for some reason untitled, though the section beginning on 383035 is titled "Shinchūgun ni tai Suru [mama] Fuhō Kōi Shinpō Tsuzuri." This second part of this reel is available under the same name in Kokuritsu Kōbun Shokan, Hensei 3-A 15, 32-4, 383035–3156. See also Diplomatic Record Office, reel A'-0012; "Shinchūgun no Fuhō Kōi," reprinted in *Seibōryoku Mondai Shiryō Shūsei*, vol. 1 (Tokyo: Fujiya Shuppan, 2004). In addition, published reports of the Tokkō regarding activities of the Allied Forces during the early Occupation in Iwate Prefecture are reproduced in Awaya Kentarō and Nakazono Hiroshi, ed., *Haisen Zengo no Shakai Jōsei*, vol. 6: *Shinchūgun no Dōkō* (Tokyo: Gendai Shiryō Shuppan, 1999).
32. JNDL, MOJ 38, reel 13, 382988–90.
33. Awaya and Nakazono, *Haisen Zengo no Shakai Jōsei*, 377.
34. Awaya and Nakazono, 370.
35. See, for example, "Re: Forwarding Information with Regard to the Trend of Reports on Unfortunate Incidents," September 15, 1945, NARA, RG 331, GHQ/SCAP, box 408, folder 14 (1-2).
36. Takemae Eiji, ed., *GHQ e no Nihon Seifu Taiō Bunsho Sōshūsei*, vol. 1 (Tokyo: Emu Tee Shuppan, 1999), 298.
37. "Re: Forwarding Information with Regard to the Trend of Reports on Unfortunate Incidents."
38. "C.L.O. No. 342: Report on the Misconduct of Allied Soldiers up to the End of September."
39. Takemae, *GHQ e no Nihon Seifu Taiō Bunsho Sōshūsei*, 1:177, 297.
40. Japanese Diplomatic Record Office, reel A'-0012. 0429 (frame 321).

41. Takemae, *GHQ e no Nihon Seifu Taiō Bunsho Sōshūsei*, 1:451.
42. Telegram, "CLO No. 41. 9th," NARA, RG 331, GHQ/SCAP, box 408, folder 14 (1-2).
43. Takemae, *GHQ e no Nihon Seifu Taiō Bunsho Sōshūsei*, 1:181, plate 345.
44. Diplomatic Record Office, reel A'-0012, 0443 (frame 328).
45. Takemae, *GHQ e no Nihon Seifu Taiō Bunsho Sōshūsei*, 1:731; "C.L.O. #354" October 23, 1945, NARA, RG 331, GHQ/SCAP, box 408, folder 14 (1-2).
46. "Misconduct among Occupation Troops," October 25, 1945, NARA, RG 331, GHQ/SCAP, box 408, folder 14 (1-2).
47. Iokibe Makoto, *Senryōki Shushōtachi no Shin Nippon* (Tokyo: Yomiuri Shimbunsha, 1997), 52–53.
48. "From: Japanese General Headquarters, Tokyo, Japan; To: Commander in Chief, Army Forces, Pacific Command, Manila Philippines; Nr: 29," August 23, 1945, NARA, RG 218, HM 1994, box 08: Chairman's File (Admiral Leahy, 1942–48), folder 43: "Japan 1946 Communications with MacArthur."
49. Iokibe, *Senryōki Shushōtachi no Shin Nippon*, 52–53.
50. "From Commander in Chief, Armed Forces, Pacific, Command, Manila, Philippines; DTG: 29/0731Z," August 29, 1945, NARA, RG 218, HM 1994, box 08: Chairman's File (Admiral Leahy, 1942–1948), folder 43: "Japan 1946 Communications with MacArthur."
51. Arisue Seizō, *Arisue Kikan no Kichō* (Fūyo Shobo: Tokyo, 1987), 89–90.
52. Arisue, 54. See also Takemae, *Inside GHQ*, 61–63. Iokibe and Takemae conflict as to the time of the meeting (10:30 a.m. vs. 8:30 a.m., respectively), but both agree that it took place on the morning of September 3, 1945.
53. Nagai Kafū, *Danchōtei Nichijō* (Tokyo: Iwanami Shoten, 1987), 288.
54. See, for example, "Shinchūgun no Fuhō Kōi: Beihei no Fuhō Kōi," JNA, Hensei, 3-A 15, 11-1, 0029-0030, 0160, 0174–75, 0318–19; JNDL, MOJ 38, reel 13, 382949, 383061, 383069; *Kagawa Ken Keisatsushi*, 205.
55. "Shinchūgun no Fuhō Kōi: Beihei no Fuhō Kōi," JNA, Hensei, 3-A 15, 11-1, 0193, 0214, 0236–37; JNDL, MOJ 38, reel 13, 383123; Takemae, *GHQ e no Nihon Seifu Taiō Bunsho Sōshūsei*, 547, 554, 555, 630.
56. "Shinchūgun no Fuhō Kōi: Beihei no Fuhō Kōi," JNA, Hensei, 3-A 15, 11-1, 0147–48, 0173.
57. "Shinchūgun no Fuhō Kōi: Beihei no Fuhō Kōi," 0101.
58. See, for example, "Shinchūgun no Fuhō Kōi: Beihei no Fuhō Kōi," 0045, 0081, 0105, 0106, 0211, 0230, 0266; JNDL, MOJ 38, reel 13, 383044, 383061, 383066, 383079, 383101, 383106, 383119, 383125.
59. "C.L.O. No. 342: Report on the Misconduct of Allied Soldiers up to the End of September."

60. Takemae, *GHQ e no Nihon Seifu Taiō Bunsho Sōshūsei*, 1:93; JNA, Hensei, 3-A 15, 11-1, 0079.

61. Harada Akira, "Naimushō Kanin Beihei ni Nusumareru," in *Zoku Naimushō Gaishi*, ed. Taikakai (Tokyo: Chihōzaimu Kyōkai, 1987), 312–14.

62. Takemae, *GHQ e no Nihon Seifu Taiō Bunsho Sōshūsei*, 1:175, report 22; JNA, Hensei, 3-A 15, 11-1, 0151–53.

63. "Shinchūgun no Fuhō Kōi: Beihei no Fuhō Kōi," JNA, Hensei, 3-A 15, 11-1, 0073, 0098, 0102, 0176, 0185, 0238, 0285, 0320, 0363.

64. "Shinchūgun no Fuhō Kōi: Beihei no Fuhō Kōi," 0093.

65. "Shinchūgun no Fuhō Kōi: Beihei no Fuhō Kōi," 0276.

66. Hiroshima Ken Keisatsu Henshū Iinkai, *Shinpen Hiroshima Ken Keisatsushi*, 883.

67. "Re: Forwarding Information with Regard to the Trend of Reports on Unfortunate Incidents."

68. Ashida Hitoshi, *Ashida Nikki*, vol. 1 (Tokyo: Iwanami Shoten, 1986), 262 (entries for June 1 and June 2, 1946). Ashida, who despite his misfortune remained resolutely pro-American, described it as the most mortifying thing he had ever experienced. Americans also robbed the compound of former prime minister Hideki Tōjō in a search for souvenirs. Takemae, *GHQ e no Nihon Seifu Taiō Bunsho Sōshūsei*, 1:575.

69. "Rengōgun Shinchūgun ni Okeru Jiko Hassei Chōsahyō," JNDL, MOJ 6, reel 2, August 30, 1945–September 25, 1945.

70. "Shinchūgun no Fuhō Kōi: Beihei no Fuhō Kōi," JNA, Hensei, 3-A 15, 11-1, 0109.

71. "Shinchūgun no Fuhō Kōi: Beihei no Fuhō Kōi," 0136–37.

72. "Shinchūgun no Fuhō Kōi: Beihei no Fuhō Kōi," 0001-0367, especially 0002 (3 counts), 0014, 0015, 0041, 0065 (abduction case), 0082 (second report of same abduction case), 0101 (rape of prostitute not tallied), 0128, 0129, 0268, 0296.

73. See JNDL, MOJ 38, reel 13, 382940–3034, especially 382944–46 (contains five cases), 383071, 383082, 383092, 383111. In addition, there are redundant reports of earlier cases that appear on 383043, 383051. For some reason the first part of this file is untitled, the section beginning on 383035 is titled "Shinchūgun ni tai Suru [mama] Fuhō Kōi Shinpō Tsuzuri." This second part of this reel is available under the same name in JNA, Hensei 3-A 15, 32-4, 383035–156.

74. See Takemae Eiji, ed., *GHQ e no Nihon Seifu Taiō Bunsetsu* (Tokyo: Eivisu Shisutemuzu, 1996), esp. 1:5; and NARA, RG 331, GHQ/SCAP, box 408, folder 14 (1-2), for correspondence from the CLO to GHQ concerning misbehavior by Allied troops.

75. See, for example, "Incoming Message: Japanese Government Radio NR C.L.O. No. 41 DTD 9 September 1945," NARA, RG 331, GHQ/SCAP, box 408, folder 14 (1-2).

76. "To the Supreme Commander for the Allied Powers from the Japanese Government; Central Liaison Office," September 3, 1945, NARA, RG 331, GHQ/SCAP, box 763, folder 8 (1-2).

77. Takemae, *GHQ e no Nippon Seifu Taiō Bunsho Sōshūsei*.

78. Takemae, *GHQ e no Nippon Seifu Taiō Bunsho Sōshūsei*, vol. 1. Rape cases appear on pages 483, 488, 528, 576 (two cases); attempted rapes are documented on 96, 485, 486, 528, 529 (two cases), 530, 561, 568 (two cases), 576 (3 cases), 577; abductions reports appear on 137, 568 (two victims); attempted abductions are on 96.

79. "C.L.O. No. 342: Report on the Misconduct of Allied Soldiers up to the End of September."

80. Catherine Burns, *Sexual Violence and the Law in Japan* (New York: Routledge Curzon, 2005), 22; John W. Dower, *Cultures of War* (New York: W. W. Norton, 2010), n. 96, 541–42; Joanna Rourke *Rape: Sex, Violence, History* (Berkeley, CA: Counterpoint, 2007), 357; Peter Schrijvers, *The GI War against Japan: American Soldiers in Asia and the Pacific during World War II* (Chippenham, U.K.: Antony Rowe, 2002), 212; Takemae, *Inside GHQ*, 67; Yuki Tanaka, *Hidden Horrors*, 103; Yuki Tanaka, "Rape and War: The Japanese Experience" in *Common Grounds: Violence against Women in War and Armed Conflict Situations* (Quezon City: Asian Center for Women's Human Rights, 1998), 174.

81. Antony Beevor, *The Second World War* (New York: Little, Brown, 2012), 776; Search on Google.com, search terms: "reported rape, Kanagawa, 1,336"; Search on Google.co.jp, search terms: "日本占領強姦神奈川, 1,336." Both conducted September 30, 2016.

82. It is hardest to establish in the case of Takemae, whose citation is inaccurate. However, as will be demonstrated below, Takemae's repetition of errors in transcription and interpretation make clear that his source was Tanaka. Takemae, *Inside GHQ*, 579n29. No such sleuthing is necessary in the cases of Beevor, Burns, or Schrivjers. All cited Tanaka.

83. Intriguingly, almost all of the Japanese-language sites citing this figure also replicate the "ten days" error, indicating that they ultimately trace their claims back to the same English-language source as the English-language sites do, i.e., Tanaka, *Hidden Horrors*, 103.

84. Yamada Meiko, *Senryōgun Ianfu* (Tokyo: Kojinsha, 1992), 36.

85. Duus Masayo, Makkaasaa no Futatsu no Bōshi, (Tokyo: Kōdansha, 1985), 79.
86. Duus, 80.
87. Duus, 79.
88. Yamada Meiko, *Senryōgun Ianfu*, 36.
89. Roger Brown also pointed this out in a post to H-Japan discussion logs. This post is no longer available online. See note 4 in chapter 7; Yuki Tanaka, *Hidden Horrors* (Boulder, CO: Westview, 1996), 103.
90. Tanaka, *Hidden Horrors*, 103.
91. "Re: Forwarding Information with Regard to the Trend of Reports on Unfortunate Incidents."
92. "Shinchūgun no Fuhō Kōi," reprinted in *Seibōryoku Mondai Shiryō Shūsei*, vol. 1 (Tokyo: Fujiya Shuppan, 2004), 9–10.
93. This information comes from conversations with Mr. Kawabata at Osaka Keisatsu Jōhō Kōkaishitsu; Mr. Murakami at Kyoto Keisatsu Jōhō Kōkaishitsu; Mr. Tateyama at Hokkaido Keisatsu Jōhō Kōkaishitsu.
94. Sarah Kovner, *Occupying Power* (Stanford, CA: Stanford University Press, 2012), 54; "Rape: Number of Offences Reported or Complaints Received," March 8, 1950, and "Statistics in re Rape," March 11, 1950, both in NARA, RG 554 (Records of General HQ, FEC), box 199, folder 250-1 #1, "Alleged Misconduct of Occupation Troops against Japanese Nationals QPMO-4." I am indebted to Professor Kovner for sharing the latter document with me.
95. Kuroda Shigeo, *Nihon Keisatsushi no Kenkyū* (Tokyo: Reibunsha, 1963), 381–83, 401–2.
96. Kuroda, 381–83.
97. Kovner, *Occupying Power*, 54; "Rape: Number of Offences Reported or Complaints Received," March 8, 1950, NARA, RG 554 (Records of General HQ, FEC), box 199, folder 250-1 #1, "Statistics in re Rape."
98. For example, in 2009, Charlotte, North Carolina, had 303 reported cases; Austin, Texas, had 266; Memphis, Tennessee, had 422; Boston had 263; Albuquerque, New Mexico, had 345; Omaha, Nebraska, had 194; St. Paul, Minnesota, had 183. Estimating from national figures according to the latest census, Charlotte, the largest of these cities, had about 176,000 males between the ages of 15 and 49. St. Paul, the smallest of them, had about 67,000 (www.neighborhoodscout.com, www.census.gov). The peak number of troops in Japan was 354,675 Americans and 40,236 from the British Commonwealth Occupation Force. This decreased to a total troop strength of 192,236 by August 1946 and to 132,828 in June 1948, where it remained until the outbreak of the Korean War in the final years of the Occupation. The average total

number of troops, the vast majority of whom were aged between 17 and
30, was about 164,000. See John J. McGrath, "Boots on the Ground: Troop
Density in Contingency Operations," *Global War on Terrorism Occasional
Paper 16* (Fort Leavenworth, KS: Combat Studies Institute Press, 2006), 28.

99. B. N. Petersen, "Weekly Summary of Events—Investigations Div, OPM
MTA," July 7, 1950, NARA, RG 331, GHQ/SCAP, box 9894: "Provost Marshal
Section," folder: "Confidential 1950."

100. Petersen, "Weekly Summary of Events—Investigations Div, OPM MTA."

101. For an example of such a false equivalence pushed by the right, see the
discussion of the *Zaitokukai* in the introduction. For an example of a left-wing
academic doing so, see Yuki Tanaka, *Hidden Horrors*, 103.

102. "Judgment of the International Military Tribunal of the Far East," excerpted
in *Documents on the Rape of Nanking*, ed. Timothy Brook (Ann Arbor:
University of Michigan Press, 1999), 259.

103. Reprinted in Brook, 214.

104. Reprinted in Brook, 214.

105. Quoted in "The Nanking Atrocity: An Interpretive Overview," in *The Nanking
Atrocity 1937–1938: Complicating the Picture*, ed. Bob Tadashi Wakabayashi
(New York: Berghahn, 2007), 49.

106. Quoted in Hua-ling Hu, *American Goddess at the Rape of Nanking: The
Courage of Minnie Vautrin* (Carbondale: University of Southern Illinois
Press, 2000), 97.

107. See the various documents titled "Cases of Disorders of Japanese Soldiers in
the Safety Zone" and "Notes on the Present Situation" reprinted in Brook,
Documents on the Rape of Nanking. The documents are case 8 (pp. 9–11); case
15 (pp. 28–38); case 17 (pp. 39–44); case 19 (pp. 45–48); case 25 (pp. 54–56); case
30 (pp. 61–63); case 32 (pp. 64–66); case 37 (pp. 77–79); case 45 (pp. 88–89);
case 48 (pp. 94–95); case 56 (pp. 116–21); case 57 (pp. 121–24); case 58 (pp.
125–34); case 61 (pp. 137–46); and case 62 (pp. 146–51). Hereafter references
to these documents will be made by case number and page number only.

108. Brook, *Documents on the Rape of Nanking*, case 222, 122; case 301, 132; case
302, 133; case 303, 133; case 436, 154; and case 428, 152. Case 307, 133, is of
the sixty-plus-year-old woman who was raped more than ten times.

109. Brook, case 60, 35; case 88, 43; case 93, 43; case 168, 62; case 173, 63; case 217,
120–21; case 264, 128; case 275, 129–30; case 289, 51; case 330, 141; case 348,
144; case 349, 144; case 374, 147; case 384, 148; case 388, 149; case 394, 149;
case 403, 150; case 404, 150; case 405, 150; case 426, 151; case 432, 153; case
434, 153; case 438, 154; case 439, 154; case 441, 154; case 407, 158; case 408,
158; case 413, 159; case 416, 159; case 417, 159.

110. Brook, case 22, 29; case 30, 30; case 87, 42–43, case 172, 62–63, case 192, 89; case 196, 94; case 225, 123; case 229, 124; case 231, 124; case 243, 126; case 252, 126; case 258, 127; case 261, 127; case 265, 128; case 267, 128; cases 271–74, 129; case 280, 130; case 284, 131; case 286, 131; case 293, 132; cases 305, 306, 133; case 317, 139; case 321, 139–40; case 323, 140; case 329, 140; case 325, 140; cases 328, 329, 141; case 333, 142; case 338, 143; cases 341, 344, 144; case 352, 144–45; cases 356–58, 361, 364, 145; cases 365, 370, 371, 146; case 377, 147–48; case 379, 148; case 387, 149; cases 401–2, 150; case 406, 151; case 430, 153; case 437, 154; case 442, 155; case 410, 158; case 412, 158–59.

111. Brook, case 78, 41.

112. Brook, case 50, 33; case 32, 33; case 94, 46; case 144, 54; case 153, 56; case 169, 62; case 200, 95; case 212, 119; case 216, 120; case 241, 126; case 282, 130; case 292, 132; case 431, 153.

113. Brook, case 172, 62–62; case 431, 153; case 212, 119.

114. Brook, case 212, 119. The MP abduction is case 187, 78.

115. Brook, case 112, 48; case 167, 61–62; case 220, 122; case 287, 131; case 291, 132; case 372, 147; case 421, 160.

116. Brook, see respectively, case 5, 10; case 44, 32; case 45, 32; case 55, 33; case 63, 36; case 18, 28; case 64, 36.

117. Brook, case 45, 32; case 89, 43; case 354, 145.

118. Brook, case 178, 65.

119. Brook, case 219, 121.

120. Brook, case 303, 133.

121. Brook, case 89, 63.

122. Brook, case 63, 36.

123. Brook, case 69, 38.

124. Brook, case 354, 145; case 428, 152.

125. Brook, case 210, 119; case 249, 126.

126. Brook, case 98, 45.

127. Brook, case 415, 158.

128. Brook, case 63, 36.

129. Brook, case 179, 66.

130. Yoshimi Yoshiaki, *Comfort Women*, trans. Suzanne O'Brien (New York: Columbia University Press, 2000), 49–51.

131. Hora Tomio, *Nitchū Sensō: Nankin Daizangyaku Jiken Shiryōshū*, vol. 1 (Tokyo: Aoki Shoten, 1985), 337. The translation quoted is from "The Nanking Atrocity: An Interpretive Overview," in Tadashi Wakabayashi, *The Nanking Atrocity 1937–1938*, 49.

132. See, for example, the claims of Hirai Kazuko and Higashinakano Shūdō and Fujioka Nobukatsu outlined in the introduction (Hirai, *Nihon Senryō to Jendaa*, 218–19); Higashinakano Shūdō and Fujioka Nobukatsu, *"Za Reipu obu Nankin" no Kenkyū* (*Research on "the Rape of Nanking"*) (Tokyo: Shōdensha, 1999), 152. See also Yuki Tanaka, *Hidden Horrors*, 103.

133. Hosokawa Morisada, *Hosokawa Nikki* (Tokyo: Chūō Kōronsha, 1979), 157. Takami Jun and Nagai Kafū made similar comments. See Takami Jun *Haisen Nikki* (Tokyo: Chūō Kōronsha, 2005), 345; Nagai Kafū, *Danchōtei Nichijō: Vol. 2* (Tokyo: Iwanami Shoten, 1987), 278.

134. Naimark, *The Russians in Germany*, 70–71.

135. James, *Europe Reborn*, 30.

136. Anonymous, *A Woman in Berlin*, trans. Philip Boehm (New York: Metropolitan Books / Henry Holt, 2005), 75.

137. Anonymous, 121.

138. Stanley Weintraub, *The Last Great Victory* (New York: Penguin, 1995), 336–37.

139. Joseph R. Starr, Office of the Chief Historian, European Command, "Fraternization with the Germans" (Frankfurt-am-Main: Headquarters, European Command, August 1947), 81.

CHAPTER 2. "THIS DEGRADING SLAVERY"

1. Sarah Kovner, *Occupying Power* (Stanford, CA: Stanford University Press, 2012), 124, 156.

2. See, for example, Hirai Kazuko, *Nihon Senryō to Jendaa* (Tokyo: Yūshisha, 2014), 30–31; Hayashi Hirofumi, "Amerika Gun no Seitaisaku no Rekishi—1950 Nendai Made," *Josei, Sensō, Jinken*, no. 7 (August 2020); Arai Eiko, "Kiristo Kyōkai no 'Panpan' Gensetsu to Magudara no Maria," in Keisen Jogakuen Daigaku Heiwa Bunka Kenkyūjo, ed., *Senryō to Sei* (Tokyo: Impakuto Shuppankai, 2007), 154.

3. This distinction appears also to have been too nice for GHQ's own clerks. Files related to the debate of prohibition of prostitution in the National Archives are included in the folder marked "Abolition of Licensed Prostitution." NARA, RG 331, GHQ/SCAP, box 9370, folder 4: "726.1 Abolition of Licensed Prostitution" (hereafter cited as RG 331, box 9370, folder 4).

4. William Manchester, *American Caesar* (New York: Dell, 1978), 560.

5. J. E. de Becker, *The Nightless City* (Tokyo: ICG Muse, 2000), 1–16; Sone Hiromi, "Prostitution and Public Authority in Early Modern Japan," trans. Akiko Terashima and Anne Walthall, in *Women and Class in Japanese History*, ed. Hitomi Tomomura, Anne Walthall, and Wakita Haruko (Ann Arbor: University of Michigan Press, 1999), 169–71.

6. Rutherford Alcock, *The Capital of the Tycoon*, vol. 2 (New York: Harper and Brothers, 1863), 272.

7. F. G. Notehelfer, ed., *Japan through American Eyes: The Journal of Francis Hall, 1859–1866* (Boulder, CO: Westview, 2001), 56.

8. Joseph V. Zaccone, Legal Consultant, "Memorandum for Record; Subject: Proposed Directive to Prohibit Prostitution," July 2, 1947, RG 331, box 9370, folder 4.

9. Sheldon Garon, *Molding Japanese Minds* (Princeton, NJ: Princeton University Press, 1997), 96.

10. Robert J. Smith and Ella Lury Wiswell, The Women of Suye Mura (Chicago: University of Chicago Press, 1982), 140–41.

11. Engelbert Kaempfer, *Kaempfer's Japan: Tokugawa Culture Observed*, trans. Beatrice M. Bodart-Bailey (Honolulu: University of Hawai'i Press, 1999), 143.

12. Public Opinion and Sociological Research Division, Civil Information and Education Section, ed., "The Japanese People Look at Prostitution," June 30, 1949, 9, NARA, RG 331, GHQ/SCAP, box 1416, folder 17: "Prostitution, Punishment of" (hereafter cited as RG 331, box 1416, folder 17).

13. Garon, *Molding Japanese Minds*, 102.

14. Garon, 96–97.

15. Cecilia S. Seigle, *Yoshiwara: The Glittering World of the Japanese Courtesan* (Honolulu: University of Hawai'i Press, 1993), 212; phone conversation, Tomatsu Hideaki, head of Jokanji temple, April 18, 2013. According to Tomatsu, the total was actually more than 25,000. This number includes all abandoned bodies of the district, not just prostitutes. Seigle states that there were 21,056 prostitutes without families registered between 1743 and 1801.

16. De Becker, *The Nightless City*, 13; Donald Richie, "Foreword," in De Becker, xi; Sone, "Prostitution and Public Authority in Early Modern Japan," 171.

17. Garon, 97.

18. Garon, 102; "Elimination of Licensed Prostitution in Japan" (Memorandum for the Record filed by Public Health and Welfare Section), January 6, 1945, RG 331, box 9370, folder 4.

19. See Yoshimi Yoshiaki, *Comfort Women*, trans. Suzanne O'Brien (New York: Columbia University Press, 2000), 203.

20. Yoshimi, 205. See also Hata Ikuhiko, *Ianfu to Senjo- no Sei* (Tokyo: Shinchōsha, 1999), 27. Yoshimi and Hayashi are on the left side of scholarly commentary in Japan, and Hata is on the right. Though Yoshimi and Hata agree on this point, they disagree on its significance. See Park Yuha, *Teikoku no Ianfu* (Tokyo: Asahi Shimbun Shuppan, 2014), 37; and Hayashi Hirofumi, *Nihongun "Ianfu" Mondai no Kakushin* (Tokyo: Kadensha, 2015), 60.

21. James H. Gordon, "Memorandum for the Record; Subject: Conference with Major Philip Weisbach, M.C, C.O. 1st Med Squadron, 1st Cavalry Division," September 30, 1945, NARA, RG 331, GHQ/SCAP, box 9370, folder 8: "Venereal Disease Control" (hereafter cited as RG 331, box 9370, folder 8).

22. B. P. W, "Memorandum for the Record; Subject: Venereal Disease in Japan," October 3, 1945; James H. Gordon, "Memorandum for the Record: Subject: Conference with Dr. H. Yosano and Dr. Fukai," October 3, 1945; H. H. Mac-Donald, "Memorandum for Record; Subject: Venereal Disease Control," October 20, 1945; and James H. Gordon, "Memorandum for the Record; Subject: Conference on Venereal Diseases," October 22, 1945, all in RG 331, box 9370, folder 8.

23. Gordon, "Memorandum for Record; Subject: Venereal Disease Control," October 22, 1945.

24. H. H. MacDonald, "Memorandum for the Record; Subject: Prostitution in Japan; Contracts; Regulations, Public and Private Prostitutes," December 29, 1945, RG 331, box 9370, folder 4.

25. MacDonald, "Memorandum for the Record; Subject: Prostitution in Japan; Contracts; Regulations, Public and Private Prostitutes," December 29, 1945; Kariya Haruo, *Edo no Seibyō* (Tokyo: Shinano, 1993), 36.

26. Gordon, "Memorandum for the Record: Subject: Conference with Dr. H. Yosano and Dr. Fukai."

27. This suggestion was made repeatedly by PHW officials, including its head, Col., later Brig. Gen. Crawford Sams. See, for example, James H. Gordon, "Memorandum for the Record; Subject: Conference on VD Control with Colonel A. G. Tuckerman, Cav., Exec Off of the 2nd Brig. 1st Cav. Div. and Exec. to the Provost Marshal General, Tokyo Area," September 29, 1945; James H. Gordon, "Memorandum for the Records," September 29, 1945; and James H. Gordon, "Memorandum for the Record; Subject: Conference with Major Philip Weisbach, M.C., C.O. 1st Med Squadron, 1st Cavalry Division," all in RG 331, box 9370, folder 8.

28. H. H. MacDonald, "Memorandum for the Record. Subject: Conference on Venereal Disease and Related Legislation," December 6, 1945, RG 331, box 9370, folder 8. The memo notes that this is the third discussion they have had on this matter, although records of the previous two are not included in the file.

29. MacDonald, "Memorandum for the Record. Subject: Conference on Venereal Disease and Related Legislation," December 6, 1945.

30. H. H. MacDonald, "Memorandum for the Record; Subject: System of Licensed Prostitution in Japan," December 11, 1945, and H. H. MacDonald, "Memorandum

for the Record. Subject: Elimination of Licensed Prostitution in Japan," January 7, 1946, RG 331, box 9370, folder 4.

31. MacDonald, "Memorandum for the Record; Subject: System of Licensed Prostitution in Japan," December 11, 1945.

32. Draft Memorandum: "AG 726.1(7 Jan 46)PH; Memorandum For: Imperial Japanese Government. Through: Central Liaison Office, Tokyo. Subject: Abolition of Licensed Prostitution in Japan," January 7, 1946, RG 331, box 9370, folder 4.

33. H. H. MacDonald, "Memorandum for the Record. Subject: Elimination of Licensed Prostitution in Japan," January 7, 1946, NARA, RG 331, box 408, folder 3-12 (1-2) 0005-1.

34. Kermit Dyke, "Check Sheet; KRD/AB/gld; From C, CI&E; To: Public Health and Welfare," December 11, 1946, RG 331, box 9370, folder 4. For Dyke's background see Takemae, *Inside GHQ*, 180–81.

35. "AG 767.7 (15 Jan 46)TH; Memorandum for: Imperial Japanese Government. Through: Central Liaison Office, Tokyo. Subject: Abolition of Licensed Prostitution in Japan," RG 331, box 9370, folder 4.

36. H. W. Allen for the Supreme Commander, "(AG 726.7 (21 Jan 46)PH; (SCAPIN-642; Memorandum for: Imperial Japanese Government. Through: Central Liaison Office, Tokyo. Subject: Abolition of Licensed Prostitution in Japan," January 21, 1946, RG 331, box 9370, folder 4.

37. See, for example, John W. Dower, *Embracing Defeat* (New York: W. W. Norton and New Press, 1999), 130; Yuki Tanaka, *Japan's Comfort Women: Sexual Slavery and Prostitution during World War II and the US Occupation* (New York: Routledge, 2002), 161; Fujime, *Sei no Rekishigaku*, 327, 384; Kramm, *Sanitized Sex* (Oakland: University of California Press, 2017), 2; Michiko Takeuchi, "'Pan-Pan Girls' Performing and Resisting Neo-colonialism(s) in the Pacific Theater," in Maria Höhn and Seungsook Moon, *Over There: Living with the U.S. Military Empire from World War II to the Present* (Durham, NC: Duke University Press, 2010), 87; Mark McLelland, *Love, Sex and Democracy in Japan during the American Occupation* (New York: Palgrave Macmillan, 2012), 57; Takemae, *Inside GHQ*, 69.

38. "AG 726.1 (Aug 46)PH; Memorandum; Subject: Information of General Application Pertaining to Memorandum Number (SCAPIN-643) AG 726.7 (21 Jan 46)PH, General Headquarters, Supreme Commander for the Allied Powers, subject: 'Abolition of Licensed Prostitution in Japan,'" August 1946, RG 331, box 9370, folder 4.

39. J. V. Zaccone, Legal Advisor, "Memorandum for the Record: Subject: Prostitution," October 10, 1946, NARA, RG 331, GHQ/SCAP, box 9370, folder 5:

"Venereal Disease Contract Tracing" (hereafter cited as RG 331, box 9370, folder 5).

40. Alfred Christian Oppler, *Legal Reform in Occupied Japan* (Princeton, NJ: Princeton University Press, 1976), 157.

41. Justin Williams Sr., *Japan's Political Revolution under MacArthur: A Participant's Account* (Athens: University of Georgia Press, 1979), 9.

42. Joseph V. Zaccone, Legal Consultant, "Memorandum for Record; Subject: Proposed Directive to Prohibit Prostitution," July 2, 1947, RG 331, box 9370, folder 4.

43. Public Opinion and Sociological Research Division, "The Japanese People Look at Prostitution" (Tokyo: General Headquarters, Supreme Commander for the Allied Powers, Civil Information and Education Section Survey Series, June 30, 1949), 1, NARA, RG 331, box 1416, folder 17.

44. Public Opinion and Sociological Research Division, "The Japanese People Look at Prostitution," 3.

45. Public Opinion and Sociological Research Division, "The Japanese People Look at Prostitution," 1.

46. Letter from Nakamura Keiichi to General MacArthur, January 19, 1948, NARA, RG 331, GHQ/SCAP, box 555, folder 19 (1-2) 250-1 #1 1948.

47. "What a Swan Would Be," flyer reproduced in "To: PSD PMO Tokyo Provost Court; From: Oshiro, Chief, Public Peace Section, MPD; Subject: Report on the Enforcement of Prostitute and etc. Control Ordinance," July 19, 1950, 6, NARA, RG 331, GHQ/SCAP, box 334: "PSD Pistols to Prostitution," folder 40: "Prostitution" (hereafter cited as RG 331, box 334, folder 40).

48. Public Opinion and Sociological Research Division, "The Japanese People Look at Prostitution," 17.

49. Garon, *Molding Japanese Minds*, 197.

50. Holly Vincele Sanders, "Prostitution in Postwar Japan: Debt and Labor" (PhD diss. Princeton University, 2005), UMI #3181618, 109.

51. "Keihokyoku Koan Hatsu Ko No. 28; To: Superintendent-General of the Metropolitan Police Board, Prefectural Governors; From: Director of the Police Affairs Bureau, Ministry of Home Affairs; Subject: Guidance and Control regarding Abolition of the System of Licensed Prostitution," May 28, 1946, NARA, RG 331, GHQ/SCAP, box 1416, folder 18: "Japanese Taxes on Prostitution." This desire to rely on persuasion and voluntary compliance was foreshadowed by a meeting between H. H. MacDonald and various Japanese officials. The orders they proposed at the time emphasized voluntary nullification of contracts. Though the "Japanese representatives assured that whether voluntarily or not, existing contracts will be cancelled," it is clear that Japanese side remained reluctant to impose nullification by fiat. See

H. H. MacDonald, "Memorandum for the Record; Subject: Proposed Japanese Legislation Abolishing Licensed Prostitution," RG 331, box 9370, folder 4.

52. J. V. Zaccone, Legal Consultant, "Memorandum for the Record: Subject: Reply to Ltr, Hgq I corp, APO 310, file AG 726.1(BA) dtd 13 Nov 46, subject: 'Abolition of Licensed Prostitution in Japan,'" January 13, 1947, RG 331, box 9370, folder 4; NARA, RG 331, GHQ/SCAP, box 477, AG Section Decimal File 1945–46, 720 to 829.1.

53. Sanders, "Prostitution in Postwar Japan," 34.

54. "AG 726.1 (6 Sep 46) PH; (SCAPIN 1183)," NARA, RG 331, GHQ/SCAP, box 4, SCAPIN 1001–700.

55. "BASIC: Ltr, Hqs I Corps, APO 301, file AG 726.1 (13 Nov 46) BA," subject: "Abolition of Licensed Prostitution in Japan," November 13, 1946, RG 331, box 9370, folder 4.

56. J. V. Saccone, Legal Consultant, "Memorandum for the Record," January 13, 1947, RG 331, box 9370, folder 4.

57. Untitled handwritten memo beginning "SCAPIN," NARA, RG 331, GHQ/SCAP, box 334: PSD "Pistols to Prostitution," folder 39: "Prostitute Law." This note summarizes the state of prostitution law then in effect in Japan as its author understood it. I have to date been unable to locate the actual memorandum on which these notes were based, but there is no doubt that an Imperial Ordinance on the subject of involuntary prostitution was issued on January 14, 1947.

58. "Chokurei Daikyūgo," January 14, 1947, National Archives of Japan Digital Archive: https://www.digital.archives.go.jp/DAS/meta/Detail _F0000000000000044654 (accessed April 12, 2016).

59. Sanders, "Prostitution in Postwar Japan," 160–61.

60. Eiji Oguma, *A Genealogy of Japanese Self-Images*, trans. David Askew (Melbourne: Transpacific Press, 2002), 221. See also chapter 3.

61. See chapter 4 for more.

62. Kanagawa Ken Keisatsushi Hensan Iinkai, ed., *Kanagawa Ken Keisatsushi*, vol. 3 (Yokohama: Kanagawa Keisatsu Honbu, 1974), 346; Shizuoka Ken Keisatsushi Hensan Iinkai, ed., *Shizuoka Ken Keisatsushi*, vol. 2 (Shizuoka: Shizuoka Keisatsu Honbu, 1979), 585; Gifu Ken Keisatsushi Hensan Iinkai, ed., *Gifu Ken Keisatsushi*, vol. 2 (Tokyo: Daiichi Hōki Shuppan, 1982), 418; Yamagata Ken Keisatsushi Hensan Iinkai, ed., *Yamagata Ken Keisatsushi*, vol. 2 (Yamagata: Tamiya Insatsujo, 1971), 996; Hokkaidō Keisatsushi Henshū Iinkai, *Hokkaidō Ken Keisatsushi, Shōwa Hen* (Sapporo: Hokkaidō Keisatsu Honbu, 1968), 570; Wakayama Ken Keisatsushi Hensan Iinkai, ed., *Wakayama Ken Keisatsushi*, vol. 2 (Tokyo: Kawakita Insatsusho, 1992), 477; Aomori Ken Keisatsushi Hensan Iinkai, ed., *Aomori Ken Keisatsushi*, vol. 2 (Hirosaki: Ono Insatsu, 1977), 562;

Hyōgo Ken Keisatsushi Hensan Iiinkai, ed., *Hyōgo Ken Keisatsushi, Shōwa Hen* (Kobe: Ishikawa Insatsu, 1975), 512.

63. MOJ (Ministry of Justice) 38, reel 13, 382955, Japanese National Diet Library.

64. Robert L. Eichelberger, diary entry, September 11, 1945, in Robert L. Eichelberger Papers, box 1, folder titled "Miscellaneous: Diary Photocopies: Diaries: July 23–October 20; October 24–December 4," Rubenstein Library, Duke University, Durham, NC.

65. See chapter 3 ("The World's Oldest Debate? Regulating Prostitution and Illicit Sexuality") in Sheldon Garon, *Molding Japanese Minds* (Princeton, NJ: Princeton University Press, 1997), 88–114, for a discussion of the state's efforts to control prostitution and sexuality in prewar Japan. See also Elise K. Tipton, "Rectifying Public Morals in Interwar Japan," *Crime, Historie & Sociétés* 5, no. 2 (April 2001): 133–48, esp. 145.

66. Crawford F. Sams, untitled memorandum, December 26, 1946, RG 331, box 9370, folder 4.

67. This suggestion was made repeatedly by PH&W officials, including its head, Col. Crawford Sams. See, for example, three items RG 331, box 9370, folder 8: James H. Gordon, "Memorandum for the Record; Subject: Conference on VD Control with Colonel A. G. Tuckerman, Cav., Exec Off of the 2nd Brig. 1st Cav. Div. and Exec. to the Provost Marshal General, Tokyo Area," September 29, 1945; James H. Gordon, "Memorandum for the Records," September 29, 1945; and James H. Gordon, "Memorandum for the Record; Subject: Conference with Major Philip Weisbach, M.C, C.O. 1st Med Squadron, 1st Cavalry Division," September 30, 1945.

68. See, for example, three items in RG 331, box 9370, folder 8: James H. Gordon, "Memorandum for the Record; Subject: Conference with Dr. H. Yosano and Dr. Fukai," October 3, 1945; James H. Gordon, "Memorandum for the Record; Subject: Conference with Dr. Yosano, Tokyo Health Department, on Venereal Disease," October 26, 1945; and James H. Gordon, "Memorandum for the Record; Subject: Visit to Omori, Hakusen, and Mukojima Geisha District," October 30, 1945.

69. See chapter 3 for more.

70. Crawford F. Sams, "Memorandum for the Chief of Staff," October 16, 1945, RG 331, box 9370, folder 8.

71. Yukiko Koshiro, *Trans-Pacific Racisms and the U.S. Occupation of Japan* (New York: Columbia University Press, 1999), 69.

72. "Bokin wa Henpu Seyo," *Niigata Nippō*, October 17, 1945, 2. See also Hirai Kazuko, *Nihon Senryō to Jendaa* (Tokyo: Yūshisha, 2014), 41.

73. Kanagawa Ken Keisatsushi Hensan Iinkai, *Kanagawa Ken Keisatsushi*, 3:352.

74. Ikeda Hirohiko, *Keisatsushochō no Shuki*, vol. 1 (Tokyo: Tsukuba Shorin, 1983), 63–104, esp. 63, 69–70, 98–100, 103–4; Hirai Kazuko, *Nihon Senryō to Jendaa*, 45–46.

75. The memorandum of this meeting (H. H. MacDonald, "Memorandum for the Record; Subject: Conference on V.D. Control," October 20, 1945, RG 331, box 9370, folder 8 gives the name of the police officer as "Hyakutoku," but his name is given in Duus Masayo, *Makasaa no Futatsu no Bōshi* (Tokyo: Kōdansha, 1985), as "Shakutoku" with the characters 釈得 (p. 32). I find Duus' rendering more convincing.

76. H. H. MacDonald, "Memorandum for the Record; Subject: Conference on V.D. Control," October 20, 1945, RG 331, box 9370, folder 8.

77. Nara Ken Keisatsushi Henshū Iinkai, ed., *Nara Ken Keisatsushi, Shōwa Hen* (Nara: Nara Keisatsu Honbu, 1978), 316; Hyōgo Ken Keisatsushi Hensan Iinkai, *Hyōgo Ken Keisatsushi, Shōwa Hen*, 115; Gifu Ken Keisatsushi Hensan Iinkai, *Gifu Ken Keisatsushi*, 2:419; Shizuoka Ken Keisatsushi Hensan Iinkai, *Shizuoka Ken Keisatsushi*, 2:586; Yamagata Ken Keisatsushi Hensan Iinkai, *Yamagata Ken Keisatsushi*, 2:997; Aomori Ken Keisatsushi Hensan Iinkai, *Aomori Ken Keisatsushi*, 2:681.

78. "Shinchūgun Aite no 'Momoiro Kōkan': Okaseba Nihonjin mo Genbatsu," *Asashi Shimbun*, May 9, 1946, 2. See also Akio Satoko, *Washinton Haitsu: GHQ ga Tokyo ni Kizanda Sengo* (Tokyo: Shinchōsha, 2003), 267–68. According to Duus Masayo, the Japanese Metropolitan Police appealed this decision to both the provost marshal and GHQ, asking that sentences for violators be reduced on the grounds that social conditions made it inevitable that such businesses needed to operate. See Duus Masayo, *Makasaa no Futatsu no Bōshi* (Tokyo: Kōdansha, 1985), 232.

79. "Japan: Prostitutes Union," *Time*, September 16, 1946, https://content.time.com/time/subscriber/article/0,33009,888318,00.html (accessed September 29, 2023).

80. "To: Mr. Fritz, PSD, GHQ; From: OSHIRO Isamu, Public Peace Section Chief, MPD; Subject: Report on the Search, Conducted on June 21, upon Houses of Ill Repute," June 28, 1950, RG 331, box 334, folder 40.

81. "Memorandum for the Record; Subject: VD and Prostitution Control under Japanese Law," September 19, 1949, RG 331, box 334, folder 40; Theodore Cohen, *Remaking Japan* (New York: Free Press / Macmillan, 1987), 96.

82. Sey Nishimura, "Promoting Public Health during the Occupation of Japan," *American Journal of Public Health* 9, no. 3 (March 2008): 428.

83. Chazono Toshimi, *Panpan to wa Dare Nanoka* (Tokyo: Impakuto Shuppankai, 2014), 202–4.

84. S. Yamashita, Chief, Oita Liaison and Coordination Office, "To: The Commanding Officer, Oita Military Government Team; From: Chief, Oita Liaison & Coordination Office; Subject: Petition Concerning the Control of Prostitutes," in James H. Gordon, Lt. Col., MC, Chief, Preventive Medicine Division, "Memorandum for Record; Subject: Visit to Kyushu and Southern Honshu," February 28, 1946, NARA, RG 331, box 9321, folder 5: "Venereal Disease Control Staff Visits."

85. Isamu Nieda, "Summary Report of Venereal Disease Control Activities in Japan, October 1945–December 1949," 18–19, NARA, RG 331, box 9321: "PH&W," folder 2–3: "October 1945–December 1949 Summary Report _VD Control; Dr. Nieda."

86. "Draft; Memorandum For: Imperial Japanese Government; Through: Central Liaison Office, Tokyo; Subject: Suppression of Prostitution," November 6, 1946, RG 331, box 9370, folder 4.

87. Thomas D. White, "AG 726.1 Surg-1; Subject: Venereal Disease Control in Army Air Force Personnel," November 20, 1946, RG 331, box 9370, folder 4.

88. Crawford F. Sams, "Suppression of Prostitution in Japan," December 26, 1946, RG 331, box 9370, folder 4.

89. Robert L. Eichelberger, "Basic: Ltr GHQ, SCAP, Subj: Suppression of Prostitution, to CG, 8th Army, APO 343, File AG-726.1 (4 Jan 47) PH, dtd 4 Jan 47," January 4, 1947, RG 331, box 9370, folder 4.

90. J. Q. Owsley, "From: Staff Medical Officer, Commander Naval Forces, Far East Command; To: Headquarters, Supreme Commander for the Allied Powers; Subject: Suppression of Prostitution," February 28, 1947, RG 331, box 9370, folder 4.

91. Ubuki Satoru, "Nihon ni Okeru Gensuibaku Kinshi Undou no Zentei: 'Hibaku Tai-ken' no Kentō" ["The Premises of the 'Ban-the-Bomb' Movement in Japan—an Investigation of the Hibaku Experience"], in *Nihon Kenkyū* 236 (April 1982): 88.

92. Sams and Elkins did not get along. Elkins' political sympathies were investigated by the Army's Counter Intelligence Corps. Sams, a staunch anti-Communist, believed Elkins to be a Communist. Elkins eventually had to leave his position and return to the United States. See Crawford F. Sams, *"Medic,"* ed. Zabelle Zakarian (Armonk, NY: M. E. Sharpe, 1998), 174–82; Duus, *Makasaa no Futatsu no Bōshi,* 235, 260.

93. Oscar M. Elkins, B.D. Consultant Venereal Disease Control, "Memorandum for Record: Subject: Proposed Amusement Tax on Houses of Prostitution in Hiroshima Ken," February 3, 1947, RG 331, box 9370, folder 4.

94. J. V. Zaccone, Legal Consultant, "Memorandum for the Record: Subject: Proposed Amusement Tax on Prostitution," March 18, 1947, RG 331, box 9370, folder 4.

95. "From: GS; To: PH&W," March 4, 1947, RG 331, box 9370, folder 4; J. V. Zaccone, Legal Consultant, "Memorandum for the Record: Subject: Proposed Amusement Tax on Prostitution," March 18, 1947, RG 331, box 9370, folder 4. The sole dissenting recommendation came from the Economic and Scientific Section. which blithely, and in fact incorrectly, argued that in view of SCAPIN 642, "prostitution carried on in established amusement places may be presumed voluntary." Furthermore, it asserted, "the imposition of a tax cannot be regarded as a form of state authorization." See W. E. L., "From: ESS/FI; To: PH&W," February 18, 1947, RG 331, box 9370, folder 4.

96. Courtney Whitney, "Check Sheet" attached to "Proposed Directive, Law to Prohibit Prostitution and Its Allied Activities; 2 from: Govt Section; to: PH&W," June 11, 1947, RG 331, box 9370, folder 4.

97. Charles A. Willoughby, "Check Sheet" attached to "Proposed Directive, Law to Prohibit Prostitution and Its Allied Activities; 3 G-2; PH&W," June 25, 1947, RG 331, box 9370, folder 4.

98. Alfred R. Hussey, "Memorandum for the Record; Subject: VD Control and Elimination of Commercialized Prostitution," July 3, 1947, RG 331, box 9370, folder 4.

99. Kovner, Occupying Power, 104; H. Meyers, "Bill for the Punishment of Prostitution and Related Activities: Public Opinion Survey," July 12, 1949, NARA, RG 331, box 1416, folder 17.

100. Robert L. Eichelberger, "BASIC: Ltr GHQ, SCAP, Subj: Suppression of Prostitution, to CG, 8th Army, APO 343, File AG-726.1 (4 Jan 47) PH, dtd 4 Jan 47," January 4, 1947, RG 331, box 9370, folder 4.

101. Duus Masayo, Makasaa no Futatsu no Bōshi (Tokyo: Kōdansha, 1985), 259.

102. Alva C. Carpenter, "Bill for the Punishment of Prostitution and Related Activities," June 15, 1948, RG 331, box 1416, folder 17.

103. Howard Myers, "Memorandum for the Record; Subject: Draft Bill for Punishment of Prostitution and Related Activities, Received 21 Jun 1949 from Attorney General's Office," June 28, 1949, RG 331, box 1416, folder 17.

104. Carpenter, "Bill for the Punishment of Prostitution and Related Activities." Carpenter resigned his commission during the Occupation and became one of the few civilian section chiefs of GHQ. See Takemae, Inside GHQ, 171.

105. Carpenter, "Bill for the Punishment of Prostitution and Related Activities." At one point in the Occupation Carpenter resigned his commission but

continued to work for the Legal Section. I was unable to determine whether he was still in the military at the time of this memo.

106. Civil Information and Education Section, GHQ, *The Japanese People Look at Prostitution*, June 30, 1949, 21, RG 331, box 1416, folder 17. The Japanese government's report on the same survey is reprinted as Kokuritsu Seron Chōsajo, ed., "Baishun ni Kan Suru Seron," in *Seibōryoku Mondai Shiryō Shūsei*, vol. 1 (Tokyo: Fujiya Shuppan, 2004), 239–53.

107. Civil Information and Education Section, GHQ, *The Japanese People Look at Prostitution*, 21.

108. Civil Information and Education Section, GHQ, *The Japanese People Look at Prostitution*, 1–6.

109. W. E. L., "From: ESS/FI; To: PH&W," February 18, 1947, RG 331, box 9370, folder 4.

110. Subject: Violation of SCAP Directive, AD 767.7 (21 Jan 46),PH Subject; Abolition n of Licensed Prostitution," March 15, 1946 and subsequent correspondence in NARA RG 331 Box 408, Folder 3-12 (1-2) 0005-1.

111. Garon, *Molding Japanese Minds*, 199–200.

112. U.S. Department of State, *Trafficking in Persons Report 2018*, 242, https://www.state.gov/documents/organization/282802.pdf, accessed April 29, 2019.

113. "Kyoto Court Hands Man Suspended Sentence for Forcing Women into Sex Trade to Clear 'Debts,'" *Japan Times*, June 25, 2019, https://www.japantimes.co.jp/news/2019/06/25/national/crime-legal/kyoto-court-hands-man-suspended-sentence-forcing- women-sex-trade-clear-debts/#.Xjef_i2B3OQ.

CHAPTER 3. PHW'S WAR ON VENEREAL DISEASE

1. Dai Jūgokai Sangiin Honkaigi Dai Nijūhachi Gō, February 27, 1953, 4, https://kokkai.ndl.go.jp/simple/dispPDF?minId=101515254X02819530227.

2. See, for example, "From: Commander Naval Activities Japan. To: Naval Activities Japan. Subject: Control of Venereal Disease," August 2, 1946, along with "Enclosure (A): 'Venereal Disease Rate per 1000 per Annum,'" NARA, RG 331, GHQ/SCAP, box 9370, folder 8: "Venereal Disease Control 1945–1946" (hereafter cited as RG 331, box 9370, folder 8). See also the various monthly reports in RG 331, box 9370, folder 8, and folder 7: "Venereal Disease Admission Rates."

3. Sams, *"Medic,"* 109.

4. See, for example, Fujime Yuki, *Sei no Rekishigaku* (Tokyo: Fuji Shuppan, 2015), 327, 418; Hirai Kazuko, *Nihon Senryō to Jendaa* (Tokyo: Yūshisha, 2014), 88; Okuda Akiko, "GHQ no Seiseisaku," in *Senryō to Sei* (Tokyo: Impakuto, 2007), 38–39.

5. See, for example, John W. Dower, *Embracing Defeat* (New York: W. W. Norton and New Press, 1999), 579n16; Yuki Tanaka, *Japan's Comfort Women: Sexual Slavery and Prostitution during World War II and the US Occupation* (New York: Routledge, 2002), 163.

6. For example, Yuki Tanaka cites documents that presented *annualized* infection *rates* as if they represented current *percentages* of infected troops. See Tanaka, *Japan's Comfort Women*, 155, 202n67. Another document Tanaka cites actually contains no statistics at all and is in fact PHW chief Crawford F. Sams' endorsement of a proposal to outlaw prostitution in Japan altogether. See Tanaka, *Japan's Comfort Women*, 161–62, 203n90, and compare to Crawford F. Sams, "Subject: Suppression of Prostitution in Japan," December 26, 1946, RG 331, box 9370, folder 4: "726.1 Abolition of Licensed Prostitution" (hereafter cited as RG 331, box 9370, folder 4).

7. For example, Yamamoto Shunichi, despite writing an otherwise essentially sound medical history repeats this basic narrative in *Nihon Baishun Seibyōshi* (Tokyo: Bunkōdo, 2002), 124–26, 130–32.

8. Takao Suzuki, *Paleopathological and Paleoepidemiological Study of Osseous Syphilis in Skulls of the Edo Period* (Tokyo: University of Tokyo Press, 1984), 4.

9. Suzuki Takao, *Hone kara Mita Nihonjin* (Tokyo: Kōdansha, 2010), 212.

10. Kariya Haruo, *Edo no Seibyō* (Tokyo: Sanichi Shobō, 1993), 27.

11. Kariya, 33.

12. Kariya, 34–36.

13. Kariya, 36–39.

14. Fukuda Masato, "Kenbai no Hajimari to Baidoku no Gensetsu," *Gengo Bunka Ronshū* 25, no. 1 (2003): 2.

15. Engelbert Kaempfer, *Kaempfer's Japan*, trans. and ed. Beatrice M. Bodart-Bailey (Honolulu: University of Hawai'i Press, 1999), 279.

16. John Z. Bowers, *When the Twain Meet* (Baltimore: Johns Hopkins University Press, 1980), 19.

17. Takao Suzuki, *Paleopathological and Paleoepidemiological Study of Osseous Syphilis in Skulls of the Edo Period* (Tokyo: University of Tokyo Press, 1984), 42.

18. Quoted in Suzuki, 4.

19. "Skeletal Remains of over 1,500 People Unearthed at Osaka Site Reveal City's Past," *Mainichi Daily News*, August 18, 2020.

20. S.v. "Toya," meaning 3, in Shogakkan, *Nihonkokugo Daijiten*; Kariya, *Edo no Seibyō*, 40–41.

21. William Willis, "Prostitution in Japan," November 26, 1867, 3, William Willis Papers, 44-9, in Yokohama Kaikō Shiryōkan, Yokohama, Japan. A more legible copy of the same report, dated September 1871, is in William Willis Papers, 44-13. Here the same information appears on 11.

22. Willis, "Prostitution in Japan," November 26, 1867, 5–6, William Willis Papers, 44-9.

23. Willis (1871 copy), 25.

24. A. Hamish Ion, "Sexual Imperialism on the China Station during the Meiji Restoration: The Control of Smallpox and Syphilis at Yokohama," *International History Review* 31, no. 4 (December 2009): 710–39.

25. Ion, 731.

26. Quoted in Kariya, 45.

27. Willis, "Prostitution in Japan" (1871 copy), 25.

28. Kariya, *Edo no Seibyō*, 111–12.

29. Ion, "Sexual Imperialism," 734.

30. Ion, 36, 39, 110.

31. William Willis, "Proposed Regulations for Mitigating Spread of Syphilis at Yokohama," October 19, 1867, 140–41, William Willis Papers, 146, in Yokohama Kaikō Shiryōkan.

32. Ion, "Sexual Imperialism."

33. James H. Gordon, "Memorandum for the Record; Subject: Conference with Dr. H. Yosano and Dr. Fukai," October 3, 1945, RG 331, box 9370, folder 8.

34. Andō Masakichi, *Wagakuni no Seibyō: Genjo to Taisaku* (Tokyo: Nippon Seibyō Yobō Kyokai, 1941), 311.

35. Ion, "Sexual Imperialism," 736; Sabine Früstuck, "Managing the Truth of Sex in Imperial Japan," *Journal of Asian Studies* 59, no. 2 (May 2000): 332–58.

36. Sey Nishimura, "Promoting Public Health during the Occupation of Japan: The Public Health Section, Kyoto Military Government Team, 1945–1949," *American Journal of Public Health* 9, no. 3 (March 2008): 427; "Table 16— Death Rates for the Ten Leading Causes of Death: Japan, 1920–1948," in GHQ/SCAP, box 9321, folder 1: "Summary Report of TB Control Activity in Japan."

37. Yamamoto Shunichi, *Baishun Seibyōshi* (Tokyo: Bunkōdō, 2002), 104.

38. Kanō Jigorō, *Kanō Jigorō Chosakushū*, vol. 1, (Tokyo: Gogatsu Shobō, 1983), 196.

39. Sabine Früstuck, *Colonizing Sex* (Berkeley: University of California Press, 2003), 89–90.

40. Sumiko Otsubo, "Feminist Maternal Eugenics in Japan," *U.S.-Japan Women's Journal. English Supplement*, no. 17 (1999): 43, 45.

41. Otsubo, 56–57.

42. Yamamoto, 105.
43. Kōseishō Yobōkyoku, *Kokumi Yūsei Zukai* (Tokyo: Issei, 1941), 74, 71, 70.
44. R. A. Vonderlehr and Lida J. Usilton, "Syphilis among Men of Draft Age in the United States," *Journal of the American Medical Association* 120, no. 17 (December 26, 1942): 1372.
45. William J. Fleming, "The Venereal Disease Problem in the United States in World War II," *Journal of the Mitchell Society*, August 1945, 195.
46. Kumai Seiichi, *Hoken Eisei Shidōsha ni Hitsuyō Naru Seibyō no Chishiki to Yobō* (Tokyo: Shindan to Chiryōsha, 1953), 12; Yoshiaki Yoshimi, *Comfort Women*, trans. Suzanne O'Brien (New York: Columbia University Press, 2002).
47. Sarah Kovner, *Occupying Power* (Stanford, CA: Stanford University Press, 2012), 32.
48. See chapter 2 for details.
49. H. H. MacDonald, "Memorandum for the Record. Subject: Elimination of Licensed Prostitution in Japan," January 7, 1946, 2, NARA, RG 331, GHQ/SCAP, box 408, folder 12 (1–2), 000-5, no. 1.
50. Robert L. Eichelberger, diary entry, September 11, 1945, in Robert L. Eichelberger Papers, box 1, folder titled "Miscellaneous: Diary Photocopies: Diaries: July 23–October 20; October 24–December 4," Rubenstein Library, Duke University, Durham, NC.
51. Sams, *"Medic,"* 17.
52. James H. Gordon, "Memorandum for the Record; Subject Conference with Major Philip Weisbach, M.C., C.O. 1st Med Squadron, 1st Cavalry Div.," September 30, 1945, RG 331, box 9370, folder 8.
53. Crawford F. Sams, "Memorandum; From: Public Health and Welfare Section; To: Chief of Staff; Subject: Summary of Venereal Disease Control Activities in the Civilian Population of Japan, September 1945 to February 1946," March 9, 1946, RG 331, box 9370, folder 8.
54. Isamu Nieda, "Summary Report of Venereal Disease Control Activities in Japan, October 1945–December 1949," 1, NARA, RG 331, GHQ/SCAP, box 9321: "PH&W," folder 2–3: "October 1945–December 1949 Summary Report _VD Control; Dr. Nieda."
55. Sams, *"Medic,"* 150.
56. Richard B. Frank, "MacArthur's Shining Hour," lecture given on November 23, 2016, at the U.S. National World War 2 International Conference, New Orleans, Louisiana, transcript, 1.
57. See, for example, "Memorandum for Record; Subject Visit to Kyushu and Southern Honshu," February 28, 1946, NARA, RG 331, GHQ/SCAP, box 9336: "C/D Reports to Far East Command," folder 5: "Venereal Disease Control Staff Visits," subfolder: "Venereal Disease Control Staff Visits, 1945-1946-1947-1948-1949"

(hereafter cited as RG 331, box 9336, folder 5, subfolder: "Venereal Disease Control Staff Visits, 1945–1948").

58. Takemae, *Inside GHQ*, 190.

59. Frank, "MacArthur's Shining Hour," 2.

60. Takemae, *Inside GHQ*, 190; Frank, "MacArthur's Shining Hour," 3–4.

61. "Preventive Vaccination Law #68, 1948," 1, NARA, RG 331, GHQ/SCAP, box 9321, folder 1: "Summary Report of TB Control Activity in Japan."

62. M. D. Dickinson, "Summary of Tuberculosis Control Activities, October 1945–December 1949," 5; and "Use of Streptomycin in the Treatment and Control of Tuberculosis in Japan," *Public Health and Welfare Technical Bulletin*, March 1949, both in NARA, RG 331, GHQ/SCAP, box 9321, folder 1: "Summary Report of TB Control Activity in Japan."

63. Sey Nishimura, "Promoting Public Health during the Occupation of Japan," 427.

64. "Table 16—Death Rates for the Ten Leading Causes of Death: Japan, 1920–1948," RG 331, GHQ/SCAP, box 9321, folder 1: "Summary Report of TB Control Activity in Japan."

65. Takemae, *Inside GHQ*, 413.

66. Frank, "MacArthur's Shining Hour," 20–21; National Institute for Education Policy Research, "School Lunch Program in Japan," n.d., 3–4, https://www .nier.go.jp/English/educationjapan/pdf/201303SLP.pdf (accessed January 16, 2023).

67. Nieda, "Summary Report," 1.

68. Nieda, 1.

69. James H. Gordon, "Memorandum for the Record; Subject: Conference with Dr. H. Yosano and Dr. Fukai," and B. P. W., "Memorandum for the Record; Subject: Venereal Disease in Japan," October 3, 1945, NARA, RG 331, box 9370, folder 8.

70. Gordon, "Memorandum for the Record; Subject: Conference with Dr. H. Yosano and Dr. Fukai."

71. C. F. S., "Prostitution and Venereal Disease in Japan and Korea," October 5, 1945, RG 331, box 9370, folder 8.

72. See Gordon, "Memorandum for the Record; Subject: Conference with Dr. H. Yosano and Dr. Fukai."

73. James H. Gordon, "Memorandum for the Record; Subject: Prevalence of Venereal Diseases in the Prostitutes of Tokyo and Yokohama," October 21, 1945, RG 331, box 9370, folder 8.

74. Crawford F. Sams, "Memorandum for the Chief of Staff," October 16, 1945, RG 331, box 9370, folder 8.

75. James H. Gordon, "Memorandum for the Record; Subject: Conference with Dr. Yosano, Tokyo Health Department, on Venereal Disease," October 26, 1945, RG 331, box 9370, folder 8.

76. James H. Gordon, "Memorandum for the Record; Subject: Conference with Colonel Shaw, Executive Officer, Office of the Provost Marshal, Tokyo and Others Regard [*sic*.] Venereal Disease Control," October 28, 1945, RG 331, box 9370, folder 8.

77. Nieda, "Summary Report," 2.

78. James H. Gordon, "Memorandum for the Record. Subject: Conference with Dr. Terada and Dr. Yosano on VD Control," November 10, 1945, and "Plan for the Use of Anti-Venereal Drugs Released to the Japanese from U.S. Army Stocks," RG 331, box 9370, folder 8.

79. Oscar M. Elkins, "Memorandum for Record: Subject: Venereal Disease Control Inspection Trip to Saitama Prefecture," November 1, 1946, RG 331, box 9336, folder 5, subfolder: "Venereal Disease Control Staff Visits, 1945–1948."

80. Okuno Akiko, "GHQ no Seiseisaku," 39. Others who make essentially the same argument about GHQ or the U.S. Army generally are Fujime Yuki, *Sei no Rekishigaku*, 327, 418; and Hirai Kazuko, *Nihon Senryō to Jendaa*, 2, 88.

81. Nieda, "Summary Report," 21.

82. Oscar M. Elkins, "Memorandum: Subject: Summary of Initial Venereal Disease Control Reports," March 28, 1947, 4, NARA, RG 331, GHQ/SCAP, box 9370: "Prostitution/Venereal Disease," folder 5: "Venereal Disease Contact Tracing" (hereafter cited as RG 331, box 9370, folder 5).

83. Gordon, "Memorandum for the Record; Subject: Conference with Dr. H. Yosano and Dr. Fukai."

84. James H. Gordon, "Memorandum for Record; Subject: Venereal Disease Control," October 22, 1945, RG 331, box 9370, folder 8; H. H. MacDonald, "Memorandum for the Record; Subject: Prostitution in Japan; Contracts; Regulations, Public and Private Prostitutes," December 29, 1945, RG 331, box 9370, folder 4.

85. James H. Gordon, "Memorandum for the Record; Subject Conference with Major Philip Weisbach, M.C., C.O. 1st Med Squadron, 1st Cavalry Div.," September 30, 1945, RG 331, box 9370, folder 8.

86. Stephen H. Duggan, "Tokyo-Yokohama Chapter Army-Navy Chaplains Association; Subject: Repression of Prostitution: To: Supreme Commander for the Allied Powers, General Headquarters," January 11, 1946, 2, RG 331, box 9370, folder 8; Sams, *"Medic,"* 106.

87. Nieda, "Summary Report," 19; Sams, *"Medic,"* 104–5; Duggan, "Tokyo-Yokohama Chapter Army-Navy Chaplains Association," 2.

88. Nieda, "Summary Report," 11, 19.
89. S. Yamashita, Chief, Oita Liaison and Coordination Office, "To: The Commanding Officer, Oita Military Government Team; From: Chief, Oita Liaison & Coordination Office; Subject: Petition concerning the Control of Prostitutes," in James H. Gordon, Lt. Col., MC, Chief, Preventive Medicine Division, "Memorandum for Record; Subject: Visit to Kyushu and Southern Honshu," February 28, 1946, RG 331, box 9336, folder 5: "Venereal Disease Control Staff Visits"; Nieda, "Summary Report," 17–18.
90. See, for example, Oscar M. Elkins, "Memorandum for Record: Subject: V.D. Inspection Trip to Chogoku [sic] Military Government Region," April 8, 1947, RG 331, box 9336, folder 5, subfolder: "Venereal Disease Control Staff Visits, 1945–1948."
91. Elkins, "Memorandum: Subject: Summary of Initial Venereal Disease Control Reports."
92. Sams, *"Medic,"* 21.
93. Sams, 156.
94. Sams, 105.
95. Sams, 109. See also chapter 2 above.
96. Sams, 109.
97. Nieda, "Summary Report," 16. See also chapter 2 above.
98. Nieda, 4.
99. Crawford F. Sams, untitled memorandum, December 26, 1946, RG 331, box 9370, folder 4.
100. H. H. MacDonald, "Memorandum for the Record: Subject: Discussion of Venereal Disease Control," October 16, 1945, RG 331, box 9370, folder 8; Ashida Hitoshi, diary entry for October 16, 1945, *Ashida Nikki*, vol. 1 (Tokyo: Iwanami Shoten, 1986), 220–21.
101. Elkins, "Memorandum: Subject: Summary Initial of Venereal Disease Control Reports," 5.
102. Sams, *"Medic,"* 22.
103. S(ylvan) E. Moulten, "Memorandum for Record; Subject: Comparative Survey of Japanese and American Serological Methods for Diagnosis of Syphilis," January 17, 1946, RG 331, box 9370, folder 8.
104. James H. Gordon, "Memorandum for Record; Subject: Conference with Prof. T. Ichikawa and Dr. K. Miyata," January 16, 1946, RG 331, box 9370, folder 8.
105. Takano Rokurō, *Yobō Igaku Nōto* (Tokyo: Kawade Shobō, 1942).
106. B. P. W., "Memorandum for Record; Subject: Venereal Disease in Japan," October 3, 1945, RG 331, box 9370, folder 8.

107. James H. Gordon, "Memorandum for the Record; Subject: Conference with Dr. T. Ichikawa, Professor of Urology, Tokyo Imperial University," October 27, 1945, RG 331, box 9370, folder 8.

108. Ikuzo Toyama, Letter to [Lt.] Col. Gordon, received January 31, 1946, RG 331, box 9370, folder 8.

109. Enclosure of letter from Toyama Ikuzo to James Gordon, received January 31, 1946, RG 331, box 9370, folder 8.

110. "SCAPIN-153; Memorandum For: The Japanese Imperial Government; Through: Central Liaison Office, Tokyo; Subject: Control of Venereal Disease," https://dl.ndl.go.jp/pid/9885216/1/1 (accessed January 22, 2023).

111. Enclosure of letter from Toyama Ikuzo to James Gordon, received January 31, 1946, RG 331, box 9370, folder 8.

112. "SCAPIN-153; Memorandum For: The Japanese Imperial Government; Through: Central Liaison Office, Tokyo; Subject: Control of Venereal Disease," https://dl.ndl.go.jp/pid/9885216/1/1 (accessed January 22, 2023).

113. Elkins, "Memorandum: Subject: Summary of Initial Venereal Disease Control Reports," 10.

114. Elkins, "Memorandum: Subject: Summary of Initial Venereal Disease Control Reports," 4.

115. Elkins, "Memorandum: Subject: Summary of Initial Venereal Disease Control Reports," 4.

116. Oscar M. Elkins, "Memorandum for Record; Subject: School for Japanese Prefectural VDCOs," December 5, 1946, and "List of the Names of the Attendants at the Course in Venereal Diseases Control (held on 5, 6 and 7 December 1946)," both in RG 331, box 9370, folder 8.

117. Elkins, "Memorandum: Subject: Summary of Initial Venereal Disease Control Reports," 9.

118. Philip E. M. Bourland, "Venereal Disease Control and Treatment Problems in Tokyo," June 6, 1946, RG 331, box 9370, folder 8.

119. Oscar M. Elkins, "Memorandum for Record; Subject: Venereal Disease Control in the Tokyo and Yokohama Areas," October 11, 1946, RG 331, box 9370, folder 8.

120. Elkins, "Memorandum for Record; Subject: Venereal Disease Control in the Tokyo and Yokohama Areas," 2.

121. Elkins, "Memorandum for Record; Subject: Venereal Disease Control in the Tokyo and Yokohama Areas."

122. "Seibyō no Sakkon wo Kataru," *Sanfujinka no Sekai* 3, no. 1 (January 1951): 81, 83, 84.

123. Nieda, "Summary Report," 10.
124. Nieda, 11.
125. Kōeki Zaidan Hōjin Kekkaku Yobōkai (Japan Anti-Tuberculosis Association), https://www.jatahq.org/about_tb/ (accessed February 14, 2023).
126. Nieda, "Summary Report."
127. For details about these visits, see RG 331, box 9336, folder 5, subfolder: "Venereal Disease Control Staff Visits, 1945–1948."
128. Oscar M. Elkins, "Memorandum for Record: Subject: Inspection of Civilian V.D. Facilities in Kyushu," May 2, 1947, 1, RG 331, box 9336, folder 5, subfolder: "Venereal Disease Control Staff Visits, 1945–1948."
129. M. D. Dickinson, "Memo for Record; Subject: Staff Visit by Dr. M. D. Dickinson," August 9, 1950, RG 331, box 9336, folder 5, subfolder: "Venereal Disease Control Staff Visits, 1949–1950."
130. Nieda, "Summary Report," 12.
131. Sams, *"Medic,"* 157.
132. Nieda, "Summary Report," 17.
133. Marta Green, "Recommendations for Repression of Prostitution," August 31, 1949, NARA, RG 331, GHQ/SCAP, box 9370: "Prostitution/Venereal Disease," folder 3: "Rehabilitation of Prostitutes" (hereafter cited as RG 331, box 9370, folder 3).
134. Marta Green, "Memorandum for Record: Rehabilitation Homes for Women," August 12, 1950, RG 331, box 9370, folder 3.
135. Esther B. Rhodes, "Memoradum: To: Mrs. Green, PH&W Section, GHQ, APO 500," February 25, 1950, RG 331, box 9370, folder 3.
136. Marta Green, "Memorandum for Record; Subject: Rough Draft of Proposed Minimum Standards for Women's Rehabilitation Homes," February 24, 1950, RG 331, box 9370, folder 3.
137. Marta Green, "Memorandum for Record; Subject: Field Trip to Kanagawa Prefecture by M. Green WD/PHW," September 28, 1949, RG 331, box 9370, folder 3.
138. Marta Green, "Memorandum for Record; Subject: Inspection of Hatogaya Joshi Rehabilitation Home for Prostitutes," September 15, 1945, RG 331, box 9370, folder 3.
139. Marta Green, "Memorandum for Record; Subject: Inspection of Jai Ryo—Rehabilitation Home for Prostitutes," September 22, 1949, RG 331, box 9370, folder 3.
140. Marta Green, "Memorandum for Record; Subject: Visit to Seiju Home—Rehabilitation Home for Prostitutes," August 24, 1949, and "Field Trip to Kanagawa Prefecture," RG 331, box 9370, folder 3.

141. Marta Green, "Memorandum for Record; Subject: Conference with Miss Goss, ESS Women's Section and Mrs. Tanino, Women Workers Section, Women & Minors Bureau, Labor Ministry," November 29, 1949, and "Memorandum for Record; Subject: Conference with Miss Williamson, CI&E Home Economics Specialist," November 28, 1949, RG 331, box 9370, folder 3.

142. Marta Green, "Memorandum for Record; Subject: Conference of the Directors of the Girls Rehabilitation Institutions in Japan," February 24, 1950, RG 331, box 9370, folder 3.

143. Marta Green, "Memorandum for Record; Subject: Rehabilitation Homes for Women," August 12, 1950, RG 331, box 9370, folder 3.

144. Nieda, "Summary Report," 14.

145. Nieda, 13.

146. M. D. Dickinson, "Memo for Record; Subject: Staff Visit by Dr. M. D. Dickinson," June 29, 1950, RG 331, box 9336, folder 5, subfolder: "Venereal Disease Control Staff Visits, 1949–1950."

147. See, for example, "Number of Cases and Rates of Venereal Diseases in Kanto Region, 1948 and 1949," statistical chart in RG 331, box 9336, folder 5, subfolder: "Venereal Disease Control Staff Visits, 1949–1950."

148. Enclosure of letter from Toyama Ikuzo to James Gordon, received January 31, 1946, RG 331, box 9370, folder 8.

149. Isamu Nieda, "Memorandum for Record; Subject: VD Inspection Trip to Ibaraki Prefecture," July 1, 1948, RG 331, box 9336, folder 5, subfolder: "Venereal Disease Control Staff Visits, 1945–1948."

150. Enclosure to Isamu Nieda, "Memorandum for Record; Subject: Staff Visit by: Dr. I Nieda," April 9, 1949, RG 331, box 9336, folder 5, subfolder: "Venereal Disease Control Staff Visits, 1949–1950."

151. Isamu Nieda, "Memorandum for Record; Subject: Staff Visit by: Dr. I. Nieda," January 26, 1949, RG 331, box 9336, folder 5, subfolder: "Venereal Disease Control Staff Visits, 1949–1950."

152. Nieda, "Summary Report," 23.

153. Dai Jūnanakai Kokkai Sangiin Hōmu Iinkai, Heikaigo Daiichi Gō, 9–10, https://kokkai.ndl.go.jp/minutes/api/v1/detailPDF/img/101715206X00119531119 (accessed February 16, 2023).

154. "From: Washington (SPMDN); To: CINCAFPAC; NR: WCL 49669," February 26, 1946, RG 331, box 9370, folder 8; Nieda, "Summary Report," 10–11.

155. Segi Mitsuo and Fukushima Ichirō, "Seibyō ni Kan Suru Tōkei," *Sanfujinka no Sekai* 3, no. 1 (January 1951): 96. The statistics for 1948 show only 4,356 deaths; however, statistics before the passage of the Venereal Disease Prevention Law of 1948, which mandated reporting, are not as reliable.

156. The number depends on whether syphilis deaths were counted among the estimated 100,000 deaths due to communicable disease through 1948.

157. "Complete Life Tables of Japan 2005," Japanese Ministry of Health, Labour, and Welfare, https://www.mhlw.go.jp/english/database/db-hw/lifetb20th /introduction.html (accessed January 10, 2023).

CHAPTER 4. "HOT AND FORCING VIOLATION"

1. Jonathan Gottschall, *The Rape of Troy* (New York: Cambridge University Press, 2008).

2. Numbers 31:17–18, 35.

3. William Shakespeare, *Henry V*, 3.3.21.

4. J. Glenn Gray, *The Warriors* (New York: Harper and Row, 1970), 67.

5. Malcolm Potts and Thomas Hayden, *Sex and War* (Dallas: Benbella Books, 2008), 3.

6. U.S. Institute of Peace, "Rape in War: Motives of Militia in the DRC," Special Report 243, June 2010; "Report of the International Commission of Inquiry on Darfur to the United Nations Secretary-General," January 25, 2005, 60, 69, 87–94.

7. International Rescue Committee Commission on Syrian Refugees, *Syria: A Regional Crisis*, January 2013, 6–7.

8. Azar Gat, *War in Human Civilization* (New York: Oxford University Press, 2006), 67–76.

9. Potts and Hayden, *Sex and War*, 154–56.

10. Rukmini Callimachi, "ISIS Enshrines a Theology of Rape," *New York Times*, August 13, 2015.

11. Potts and Hayden, *Sex and War*, 9–10.

12. *Warburton Mission II Report*, http://www.womenaid.org/press/info /humanrights/warburtonfull.htm (accessed February 19, 2023).

13. See chapter 1.

14. Steven Pinker, *The Blank Slate* (New York: Viking, 2002), 368.

15. International Rescue Committee Commission on Syrian Refugees, *Syria: A Regional Crisis*, January 2013, 6.

16. Michael Bilton and Kevin Sim, *Four Hours in My Lai* (New York: Penguin, 1992), 128–29.

17. Lorenzo Tondo and Isobel Koshiw, "Evidence Some Ukrainian Women Raped before Being Killed Say Doctors," *The Guardian*, April 25, 2022, https://www.theguardian.com/world/2022/apr/25/evidence-ukraine -women-raped-before-being-killed-say-doctors-russia-war.

18. James M. Scott, *Rampage* (New York: W. W. Norton, 2018), 338.

19. Aki Peritz and Tara Maller, "The Islamic State of Sexual Violence," *Foreign Policy*, September 16, 2014.

20. International Rescue Committee Commission on Syrian Refugees, *Syria: A Regional Crisis*, January 2013, 6.

21. Nicholas Thompson, *The Hawk and the Dove: Paul Nitze, George Kennan and the History of the Cold War* (New York: Henry Holt, 2009), 211.

22. John Ferling, *Whirlwind* (New York: Bloomsbury, 2015), 59.

23. David Hackett Fischer, *Washington's Crossing* (New York: Oxford University Press, 2004), 178–79.

24. Bob Tadashi Wakabayashi, "Opium, Expulsion, Sovereignty: China's Lessons for Bakumatsu Japan," *Monumenta Nipponica* 47, no. 1 (Spring 1992): 14.

25. Keith L. Jackson, "'Black Horror on the Rhine,'" *Journal of Modern History* 42, no. 4 (December 1970): 606–27. See especially 617–20.

26. Jackson, 626.

27. "Memorandum of Chancellor Scharffenberg, German Embassy, Nanking Office," January 13, 1938, reprinted in John Rabe, *The Good Man of Nanking: The Diaries of John Rabe*, ed. Erwin Wickert, trans. John E. Woods (New York: Alfred A. Knopf, 1998), 132.

28. Neil Kagan and Steven G. Hyslop, *The Secret History of World War II* (Washington, DC: National Geographic, 2016), 170.

29. Robert Shaffer, "A Rape in Beijing, December 1946: GIs, Nationalist Protests, and U.S. Foreign Policy," *Pacific Historical Review* 69, no. 1 (February 2000): 31–64.

30. Ben Hubbard, "Libyan Spy Files Detail Gadhafi Regime's Collapse," *Pittsburgh Post-Gazette*, September 5, 2011. The same accusation was made against the Gadhafi regime, whose forces have more credibly been reported participating in war rape. Pascale Harter, "Libya Rape Victims 'Face Honour Killings,'" *BBC News*, June 14, 2011.

31. Douglas Brinkley, "Painting to Sound the Alarm in the Wake of Pearl Harbor," *New York Times*, December 8, 2003.

32. Ironically, considering the brutalities meted out to other women captured by the Japanese, the nurses taken on Corregidor were treated relatively decently, at least initially. John C. McManus, *Fire and Fortitude* (New York: Penguin, Random House, 2019), 470–71.

33. Eiji Oguma, *A Genealogy of Japanese Self-Images*, trans. David Askew (Melbourne: Transpacific Press, 2002), 221.

34. John F. Embree, *A Japanese Village: Suye Mura* (London: Kegan Paul, Trench, Trubner and Co., 1946), 150.

35. *Makete Katsu* (TV mini-series), episode 1, teleplay by Sakamoto Yūji, dir. Yanagawa Tsuyoshi, NHK, 2012.

36. Bōeichō Bōeikenshūjo Senshishitsu, ed., *Senshi Sōsho: Hondo Kessen Junbi*, vol. 2: *Kyūshū no Bōei* (Tokyo: Asagumo Shinbunsha, 1972), 165, 239, 247, 433.

37. Bōeichō Bōeikenshūjo Senshishitsu, 2:12, 271–72, 408–11, 422–23, 445–46; Gunjishigakkai, *Kimitsu Sensō Nisshi*, vol. 2 (Tokyo: Kinseisha, 1998), 726, 734, 742, 751.

38. Handō Kazutoshi, *Sensō to iu Mono* (Tokyo: PHP, 2021), 140–41.

39. Yamada Fūtarō, *Senchūha Fusen Nikki* (Tokyo: Kōdansha, 2002), 639.

40. Sarah Kovner, *Occupying Power* (Stanford, CA: Stanford University Press, 2012), 49.

41. *Waga Kokyō wa Saipan* (NHK Nagoya), broadcast November 11, 2005.

42. Denis Warner and Peggy Warner with Sadao Seno, *The Sacred Warriors* (New York: Van Nostrand Reinhold, 1982), 89.

43. D. Warner and P. Warner, 315–16.

44. Handō Kazutoshi, *Sensō to iu Mono* (Tokyo: PHP, 2021), 138–40.

45. Handō, 140.

46. "Understanding Himeyuri," Himeyuri Peace Museum English website, https://www.himeyuri.or.jp/EN/war.html (accessed August 26, 2022).

47. Oshiro Masayasu, *Okinawasen: Minshū no Me de Toraeru Sensō* (Tokyo: Kobunsha, 1988), 40.

48. Haruko Taya Cook and Theodore Cook, *Japan at War: An Oral History* (New York: New Press, 1992), 367. I also heard harrowing, though secondhand, testimony of such events on the island of Zamami in the Kerama Islands in Okinawa Prefecture.

49. Norma Field, *In the Realm of a Dying Emperor: Japan at Century's End* (New York: Vintage, 1993), 56–59.

50. The Pacific War Research Society, *Japan's Longest Day* (Tokyo: Kōdansha International, 1980), 295.

51. Handō, *Sensō to iu Mono*, 141–42.

52. Okayama Ken Keisatsushi Hensan Iinkai, *Okayama Ken Keisatsushi*, vol. 2 (Okayama: Okayama Bijutsu Shikō, 1976), 204.

53. Yamagata Ken Keisatsushi Hensan Iinkai, *Yamagata Ken Keisatsushi*, vol. 2 (Yamagata: Tamiya Insatsujo, 1971), 996.

54. See Hokkaidō Keisatsushi Henshū Iinkai, ed., *Hokkaidō Keisatsushi, Shōwa Hen* (Sapporo: Hokkaidō Keisatsu Honbu, 1968), 569; Aomori Ken Keisatsushi Hensan Iinkai, ed., *Aomori Ken Keisatsushi*, vol. 2 (Hirosaki: Ono Insatsu, 1977), 680; Gifu Ken Keisatsushi Hensan Iinkai, ed., *Gifu Ken Keisatsushi*, vol.

2 (Tokyo: Daiichi Hōki Shuppan, 1982), 391, 401, 418; Shizuoka Ken Keisatsushi Hensan Iinkai, ed., *Shizuoka Ken Keisatsushi*, vol. 2 (Shizuoka: Shizuoka Keisatsu Honbu, 1979), 579, 585; Kanagawa Ken Keisatsushi Hensan Iinkai, ed., *Kanagawa Ken Keisatsushi*, vol. 3 (Yokohama: Kanagawa Keisatsu Honbu, 1974), 20–21; Chiba Ken Keisatsushi Hensan Iinkai, ed., *Chiba Ken Keisatsushi*, vol. 2 (Tokyo: Tōkyō Horei Shuppan, 1987), 460; Saitama Ken Keisatsushi Hensan Iinkai, ed., *Saitama Ken Keisatsushi* (Tokyo: Tōkyō Horei Shuppan, 1977); Aichi Ken Keisatsushi Henshū Iinkai, ed., *Aichi Ken Keisatsushi* (Nagoya: Aichi Ken Keisatsu Honbu, 1971), 12; Tottori Ken Keisatsushi Hensan Iinkai, ed., *Tottori Ken Keisatsushi*, vol. 1 (Tottori City: Yatani Insatsusho, 1981), 1071, 1075; Wakayama Ken Keisatsushi Hensan Iinkai, ed., *Wakayama Ken Keisatsushi*, vol. 2 (Tokyo: Kawakita Insatsusho, 1992), 477; Kyōtofu Keisatsushi Henshū Iinkai, ed., *Kyōtofu Keisatsushi*, vol. 3 (Kyōto: Kyōto Keisatsu Honbu, 1980), 586; Ōsaka Fu Keisatsushi Hensan Iinkai, ed., *Ōsaka Fu Keisatsushi*, vol. 3 (Ōsaka: Ōsaka Fu Keisatsu Honbu, 1973), 16–19, 21; Hyōgo Ken Keisatsushi Hensan Iinkai, *Hyōgo Ken Keisatsushi, Shōwa Hen* (Kobe: Ishikawa Insatsu, 1975), 512–13; Kagawa Ken Keisatsushi Kenshū Iinkai, ed., *Kagawa Ken Keisatsushi* (Nagano: Tōkyō Horei Shuppan, 1957), 156–57; Kōchi Ken Keisatsushi Hensan Iinkai, ed., *Kōchi Ken Keisatsushi Shōwa Hen* (Sagawa: Sagawa Insatsusho, 1979), 100, 105; Ehime Ken Keisatsushi Hensan Iinkai, ed., *Ehime Ken Keisatsushi*, vol. 12 (Imabari: Hara Insatsu, 1978), 562, 565; Okayama Ken Keisatsushi Hensan Iinkai, *Okayama Ken Keisatsushi*, vol. 2 (Okayama: Okayama Bijutsu Shikō, 1976), 204; Shimane Ken Keisatsushi Hensan Iinkai, ed., *Shimane Ken Keisatsushi Shōwa Hen* (Tokyo: Toppan Insatsu, 1984), 441; Fukuoka Ken Keisatsushi Hensan Iinkai, *Fukuoka Ken Keisatsushi*, vol. 1 (Fukuoka: Fukuoka Keisatsu Honbu, 1980).

55. "Manga Gakkō," *Asahi Gurafu*, August 17, 1955, 23.
56. JNDL Japanese Army and Navy Archives, reel 229, T1555, 02462.
57. JNDL Japanese Army and Navy Archives, reel 229, T1555, 02497.
58. JNDL Japanese Army and Navy Archives, reel 229, T1554, 02446.
59. Awaya Kentarō and Nakazono Hiroshi, ed., *Haisen Zengo no Shakai Jōsei*, vol. 6: *Shinchūgun no Dōkō* (Tokyo: Gendai Shiryō Shuppan, 1999), 410.
60. "Arienu Ryakudatsu Bōkō," *Asahi Shimbun*, August 19, 1945, 2.
61. Fukuoka Ken Keisatsushi Hensan Iinkai, *Fukuoka Ken Keisatsushi*, 1:519.
62. Okayama Ken Keisatsushi Hensan Iinkai, *Okayama Ken Keisastushi*, 2:487.
63. JNDL Japanese Army and Navy Archives, reel 229, T1555, 02450.
64. Gifu Ken Keisatsushi Hensan Iinkai, *Gifu Ken Keisatsushi*, 2:419.
65. Kōchi Ken Keisatsushi Hensan Iinkai, *Kōchi Ken Keisatsushi Shōwa Hen*, 105.

66. William C. Chase, *Front Line General* (Houston: Pacesetter Press, 1975), 127.
67. Patrick Barn "Joriku Suru Beiheitachi Yo, Mamore Genjū na Kiritsu," *Asahi Shimbun*, August 19, 1945, 2.
68. Hora Tomio, *Nitchū Senso̅: Nankin Daizangyaku Jiken Shiryo̅shū*, vol. 1 (Tokyo: Aoki Shoten, 1985), 337. Portions of this directive are translated in "The Nanking Atrocity: An Interpretive Overview," in Bob Tadashi Wakabayashi, ed., *The Nanking Atrocity 1937–1938: Complicating the Picture* (New York: Berghahn Books, 2007), 49.
69. Nagai Kafū, *Dancho̅tei Nichijo̅*, vol. 2 (Tokyo: Iwanami Bunko, 1987), 143–44. See also Eri Hotta, *Japan 1941: Countdown to Infamy* (New York: Alfred A. Knopf, 2014), 154.
70. Michihiko Hachiya, *Hiroshima Diary: The Journal of a Japanese Physician, August 6, 1945–September 30, 1945*, trans. Warner Wells (Chapel Hill: University of North Carolina Press, 1955), 194.
71. Field, *In the Realm of a Dying Emperor*, 59.
72. Quoted in Tokkō report from Iwate Prefecture in Awaya and Nakazono, 406.
73. Awaya and Nakazono, 404, 408.
74. One encounter has an American officer stopping at a Japanese police station to inform the officer on duty that Japanese women should avoid being barefoot and should not wear skirts or simple dresses. He also asked that women refrain from "tempting us" by dressing up, wearing lipstick, or drawing eyebrows, as this could become the source of mistaken ideas. See *Asahi Shimbun*, September 12, 1945, 1, bottom (article name is unclear).
75. "Kokorozukai ga Sugite ka? Nyūjō Sōsō no Kanzume," *Asahi Shimbun*, September 12, 1945, 2.
76. Hokkaido Keisatsushi Henshū Iinkai, *Hokkaido Keisatsushi, Sho̅wa Hen* (Sapporo: Hokkaidō Keisatusu Honbu, 1968), 576.
77. Yamagata Ken Keisatsushi Hensan Iinkai, *Yamagata Ken Keisatsushi*, 2:896.
78. Shimane Ken Keisatsushi Hensan Iinkai, *Shimane Ken Keisatsushi Sho̅wa Hen*, 442.

CHAPTER 5. "THE ABSURDITY OF HISTORY"

1. David G. Gilmore, *Manhood in the Making* (New Haven, CT: Yale University Press, 1990), 222–23.
2. Mark McLelland, *Love, Sex, and Democracy in Japan during the American Occupation* (New York: Palgrave Macmillan, 2012), 95–116.
3. Kubushiro Ochimi, "Konketsuji no Atarashii Shomondai," *Nyū Eiji*, March 1953.
4. "Ippan Jidō to Kubetsu Sezu," *Asahi Shimbun*, August 20, 1953, 13, gives a figure of 4,972 based on a Ministry of Health survey. Zenkoku Shakai Fukushi

Kyōgikai, "Igai ni Sukunakatta Konketsuji," *Shakai Jigyō* 35, no. 12 (1952), gives a figure of 1,644, excluding the prefectures of Tokyo (the most populous), Gifu and Wakayama. "Konketsuji wa Gosenjūsannin," *Asahi Shimbun*, December 24, 1952, 7, gives a figure of 5,013 based on a Ministry of Health survey of obstetricians and midwives that excluded Yamagata Prefecture and had a response rate of 77 percent.

5. See, for example, Ishikawa Tatsuzō, "Tokubetsu Kikaku: Fujin Sanseiken Bōkokuron," *Sandei Mainichi* 50, no. 9 (2734): 16–21.

6. Pharr, "The Politics of Women's Rights," 231.

7. "Fujin Sanseiken ni tai Suru Kakusō no Ikō Chōshu," Japanese National Archive (Kokuritsu Kōbun Shokan), Hensei, 3-A, 15, 34-2, http://www.jacar .go.jp/DAS/meta/ (accessed April 18, 2016).

8. Quoted in Nishi Kiyoko, *Senryōka no Nihon Fujin Seisaku* (Tokyo: Domesu Shuppan, 1985), 65.

9. "Fujin Sanseiken ni tai Suru Kakusō no Ikō Chōshu," 5.

10. Douglas MacArthur, *Reminiscences* (New York: McGraw-Hill, 1964), 282–83.

11. See State War Navy Coordinating Committee, "SWNCC 150/4: Politico-Military Problems in the Far East: United States Initial Post-Defeat Policy Relating to Japan," September 21, 1945, http://www.ndl.go.jp/constitution/e /shiryo/01/022shoshi.html (accessed February 23, 2016). The earlier versions of this document are available at the same location.

12. Pharr, "The Politics of Women's Rights," 226.

13. State War Navy Coordinating Committee, "SWNCC 150/4," September 21, 1945.

14. Courtney Whitney, *MacArthur: His Rendezvous with History* (New York: Knopf, 1956), 213.

15. "GHQ no Fujin Mondai: Testimony of Katō Shizue," in *Senryōka no Nihon Fujin Seisaku*, ed. Nishi Kiyoko (Tokyo: Domesu Shuppan, 1985), 58–59.

16. Takemae Eiji, *Inside GHQ* (New York: Continuum, 2002), 240.

17. Takemae, 240.

18. Pharr, "The Politics of Women's Rights," 230.

19. Beate Sirota Gordon, interview by Suzuki Akinori, fall 1992, video in author's possession.

20. Sirota Gordon interview.

21. Sirota Gordon interview.

22. Sirota Gordon interview.

23. Quoted in Margalit Fox, "Beate Gordon, Long-Unsung Heroine of Japanese Women's Rights, Dies at 89," *New York Times*, January 1, 2013, http://www .nytimes.com/2013/01/02/world/asia/beate-gordon-feminist-heroine-in-japan -dies-at-89.html?_r=0.

24. Sirota Gordon interview. In this interview Gordon makes clear that she was well aware that women often exercised far more power within the household than they did in public.

25. Pharr, "The Politics of Women's Rights," 232.

26. The pamphlet featured artwork put together by a team led by Frances Baker née Wismer and later Blakemore. See Michiyo Morioka, *An American Artist in Tokyo: Francis Blakemore 1906–1997* (Seattle: Marquand Books, 2007), 88.

27. Minamikata Satoshi, "A Brief Sketch on Equality of the Sexes and Division of Matrimonial Property at Divorce—Revision of the Family Law since 1945," *Hosei Riron* 35, no. 2 (2002): 127.

28. Kurt Steiner, Far Eastern Section, "Postwar Changes in the Japanese Civil Code," *Washington Law Review* 25, no. 3 (August 1950): 292.

29. Steiner, 194.

30. See chapter 4.

31. Richard J. Smethurst, *A Social Basis for Prewar Japanese Militarism* (Berkeley: University of California Press, 1974).

32. Elise K. Tipton, *The Japanese Police State* (Honolulu: University of Hawai'i Press, 1990), 121–22.

33. Ian W. Toll, *Pacific Crucible* (New York: W. W. Norton, 2012), 96–98.

34. Eiko Ikegami, *The Taming of the Samurai* (Cambridge, MA: Harvard University Press, 1998); Marius B. Jansen, *The Making of Modern Japan* (Cambridge, MA: Belknap Press of Harvard University, 2000), 103.

35. Toll, *Pacific Crucible*, 96–98.

36. Tōjō Hideki, "Senjinkun," http://www.library.pref.nara.jp/event/booklist /W_2013_02/senjinkun.html (accessed April 19, 2016.

37. Saitama Ken, ed., *Shinpen Saitama Kenshi*, vol. 7 (Tokyo: Kabushikigaisha Gyōsei, 1991), 80–81; Tottori Ken Keisatsushi Hensan Iinkai, ed., *Tottori Ken Keisatsushi*, vol. 1 (Tottori City: Yatani Insatsusho, 1981), 1:1077.

38. Spencer A. Sherman and Janice Fuhrman, *Occupied Japan: An Experiment in Democracy* (Oregon Public Broadcasting and Look East Productions, 1996).

39. Mitsuo Fuchida, *For That One Day*, trans. Douglas T. Shinsato and Tadanori Urabe (Kameula, HI: eXperience, 2011), 199.

40. Sherman and Fuhrman, *Occupied Japan*.

41. Sherman and Fuhrman.

42. Phone conversation with Itō Bungaku, June 10, 2012.

43. Faubion Bowers discusses the lack of sanitary facilities in Tokyo during the early Occupation in Sherman and Fuhrman, *Occupied Japan*.

44. *Jitsuroku Nihon Senryō: GHQ Nihon Kaizō no Shichi nen* (Tokyo: Gakshū Kenkyūsha, 2005), 21.

45. *Jitsuroku Nihon Senryō,* 21.

46. Yamada Fūtarō, *Senchūha Fusen Nikki* (Tokyo: Kōdansha, 2002), 560; Nagai Kafū, *Danchōtei Nichijō* (Tokyo: Iwanami Shoten, 1987), 285.

47. Kawai Michi, *Suraidingu Doa,* trans. Nakamura Taeko (Tokyo: Keisenjogakuin, 1995), 143. This autobiography was originally written in English under the title *Sliding Doors,* then translated into Japanese. I had access to only the translation.

48. Harry E. Wildes, *Typhoon in Tokyo* (New York: Macmillan, 1954), 16.

49. See chapter 1.

50. Tottori Ken Keisatsushi Hensan Iinkai, *Tottori Ken Keisatsushi,* 1:1089–93; Gifu Ken Keisatsushi Hensan Iinkai, ed., *Gifu Ken Keisatsushi,* vol. 2 (Tokyo: Daiichi Hōki Shuppan, 1982), 2419–20; Aomori Ken Keisatsushi Hensan Iinkai, ed., *Aomori Ken Keisatsushi,* vol. 2 (Hirosaki: Ono Insatsu, 1977), 679–80; Shimane Ken Keisatsushi Hensan Iinkai, ed., *Shimane Ken Keisatsushi Shōwa Hen* (Toppan Insatsu, 1984), 438; Nara Ken Keisatsushi Henshū Iinkai, ed., *Nara Ken Keisatsushi, Shōwa Hen* (Nara: Nara Keisatsu Honbu, 1978), 314; Kanagawa Ken Keisatsushi Hensan Iinkai, ed., *Kanagawa Ken Keisatsushi,* vol. 3 (Yokohama: Kanagawa Keisatsu Honbu, 1974), 371–72. However, at least one officer was duly impressed to see that American officers, including the Supreme Commander, often returned the salute. See Harada Hiroshi, *MP no Jiipu Kara Mita Senryōka no Tokyo* (Tokyo: Sōshisha, 1994), 18.

51. Kōchi Ken Keisatsushi Hensan Iinkai, ed., *Kōchi Ken Keisatsushi Showa Hen* (Sagawa, Kochi: Sagawa Insatsusho, 1979), 109, 110; *Kanagawa Ken Keisatsushi,* 3:371.

52. *Kōchi Ken Kesatsushi, Shōwa Hen,* 109.

53. See chapter 2.

54. *The Big Picture,* episode "Japan: Our Far East Partner," NARA ARC Identifier 2569524 / Local Identifier 111-TV-254, https://www.youtube.com/watch?v=tGJODnjAUUA (accessed October 2, 2023).

55. Oguma Eiji, *"Minshu" to "Aikoku"* (Tokyo: Shinyōsha, 2002), 276.

56. Oguma, 389.

57. Quoted in Oguma, 279.

58. Quoted in Oguma, 279.

59. Izuoka Manabu, "Karikomi to Seibyōin: Sengo Kanagawa no Sei Seisaku," in Keisen Jogakuen Daigaku Heiwa Bunka Kenkyūjo, ed., *Senryō to Sei* (Tokyo: Impakuto Shuppankai, 2007), 120–21.

60. Ehime Ken Keisatsushi Hensan Iinkai, *Ehime Ken Keisatsushi,* 564. See also Tottori Ken Keisatsushi Hensan Iinkai, *Tottori Ken Keisatsushi,* 1099–1100.

61. Sheldon Garon, *Molding Japanese Minds* (Princeton, NJ: Princeton University Press, 1997), 106–8.

62. Yamamoto Akira quoted in Oguma, *"Minshu" to "Aikoku,"* 276.

63. Nagai Kafu, *Danchoutei Nichijo (ge)* (Tokyo: Iwanami Shoten, 1988), 139 (entry for May 12, 1941).

64. Yamada Fūtarō, *Senchūha Fusen Nikki* (Tokyo: Kōdansha, 2002), 438–39.

65. Sōmuchō Tōkekyoku (Statistics Bureau, Management and Coordination Agency), ed., *Nihon Chōki Tōkei Sōran Daiikkan* (*Historical Statistics of Japan, Vol. 1*) (Tokyo: Nihon Tōkei Kyōkai [Japan Statistical Association], 1987).

66. Lee K. Pennington, *Casualties of History* (Ithaca, NY: Cornell University Press, 2015), 197.

67. "C.L.O. No. 1415 (1.3) Cases of Murder and Intimidation by Japanese against U.S. Servicemen," December 28, 1945, 22, NARA, SCAP Records, box 408, envelope in front of box.

68. "Investigation reports on the prostitutes and those who have offered them the places of prostitution," June 1950, NARA, RG 331, GHQ/SCAP, box 334: "PSD Pistols to Prostitution," folder 40: "Prostitution."

69. Faubion Bowers speaking in Spencer A. Sherman and Janice Fuhrman, *Occupied Japan: An Experiment in Democracy* (Oregon Public Broadcasting and Look East Productions, 1996).

70. Bowers in Sherman and Fuhrman.

71. Digest of undated anonymous letter to General MacArthur received on September 23, 1947, NARA, RG 331, box 502, folder 7 (1–2), 250-1 (hereafter cited as RG 331, box 502, folder 7 [1–2]).

72. Digest of anonymous letter to General MacArthur dated August 3, 1947, RG 331, box 502, folder 7 (1–2), 250-1, no. 1. See also digest of letter dated October 3, 1947, from Chiyoda Mikichi to General MacArthur, RG 331, box 502, folder 7 (1–2).

73. Digest of anonymous undated letter to General MacArthur received on September 23, 1947, RG 331, box 502, folder 7 (1–2), 250-1, no. 1.

74. Digest of anonymous letter to General MacArthur dated January 11, 1947, RG 331, box 502, folder 7 (1–2), 250-1, no. 1.

75. The American was subsequently sentenced to life in prison, but the base commander reduced the term to twenty years of hard labor. "PFC. Collier's Sentence Reduced to Twenty Years Hard Labor," NARA, RG 331, GHQ/SCAP, box 24: "Courtmartials [*sic*]," folder 3: "Courtmartials [*sic*], 1946–."

76. Takami Jun, *Haisen Nikki* (Tokyo: Chūō Kōronsha, 2005), 382–83.

77. Quoted in Hayashi Kaori, Tamura Keiko, and Takatsu Fumiko, *Sensō Hana-yome* (Tokyo: Fuyō Shobō Shuppan, 2002), 88.

78. Kawai Michi, *Suridingu Doa*, trans. Nakamura Taeko (Tokyo: Keisenjogakuin, 1995), 145.
79. Doc. No. 33735, letter from Yokoyama Masayoshi to General MacArthur, August 11, 1947, RG 331, box 502, folder 7 (1–2), 250-1, no. 1.
80. Harada Hiroshi, *MP no Jiipu Kara Mita Senryōka no Tokyo* (Tokyo: Sōshisha, 1994), 61.
81. "Public Displays of Affection," March 23, 1946, RG 331, box 502, folder 7 (1–2), 250-1, no. 2.
82. John D. Glismann, "To: Colonel Devin Kinki Military Government Region; Subject: Operation of Kyoto City Vice-Squads," February 17, 1948, NARA, RG 331, GHQ/SCAP, box 9336: "C/D Reports to Far East Command," folder 5: "Venereal Disease Control Staff Visits, 1945-1946-1947-1948-1949" (hereafter cited as RG 331, box 9336, folder 5).
83. Order of "9 AM 18 February 1948," RG 331, box 9336, folder 5.
84. M. D. Dickinson, "Memo for Record; Subject: Staff Visit—Dr. Dickinson," July 7, 1950, RG 331, box 9336, folder 5, subfolder: "Venereal Disease Staff Visits, 1949–1950."
85. Peggy Hayama interviewed in Sherman and Fuhrman, *Occupied Japan*.
86. See, for example, Shibata Hideaki, *Senryōki no Seibōryoku* (Tokyo: Shin Nihon Shuppansha, 2022).
87. Hayashi, Tamura, and Takatsu, *Sensō Hanayome*, 1, 10, 11.
88. Hayashi, Tamura, and Takatsu, 212.
89. Sumiya Etsuji and Takenaka Katsuo, eds., *Gaishō: Jittai to Sono Shuki* (Tokyo: Yūkōsha, 1949), 224–25. See also Chazono Toshimi, *Panpan to wa Dare Nanoka* [*Who Are the Panpan?*] (Tokyo: Impakuto Shuppankai, 2014), 185–86. *Gaishō* was printed when censorship was still in effect, and the soldier's nationality is omitted.
90. Sumiya and Takenaka, *Gaishō*, 235–36. See also Chazono, *Panpan to wa Dare Nanoka*, 186–87. In this young woman's case, this was her second arrest. She had been in a relationship with a foreigner while working at a cabaret in Ōsaka. During that relationship she had been rounded up and examined; she tested positive for VD and was cured after treatment.
91. Sumiya and Takenaka, *Gaishō*, 72, 86, 92.
92. Chazono, *Panpan to wa Dare Nanoka*, 172.
93. Ichikawa Fusae, "'Dokuritsu' Nippon no Fujin Mondai" ["Women's Issues in 'Independent' Japan"], *Tōyō Keizai Shimpō Bessatsu*, May 1952, 54–55.
94. Hayashi, Tamura, and Takatsu, *Sensō Hanayome*, 19.
95. Sherman and Furhman

CHAPTER 6. *PANPAN* LITERATURE

1. AFI, "AFI's 100 Years . . . 100 Heroes and Villains," archived at https://web .archive.org/web/20110807135547/http://connect.afi.com/site/DocServer /handv100.pdf?docID=246 (accessed October 2, 2023).

2. Harper Lee, *To Kill a Mockingbird* (New York: Grand Central Publishing, 1982), 251.

3. Kanzaki Kiyoshi, *Ketteiban: Kanzaki Repōto* (Tokyo: Gendaishi Shuppankai, 1974), 161–62.

4. Michael Molasky, *The American Occupation of Japan and Okinawa: Literature and Memory* (New York: Routledge, 1999), 11–12.

5. Oguma Eiji, *"Minshu" to "Aikoku"* (Tokyo: Shinyōsha, 2002), 259.

6. Chazono Toshimi, *Panpan to wa Dare Nanoka* [*Who Are the Panpan?*] (Tokyo: Impakuto Shuppankai, 2014), 10–11, 90–95, 254.

7. Molasky, *The American Occupation of Japan and Okinawa*, 113.

8. Nihon Kyōsantō Chūō Iinkai, ed., *Nihon Kyosantō no Gojūnen* (Tokyo: Nihon Kyōsantō Chūōiiinkai Shuppankyoku, 1972), 140.

9. Yanaginuma Masaharu, *Nihon Kyōsantō Undōshi, Sengohen* (Tokyo: Keibunkaku, 1953), 291.

10. Nihon Kyōsantō Sendenkyōikubu and Nihon Kyōsantō Tōkyōtō Iinkai Sendenkyōikubu, "Heiwa he no Fujin no Yōkyū wo Hiroi Tōistu Sensen e," in *Tatakai wa Jinmin no Shinrai no Moto ni*, ed. Nihon Kyōsantō Sendenkyōikubu and Nihon Kyōsantō Tōkyōtō Iinkai Sendenkyōikubu (Tokyo: Nihon Kyōsantō Tōkyōtō Iinkai, 1950), 96–99.

11. Tokuda Kyūichi, "Minzoku no Dokuritsu no Tame ni Zenjinmin Shokun ni Utau," in *Nihon Kyōsantō Gojūnen Mondai Shiryōshu*, vol. 1 (Tokyo: Shin Nippon Shuppansha, 1957), 35–39.

12. Tokuda Kyūichi, "Atarashii Jōsei to Kore ni tai Suru Wagatō no Seisaku," in *Nihon Kyōsantō Gojūnen Mondai Shiryōshu*, 1:13. Though Tokuda's use of this term certainly gave his argument rhetorical flourish, it was something he likely did not say lightly. According to a posthumous tribute by his brother, both of Tokuda's grandmothers were from impoverished families that sold them into prostitution in Okinawa, a profession they both escaped only by becoming concubines of Kagoshima traders. See Tōyō Shokan, ed., *Kaisō no Tokuda Kyūichi* (Tokyo: Tōyō Shokan, 1955), 17–18.

13. "Translation: Immediate Demands," Enclosure to Foreign Service Despatch 482 from USPOLAD Tokyo to the Department of State, Washington, Subject: New Policy Directives of Japan Communist Party, September 27, 1951, NARA, RG 84, entry no. 2828, Tokyo Office of the U.S. Political Advisor Classified General Records, box 68, folder 350.21: "Communism July–September 1951."

14. See, for example, Nikkan Rōdō Tsūshinsha, ed., *Saikin ni Okeru Nikkyō no Kinhonteki Senryaku Senjutsu* (Tokyo: Nikkan Rōdō Tsūshinsha, 1953), 1; Nihon Kyōsantō Chōsaiinkai, ed., *Senryōka Nihon no Bunseki: Amerika wa Nihon wo Dō Shihaishiteiruka* (Kyoto: Sanichishobō, 1953), 254.

15. Fujiwara Michiko, Address to the Japanese Diet, February 27, 1953, http://kokkai.ndl.go.jp/SENTAKU/sangiin/015/0512/01502270512028c.html; http://library.cqpress.com/cqresearcher/document.php?id=cqresrre1952070800 (both accessed October 4, 2023).

16. "Baishun Torishimari Beigun no Kenkatsugai" ["Outlawing Prostitution outside Purview of American Military"], *Asahi Shimbun*, July 24, 1952, 1. Fujiwara's far more dramatic portrayal has come to be accepted by many who write on postwar prostitution in Japan and relations between GIs and Japanese Women. See, for example, Hirai Kazuko, *Nihon Senryō to Jendaa* [*The Japanese Occupation and Gender*] (Tokyo: Yūshisha, 2014), 76.

17. Fujiwara Michiko, Address to the Japanese Diet, February 27, 1953, http://kokkai.ndl.go.jp/SENTAKU/sangiin/015/0512/01502270512028c.html; http://library.cqpress.com/cqresearcher/document.php?id=cqresrre1952070800 (both accessed October 4, 2023).

18. Kokka Chihō Keisatsu Honbu Keijibu Chōsa Tōkeika, ed., *Hanzai Tōkeisho: Daiichibu: Shōwa Nijūnananen* (Tokyo: Okumura Insatsu, 1953), 332.

19. Kokka Chihō Keisatsu Honbu Keijibu Chōsa Tōkeika, 332.

20. Kokka Chihō Keisatsu Honbu Keijibu Chōsa Tōkeika, 332.

21. Kokka Chihō Keisatsu Honbu Keijibu Chōsa Tōkeika, 10, 44.

22. These figures are derived by using the following figures for populations: for Japanese men, the average of 1950 and 1955 census figures for the total number of men between the ages of fifteen and forty-nine in 1952 (respectively 20,117,222 and 22,060,767, to obtain a figure of 21,088,994). Though this is admittedly a rough estimate, given a growing population it can reasonably be assumed that the figures for 1950 and 1955 represent lower and upper bounds for the population. This would lead to a rape rate of between 11.15 and 12.23 per 100,000. The figure for resident Koreans is based on the assumption that all reported rapes were committed by men and that men made up half the population of the approximately 600,000 Korean residents. As for the American servicemen, the number is derived by taking the number of reported rapes and dividing it by 2.6 on the grounds that the American troop strength at the time of the return of sovereignty in April 1952 was approximately 260,000. See Takemae Eiji, *Inside GHQ* (New York: Continuum, 2002), 126.

23. "A Korean Movement concerning the Asakusa Murder of GI Case," April 10, 1951, NARA, RG 331, box 351, folder 7: "000.5A Crimes." For other examples

of the despairing criminality trope see, for example, Mizuno Hiroshi, ed., *Shi ni Nozonde Uttaeru* (Tokyo: Tōgosha, 1982), 174–85; Gotō Ben, *Kuroi Haru* (Tokyo: Tōgosha, 1985), 126–31, 150–52; Fujiwara Shinji, *Minna ga Miteiru Mae de* (Tokyo: Masushobō, 1955), 169, 173, 177, 198; Fujiwara Shinji, *Zoku Minna ga Miteiru Mae de* (Tokyo: Masushobō, 1955), 51, 178.

24. Harry E. Wildes, *Typhoon in Tokyo* (New York: Macmillan, 1954), 284.

25. Hessel Tiltman, "Anti-American Feeling Is Seething in Japan," *Washington Post*, October 12, 1952.

26. Quoted in Inui Takashi, *Nippon wa Kurutteru* (Tokyo: Dōkōsha Isobe Shobō, 1953), 259.

27. Richard L.-G. Deverall, *The Great Seduction* (Tokyo: International Literature Printing, 1953), iii.

28. Hessell Tiltman, "Malicious Lies Stir Japanese against U.S.," *Washington Post*, July 12, 1953, B1.

29. Japanese Diplomatic Archives, A-0134/10 0156-0157.

30. Harry E. Wildes, "The War for the Mind of Japan," *Annals of the Political Academy of Social Science* 294 (July 1954): 2.

31. Wildes, "The War for the Mind of Japan," 2.

32. Kanzaki Takeshi, ed., *Kanzaki Kiyoshi no Tsuioku* (Tokyo: Uniaato, 1981), 106–10.

33. Kokkai Gijiroku Tōroku, April 14, 1954; July 7, 1955; March 5, 1957; October 9, 1959; June 6, 1963; March 25, 1965.

34. Kanzaki Takeshi, *Kanzaki Kiyoshi no Tsuioku*, 45.

35. Kanzaki Takeshi, 45.

36. See, for example, Shimamoto Shizuo, "Sensei no Techō Yori: Wakai Kateikyōshi," *Shōjo no Tomo*, August 1936, 208–21; Shimamoto Shizuo, "Hakuboku Nikki: Joōsama Funshitsu," *Shōjo no Tomo*, January 1937, 182–93; Shimamoto Shizuo, "Kokuban Romansu: Kyōshitsu wo Kirei ni," *Shōjo no Tomo*, January 1939, 190–201; Shimamoto Shizuo, "Kokuban Romansu: Tōban Nisshi Yori," *Shōjo no Tomo*, August 1941, 184–93.

37. Kanzaki Takeshi, *Kanzaki Kiyoshi no Tsuioku*, 38, 78–79, 109.

38. See, for example, Shimamoto Shizuo, "Mokuren Jūgun," in *Jogakusei Jidai* (Tokyo: Kokuminsha, 1943), 152–77, esp. 175–77; Shimamoto Shizuo, "Kaigun Kenkin," in *Jogakusei Jidai*, 91.

39. Shimamoto, "Mokuren Jūgun," 175–76.

40. Shimamoto Shizuo, "Kokuban Romansu: Murasaki Butai," *Shōjo no Tomo*, November 1939, 186–97; Shimamoto Shizuo, "Sensei no Techō Yori: Imon Nikki," *Shōjo no Tomo*, November 1936, 122–33.

41. Shimamoto Shizuo, *Shōjo Kotekitai* (Tokyo: Jitsugyō no Nihonsha, 1942), 3.

42. Shimamoto Shizuo, "Kokuban Romansu: Eigo no Sensei," *Shōjo no Tomo*, September 1942, 138–45.

43. Kanzaki Kiyoshi, *Aizu Rōjō* (Tokyo: Kokuminsha, 1945), 236.

44. Kanzaki Takeshi, *Kanzaki Kiyoshi no Tsuioku*, 30.

45. "'Amerikagata' Seikōdō no Dentatsushatachi no Jittai," *Shūkan Posuto*, September 1973, 80–81.

46. Kanzaki Takeshi, *Kanzaki Kiyoshi no Tsuioku*, 110.

47. "Summary of Information; Subject: Japan-China Friendship Association (Nippon Chugoku Yuko Kyokai)," December 22, 1951, NARA, RG 84, Entry #2828 Tokyo Office of the U.S. Political Advisor Classified General Records, box 68, file "350.21 Communism October–December 1951."

48. Deverall, *The Great Seduction*, 333–34.

49. See Oguma Eiji, *"Minshu" to "Aikoku"* (Tokyo: Shinyōsha, 2002), chap. 7, esp. 255–87.

50. Chazono, *Panpan to wa Dare Nanoka*, 63.

51. Oguma, *"Minshu" to "Aikoku,"* 275–76.

52. Kanzaki Kiyoshi, "Nihon Josei no Kokusaisei to Baishōsei," *Kaizō* 10, no. 33 (October 1952): 76–82.

53. Kanzaki Kiyoshi, *Ketteiban*, 312, http://kokkai.ndl.go.jp/SENTAKU/sangii n/026/0462/02603050462008a.html (accessed October 4, 2023).

54. Kanzaki Kiyoshi, *Ketteiban*, 196.

55. Kanzaki Kiyoshi, *Ketteiban*, 169–70, 200–201, 222; Kanzaki Kiyoshi, *Sengo Nippon no Baishun Mondai*, 55.

56. Kanzaki Kiyoshi, *Ketteiban*, 6, 156.

57. Kanzaki Kiyoshi, *Ketteiban*, 136–38. Kaburagi presents essentially the same story in his "memoir." See Tanaka Kimiko, *Onna no Bōhatei*, 3, 44; Kaburagi Seiichi, *Hiroku: Shinchūgun Ian Sakusen* (Tokyo: Banchō Shobō, 1972), 26, 27, 96. Dower repeats this story, unaltered and essentially unchallenged in John W. Dower, *Embracing Defeat* (New York: W. W. Norton / New Press, 1999), 128–29. Yuki Tanaka presents a similar story with a possible but still not plausible timeline substituted for that of his source material; see Yuki Tanaka, *Japan's Comfort Women* (London: Routledge, 2002), 147. Even Molasky abandons his usual admirable skepticism when it comes to this story (*The American Occupation of Japan and Okinawa*, 109).

58. Kanagawa Ken Keisatsushi Hensan Iinkai, ed., *Kanagawa Ken Keisatsushi*, vol. 3 (Yokohama: Kanagawa Keisatsu Honbu, 1974), 48–52; Takemae, *Inside GHQ*, 53.

59. Kanagawa Ken Keisatsushi Hensan Iinkai, *Kanagawa Keisatsushi*, 3:52; Arisue Seizō, *Shūsen Hishi: Arisue Kikan no Shuki* (Tokyo: Fuyō Shobō Shuppan, 1987), 89–90.

60. *Ashida Nikki*, 1:214; "Fujoshi e no bōkō wa kaimu," *Asahi Shimbun*, September 11, 1945, 2; Hokkaido Police History, 2:562; *Shōwa Niman Nichi no Zenkiroku*, vol. 7: *Haikyo kara no Shuppatsu* (Tokyo: Kodansha, 1989), 144. There is some discrepancy in the records regarding when the first troops entered Tokyo. For example, the Chiba police history records that elements of the First Cavalry Division moved into the Yoyogi Drill Field and the Dai-ichi Hotel as early as September 2; see Chiba Ken Keisatsushi Hensan Iinkai, ed., *Chiba Ken Keisatsushi*, vol. 2 (Tokyo: Tōkyō Horei Shuppan, 1987), 469. But according to William C. Chase, who was then commander of the First Cavalry division, he and an associated detail were the first Americans into the wards of Tokyo (as opposed to Tokyo Prefecture). They first ventured into the city on September 5, 1945. William C. Chase, *Front Line General* (Houston: Pacesetter Press, 1975), 128.
61. Kanzaki Kiyoshi, *Ketteiban*, 214–16.
62. Kanzaki Kiyoshi, *Ketteiban*, 128. The Home Ministry order is described in Kanagawa Ken Keisatsushi Hensan Iinkai, *Kanagawa Keisatsushi*, 3:346.
63. Robert Eichelberger, diary entry for August 26, 1945, Robert Eichelberger Papers, Duke University Library Special Collections, Durham, NC.
64. Kanzaki Kiyoshi, Ketteiban, 143. The same story is repeated in Hashimoto Yoshio, *Hyakuokuen no Baishun Ichiba* (Tokyo: Saikō shinsha, 1958), 230.
65. Kanzaki Kiyoshi, *Ketteiban*, 201.
66. Kanzaki Kiyoshi, *Ketteiban*, 196–202.
67. See, for example, Yuki Tanaka, *Japan's Comfort Women* (London: Routledge, 2002), 159, 174; Hirai Kazuko, *Nihon Senryō to Jendaa*, 112, 138, 139.
68. "Kyōdō Benjo," *Nihon Kokugo Daijiten*, vol. 4 (Tokyo: Shogakkan, 2006), 478; "Kōshū Benjo," in *Nihon Zokugo Daijiten*, ed. Yonekawa Akihiko (Tokyo: Tōkyōdō Shuppan, 2006), 227. For an actual usage of such a term by an IJA medical officer in 1939, see Asō Tetsuo, "Karyūbyō no Sekkyokuteki na Yobōhō," in *Jūgonen Sensō Juyō Bunken Shiriizu*, vol. 1: *Gun Ikan no Senjō Hōkoku Ikenshū* (Tokyo: Fuji Shuppan, 1990), 68. (The page number in the original report is 16.)
69. Quoted in Yoshimi Yoshiaki, *Comfort Women*, trans. Suzanne O'Brien (New York: Columbia University Press, 2000), 199.
70. Miyagi Tamayo, "Baishun Gyōsha ni Tai Atari Shite," *Chūō Kōron*, May 1958, 120–23. See also Holly Vincele Sanders, "Prostitution in Postwar Japan: Debt and Labor" (PhD diss., Princeton University, 2005), 166. Another example of prostitutes being referred to as toilets can be seen in a debate of the Shizuoka Prefectural assembly is discussed by Hirai Kazuko in *Nihon Senryō to Jendaa*, 176.

71. Chazono, *Panpan to wa Dare Nanoka*, 66; Tanaka Masakazu, "Kontakuto Zoon toshite no Senryōki Nippon: 'Kichi no Onnatachi' wo Megutte ["Occupied Japan as a Contact Zone: Concerning 'Women of the Bases"], *Kontakuto Zoon*, no. 4 (2011): 170.

72. Chazono, *Panpan to wa Dare Nanoka*, 67.

73. Esashi Akiko, "Yokahama Beru Epokku no Onna: Kitabayashi Yoshiko," *Shinokai Kenkyūshi No. 3: Jidai no Mezame wo Yomu* (July 1996): 120–32.

74. See, for example, Kitabayashi Tōma, "Machi no Kokusai Musume," *Bundan Andepandan*, no. 1 (1930); Kitabashi Tōma, *Kyoryūchi no Oka* (Tokyo: Ōya Shoten, 1932).

75. Kida Junichirō, "Kanagawa Bunka wo Kizuita Hitobito, No. 22: Sakka Kitabayashi Tōma," *Best Partner* 25, no. 10 (October 2013): 36–41; Kitabayashi Tōma, "Boku ha Hōsōkyokuchō," *Hōsō Bunka* 12, no. 2 (February 1957): 30.

76. Kitabayashi Tōma, "Sendensen ho Ikani Tatakawaretaka," in *Daitōa Sensō: Rikugun Hōdōhanin Shuki: Biruma Kensetsusen*, ed. Bunka Hōkōkai (Tokyo: Dai Nippon Yūbenkai, Kōdansha, 1943), 42–45.

77. Kitabayashi Yoshiko, "Beigun Gyōjō Hiroku: Yokohama no Higeki," *Fuji* 6, no. 1 (January 1953): 80–90. Compare the crimes described with actual cases in "Shinchūgun no Fuhō Kōi: Beihei no Fuhō Kōi No. 10," "Rengōgun Shinchūgun ni Okeru Jiko Hassei Chōsahyō," and the CLO reports in Takemae, *GHQ e no Nihon Seifu Taiō Bunsho Sōshūsei*, vol. 1 (Tokyo: Emu Tee Shuppan, 1999). A later version of Kitabayashi's essay appears in Gotō Ben, *Kuroi Haru* (Tokyo: Tōgosha, 1985). Compare the cases in Gotō Ben, *Kuroi Haru*, 267–68, 276, 271–72; JNA Hensei 3A 15, 11-1, 0296, 0254; MOJ 38, reel 13, 383082, 383003, 383122; and Takemae, *GHQ e no Nihon Seifu Taiō Bunsho Sōshūsei*, 1:568, case 83; 1:576, case 8; 2:882, (III) Atsugi District.

78. Esashi Akiko, "Yokahama Beru Epokku no Onna," 132.

79. Deverall, *The Great Seduction*, 113–48.

80. Deverall, 148.

81. Molasky, *The American Occupation of Japan and Okinawa*, 122.

82. Molasky, 123n48, 216. In this note, Molasky gives the man's name as Hihara Hinenori. In an email exchange he informed the author that this was a mistake and that it should have been rendered as "Shigenori."

83. Deverall, *The Great Seduction*, 113.

84. Yamazaki Yasuo, *Chosha to Shuppansha, No. 2* (Tokyo: Gakufū Shoin, 1955), 81–82.

85. Michiba Chikanobu and Toka Kōji, "Bungaku Zasshi *Jinminbungaku* no Jidai," *Wakō Daigaku Gendai Ningen Gakubu Kiyō*, no. 3 (March 2010): 209–11.

86. Michiba and Toka, 210.

87. Michiba and Toka, 211.

88. Jinminbungaku Henshūbu, "*Jinmin Bungaku* Tōmen no Kadai," *Jinmin Bungaku*, November 1952, reprinted in *Jinmin Bunkagaku Fukkokuban* (Tokyo: Fuji Shuppan, 2011), 7:6–7.

89. Yamazaki Yasuo, *Chosha to Shuppansha, No.* 2, 81–82.

90. Toba Kōji, "Kaisetsu *Jinmin Bungaku* Ron," in Toba Kōji, Michiba Chikanobu, and Shibazaki Kōzaburō, "*Jinmin Bungaku:* Kaisetsu, Kaidai, Kaisō, Sōmokuji, Sakuin" (Tokyo: Fuji Shuppan, 2011), 16.

91. Kashii Toshie, "Dassō," *Jinmin Bungaku*, May 1952, 115–20; Kashii Toshie, "Izukoe," *Jinmin Bungaku*, October 1952, 106–21. Both reprinted in *Jinmin Bunkagaku Fukkokuban* (Tokyo: Fuji Shuppan, 2011), vols. 5 and 7, respectively.

92. Yamazaki Yasuo, *Chosha to Shuppansha, No.* 2, 81–82.

93. Jiji Mondai Kenkyūjo, ed., *Beigun Kichi: Dare no Tame no Mono Ka* (Tokyo: Shadan Hōjin Jiji Mondai Kenkyūjo, 1968), 234–35.

94. Fukuda Tsuneari, *Heiwaron ni tai Suru Gimon* (Tokyo: Bungei Shunjūshinsha, 1955), 48.

95. Jiji Mondai Kenkyūjo, *Beigun Kichi*, 237.

96. Kanda Masao and Kubota Yasutarō, *Uchinada: Gunji Kichi Hantai Tōsō no Jittai* (Tokyo: Shakai Shobō, 1953), 149, 221; "Sengo Rōdō Undōshi," *Gakushū no Tomo*, no. 92, 76.

97. *Rōdō Keizai Shunpō*, no. 8 (213) (January 1954): 30.

98. "Kichi Nōmin to Kanri Kōjō Rōdōsha," *Chūō Kōron* 69, no. 1 (784) (January 1954): 158.

99. "Machi kara Mura kara," *Shin Josei*, no. 45 (September 1954): 143.

100. Kyōtofu Rōdō Keizai Kenkyūjo, ed., *Kyōto Rōdō Undōshi Nenpyō* (Kyoto: Kyōtofu Rōdō Keizai Kenkyūjo, 1965), 18.

101. Kanda Masao and Kubota Yasutarō, *Uchinada: Gunji Kichi Hantai Tōsō no Jittai* (Tokyo: Shakai Shobō, 1953), 276; Ōkochi Kazuo, ed., *Shiryō: Sengo Nijūnenshi*, vol. 4, *Rōdō* (Tokyo: Nihon Hyōronsha, 1966), 233.

102. Sugita Tomoe, "Nippon no Teisō: Tsuma to Natta Watashi no Kunō," *Shin Josei*, no. 29 (June 1953), reprinted in *Shin Josei Fukkokuban* (Tokyo: Fuji Shuppan, 2010), 8:147–65.

103. Sugita Tomoe.

104. Yamazaki Yasuo, *Chosha to Shuppansha No.* 2 (Tokyo: Gakufū Shoin, 1955), 92.

105. Chūgokugo Gakshū Sōsho Henshū Iinkai, ed., *Chūgokugo Gakshū Sōsho, 5, Gendai Chūgokugo Sakubun* (Tokyo: Kōnan Shoin, 1956), 136; Sōhyō Osaka Chihō Hyōgikai, ed., *Sohyō Osaka Chihyō Jūnenshi Nenpyō* (Osaka: Osaka Rōdōkumiai Sōhyōgikai Osaka Chihō Hyōgikai, 1961), 208.

106. Mizuno, *Shi ni Nozonde Uttaeru*, 302.
107. Mizuno Hiroshi and Kanzaki Kiyoshi, "Kichi no naka no Junketsu," *Shin Josei*, no. 31 (August 1953), reprinted in *Shin Josei Fukkokuban*, 8:58–65.
108. Mizuno and Kanzaki, 59.
109. Mizuno and Kanzaki, 59.
110. Tamura Keiko, "Senryō ni Okeru Deai kara Kekkon made," in Hayashi Kaori, Tamura Keiko, and Takatsu Fumiko, *Sensō Hanayome* (Tokyo: Fuyō Shobō Shuppan, 2002), 127.
111. Katsura Sanshi and Gotō Ben, "Sanshi no Honma Dekka," *Shūkan Yomiuri*, May 26, 1991, 130–34.
112. Kitabayashi Tōma, "Fujin no Rikkōho," *Seikai Ōrai* 21, no. 3 (March 1955), 180–85.
113. Email to author from Michael Molasky, January 18, 2005.
114. Email to author from Michael Molasky, January 18, 2005.
115. See, for example, Tanaka, *Japan's Comfort Women*, 149. For some reason Tanaka refers to Gotō as "Itsushima Tsutomu," an alternative reading for the characters in his name, but one under which Gotō has not published.
116. The embellishments are all in Kitabayashi's contribution. The rest is pure invention.
117. Gotō Tsutomu, *Tokyo no Teisō* (Tokyo: Seishun Shuppansha, 1958) and *Kinjirareta Chitai* (Tokyo: Chiseisha, 1958).
118. Gotō Tsutomu, "Beigun Seihanzaishi," *Shinsō* 64 (1954): 43.
119. Gotō Ben, *Kuroi Haru* (Tokyo: Tōgosha, 1985), 85.
120. Japanese National Diet Library Online Catalog, search terms "ノストラダムス, 五島勉."
121. See Gotō Ben, *Nosutradamusu no Daiyogen, Semarikuru 1999nen Nana no Tsuki, Jinrui Metsubo no Hi* (Tokyo: Shōdensha, 1981).
122. Gotō Ben, *Nihon Gembaku Kaihatsu no Shinjitsu* (Tokyo: Shōdensha, 2001).
123. Gotō Ben, *Uchūjin Nazo no Isan* (Tokyo: Shōdensha, 1988).
124. See Gotō Ben, *Hitoraa no Shūmatsu Yōgen: Sokkin ni Kattata 2039nen* (Tokyo: Shōdensha, 2015) and *1999nen Ikō: Hitoraa Dake ni Mieta Kyōfu no Miraizu* (Tokyo: Shodensha, 1988).
125. Harada Minoru, "Nosutoradamusu, '1999 Nen Jinrui Zetsumetsusetsu' no Giman to Zaiaku," *Seiron*, June 1999, 288–300.
126. Wikipedia, s.v. "Gotō Ben," https://ja.wikipedia.org/wiki/五島勉 (accessed November 8, 2022).
127. Gotō Ben, *Kuroi Haru* (Tokyo: Tōgosha, 1985), ii.
128. Gotō Tsutomu, *Tokyo no Teisō* (Tokyo: Seishun Shuppansha, 1958), 4.
129. Gotō Tsutomu, *Kinjirareta Chitai* (Tokyo: Chiseisha, 1958), 189.

130. Hosokawa Morisada, *Jōhō Tennō in Tassezu, Gekan*, vol. 2 (Tokyo: Dōkōsha Isobe Shobō, 1953), 428–29.

131. Watanabe Sadao, interview with Tokyo FM Radio, October 9, 2022, https:// news.audee.jp/news/fJgPaExeLE.html?showContents=detail; Duus Masayo, *Haisha no Okurimono* (Tokyo: Kōdansha, 1995), 217; "RAA Kyōkai Enkakushi" (Tokyo: Nisshinsha, 1949), 38–39, 56, reprinted in *Seibōryoku Mondai Shiryō Shūsei*, vol. 1 (Tokyo: Fuji Shuppan, 2004), 320–21, 329.

132. Gotō Tsutomu, *Zoku Nippon no Teisō*, 40.

133. "RAA Kyōkai Enkakushi" (Tokyo: Nisshinsha, 1949), 16, reprinted in *Seibōryoku Mondai Shiryō Shūsei*, vol. 1 (Tokyo: Fuji Shuppan, 2004), 309.

134. Yanatori Mitsuyoshi, *Furin no Seitai* (Tokyo: Saikō Shinsha, 1958); Miura Hiroto, *Hadaka Nihonshi* (Tokyo: Saikō Shinsha, 1958); Enomoto Shunkichi, *Nikutai no Junrei* (Tokyo: Saikō Shinsha, 1958).

135. Chase, *Front Line General*, 129.

136. Hashimoto, *Hyakuokuen no Baishun Ichiba*, 91.

137. Hashimoto, 103, 116, 124.

138. Hashimoto, 120–24.

139. "RAA Kyōkai Enkakushi," 40; *Seibōryoku*, 321.

140. Hashimoto, *Hyakuokuen no Baishun Ichiba*, 200.

141. Hashimoto, 85

142. See the series of articles called "Sengo Baishun Shi," *Naigai Times*, February 7, 1961–March 12, 1961.

143. "Sengo Baishunshi: Okasareta Tsubomi: Kutsū mo Itsuka Kairaku e," *Naigai Taimusu*, February 23, 1961, 7; "Sengo Baishunshi: Kuro no Miryoku ni Onna mo Kizetsu," *Naigai Taimusu*, March 11, 1961, 9. Kaburagi Seiichi tells this story as his own in his *Hiroku: Shinchūgun Ian Sakusen* (Tokyo: Banchō Shobō, 1972), 45–46.

144. Kobayashi Daijirō and Murase Akira, *Minna wa Shiranai Kokka Baishun Meirei* (Tokyo: Yūzankaku Shuppan, 1992), 258–60.

145. Kobayashi and Murase, 251–52.

146. Kobayashi and Murase, 55, 69. See also "Sengo Baishunshi #26," *Naigai Timusu*, March 9, 1961, 7; "Sengo Baishunshi #29," *Naigai Taimusu*, March 12, 1961, 9. This is one case where the original articles are somewhat toned down when published in the book, since prostitution would probably not be as popular with a general audience as it was with readers of the *Naigai Taimusu*.

147. See, for example, Ozawa Shōichi and Ei Rokusuke, *Iro no Michi* (Tokyo: Chikuma Shobō, 2007), 202–15.

148. "Female Floodwalls" is not a literal translation, which would be something akin to "Woman Floodwalls," or "Woman Wavebreaks." "Female Floodwalls" is originally Molasky's translation of the title, and I have adopted it as more elegant than my own.

149. Compare Kaburagi, *Hiroku*, 39–49, 41–43, 44–45, 45, 257, 258, 259–60, with Kobayashi and Murase, *Minna wa Shiranai Kokka Baishun Meirei*, 33–34, 35–37, 32, 39, 62, 62, 64, 67–69, respectively.

150. Kaburagi, *Hiroku*, 33–34.

151. Though Itō maintained a blog on which he treats the book as if it were a genuine testimonial, he confirmed in a telephone conversation with the present writer that it was nothing of the sort.

152. Kaburagi Seichi, "Jo ni kaete," in Tanaka Kimiko, *Onna no Bōhatei* (Tokyo: Dainishobō, 1957), 3; email from Koizumi Katsurō, June 5, 2012.

153. Kaburagi, *Shinchūgun Ian Sakusen*, 261; email from Public Relations Department, *Bungei Shunjū*, June 10, 2012.

154. Kaburagi, *Shinchūgun Ian Sakusen*, 261; email from Watanabe Jin, Public Relations Department, Keiō Gijuku University.

155. "Keiō Kokusai Byōin Setsuritsu Kaibunsho wo Meguru Tenya Wanya," *Shūkan Posuto*, May 12, 1978, 178–80.

156. Kaburagi, *Shinchūgun Ian Sakusen*, 261; email from Toyoda Hiroshi, IT Specialist ("Hōmupeiji Tantō") Musashino Kōgyō, June 20, 2012.

157. Tanaka Kimiko, *Onna no Bōhatei*, 2; Kaburagi, *Shinchūgun Ian Sakusen*, 56.

158. Tanaka Kimiko, *Onna no Bōhatei*, 2; Kaburagi, *Shinchūgun Ian Sakusen*, 260.

159. Kaburagi, *Shinchūgun Ian Sakusen*, 58–59, 255–56.

160. Tanaka Kimiko, *Onna no Bōhatei*, 75–80; Kaburagi, *Shinchūgun Ian Sakusen*, 132–37.

161. Phone conversation with Itō Bungaku, June 10, 2012.

162. Sakaguchi Yūzō, ed., "RAA Kyōkai Enkakushi" (Tokyo: Nisshinsha, 1949), 16, reprinted in *Seibōryoku Mondai Shiryō Shūsei*, vol. 1 (Tokyo: Fujiya Shuppan, 2004), 309.

163. Inoue Setsuko, "Senryōgun Ianjo kara no Shuppatsu," *Gekkan Jōkyō to Shutai*, no. 227 (November 1994): 82–83.

164. Molasky, *The American Occupation of Japan and Okinawa*, 129.

165. Fujiwara Shinji, *Minna ga Miteiru Mae de* (Tokyo: Masu Shobō, 1955), 217, and *Zoku Minna ga Miteiru Mae de* (Tokyo: Masu Shobō, 1955), 229.

166. See, for example, Gotō Ben, *Kuroi Haru*, 64; Fujiwara Shinji, *Minna ga Miteiru Mae de*, 79, 185; Hashimoto, *Hyakuokuen no Baishun Ichiba*, 6, 12, 71, 88, passim.

167. Kanzaki Kiyoshi, *Ketteiban*, 181.
168. Mizuno, *Shi ni Nozonde Uttaeru*, 22; Yamada Meiko, *Senryōgun Ianfu* (Tokyo: Kōjinsha, 1992), 84.
169. Gotō Ben, *Kuroi Haru*, 151.
170. Watanabe Sumiko, *Aoime no Koibitotachi* (Tokyo: Dainishobō, 1959), 199, 201; Gotō, *Zoku Nippon no Teisō*, 50, 169; Hashimoto, *Hyakuokuen no Baishun Ichiba*, 63.
171. Takasaki Setsuko, *Konketsuji* (Tokyo: Dōkōsha Isebeshobō, 1952), 30, 51, 52, 63, 64, 96, 99, 106, 108, 109, 230, 238, 240, 241, 244, 245, 246, 248, 261, 263, 265.
172. Tanaka Kimiko, *Onna no Bōhatei*, 75; Fujiwara Shinji, *Minna ga Miteiru Mae de*, 104; Fujiwara Shinji, *Zoku Minna ga Miteiru de*, 110; Fujiwara Shinji, *Hazukashimeraretemo* (Tokyo: Tora Shobō, 1952), 122.
173. See, for example, Gotō Ben, *Kuroi Haru*, 62–64, 113–15, 127–31; Fujiwara Shinji, *Minna ga Miteiru Mae de*, 149–84, and *Zoku Minna ga Miteiru Mae de*, 3–34, 35–61.
174. See, for example, the story of the women who committed suicide after being recruited into the RAA in Kaburagi, *Shinchūgun Ian Sakusen*. A nearly identical story with only minimal changes in detail appears in Makabe Hiroshi, "Ikenie ni Sareta Nanamannin no Musemetachi," in *Tokyo Yammichi Kōbō Shi*, ed. Tokyo Yakeato Yamiichi o Kiroku Suru Kai (Tokyo: Sōfūsha, 1978), 192–217. Citing this later source, John W. Dower, in *Embracing Defeat*, introduced it to the English-speaking world.
175. Fujiwara Shinji, *Minna ga Miteiru Mae de* and *Zoku Minna ga Miteiru Mae de*.
176. Mizuno, *Shi ni Nozonde Uttaeru*, 293–94.
177. Yamada, *Kokusaku*, 90–91.
178. Dower, *Embracing Defeat*, 579–80.
179. Kanagawa Ken Keisatsushi Hensan Iinkai, *Kanagawa Keisatsushi*, 3:361–63.
180. The figures of fifteen and sixty appear in Kanzaki Kiyoshi, *Ketteiban*, 138; Makabe, "Ikenie ni Sareta Nanamannin no Musemetachi," 207; Yamada Meiko, *Senryōgun Ianfu* (Tokyo: Kōjinsha, 1992), 37; Hashimoto, *Hyakuokuen no Baishun Ichiba*, 53; Dower, *Embracing Defeat*, 129; and Tanaka, *Japan's Comfort Women*, 147. Kobayashi and Murase claim that the number served ranged from 40 to 60 (*Minna wa Shiranai Kokka Baishun Meirei*, 47). Tanaka gives the figure of 150,000 in both his *Japan's Comfort Women*, 162, and an interview with Eric Talmadge quoted in Talmadge, "GIs Frequented Japan's 'Comfort Women,'" *Washington Post*, April 25, 2007. Tanaka's ultimate source for this claim is the PHW document referred to in chapter 2 (H. H. MacDonald, "Memorandum for the Record; Subject: Prostitution in Japan; Contracts;

Regulations, Public and Private Prostitutes," December 29, 1945, NARA, RG 331, box 9370, folder 4: "726.1 Abolition of Licensed Prostitution") that estimates *the total number of women working in prostitution in the whole of Japan*, not just those catering to the American troops who had only just arrived. Moreover, it was an estimate that was judged "not accurate."

181. The maximum number of Allied troops in Japan was 354,675 in December 1945. John J. McGrath, "Boots on the Ground: Troop Density in Contingency Operations," *Global War on Terrorism Occasional Paper 16* (Fort Leavenworth, KS: Combat Studies Institute Press, 2006), 28.

182. The 70,000 figure first appeared in Gotō (*Zoku Nippon no Teisō*, 40) and was subsequently taken up by Kobayashi and Murase (*Minna wa Shiranai Kokka Baishun Meirei*, 68) and Kaburagi, *Shinchūgun Ian Sakusen*, 260. It also appears in Kanzaki Kiyoshi, "Ikeda Hayato to Sengo no Baishun," *Ushio*, June 1972, 232–37; and Yamada Meiko, *Senryōgun Ianfu*, 8, 239. Makabe Hiroshi incorporates the figure into the title of his article in "Ikenie ni Sareta Nanamannin no Musemetachi." See also Takemae, *Inside GHQ*, 68; Fujime Yuki, *Sei no Rekishigaku* (Tokyo: Fuji Shuppan, 2015), 327, 384.

183. Hirai, *Nihon Senryō to Jendaa*, 37.

184. Gotō Tsutomu, *Anata no Shiranai Toki ni: Sengo Zankoku Monogatari* (Tokyo: Daiwa Shobō, 1965), 5; Gotō Tsutomu, *Sengo Zankoku Monogatari: Anata no Shiranai Toki ni* (Tokyo: Daiwa Shobō, 1968), 5.

185. In Fujiwara's case the fraud was so obvious he was, by his own accounts, inundated with mail denouncing his work as lies. He responded to the charge by asserting that there were some parts that were true and others were the result of his making composite characters, so it was "difficult" to say whether what he wrote was true but that people living near the bases had certainly suffered worse.

186. Kanzaki Kiyoshi, "Nihon Josei no Kokusaisei to Baishōsei," *Kaizō* 33, no. 10 (October 1952): 76–77.

CHAPTER 7. A NEW GENERATION OF MYTHMAKERS

1. See, for example Kitabayashi Yoshiko, "Beigun Gyōjō Hiroku: Yokahama no Higeki," *Fuji* 6, no. 1 (January 1953): 86; Kaiya Mitsuo, "*Nippon no Teisō wo Yomite*," *Shinjin Bungei* 4, no. 7 (August 1953): 51.

2. Yamazaki Yasuo, *Chosha to Shuppansha No. 2* (Tokyo: Gakufū Shoin, 1955), 81–82.

3. Roger Brown, post to H-Japan discussion logs, formerly available online at http://h-net.msu.edu/cgi-bin/logbrowse.pl?trx=vx&list=h-japan&month=0410&week=b&msg=JoAq%2B3/KvV4MdI3m1nxJLg&user=&pw=. See "Subject:

U.S. Occupation and Rapes (E/J)," October 12, 2004. See note 4 below; Yuki Tanaka, *Hidden Horrors* (Boulder, CO: Westview, 1996), 103.

4. Yuki Tanaka, post to H-Japan, October 20, 2004, formerly available online at http://h-net.msu.edu/cgi-bin/logbrowse.pl?trx=vx&list=h-japan&month =0410&week=c&msg=U%2BkA63yfB4ifDr1GDuJIUQ&user=&pw=. Though this post is no longer available online, Roger Brown was kind enough to send me a copy of the original post. The same post is discussed in Sarah Kovner, *Occupying Power* (Stanford, CA: Stanford University Press, 2012), 178n33.

5. John W. Dower, *Cultures of War* (New York: W. W. Norton and New Press, 2010), 541–42n96.

6. Antony Beevor, *The Second World War* (New York: Little, Brown, 2012), 776, 833.

7. Yuki Tanaka, *Hidden Horrors: Japanese War Crimes in World War II*, 2nd ed. (Lanham, MD: Rowman and Littlefield, 2018), 115, 280.

8. Yuki Tanaka, "War, Rape and Patriarchy: The Japanese Experience," *Asia-Pacific Journal: Japan Focus* 18, issue 1, no. 1 (December 31, 2019).

9. Yuki Tanaka, *Japan's Comfort Women* (London: Routledge, 2002), 127. Tanaka's dates here are erroneous. *Nippon no Teisō* was published in 1953, and *Kuroi Haru* is the name of the reissue of *Zoku Nippon no Teisō*. Under that title it was published in 1953, but it was not published under the name *Kuroi Haru* until 1985.

10. Gotō Ben, *Kuroi Haru* (Tokyo: Tōgosha, 1985), ii.

11. Tanaka, *Japan's Comfort Women*, 130; Gotō Ben, "Waga Seidashi no Sao," *Gendai* 14, no. 12 (December 1980): 312–13.

12. Tanaka, *Japan's Comfort Women*, 149; Gotō, *Kuroi Haru*, 229–67.

13. Tanaka, *Japan's Comfort Women*, 200n21. Tanaka also makes reference to this episode in *Hidden Horrors*.

14. Gotō, *Kuroi Haru*, 30–36.

15. Hiroshima Ken Keisatsu Henshū Iinkai, ed., *Shinpen Hiroshima Ken Keisatsushi* (Hiroshima: Kyōdō Insatsu Tōsho, 1974), 879.

16. Hiroshima Ken Keisatsu Henshū Iinkai, *Shinpen Hiroshima Ken Keisatsushi*, 884–85.

17. Australian War Memorial, "British Commonwealth Occupation Force 1945–52," https://www.awm.gov.au/articles/atwar/bcof (accessed July 5, 2019).

18. Hiroshima Ken Keisatsu Henshū Iinkai, *Shinpen Hiroshima Ken Keisatsushi*, 877.

19. Hiroshima Ken Keisatsu Henshū Iinkai, 891–92.

20. Tanaka, *Japan's Comfort Women*, 126, 136.

21. Tanaka, *Japan's Comfort Women*, 140.

22. Tanaka, *Japan's Comfort Women*, 139.

23. Kanzaki Kiyoshi, *Ketteiban: Kanzaki Repōto* (Tokyo: Gendaishi Shuppankai, 1974), 137.

24. Kaburagi Seiichi, *Shinchūgun Ian Sakusen* (Tokyo: Banchō Shobō, 1972), 26–27.

25. Kaburagi, 25.

26. Kanzaki Kiyoshi, *Ketteiban*, 136.

27. Tanaka, *Japan's Comfort Women*, 116–17.

28. General of the Army Douglas MacArthur's General Staff, *Reports of General MacArthur: MacArthur in Japan: The Occupation: Military Phase, Vol. 1 Supplement*, facsimile reprint ed. (Washington, DC: U.S. Government Printing Office, 1994), 47.

29. Tanaka, *Japan's Comfort Women*, 147.

30. Benis M. Frank and Henry I. Shaw Jr., *Victory and Occupation: History of the U.S. Marine Corps Operations in World War II*, vol. 5, part 2 (Washington, DC: Historical Branch, G-3 Division, U.S. Marine Corps, 1968), 485–87.

31. Robert Eichelberger, diary entry for August 19, 1945, in box 1, folder titled "Miscellaneous: Diary Photocopies: Diaries: July 23–October 20; October 24–December 4," Robert L. Eichelberger Papers, Rubenstein Library, Duke University, Durham, NC.

32. Crawford F. Sams and Zabelle Zakarian, eds., *Medic* (Armonk, NY: M. E. Sharpe, 1998), 5.

33. Stanley Falk, conversation with author, August 27, 2021.

34. Tanaka, *Japan's Comfort Women*, 163.

35. Tanaka, *Japan's Comfort Women*, 164.

36. Wikipedia, s.v. "Rape during the Occupation of Japan," https://en.wikipedia .org/wiki/Rape_during_the_occupation_of_Japan (accessed January 2, 2020).

37. Due to Tanaka's somewhat nonstandard method of citation, this may not be immediately clear. A number of times, he cites chapters in both Mizuno Hiroshi, ed., *Shi ni Nozonde Uttaeru* (Tokyo: Tōgosha, 1982), and Gotō, *Kuroi Haru*, as if they were actually written by the "women" that "Mizuno" and Gotō largely invented. In other places he cites the work of different authors who in turn have simply taken from Mizuno, Gotō, Kanzaki, Kaburagi, or Kobayashi and Murase. The citations in question are notes 23 (this is through two intervening sources, but ultimately it is Gotō, *Kuroi Haru*), 25–26, 69–74, 76–82, 84–86, in chapter 5 as well as notes 1, 3, 20 (here again the reference is indirect, but the ultimate source is Gotō), 21, 25–27, 29–31, 34–36, 38–43, 47–48, 50–53, 57, 63–64, 92, 94, 96–97, 99, 100, 102–4, in chapter 6. See the relevant notes in Tanaka, *Japan's Comfort Women*, 195–203.

38. Tanaka, *Japan's Comfort Women*, 127–31, 199nn69–82, 84–86.

39. Tanaka, *Japan's Comfort Women*, 126.

40. Hiroshima Ken Keisatsu Henshū Iinkai, *Shinpen Hiroshima Ken Keisatsushi*, 884–85.

41. Hiroshima Ken Keisatsu Henshū Iinkai, 888–89. Sarah Kovner has also pointed out that Tanaka recorded the wrong numbers for rape. See Sarah Kovner, *Occupying Power* (Stanford, CA: Stanford University Press, 2012), 53.

42. Hiroshima Ken Keisatsu Henshū Iinkai, *Shin Hen Hiroshima Ken Keisatsushi*, 884–85. Tanaka's reference is to 888–89, but the text makes clear that he was also referring to information that appears on 884–85. See Tanaka, *Japan's Comfort Women*, 199n67.

43. Tanaka, *Japan's Comfort Women*, 158–59.

44. Tanaka, *Japan's Comfort Women*, 161.

45. Eric Talmadge, "GIs Frequented Japan's 'Comfort Women,'" *Washington Post*, April 25, 2007.

46. H. H. MacDonald, "Memorandum for the Record. Subject: Conference on Venereal Disease and Related Legislation," December 6, 1945, NARA, RG 331, GHQ/SCAP, box 9370, folder 8: "Venereal Disease Control."

47. Tanaka, *Japan's Comfort Women*, 160.

48. Tanaka, *Japan's Comfort Women*, 156, 158, 159.

49. Tanaka, *Japan's Comfort Women*, 160.

50. Tanaka, *Japan's Comfort Women*, 160.

51. John W. Dower, *Embracing Defeat* (New York: W. W. Norton / New Press, 1999), 579–80nn4–30, 124, 597n6.

52. Dower, *Embracing Defeat*, 579–80nn4, 7, 8, 12, 13, 14, 16, 17, 20, 21, 22, 24, 27, 28, 30.

53. Dower, *Embracing Defeat*, 579–80nn7, 8, 12, 17, 20, 21.

54. Dower, *Embracing Defeat*, 579n8.

55. Dower, *Embracing Defeat*, 579n13, 580nn22, 25.

56. Dower, *Embracing Defeat*, 579n16.

57. Dower, *Embracing Defeat*, 579nn14, 17, 580nn28, 30.

58. Dower, *Embracing Defeat*, 579nn20, 24.

59. Dower, *Embracing Defeat*, 123.

60. Hirohito's surrender message can be heard on YouTube, https://www.youtube.com/watch?v=RFVzDGSiojs (accessed January 28, 2023). A brief excerpt of the Otoki recording is played in the 2017 NHK docudrama *Sengo Zero Nen: Tokyo Burakku Hooru*, broadcast August 15, 2015, https://www.nhk.or.jp/archives/shogenarchives/postwar/sengozeronen/onnatachi/ (accessed February 19, 2023). Otoki speaks from about the 0:40 mark to about 0:59.

61. Richard Nixon Presidential Library and Museum, "'Smoking Gun': Richard Nixon and Bob Haldeman discuss the Watergate break-in, June 23, 1972," YouTube video, https://www.youtube.com/watch?v=ehKRQoN-dIg (accessed January 28, 2023).

62. Iwanaga Shinkichi, *Hōso no Chishiki Shiriizu No. 3: Hōdō/Kyōyō Bangumi* (Tokyo: Dōbunkan, 1956), 82–83.

63. Fujikura Shūichi, *Maiku Yodan* (Tokyo: Ryūbundō Shuppan, 1948), 105.

64. Nihon Hōsō Shuppan Kyōkai, ed., *Rajio Shakai Tanbō* (Tokyo: Nihon Hōsō Shuppan Kyōkai, 1949), 158–67.

65. Ozaki Yoshimitsu, "NHK Rajio Bangumi 'Gaitō Rokuon' Seishōnen no Furyōka wo Dōshite Fuseguka: Gaado Shitano Musumetachi no Mojika Shiryō," *Notre Dame Seishin University Kiyō Studies in Foreign Languages and Literature: Studies in Culture, Studies in Japanese Language and Literature* 45, no. 1 (2021): 88.

66. Ozaki, 94.

67. Ozaki, 77.

68. See, for example, "Rakuchō no Otoki Gairoku kara Kōsei Monogatari," *Asahi Shimbun*, February 9, 1948, 4.

69. Dower, *Embracing Defeat*, 124, 579n5.

70. Fujikura later wrote an embellished account of this encounter in 1948 (Fujikura Shūichi, *Maiku Yodan*, [Tokyo: Ryūbundō, 1948], 109-110.) He then further embellished the story in Fujikura Shūichi, *Maiku to Tomo ni*, (Tokyo: Dainippon Yūbenkai Kōdansha, 1952), 148. Dower's account contains a verbatim quotation from this latter embellishment. However, it is unclear where Dower got it. The source he cites, *Dokumento: Shōwa Sesōshi Sengohen*, discusses prostitution in other locations, but makes no mention of Otoki. Another source Dower employed in his narrative (Takahashi Kazuo, "Yami no Onnatachi" in Ino Kenji, [Tokyo Yamiichi Kōbōshi, 1978], 223) has an extended quotation that is clearly derived from Fujikura's 1948 account, but this is not the version that Dower used.

71. Dower, *Embracing Defeat*, 123.

72. Ozaki Yoshimitsu, "NHK Rajio Bangumi," 89.

73. Ozaki, 78.

74. Ozaki, 78, 89. Some of this portion of the interview can be heard in the excerpt broadcast by NHK in its *Sengo Zero Nen: Tokyo Burakku Hooru*.

75. Fujikura, *Maiku Yodan*, 66–67.

76. Dower, *Embracing Defeat*, 124.

77. Dower, *Embracing Defeat*, 126.

78. Dower, Embracing Defeat, 127.

79. Dower, *Embracing Defeat*, 129

80. Dower, *Embracing Defeat*, 129.

81. Dower, *Embracing Defeat*, 130.

82. Dower, *Embracing Defeat*, 130, 579n16.

83. Ian Buruma, *Year Zero* (New York: Penguin Press, 2013), 38, 342n38.

84. Wikipedia, s.v. "Rape during the Occupation of Japan," https://en.wikipedia
.org/wiki/Rape_during_the_occupation_of_Japan#cite_note-FOOTNOT
EDower1999579-23; s.v. "Rape during the Occupation of Japan," https://ja
.wikipedia.org/wiki/占領期日本における強姦-cite_note-FOOTNOTED
ower1999579-13; s.v. "Rape during the Occupation of Japan," https://
fr.wikipedia.org/wiki/Viols_durant_l%27occupation_du_Japon#cite_
note-Dower1999579-18; s.v. "Rape during the Occupation of Japan," https://
it.wikipedia.org/wiki/Stupri_durante_l%27occupazione_del_Giappone#cite
_note-Dower-8 (all accessed September 20, 2022).

85. Wikipedia, s.v. "Rape during the Occupation of Japan," https://en.wikipedia
.org/wiki/Rape_during_the_occupation_of_Japan#CITEREFBuruma2013;
s.v. "Rape during the Occupation of Japan," https://ja.wikipedia.org/wiki
/占領期日本における強姦#CITEREFBuruma2013; s.v. "Rape during the Occupation of Japan," https://fr.wikipedia.org/wiki/Viols_durant_l%27occupation
_du_Japon#cite_note-Buruma201338-19 (all accessed January 31, 2023).

86. Yoshimi Kaneko, *Baishō no Shakaishi* (Tokyo: Yūzankaku Shuppan, 1984),
198; Kobayashi Daijirō and Murase Akira, *Minna wa Shiranai Kokka Baishun
Meirei* (Tokyo: Yūzankaku Shuppan, 1992), 69.

87. Gotō Tsutomu, *Zoku Nippon no Teisō* (Tokyo: Sōjusha, 1953), 64.

88. Dower, *Embracing Defeat*, 579n7.

89. Dower, *Embracing Defeat*, 579–80nn8, 12, 17, 20, 21.

90. See Dower, 579n12; Yoshimi Kaneko, *Baishō no Shakaishi*, 198.

91. Kanzaki Kiyoshi, *Ketteiban*, 162.

92. Dower, *Embracing Defeat*, 129.

93. Dower, Embracing Defeat, 129, 579n13.

94. Yoshikawa Sachiko (Yukiko), "Akumu no Yōna RAA no Hibi," *Ushio*, no. 154
(June 1972): 164–65.

95. Tanaka Kimiko, *Onna no Bōhatei* (Tokyo: Daini Shobō, 1957), 47–53; Kaburagi
Seiichi, *Hiroku Shinchūgun Ian Sakusen* (Tokyo: Banchō Shobō, 1972),
100–106.

96. Dower, *Embracing Defeat*, 130.

97. Kabushiki Gaisha Kōdansha, *Shōwa Nimannichi Zenkiroku*, vol. 7: *Haikyo
kara no Shuppatsu* (Tokyo: Kōdansha, 1989), 270.

98. Yoshimi Kaneko, *Baishō no Shakaishi*, 196; Kobayashi and Murase, *Minna
wa Shiranai Kokka Baishun Meirei*, 62.

99. Gotō Tsutomu, *Zoku Nippon no Teisō*, 39.

100. Dower, *Embracing Defeat*, 579n17, Yoshimi Kaneko, *Baishō no Shakaishi*, 210–12.

101. Dower, *Embracing Defeat*, 579n17; Takahashi Kazuo, "Yami no Onnatachi," in Tokyo Yakeato Yamiichi wo Kiroku Suru Kai, ed., *Tokyo Yamiichi Kōbōshi* (Tokyo: Sōfusha, 1978), 226.

102. Kanzaki Kiyoshi, *Ketteiban*, 384. It should be noted that the First Cavalry Division was in Japan and played a prominent role in the Occupation; it was the first American unit to enter Tokyo. Kanzaki showed elsewhere, however, that he understood the difference between a cavalry division and an infantry division, and that the First Cavalry was the latter. See Kanzaki Kiyoshi, *Ketteiban*, 141. The reason for this error is that he is repeating Kaburagi's mistake.

103. Kaburagi, *Hiroku Shinchūgun Ian Sakusen*, 258.

104. Kobayshi and Murase, *Minna wa Shiranai Kokka Baishun Meirei*, 64.

105. Gotō Tsutomu, *Zoku Nippon no Teisō*, 39.

106. Dower, *Embracing Defeat*, 131.

107. See chapter 2.

108. J. V. Zaccone, "Memorandum for Record: Subject: Prostitution," October 10, 1946, NARA, RG 331, GHQ/SCAP, box 9370, folder 5: "Venereal Disease Contact Tracing."

109. Rōdōshō Fujinshōnen Kyoku, ed., *Baishunfu Narabi ni Sono Aitegata ni tsuite no Chōsa, Fujin Kankei Shiryō Shiriizu Chōsa Shiryō, Daijūni (no. 12)* (Tokyo: Rōdōshō Fujinshōnen Kyoku, 1953), 21.

110. John J. McGrath, "Boots on the Ground: Troop Density in Contingency Operations," *Global War on Terrorism Occasional Paper 16* (Fort Leavenworth, KS: Combat Studies Institute Press, 2006), 28; Bureau of Statistics, Office of the Prime Minister, *Population Census of 1950*, vol. 3: *Results of Ten Percent Sample Tabulation, Part 1* (Tokyo: Sōmushō Tōkeikyoku, 1952), 24–25, https://www.e-stat.go.jp/en/stat-search/files?page=1&layout=datalist&toukei=0020 0521&bunya_l=02&bunya_s=0201&tstat=000001036869&cycle=0&tclass1 =000001038437&result_page=1&tclass2val=0.

111. Daijūsankai Kokkai Shūgiin Gyōsei Kansatsu Tokubetsu Iinkaigiroku Daijūichigō (no. 11), February 29, 1952, 4–5.

112. Tamura Taijirō, *Nikutai no Mon* in *Gendai Chōhen Shōsetsu Zenshū*, vol. 13 (Tokyo: Shunyōdō, 1949), 399–402, 414–15.

113. Molasky, *The American Occupation of Japan and Okinawa*, 119.

114. Takemae Eiji, *Inside GHQ* (New York: Continuum, 2002), 67.

115. Robert L. Eichelberger with Milton Mackaye, *Our Jungle Road to Tokyo* (New York: Viking, 1950), 273–74.

116. Takemae, *Inside GHQ*, 579n33.

117. See, for example, Hayashi Hirofumi, ed., *Nihon Senryōki Seibaibai Kankei GHQ Shiryō*, vol. 5 (Tokyo: Sōtensha, 2016), 33–34, 39–40, and compare to the handwritten numbers at the bottom of the page. Hayashi's ordering is correct.

118. Hayashi Hirofumi, "Kaidai," in *Nihon Senryōki Seibaibai Kankei GHQ Shiryō*, vol. 1, ed. Hayashi Hirofumi (Tokyo: Sōtensha, 2016), ix.

119. Hayashi Hirofumi, "Higashi Ajia no Beigun Kichi to Seibaibai," *Amerikashi Kenkyū*, no. 29 (August 2006): 8–10.

120. See, for example, Hayashi Hirofumi, "Higashi Ajia no Beigun Kichi to Seibaibai," 4; Hayashi Hirofumi, "Amerikagun no Seitaisaku no Rekishi, 1950 Nendai Made," *Josei, Sensō, Jinken*, no. 7 (March 2005): 8.

121. Dai Jūroku Kokkai Shūgiin, Gaimuiinkai Giroku Daijūnigō (Sixteenth Diet Assembly, House of Representatives, Twelfth Meeting of the Foreign Affairs Committee), 26–27, https://kokkai.ndl.go.jp/minutes/api/v1/detailPDF/img/101603968X01219530710#page=1, (accessed October 12, 2023).

122. Hayashi Hirofumi, "Higashi Ajia no Beigun Kichi to Seibaibai," 6–7.

123. Kanzaki Kiyoshi, *Sengo Nihon no Baishun Mondai* (Tokyo: Shakai Shobō, 1954), 82–83.

124. Hayashi Hirofumi, "Amerikagun no Seitaisaku no Rekishi, 1950 Nendai Made," 8–10.

125. Gotō Tsutomu, *Zoku Nippon no Teisō* (Tokyo: Sōjusha, 1953), 33.

126. Hayashi Hirofumi, ed., *Nihon Senryōki Seibaibai Kankei GHQ Shiryō*, vol. 7 (Tokyo: Sōtensha, 2016), 290.

127. Hayashi Hirofumi, "Amerikagun no Seitaisaku no Rekishi, 1950 Nendai Made," 14.

128. Hayashi Hirofumi, ed., *Nihon Senryōki Seibaibai Kankei GHQ Shiryō*, vol. 4 (Tokyo: Sōtensha, 2016), 82.

129. Venereal Disease Control—Character Guidance Council Meetings in Hayashi Hirofumi, ed., *Nihon Senryōki Seibaibai Kankei GHQ Shiryō*, 8:98—319.

130. See, for example, the comments of Military Government Health Officers reprinted in Hayashi Hirofumi, *Nihon Senryōki Seibaibai Kankei GHQ Shiryō*, 8:16–24.

131. Hayashi Hirofumi, "Amerikagun no Seitaisaku no Rekishi, 1950 Nendai Made," *Josei, Sensō, Jinken*, no. 7 (March 2005): 14.

132. Hayashi Hirofumi, ed., *Nihon Senryōki Seibaibai Kankei GHQ Shiryō*, vol. 7 (Tokyo: Sōtensha, 2016). This volume contains documents from the folders on the rehabilitation of prostitutes and the decision to ban licensed prostitution. The rights of the women involved were in fact the major point of most of these documents.

133. Hayashi Hirofumi, "Amerikagun no Seitaisaku no Rekishi, 1950 Nendai Made," 18n50.

134. Hayashi Hirofumi, "[Summary] 'A Historical Study of the US Military's Policy toward Prostitution,'" http://hayashihirofumi.g1.xrea.com/eng14.htm (accessed February 5, 2023).

135. Hayashi Hirofumi, "Amerikagun no Seitaisaku no Rekishi, 1950 Nendai Made," *Josei, Sensō, Jinken*, no. 7 (March 2005): 8.

136. Hayashi Hirofumi, "Amerikagun no Seitaisaku no Rekishi, 1950 Nendai Made," 18n51.

137. James H. Gordon, "Memorandum for the Record; Subject: Conference on V.D. Control," October 21, 1945, NARA, RG 331, box 9370, folder 8: "Venereal Disease Control." This document is also reproduced in Hayashi, *Nihon Senryōki Seibaibai Kankei GHQ Shiryō*, 4:35–36.

138. Robert Kramm, *Sanitizing Sex* (Oakland: University of California Press, 2017), 75–76.

139. Kramm, 207.

140. Fujime Yuki, *Sei no Rekishigaku* (Tokyo: Fuji Shuppan, 2015), 326.

141. Fujime Yuki, 327.

142. Fujime Yuki, 381, 383, 395.

143. Fujime Yuki, 326, 327, 418.

144. Hirai Kazuko, Nihon Senryō to Jendaa, (Tokyo: Yūshisha, 2014). For examples of Kanzaki see Hirai, 14, 30, 98, 112, 138–139, 213. For examples of Kobayshi and Murase see Hirai, 26, 37, 51, 79. For example of Kaburagi see pp. 26, 36.

145. Hirai Kazuko, *Nihon Senryō to Jendaa*, 8.

146. Hirai Kazuko, 23n26.

147. Hayakawa Norio, "Senryōgun Heishi no Ian to Baibaishunsei no Saihen," in *Senryō to Sei* (Tokyo: Impakuto Shuppankai, 2007), 75n5, 76n10, 77n17, 78n29; Sugiyama Akiko, "Haisen to RAA," *Joseigaku Nenpō*, no. 9 (1988): 35–40, 42, 44; Tanaka Masakazu, "Kontakuto Zoon toshite no Senryōki Nippon," in *Kontakuto Zoon*, no. 4 (2011): 166–68, 173–75; Furukubo Sakura, "Haisengo Nihon ni Okeru Gaishō to iu Mondai," *Jinken Mondai Kenkyū*, no. 1 (2001); Makabe Hiroshi, "Ikenie ni Sareta Nanamannin no Musumetachi," in *Tokyō Yamiichi Kōbōshi* (Tokyo: Sōfūsha, 1978), 199, 207, 208, 210, 214, 215; Takahashi Kazuo, "Yami no Onnatachi," in *Tokyō Yamiichi Kōbōshi*, 219–21; Kishi Kensuke, *Sengo Zeronen: Tokyō Burakku Hooru* (Tokyo: NHK Shuppan, 2018), 110, 117, 118, 126; Murakami Katsuhiko, *Shinchūgun Muke Tokushu Ianjo RAA* (Tokyo: Chikuma Shobō, 2022), 49–51, 59–64, 66–67, 75–77, 89, 91; Shibata Hideaki, *Senryōki no Seibōryoku* (Tokyo: Shin Nippon Shuppansha, 2022), 53, 63–67, 69, 73–74, 84, 134, 151–52.

148. Yamada Meiko, *Senryōgun Ianfu* (Tokyo: Kōjinsha, 1992); Yamada Meiko, *Nippon Kokusaku Ianfu* (Tokyo: Kōjinsha, 1996); Inoue Setsuko, *Senryōgun Ianjo* (Tokyo: Shinhyōron, 1995).

CONCLUSION

1. Karl Popper, *The Open Society and Its Enemies* (Princeton, NJ: Princeton University Press, 2013), 635n59.
2. Yasuoka Akio, conversation with author, August 1, 2023.
3. For an example of a false report, see "Basic: Ltr, GHQ, AG 000.5 (12 Oct 45) GA, dtd 14 Oct 45, subj, 'Misconduct among Occupation Troops," RG 331, GHQ/SCAP, box 408, folder 14-(1–2). For an example of an unreported rape, see B. N. Petersen, "Weekly Summary of Events—Criminal Investigations Div, OPM MTA," December 16, 1950, NARA, RG 331, GHQ/SCAP, box 9894: "Provost Marshal Section," folder: "Confidential 1950."
4. Hessell Tiltman, "Malicious Lies Stir Japanese against U.S.," *Washington Post*, July 12, 1953, B1.
5. Fujiwara Michiko, Address to the Japanese Diet, February 27, 1953, http://kokkai.ndl.go.jp/SENTAKU/sangiin/015/0512/01502270512028c.html; http://library.cqpress.com/cqresearcher/document.php?id=cqresrre1952070800.
6. ARA, RG 331, box 290, folder 16; "Rengōgun ni yoru fuhō kōi" (Japanese, handwritten) for May 1946, "Table of Misconducts Committed by Allied Servicemen" (typescript) for May 1946, NARA, RG 331, box 290, folder 16.
7. Toshikazu Kaze, *Journey to the Missouri* (New Haven, CT: Yale University Press, 1950), 14.
8. Harry Emerson Wildes, "The War for the Mind of Japan," in "America and a New Asia," special issue, *Annals of the American Academy of Political and Social Science* 294 (July 1954): 2, 6.
9. See, for example, Ōya Sōichi, "Ichiban Toku wo Shita no wa Onna," *Bungei Shunjū* 30, no. 9 (June 1952): 199.
10. Kanzaki Kiyoshi, *Ketteiban: Kanzaki Repōto* (Tokyo: Gendaishi Shuppankai, 1974), 161–62.
11. Mark McLelland, *Love, Sex and Democracy in Japan during the American Occupation* (New York: Palgrave Macmillan, 2012), 56.
12. Oguma Eiji, *"Minshu" to "Aikoku"* ["Democracy" and "Patriotism"] (Tokyo: Shinyōsha, 2002), 275.
13. Kovner, *Occupying Power*. A similar dynamic was also at work in occupied Germany. See Petra Goedde, *GIs and Germans* (New Haven, CT: Yale University Press, 2003).
14. Kita Yasutoshi, *Shirasu Jirō: Senryō wo Seotta Otoko*, vol. 1 (Tokyo: Kōdansha, 2013), Kindle edition, location 2460/2817.

15. Quoted in Igarashi Yoshikuni, *Haisen no Kioku* (Tokyo: Chūō Kōron Shinsha, 2007), 109–10. For more on the DDT disinfection program see Takemae, *Inside GHQ*, 410–11.

16. Igarashi, 110.

17. See Tiltman, "Malicious Lies Stir Japanese against U.S."

18. Quoted in Oguma, *"Minshu" to "Aikoku,"* 269.

19. Oguma, 364.

20. Gotō Ben, *Kuroi Haru* (Tokyo: Tōgosha, 1985), 197.

21. Quoted in Oguma, *"Minshu" to "Aikoku,"* 277.

22. See, for example, Itagaki Naoko, "Konketsuji no Ryōshin," *Kaizō*, March 1953, 163, or "Aoime no Ichinensei," *Shūkan Asahi*, March 1, 1953, 4–11. Contempt for mixed-race children was not entirely limited to anti-Americans. For a generally low evaluation of mixed-race children from a pro-American activist, see Uemura Tamaki, "Panpan no Atarashii Michi wo Hiraku Tame ni wa," *Fujin Kōron*, May 1952, 38.

23. Kanzaki Kiyoshi, Testimony before Japanese National Diet on April 14, 1954 (Dai Jūkyū Kai Shūgiin Naikaku Iinkaiin Kōchōkai Dainigō, 21. https://kokkai .ndl.go.jp/minutes/api/v1/detailPDF/img/101904914X00219540414#page=1, (accessed October 12, 2023).

24. Morita Akio, "No to Ieru Nippon ni Nare" in Ishihara Shintarō and Morita Akio, *No to Ieru Nippon* (Tokyo: Kobunsha, 1989), 105–15.

25. "Playboy Interview, Shintaro Ishihara," *Playboy*, October 1990, 68.

26. Ishihara Shintarō, *"Chichi" Nakushite Kuni Tatazu* (Tokyo: Kōbunsha, 1997), 81.

27. Ishihara Shintarō, *Kokka Naru Genei* (Tokyo: Bungeishunjū, 1999), 668.

28. Shirai Satoshi and Uchida Tatsuru, *Nihon Sengo Shiron* (Tokyo: Asahi Shimbun Shuppan, 2021).

29. Kobayashi Yoshinori, *Shingōmanizmu Sengen*, vol. 12: *Taga tame ni Pochi wa Naku* (Tokyo: Shogakkan, 2002), 111, 107.

30. Kobayashi Yoshinori, *Shingōmanizmu Sengen*, 12:108–11.

31. Tsurumi Shunsuke, Satō Tadao, and Kita Morio, eds., Gendai Manga 15: Manga Sengoshi, 1: Seiji Hen, (Tokyo: Chikuma Shobō, 1970), 263.

32. Yasuoka Akio, interview with author, July 18, 2023.

33. "CCAS Statement of Purpose," Committee of Concerned Asian Scholars, *Bulletin of Concerned Asian Scholars* 1, no. 1 (May 1968).

34. "Policy Statement: Japan," Committee of Concerned Asian Scholars, *Bulletin of Concerned Asian Scholars* 2, no. 1 (October 1969): 8.

35. "Policy Statement: Japan," 26.

36. John W. Dower, *Cultures of War* (New York: W. W. Norton and New Press, 2010), 316.

37. Dower, 541–52n96.

38. John W. Dower with Patrick Lawrence and Herbert Bix, "Japan and the United States: Reflections on War, Empire, Race and Culture: John W. Dower in Conversation with Patrick Lawrence," *Asia Pacific Journal: Japan Focus* 17, issue 2, no. 2 (January 15, 2019): 6.

39. Takemae Eiji, "Early Postwar Reformist Parties," in *Democratizing Japan: The Allied Occupation*, ed. Robert E. Ward and Sakamoto Yoshikazu (Honolulu: University of Hawai'i Press, 1987), 358.

40. Yuki Tanaka, "A Response to the Letter from Mr. D. H. Garrett," *Asia-Pacific Journal: Japan Focus* 10, issue 54, no. 157 (December 31, 2012).

41. Yuki Tanaka, "War, Rape and Patriarchy: The Japanese Experience," *Asia-Pacific Journal: Japan Focus* 18, issue 1, no. 1 (December 31, 2019).

42. "Ask Hayashi Hirofumi, Author of *Beigun Kichi no Rekishi*," *Anpo Haki* (*Anpo-haki Chūō Iinkai*), no. 374, June 15, 2012, http://hayashihirofumi.g1.xrea.com /paper112.htm.

43. Hirai Kazuko, *Nihon Senryō to Jendaa*, 3–4.

44. Hirai Kazuko, 3–4.

45. Ōya Sōichi, "Ichiban Toku wo Shita no wa Onna," *Bungei Shunjū* 30, no. 9 (June 1952): 194–99, esp. 199.

46. Rōdōkyoku Fujinshōnenkyoku, ed., *Fujin wa Nani wo Kangaeteiruka* (Tokyo: Rōdōshō Fujinshōnenkyoku, 1952), 12.

47. Tanaka, *Japan's Comfort Women*, 140.

48. Shibata Hideaki, *Senryōki no Seibōryoku* (Tokyo: Shin Nihon Shuppansha, 2022), 183.

49. Shibata Hideaki, 218, 223.

50. Shibata Hideaki, 234.

51. Edward Gibbon, *The History of the Decline and Fall of the Roman Empire*, vol. 1 (London: Allen Lane and Penguin Press, 1994), 527.

SELECTED BIBLIOGRAPHY

Akio Satoko. *Washinton Haitsu: GHQ ga Tokyo ni Kizanda Sengo.* Tokyo: Shinchōsha, 2003.

Alcock, Rutherford. *The Capital of the Tycoon.* Vol. 2. New York: Harper and Brothers, 1863.

Andō Masakichi. *Wagakuni no Seibyō: Genjo to Taisaku.* Tokyo: Nippon Seibyō Yobō Kyokai, 1941.

Anonymous. *A Woman in Berlin.* Translated by Philip Boehm. New York: Metropolitan Books / Henry Holt, 2005.

Aomori Ken Keisatsushi Hensan Iinkai, ed. *Aomori Ken Keisatsushi.* Vol. 2. Hirosaki: Ono Insatsu, 1977.

Ashida Hitoshi. *Ashida Nikki.* Vol. 2. Tokyo: Iwanami Shoten, 1986.

Awaya Kentarō and Nakazono Hiroshi, eds. *Haisen Zengo no Shakai Jōsei,* vol. 6: *Shinchūgun no Dōkō.* Tokyo: Gendai Shiryō Shuppan, 1999.

Beevor, Antony. *The Second World War.* New York: Little, Brown, 2012.

Bilton, Michael, and Kevin Sim. *Four Hours in My Lai.* New York: Penguin, 1992.

Boeichō Boeikenshūjo Senshishitsu, ed. *Senshi Sōsho: Hondo Kessen Junbi,* vol. 2: *Kyūshū no Boei.* Tokyo: Asagumo Shinbunsha, 1972.

Bowers, John Z. *When the Twain Meet.* Baltimore: Johns Hopkins University Press, 1980.

Brook, Timothy, ed. *Documents on the Rape of Nanking.* Ann Arbor: University of Michigan Press, 1999.

Bureau of Statistics, Office of the Prime Minister. *Population Census of 1950,* vol. 3: *Results of Ten Percent Sample Tabulation, Part 1.* Tokyo: Sōmushō Tōkeikyoku, 1952.

Buruma, Ian. *Wages of Guilt: Memories of War in Germany and Japan.* London: Jonathan Cape, 1994.

———. *Year Zero: A History of 1945.* New York: Penguin Press, 2013.

Chase, William C. *Front Line General.* Houston: Pacesetter, 1975.

Chazono Toshimi. *Panpan to wa Dare Nanoka*. Tokyo: Impakuto Shuppankai, 2014.

Chiba Ken Keisatsushi Hensan Iinkai, ed. *Chiba Ken Keisatsushi*. Vol. 2. Tokyo: Tokyo Horei, 1987.

Chūgokugo Gakshū Sōsho Henshū Iinkai, ed. *Chūgokugo Gakshū Sōsho*, vol. 5: *Gendai Chūgokugo Sakubun*. Tokyo: Kōnan Shoin, 1956.

Cohen, Theodore. *Remaking Japan*. New York: Free Press / Macmillan, 1987.

Cook, Haruko Taya, and Theodore Cook. *Japan at War: An Oral History*. New York: New Press, 1992.

De Becker, J. E. *The Nightless City, or the "History of the Yoshiwara Yukwaku."* Tokyo: ICG Muse, 2000.

Deverall, Richard L.-G. *The Great Seduction*. Tokyo: International Literature Printing, 1953.

Dower, John W. *Cultures of War*. New York: W. W. Norton / New Press, 2010.

———. *Embracing Defeat: Japan in the Wake of World War II*. New York: W. W. Norton, 1999.

———. "The Eye of the Beholder: Background Notes of the US-Japan Military Relationship." *Bulletin of Concerned Asian Scholars* 2, no. 1 (October 1969): 15–31.

Dower, John W., with Patrick Lawrence and Herbert Bix. "Japan and the United States: Reflections on War, Empire, Race and Culture: John W. Dower in Conversation with Patrick Lawrence." *Asia Pacific Journal: Japan Focus* 17, issue 2, no. 2 (January 15, 2019), Article ID 5236, https://apjjf.org/-Patrick-Lawrence--John-W--Dower/5236/article.pdf (accessed October 15, 2023).

Dower, John W., Miura Yōichi, and Takahashi Tadaaki, trans. *Haiboku wo Dakishimete*. Vol. 1. Tokyo: Iwanami Shoten, 2001.

Duus Masayo. *Makasaa no Futatsu no Bōshi*. Tokyo: Kōdansha, 1985.

Ehime Ken Keisatsushi Hensan Iinkai, ed. *Ehime Ken Keisatsushi*. Vol. 2. Imabari: Hara Insatsu, 1978.

Eichelberger, Robert L., with Milton Mackaye. *Our Jungle Road to Tokyo*. New York: Viking, 1950.

Embree, John F. *A Japanese Village: Suye Mura*. London: Kegan Paul, Trench, Trubner and Co., 1946.

Esashi Akiko. "Yokahama Beru Epokku no Onna: Kitabayashi Yoshiko." *Shinokai Kenkyūshi No. 3: Jidai no Mezame wo Yomu*, July 1996, 112–37.

Esashi Akiko and Shinokai, eds. *Jidai wo Hiraita Onnatachi: Kanagawa no Hyaku Sanjū Ichin Nin*. Yokohama: Kanagawa Shinbunsha, 2005.

Field, Norma. *In the Realm of a Dying Emperor: Japan at Century's End*. New York: Vintage, 1993.

Fischer, David Hackett. *Washington's Crossing.* New York: Oxford University Press, 2004.

Fleming, William J. "The Venereal Disease Problem in the United States in World War II." *Journal of the Mitchell Society* (August 1945): 195–200.

Frank, Bennis M., and Henry I. Shaw Jr. *Victory and Occupation: History of the U.S. Marine Corps Operations in World War II.* Vol. 5, part 2. Washington, DC: Historical Branch, G-3 Division, U.S. Marine Corps, 1968.

Frank, Richard B. "MacArthur's Shining Hour." Lecture given November 23, 2016, at the U.S. National World War II International Conference, New Orleans, LA.

———. "MacArthur's Shining Moment." Unpublished manuscript.

Früstuck, Sabine. *Colonizing Sex.* Berkeley: University of California Press, 2003.

Fujikura Shūichi. *Maiku Yodan.* Tokyo: Ryūbundō Shuppan, 1948.

Fujime, Yuki. *Sei no Rekishigaku [A History of Sexuality].* 1997. Reprint, Tokyo: Fuji Shuppan, 2015.

Fujiwara Shinji. *Minna ga Miteiru Mae de.* Tokyo: Masushobō, 1955.

———. *Zoku Minna ga Miteiru Mae de.* Tokyo: Masushobō, 1955.

Fukuda Masato. "Kenbai no Hajimari to Baidoku no Gensetsu." *Gengo Bunka Ronshū* 25, no. 1 (2003): 1–15.

Fukuda Tsuneari. *Heiwaron ni tai Suru Gimon.* Tokyo: Bungei Shunjūshinsha, 1955.

Fukuoka Ken Keisatsushi Hensan Iinkai. *Fukuoka Ken Keisatsushi.* Vol. 1. Fukuoka: Fukuoka Keisatsu Honbu, 1980.

Garon, Sheldon. *Molding Japanese Minds.* Princeton, NJ: Princeton University Press, 1997.

Gat, Azar. *War in Human Civilization.* New York: Oxford University Press, 2006.

Gayn, Mark. *Japan Diary.* New York: William Sloane Associates, 1948.

Gifu Ken Keisatsushi Hensan Iinkai, ed. *Gifu Ken Keisatsushi.* Vol. 2. Gifu: Daiichi Hōki Shuppan, 1982.

Gilmore, David G. *Manhood in the Making.* New Haven, CT: Yale University Press, 1990.

Gordon, Beate Sirota. *The Only Woman in the Room: A Memoir.* Tokyo: Kōdansha International, 1997.

Gotō Ben. *Hitoraa no Shūmatsu Yogen:Sokkin ni Kattata 2039nen.* Tokyo: Shōdensha, 2015.

———. *Isuramu vs. Amerika: Owarinaki Tatakai no Hiyōgen.* Tokyo: Seishun Shuppansha, 2002.

———. *Karuma no Hōsoku: Seimei Tensho no Himitsu Anata no Shigo Dōunaruka.* Tokyo: Shōdensha, 1980.

———. *Kuroi Haru.* Tokyo: Tōgosha, 1985.

———. *Nihon Gembaku Kaihatsu no Shinjitsu.* Tokyo: Shōdensha, 2001.

———. *1999nen Ikō: Hitoraa Dake ni Mieta Kyōfu no Miraizu.* Tokyo: Shōdensha, 1988.

———. *Nosutradamusu no Daiyogen, Semarikuru 1999nen Nanantsuki, Jinrui Metsubō no Hi.* Tokyo: Shōdensha, 1981.

———. *Uchūjin Nazo no Isan.* Tokyo: Shōdensha, 1988.

Gotō Tsutomu. "Beigun Seihanzaishi." *Shinsō* 64 (1954): 42–50.

———. *Kinjirareta Chitai.* Tokyo: Chiseisha, 1958.

———. *Tokyo no Teisō.* Tokyo: Seishun Shuppansha, 1958.

———. *Zoku Nippon no Teisō.* Tokyo: Sōjusha, 1953.

Gottschall, Jonathan. *The Rape of Troy.* New York: Cambridge University Press, 2008.

Gray, J. Glenn. *The Warriors.* New York: Harper and Row, 1970.

Gunjishigakkai, ed. *Kimitsu Sensō Nisshi.* Vol. 2. Tokyo: Kinseisha, 1998.

Hachiya, Michihiko. *Hiroshima Diary: The Journal of a Japanese Physician, August 6, 1945–September 30, 1945.* Translated by Warner Wells. Chapel Hill: University of North Carolina Press, 1955.

Hall, John Whitney. "Foundations of the Modern Japanese Daimyo." *Journal of Asian History* 20, no. 3 (May 1961): 317–29.

Harada Hiroshi. *MP no Jiipu Kara Mita Senryōka no Tokyo.* Tokyo: Sōshisha, 1994.

Hashimoto Yoshio. *Hyakuokuen no Baishun Ichiba.* Tokyo: Saikō Shinsha, 1958.

Hata Ikuhiko. *Ianfu to Senjō no Sei.* Tokyo: Shinchōsha, 1999.

Hayashi Hirofumi. "Amerika Gun no Seitaisaku no Rekishi—1950 Nendai Made." *Josei, Sensō Jinken,* no. 7.

———. "Higashi Ajia no Beigun Kichi to Seibaibai." *Amerikashi Kenkyū,* no. 29, August 2006.

———, ed. *Nihon Senryōki Seibaibai Kankei GHQ Shiryō.* Vols. 1–9. Tokyo: Sōtensha, 2016–17.

Hayashi Kaori, Tamura Keiko, and Takatsu Fumiko. *Sensō Hanayome.* Tokyo: Fuyō Shobō Shuppan, 2002.

Higashinakano, Shūdō, and Nobukatsu Fujioka. *"Za Reipu obu Nankin" no Kenkyū.* Tokyo: Shōdensha, 1999.

Hirai Kazuko. *Nihon Senryō to Jendaa.* Tokyo: Yūshisha, 2014.

Hora Tomio. *Nitchū Sensō: Nankin Daizangyaku Jiken Shiryōshū.* Vol. 1. Tokyo: Aoki Shoten, 1985.

Hosokawa Morisada. *Hosokawa Nikki.* Tokyo: Chūō Kōronsha, 1979.

Hua-ling Hu. *American Goddess at the Rape of Nanking: The Courage of Minnie Vautrin.* Carbondale: University of Southern Illinois Press, 2000.

Hume, Bill. *Babysan: A Private Look at the Japanese Occupation.* Tokyo: Kasugi Bōeki K. K., 1953.

Hyōgo Ken Keisatsushi Hensan Iinkai, ed. *Hyōgo Ken Keisatsushi, Shōwa Hen.* Kōbe: Ishikawa Insatsu, 1975.

Ichikawa Fusae. "'Dokuritsu' Nippon no Fujin Mondai." *Tōyō Keizai Shinpō Bessatsu,* May 1952, 51–55.

Igarashi Yoshikuni. *Haisen no Kioku.* Tokyo: Chūō Kōron Shinsha, 2007.

Ikegami, Eiko. *The Taming of the Samurai.* Cambridge, MA: Harvard University Press, 1998.

Inoue Setsuko. *Senryōgun Ianjo.* Tokyo: Shinpyōron, 1992.

Inui Takashi. *Nippon ha Kurutteru.* Tokyo: Dōkōsha Isobe Shobō, 1953.

Iokibe Makoto. *Senryōki Shushōtachi no Shin Nippon.* Tokyo: Yomiuri Shinbunsha, 1997.

Ion, A. Hamish. "Sexual Imperialism on the China Station during the Meiji Restoration: The Control of Smallpox and Syphilis at Yokohama." *International History Review* 31, no. 4 (December 2009): 711–39.

Ishihara Shintarō. *"Chichi" Nakushite Kuni Tatazu.* Tokyo: Kōbunsha, 1997.

———. *Kokka Naru Genei.* Tokyo: Bungeishunjū, 1999.

Ishihara Shintarō and Morita Akio. *No to Ieru Nippon.* Tokyo: Kōbunsha, 1989.

Ishikawa Tatsuzō. "Tokubetsu Kikaku: Fujin Sanseiken Bōkokuron." *Sandei Mainichi* 50, no. 9 (2734): 16–21.

Itagaki Naoko. "Konketsuji no Ryōshin." *Kaizō,* March 1953, 163.

Iwanaga Shinkichi. *Hōso no Chishiki Shiriizu No. 3: Hōdō Kyōyō Bangumi.* Tokyo: Dōbunkan, 1956.

Jackson, Keith L. "'Black Horror on the Rhine.'" *Journal of Modern History* 42, no. 4 (December 1970): 606–27.

Jiji Mondai Kenkyūjo, ed. *Beigun Kichi: Dare no Tame no Mono Ka.* Tokyo: Shadan Hōjin Jiji Mondai Kenkyūjo, 1968.

Jinmin Bungaku Henshūbu. *"Jinmin Bungaku Tōmen no Kadai." Jinmin Bungaku,* November 1952, reprinted in *Jinmin Bunkagaku Fukkokuban.* Vol. 7. Tokyo: Fuji Shuppan, 2011.

Jūgonen Sensō Juyō Bunken Shiriizu, vol. 1: *Gunikan no Senjō Hōkoku Ikenshū.* Tokyo: Fuji Shuppan, 1990.

Kabushikigaisha Kōdansha, ed. *Shōwa Nimanhi no Zenkiroku,* vol. 7: *Haikyo kara no Shuppatsu.* Tokyo: Kabushikigaisha Kōdasha, 1989.

Kaempfer, Engelbert. *Kaempfer's Japan.* Translated and edited by Beatrice M. Bodart-Bailey. Honolulu: University of Hawai'i Press, 1999.

Kagawa Ken Keisatsushi Kenshū Iinkai, ed. *Kagawa Ken Keisatsushi.* Nagano: Tōkyō Horei Shuppan, 1957.

Kaiya Mitsuo. *"Nippon no Teisō wo Yomite." Shinjin Bungei* 4, no. 7 (August 1953): 51–53.

Kanagawa Ken Keisatsushi Hensan Iinkai, ed. *Kanagawa Ken Keisatsushi*. Yokohama: Kanagawa Keisatsu Honbu, 1974.

Kanda Masao and Kubota Yasutarō. *Uchinada: Gunji Kichi Hantai Tōsō no Jittai*. Tokyo: Shakai Shobō, 1953.

Kanō Jigorō. *Kanō Jigorō Chosakushū*. Tokyo: Gogatsu Shobō, 1983.

Kanzaki Kiyoshi. *Aizu Rōjō*. Tokyo: Kokuminsha, 1945.

———. *Baishun: Ketteiban Kanzaki Repōto*. Tokyo: Gendaishi Shuppankai, 1974.

———. "Nihon Josei no Kokusaisei to Baishōsei." *Kaizō* 10, no. 33 (October 1952): 76–82.

———. "Ruporutaaju Yokosuka: Nihon no Reddo Rain." *Fujin Kōron*, November 1952, 171–75.

———. *Sengo Nihon no Baishun Mondai*. Tokyo: Shakai Shobo, 1954.

Kanzaki Takeshi, ed. *Kanzaki Kiyoshi no Tsuioku*. Tokyo: Uniaato, 1981.

Kariya Haruo. *Edo no Seibyō*. Tokyo: Sanichi Shobō, 1993.

Kashii Toshie. "Dassō." *Jinmin Bungaku*, May 1952, 115–20. Reprinted in *Jinmin Bunkagaku Fukkokuban*, vol. 5. Tokyo: Fuji Shuppan, 2011.

———. "Izukoe." *Jinmin Bungaku*, October 1952, 106–21. Reprinted in *Jinmin Bunkagaku Fukkokuban*. Tokyo: Fuji Shuppan, 2011.

Katsura Sanshi and Gotō Ben. "Sanshi no Honma Dekka." *Shūkan Yomiuri*, May 26, 1991.

Kawai Michi. *Suraidingu Doa*. Translated by Nakamura Taeko. Tokyo: Keisenjogakuin, 1995.

Keisen Jogakuen Daigaku Heiwa Bunka Kenkyūjo, ed. *Senryō to Sei*. Tokyo: Impakuto Shuppankai, 2007.

"Kichi Nōmin to Kanri Kōjō Rōdōsha." *Chūō Kōron* 69, no. 1 (January 1954): 158–61.

Kida Junichirō. "Kanagawa Bunka wo Kizuita Hitobito. No. 22: Sakka Kitabayashi Tōma." *Best Partner* 25, no. 10 (October 2013): 36–41.

Kishi Kensuke. *Sengo Zeronen: Tokyō Burakku Hooru*.Tokyo: NHK Shuppan, 2018.

Kita Yasutoshi. *Shirasu Jirō: Senryō wo Seotta Otoko*. Tokyo: Kōdansha, 2013.

Kitabayashi Tōma. "Fujin no Rikkōho." *Seikai Ōrai* 21, no. 3 (March 1955): 180–85.

———. *Kyoryūchi no Oka*. Tokyo: Ōya Shoten, 1932.

———. "Machi no Kokusai Musume." *Bundan Andepandan*, no. 1 (1930): 143.

———. "Sendensen ho Ikani Tatakawaretaka." In *Daitōa Sensō: Rikugun Hōdōhanin Shuki: Biruma Kensetsusen*, edited by Bunka Hōkōkai. Tokyo: Dai Nippon Yūbenkai, Kōdansha, 1943.

Kitabayashi Yoshiko. "Beigun Gyōjō Hiroku: Yokohama no Higeki." *Fuji* 6, no. 1 (January 1953).

Kobayashi Dajiro, and Murase Akira. *Minna wa Shiranai Kokka Baishun Meirei*. Tokyo: Yuzankaku Shuppan, 1992.

Kobayashi Yoshinori. *Shingōmanizmu Sengen*, vol. 12: *Taga Tame ni Pochi wa Naku*. Tokyo: Shogakkan, 2002.

Kōchi Ken Keisatsushi Hensan Iinkai, ed. *Kōchi Ken Keisatsushi Showa Hen*. Sagawa, Kochi: Sagawa Insatsusho, 1979.

Kokka Chihō Keisatsu Honbu Keijibu Chōsa Tōkeika, ed. *Hanzai Tōkeisho: Dai-ichibu: Shōwa Nijūnananen*. Tokyo: Okumura Insatsu, 1953.

Kōseishō Yobōkyoku, *Kokumin Yūsei Zukai*. Tokyo: Issei, 1941.

Koshiro, Yukiko. *Trans-Pacific Racisms and the U.S. Occupation of Japan*. New York: Columbia University Press, 1999.

Kovner, Sarah. *Occupying Power: Sex Workers and Servicemen in Postwar Japan*. Stanford, CA: Stanford University Press, 2012.

Kramm, Robert. *Sanitizing Sex*. Berkeley: University of California Press, 2017.

Kumai Seiichi. *Hoken Eisei Shidōsha ni Hitsuyō Naru Seibyō no Chishiki to Yobō*. Tokyo: Shindan to Chiryōsha, 1953.

Kuroda Shigeo. *Nihon Keisatsushi no Kenkyū*. Tokyo: Reibunsha, 1963.

Kyōtofu Keisatsushi Henshū Iinkai, ed. *Kyōtofu Keisatsushi*. Vol. 3. Kyoto: Kyōto Keisatsu Honbu, 1980.

Kyōtofu Rōdō Keizai Kenkyūjo, ed. *Kyōto Rōdō Undōshi Nenpyō*. Kyoto: Kyōtofu Rōdō Keizai Kenkyūjo, 1965.

Lifton, Robert J. *Destroying the World to Save It*. New York: Metropolitan, 1999.

MacArthur, Douglas. *Reminiscences*. New York: McGraw-Hill, 1964.

"Machi kara Mura kara." *Shin Josei*, no. 45 (September 1954).

Manchester, William. *American Caesar*. New York: Dell, 1978.

McGrath, John J. "Boots on the Ground: Troop Density in Contingency Operations." *Global War on Terrorism Occasional Paper 16*. Fort Leavenworth, KS: Combat Studies Institute Press, 2006.

McGregor, Richard. *Asia's Reckoning*. New York: Viking, 2017.

McLelland, Mark. *Love, Sex and Democracy in Japan during the American Occupation*. New York: Palgrave Macmillan, 2012.

Michiba Chikanobu and Toka Kōji. "Bungaku Zasshi *Jinminbungaku* no Jidai." *Wakō Daigaku Gendai Ningen Gakubu Kiyō*, no. 3 (March 2010): 209–37.

Mizuma Masanori. "Fuin Sareteita Senryōka no Beihei 'Nihonjin Fujoshi Ryōjoku Jiken' Fairu." *Sapio*, April 11, 2007.

Mizuno Hiroshi, ed. *Nippon no Teisō*. Tokyo: Sōjusha, 1953.

———. *Shi ni Nozonde Uttaeru*. Tokyo: Tōgosha, 1982.

Mizuno Hiroshi and Kanzaki Kiyoshi. "Kichi no naka no Junketsu." *Shin Josei*, no. 31 (August 1953). Reprinted in *Shin Josei Fukkokuban*, vol. 8. Tokyo: Fuji Shuppan, 2010.

Molasky, Michael. *The American Occupation of Japan and Okinawa: Literature and Memory*. New York: Routledge, 1999.

Morioka, Michiyo. *An American Artist in Tokyo: Francis Blakemore 1906–1997*. Seattle: Marquand Books, 2007.

Murakami Katsuhiko. *Shinchūgun Muke Tokushu Ianjo RAA*. Tokyo: Chikuma Shobō, 2022.

Nagai Kafū. *Danchōtei Nichijō*. Tokyo: Iwanami Shoten, 1987.

Naimark, Norman H. *The Russians in Germany*. Cambridge, MA: Harvard University Press, 1995.

Nara Ken Keisatsushi Henshū Iinkai, ed. *Nara Ken Keisatsushi, Shōwa Hen*. Nara: Nara Keisatsu Honbu, 1978.

Nihon Hōsō Shuppan Kyōkai, ed. *Rajio Shakai Tanbō*. Tokyo: Nihon Hōsō Shuppan Kyōkai, 1949.

Nihon Kokugo Daijiten. Vol. 4. Tokyo: Shogakkan, 2006.

Nihon Kyōsantō Chōsaiinkai, ed. *Senryōka Nihon no Bunseki: Amerika wa Nihon wo Dō Shihaishiteiruka*. Kyoto: Sanichishobō, 1953.

Nihon Kyōsantō Sendenkyōikubu and Nihon Kyōsantō Tōkyōtō Iinkai Sendenkyōikubu, eds. "Heiwa e no Fujin no Yōkyū wo Hiroi Tōitsu Sensen e." *Tatakai ha Jinmin no Shinrai no Moto ni*. Tokyo: Nihon Kyōsantō Tōkyōtō Iinkai, 1950.

Nikkan Rōdō Tsūshinsha, ed. *Saikin ni Okeru Nikkyō no Kinhonteki Senryaku Senjutsu*. Tokyo: Nikkan Rōdō Tsūshinsha, 1953.

Nishimura, Sey. "Promoting Public Health during the Occupation of Japan." *American Journal of Public Health* 9, no. 3 (March 2008): 424–34.

Notehelfer, F. G., ed. *Japan through American Eyes: The Journal of Francis Hall, 1859–1866*. Boulder, CO: Westview, 2001.

Ōba Akira. "Nihon no Engan Bōei no Henkan to Sono Jidashiteki Haikei." *Bōei Shisetsu to Gijutsu*, no. 15.

Oguma, Eiji. *A Genealogy of "Japanese" Self-Images*. Translated by David Askew. Melbourne: Trans Pacific Press, 2002.

———. *"Minshu" to "Aikoku."* Tokyo: Shinyōsha, 2002.

Okayama Ken Keisatsushi Hensan Iinkai, ed. *Okayama Ken Keisatsushi*. Vol. 2. Okayama: Okayama Bijutsu Shikō, 1976.

Oppler, Alfred Christian. *Legal Reform in Occupied Japan*. Princeton, NJ: Princeton University Press, 1976.

Ōsaka Fu Keisatsushi Hensan Iinkai, ed. *Ōsaka Fu Keisatsushi*. Vol. 3. Ōsaka: Ōsaka Fu Keisatsu Honbu, 1973.

Ōshiro Masayasu. *Okinawasen: Minshū no Me de Toraeru Sensō*. Tokyo: Kōbunsha, 1988.

Ōtake Bungo. "Nikutai to Bōhatei." *Diyamondo*, May 1952.

Otsubo, Sumiko. "Feminist Maternal Eugenics in Japan." *U.S.-Japan Women's Journal, English Supplement*, no. 17 (1999): 39–76.

Ōya Sōichi "Ichiban Toku wo Shita no ha Onna." *Bungei Shunjū* 30, no. 9 (June 1952): 194–99.

Ozaki Yoshimitsu. "NHK Rajio Bangumi Gaitō Rokuon Seishōnen no Furyōka wo Dōshite Fuseguka: Gaado Shitano Musumetachi no Mojika Shiryō." *Notre Dame Seishin University Kiyō Studies in Foreign Languages and Literature: Studies in Culture, Studies in Japanese Language and Literature* 45, no. 1 (2021): 77–96.

Ozawa Shōichi and Ei Rokusuke. *Iro no Michi*. Tokyo: Chikuma Shobō, 2007.

Park Yuha. *Teikoku no Ianfu*. Tokyo: Asahi Shimbun Shuppan, 2014.

Peritz, Aki, and Tara Maller. "The Islamic State of Sexual Violence." *Foreign Policy*, September 16, 2014, https://foreignpolicy.com/2014/09/16/the-islamic-state-of-sexual-violence/.

Pharr, Susan J. "The Politics of Women's Rights." In *Democratizing Japan*, edited by Robert E. Ward and Yoshikazu Sakamoto, 221–52. Honolulu: University of Hawai'i Press, 1987.

"Playboy Interview, Shintaro Ishihara." *Playboy*, October 1990.

Potts, Malcolm, and Thomas Hayden. *Sex and War: How Biology Explains Warfare and Terrorism and Offers a Path to a Safer World*. Dallas: Benbella Books, 2008.

Public Opinion and Sociological Research Division, Civil Information and Education Section, ed. "The Japanese People Look at Prostitution." June 30, 1949.

"Report of the International Commission of Inquiry on Darfur to the United Nations Secretary-General." January 25, 2005.

Rōdō Keizai Shunpō, no. 8 (213) (January 1954).

Rōdōkyoku Fujinshōnenkyoku, ed. *Fujin ha Nani wo Kangaeteiruka*. Tokyo: Rōdōshō Fujinshōnenkyoku, 1952.

Rōdōshō Fujinshōnen Kyoku, ed. *Baishunfu Narabi ni Sono Aitegata ni tsuite no Chōsa, Fujin Kankei Shiryō Shiriizu Chōsa Shiryō, Daijūni*. No. 12. Tokyo: Rōdōshō Fujinshōnen Kyoku, 1953.

Saitama Ken, ed. *Shinpen Saitama Kenshi*. Vol. 7. Kabushikigaisha Gyōsei, 1991.

Saitama Ken Keisatsushi Hensan Iinkai, ed. *Saitama Ken Keisatsushi*. Tokyo: Tōkyō Horei Shuppan, 1977.

Sams, Crawford F. *"Medic": The Mission of an American Military Doctor in Occupied Japan and Wartorn Korea*. Edited by Zabelle Zakarian. Armonk, NY: M. E. Sharpe, 1998.

Sanders, Holly Vincele. "Prostitution in Postwar Japan: Debt and Labor." PhD diss., Princeton University, 2005.

Segi Mitsuo and Fukushima Ichirō. "Seibyō ni Kan Suru Tōkei." *Sanfujinka no Sekai* 3, no. 1 (January 1951): 91–97.

Seibōryoku Mondai Shiryō Shūsei. Vol. 1. Tokyo: Fujiya Shuppan, 2004.

"Seibyō no Sakkon wo Kataru." *Sanfujinka no Sekai* 3, no. 1 (January 1951): 79–90.

Seigle, Cecilia S. *Yoshiwara: The Glittering World of the Japanese Courtesan.* Honolulu: University of Hawai'i Press, 1993.

"Sengo Rōdō Undōshi." *Gakushū no Tomo*, no. 92.

Shaffer, Robert. "A Rape in Beijing, December 1946: GIs, Nationalist Protests, and U.S. Foreign Policy." *Pacific Historical Review* 69, no. 1 (February 2000): 31–64.

Shibata Hideaki. *Senryōki no Seibōryoku.* Tokyo: Shin Nihon Shuppansha, 2022.

Shimamoto Shizuo. "Hakuboku Nikki: Joōsama Funshitsu." *Shojō no Tomo*, January 1937, 182–93.

———. *Jogakusei Jidai.* Tokyo: Kokuminsha, 1943.

———. "Kokuban Romansu: Eigo no Sensei." *Shōjo no Tomo*, September 1942.

———. "Kokuban Romansu: Kyōshitsu wo Kirei ni." *Shōjo no Tomo*, January 1939, 190–201.

———. "Kokuban Romansu: Tōban Nisshi Yori." *Shōjo no Tomo*, August 1941, 184–93.

———. "Sensei no Techō Yori: Wakai Kateikyōshi." *Shōjo no Tomo*, August 1936, 208–21.

Shimane Ken Keisatsushi Hensan Iinkai, ed. *Shimane Ken Keisatsushi: Shōwa Hen.* Toppan Insatsu, 1984.

"Shin Ōkubo de Matamoya Zaitokukai Demo Nigatsu Kokonoka 'Yoi Kankokujin mo, Warui Kankokujin mo Dochiramo Korose' no Purakaado Age." *Nikkan Berita*, February 10, 2013.

Shirai Satoshi. *Nihon Sengo Shiron.* Tokyo: Tokuma Shoten, 2015.

Shirai Satoshi and Uchida Tatsuru. *Nihon Sengo Shiron.* Tokyo: Asahi Shimbun Shuppan, 2021.

Shizuoka Ken Keisatsushi Hensan Iinkai, ed. *Shizuoka Ken Keisatsushi.* Vol. 2. Shizuoka: Shizuoka Keisatsu Honbu, 1979.

Smethurst, Richard J. *A Social Basis for Prewar Japanese Militarism.* Berkeley: University of California Press, 1974.

Sōhyō Osaka Chihō Hyōgikai, ed. *Sohyō Osaka Chihō Jūnenshi Nenpyō.* Osaka: Osaka Rōdōkumiai Sōhyōgikai Osaka Chihō Hyōgikai, 1961.

Sōmuchō Tōkeikyoku [Statistics Bureau, Management and Coordination Agency], ed. *Nihon Chōki Tōkei Sōran (Historical Statistics of Japan).* Vol. 1. Tokyo: Nihon Tōkei Kyōkai [Japan Statistical Association], 1987.

Starr, Joseph R., Office of the Chief Historian, European Command. "Fraternization with the Germans." Frankfurt am Main: Headquarters, European Command, August 1947.

Sugita Tomoe. "Nippon no Teisō: Tsuma to Natta Watashi no Kunō." *Shin Josei*, no. 29 (June 1953): 147–64. Reprinted in *Shin Josei Fukkokuban*. Tokyo: Fuji Shuppan, 2010.

Sumiya Etsuji and Takenaka Katsuo, eds. *Gaishō: Jittai to Sono Shuki*. Tokyo: Yūkōsha, 1949.

Suzuki Takao. *Hone kara Mita Nihonjin*. Tokyo: Kōdansha, 2010.

———. *Paleopathological and Paleoepidemiological Study of Osseous Syphilis in Skulls of the Edo Period*. Tokyo: University of Tokyo Press, 1984.

Takano Rokurō. *Yobō Igaku Nōto*. Tokyo: Kawade Shobō, 1942.

Takasaki Setsuko. *Konketsuji*. Tokyo: Dōkōsha Isebeshobō, 1952.

Takemae Eiji. "Early Postwar Reformist Parties." In *Democratizing Japan: The Allied Occupation*, edited by Robert E. Ward and Sakamoto Yoshikazu. Honolulu: University of Hawai'i Press, 1987.

———, ed. *GHQ e no Nihon Seifu Taiō Bunsho Sōshūsei*. Tokyo: Emu Ti Shuppan, 1994.

———. *Inside GHQ: The Allied Occupation of Japan and Its Legacy*. New York: Continuum, 2002.

Tamura Taijirō. *Nikutai no Mon* in *Gendai Chōhen Shōsetsu Zenshū*. Vol. 13. Tokyo: Shunyōdō, 1949.

Tanaka Masakazu. "Kontakuto Zoon Toshite no Senryōki Nippon: 'Kichi no Onnatachi.'" *Kontakuto Zoon*, no. 4 (2011): 163–89.

Tanaka, Yuki. *Hidden Horrors: Japanese War Crimes in World War II*. Boulder, CO: Westview, 1996.

———. *Hidden Horrors: Japanese War Crimes in World War II*. 2nd ed. Lanham, MD: Rowman and Littlefield, 2018.

———. *Japan's Comfort Women: Sexual Slavery and Prostitution during World War II and the US Occupation*. New York: Routledge, 2002.

Thompson, Nicholas. *The Hawk and the Dove: Paul Nitze, George Kennan and the History of the Cold War*. New York: Henry Holt, 2009.

Tipton, Elise K. *The Japanese Police State*. Honolulu: University of Hawai'i Press, 1990.

Toba Kōji. "Kaisetsu *Jinmin Bungaku* Ron." In Toba Kōji, Michiba Chikanobu, and Shibazaki Kōzaburō, *Jinmin Bungaku: Kaisetsu, Kaidai, Kaisō, Sōmokuji, Sakuin*. Tokyo: Fuji Shuppan, 2011.

Tokuda Kyūichi. *Nihon Kyōsantō Gojūnen Mondai Shiryōshu*. Vol. 1. Tokyo: Shin Nippon Shuppansha, 1957.

Tōkyō Yakeato Yamiichi o Kiroku Suru Kai, ed. *Tōkyō Yamiichi Kōbō Shi*. Tokyo: Sōfūsha, 1978.

Toll, Ian W. *Pacific Crucible*. New York: W. W. Norton, 2012.

Tomomura, Hitomi, Anne Walthall, and Wakita Haruko, eds. *Women and Class in Japanese History*. Ann Arbor: University of Michigan Press, 1999.

Tottori Ken Keisatsushi Hensan Iinkai, ed. *Tottori Ken Keisatsushi*. Vol. 1. Tottori City: Yatani Insatsusho, 1981.

Tōyō Shokan, ed. *Kaisō no Tokuda Kyūichi*. Tokyo: Tōyō Shokan, 1955.

Tsou Jung (Zou Rong). *The Revolutionary Army*. Translated by John Lust. The Hague: Mouton, 1968.

Tsurumi Shunsuke, Satō Tadao, and Kita Morio, eds. Gendai Manga 15: Manga Sengoshi I: Seiji Hen. Tokyo: Chikuma Shobō, 1970.

———. *Gendai Manga 15: Manga Sengoshi II: Shakai Fūzoku Hen*. Tokyo: Chikuma Shobō, 1970.

Uemura Tamaki, "Panpan no Atarashii Michi wo Hiraku Tame ni wa." *Fujin Kōron*, May 1952.

U.S. Institute of Peace. "Rape in War: Motives of Militia in the DRC." Special Report 243, June 2010.

Vonderlehr, R. A., and Lida J. Usilton. "Syphilis among Men of Draft Age in the United States." *Journal of the American Medical Association* 120, no. 17 (December 1942): 1369–72.

Wakabayashi, Bob Tadashi, ed. *The Nanking Atrocity 1937–1938: Complicating the Picture*. New York: Berghahn Books, 2007.

———. "Opium, Expulsion, Sovereignty: China's Lessons for Bakumatsu Japan." *Monumenta Nipponica* 47, no. 1 (Spring 1992): 1–25.

Wakayama Ken Keisatsushi Hensan Iinkai, ed. *Wakayama Ken Keisatsushi*. Vol 2. Tokyo: Kawakita Insatsusho, 1992.

Watanabe Sumiko. *Aoime no Koibitotachi*. Tokyo: Dainishobō, 1959.

Weintraub, Stanley. *The Last Great Victory*. New York: Penguin, 1995.

Whitney, Courtney. *MacArthur: His Rendezvous with History*. New York: Knopf, 1956.

Wildes, Harry E. *Typhoon in Tokyo*. 1954. Reprint, New York: Macmillan, 1958.

———. "The War for the Mind of Japan." In "America and a New Asia," special issue, *Annals of the American Academy of Political and Social Science* 294 (July 1954): 1–7.

Williams, Justin, Sr. *Japan's Political Revolution under MacArthur: A Participant's Account*. Athens: University of Georgia Press, 1979.

Yamada Fūtarō. *Senchūha Fusen Nikki*. Tokyo: Kōdansha, 2002.

Yamada Meiko. *Nippon Kokusaku Ianfu*. Tokyo: Kōjinsha, 1996.

———. *Senryōgun Ianfu*. Tokyo: Kōjinsha, 1992.

Yamagata Ken Keisatsushi Hensan Iinkai, ed. *Yamagata Ken Keisatsushi*. Vol. 2. Yamagata: Tamiya Insatsusho, 1971.

Yamamoto Shunichi. *Nihon Baishun Seibyōshi*. Tokyo: Bunkōdo, 2002.

Yamazaki Yasuo. *Chosha to Shuppansha, No. 2*. Tokyo: Gakufū Shoin, 1955.

Yanaginuma Masaharu. *Nihon Kyōsantō Undōshi, Sengohen*. Tokyo: Keibunkaku, 1953.

Yonekawa Akihiko, ed. *Nihon Zokugo Daijiten*. Tokyo: Tōkyōdō Shuppan, 2006.

Yosano Hikaru. "Haisen Hiwa: Senryōgun Ian Bibōroku." *Shinchō 45*, May 1990, 132–43.

Yoshiaki, Yoshimi. *Comfort Women: Sexual Slavery in the Japanese Military during World War II*. Translated by Suzanne O'Brien. New York: Columbia University Press, 2000.

Yoshikawa Sachiko (Yukiko). "Akumu no Yōna RAA no Hibi." *Ushio*, no. 154 (June 1972): 164–65.

Yoshimi, Kaneko. *Baishun no Shakaishi [A Social History of Prostitution]*. Tokyo: Yuzankaku Shuppan, 1984.

Zenkoku Shakai Fukushi Kyōgikai. "Igai ni Sukunakatta Konketsuji." *Shakai Jigyō* 35, no. 12 (1952): 46.

INDEX

Page numbers in italics indicate figures and tables.

public prostitutes, 81, 206. *See also* licensed prostitutes/prostitution
Public Safety Division (PSD), GHQ, 35–36, 37–38, 51–54

RAA (Recreation and Amusement Association), 175–8, 192, 210
Rabe, John, 40–41
Rakuchō no Otoki, 200, 201, 298*n*60, 299*n*74
"Rape during the Occupation of Japan" (Wikipedia), 196
Rape of Nanking, The (Chang), 4
Rape of Nanking, The, 3, 40–43 254n133, 111, 120–1
rapes: on American bases, lurid tales of, 165–70; Arisue Seizō on other GI crimes more significant than, 34; Bangladesh's war for independence and, 108; Bosnian camps for, 109; challenging myth of, 8–9, 244–5*n*24; claims of Allied Occupation after World War II of, 2–8, 244*n*14; CLO records of GI criminal activity including, 31; by conquerors of conquered, Japanese fears of, 63; definitions, reports, and stigma of, 39; discourse on Japanese nationalist interests and, 16; Fujiwara's allegations of, 154; by GI gang, reported to Supreme Commander, 30; initial phase of Occupation and, 19, 188–9, 220; intimate association between war and, 14; Japanese media on early Occupation and, 20–21; Japanese police on early Occupation and, 23, 189; *To Kill a Mockingbird* on crime of, 150–1; as metaphor for defeat and occupation, 225, 226; during Occupation vs. in midsized American cities, 38, 251*n*98; propaganda, anti-American campaign and, 152; propaganda, Kitabayashi Yoshiko and Kitabayashi Tōma and, 164–5; rarity of, initial phase of Occupation and, 29; reported, statistical chart of, 236–41; war associated with, 107–8. *See also* mass rape legend; war rape
Rice, George, 212–3
Richmon, Irving, 91
robbery, by American GIs, 26, 28

romance, GI–Japanese: brothels to prevent, 138; Japanese reluctance to believe in, 151; Kanzaki's writing against, 159; life in occupied Japan and, 139–43, *140*, *141*; resentment of, 143, 151–2; "Tokyo Joe" cartoon of, *145*; women harassed for, 145–6, 148, 149, 281*n*90
Rosenberg, Alfred, 111
rumors, Occupation of Japan and, 107–8, 119–21
Ryūkyū pox, 80. *See also* syphilis

Safety Zone, Nanjing, China, 40–41
Saikō Shinsha, 176
Saitō, Old Man, 22, 133
Sakurai Makoto, 1
Salvarsan (antisyphilitic drug), 96
Samejima Tsuruko, 169
Sams, Crawford F.: Elkins' political sympathies and, 262*n*92; GHQ's pro-prostitution policy and, 211; Hayashi's rants on, 213; Hayashi's sexual depiction of, 232; on nationwide public health program, 102; on occupying and VD, 79; PHW in Japan and, 87–88, *94*, 105; in PHW photo, *89*; results focus of, 93; road from Yokohama to Tokyo and, 195; on tolerance of peoples of other lands, 95; on VD and prostitution, 69–70, 90–91
San Francisco Peace Treaty, 225
Sanitizing Sex (Kramm), 214
Sankirai (Chinese medicine for syphilis), 81
sarin gas attacks, 173
Sasebō disease, 78
SCAP (Supreme Commander Allied Powers). *See* General Headquarters
SCAPIN 153 (infectious diseases order), 97
SCAPIN 642 (prostitution prohibition order), 55, 57–58, 62, 75, 130
SCAPIN 1183 (Japanese police directive translations order), 62
scarlet fever vaccinations, 88
Scharffenberg, Paul, 111
Schell, James, 66–67
school lunch program, PHW and, 89–90
Schrijvers, Peter, 250*n*82
Second World War, The (Beevor), 31

ABOUT THE AUTHOR

Brian P. Walsh has lived, worked, and studied in Japan for seventeen years. He received a master's degree in Japan studies from the University of Washington in 2003 and a PhD in modern Japanese history from Princeton University in 2016. His principal areas of study are U.S.-Japan relations in the 1940s and 1950s and the postwar development of a new Japanese national identity in the wake of its catastrophic defeat in World War II. He teaches Japanese history and international relations at Kwansei Gakuin University.